# Hubbell Trading Post

# Hubbell Trading Post
*Trade, Tourism, and the Navajo Southwest*

Erica Cottam

University of Oklahoma Press : Norman

Library of Congress Cataloging-in-Publication Data
Cottam, Erica, 1985–
  Hubbell Trading Post : trade, tourism, and the Navajo southwest / Erica Cottam.
     pages cm
  Includes bibliographical references and index.
  ISBN 978-0-8061-4837-3 (hardcover)
  ISBN 978-0-8061-6752-7 (paper)
  1. Hubbell Trading Post National Historic Site (Ganado, Ariz.)—History. 2. Navajo Indians—Commerce. 3. Hubbell Trading Post National Historic Site (Ganado, Ariz.) 4. Hubbell, John Lorenzo. 5. Indian traders—Arizona—Ganado—Biography. 6. Hubbell family. 7. Navajo Indian Reservation—History.
     I. Title.

  F819.G36C65 2015
  979.1'37—dc23

2015001127


The paper in this book meets the guidelines for permanence and durability of the Committee on Production Guidelines for Book Longevity of the Council on Library Resources, Inc. ∞

Copyright © 2015 by the University of Oklahoma Press, Norman, Publishing Division of the University. Paperback published 2020. Manufactured in the U.S.A.

All rights reserved. No part of this publication may be reproduced, stored in a retrieval system, or transmitted, in any form or by any means, electronic, mechanical, photocopying, recording, or otherwise—except as permitted under Section 107 or 108 of the United States Copyright Act—without the prior written permission of the University of Oklahoma Press. To request permission to reproduce selections from this book, write to Permissions, University of Oklahoma Press, 2800 Venture Drive, Norman OK 73069, or email rights.oupress@ou.edu.

To my mother

# Contents

List of Illustrations    ix
Acknowledgments    xi

Introduction    3
1. Drifting into Navajo Country: Juan Lorenzo Hubbell and the Navajos    10
2. Traders to the Navajos: Early Trading Posts in the Pueblo Colorado Valley    32
3. Laying the Foundations: The Daily Business of the Hubbell Trading Post, 1878–1900    53
4. The Rise of an Empire: Expansion and Evolution, 1900–1914    73
5. Troubled Times: Changing Fortunes, 1915–1929    99
6. "No Misrepresentations, No Shams, and No Counterfeits": Tourism and the Curio Trade    123
7. "Seekers of Beauty" and "Adventurers into the Buried Long Ago": Visitors to the Post    150
8. "The Worst They Ever Knew": The Great Depression and World War II, 1930–1945    184
9. A New Era: Becoming a National Historic Site, 1945–1967    213

Notes    235
Bibliography    319
Index    339

# Illustrations

*Figures*

Navajo boy herding sheep   16
Navajos under juniper tree   27
Hubbell-Gutiérrez family   29
Young J. L. Hubbell   34
Leonard Trading Post   40
The bullpen   45
The Hubbell family   51
Navajos shearing sheep   60
E. A. Burbank oil painting   71
Navajo horse racers   72
Adele and Barbara Hubbell   75
Arizona statehood   81
Lorenzo, Jr.   85
Hubbells in and on automobile   88
Roman and Alma   95
Alma Hubbell and baby John   103
Hubbell children with pets   116
Roman and Dorothy   118
J. L. with grandson, Jack   121
Navajo weaver   126
J. L.'s office with rug paintings   134
J. L. buying blankets   139
Navajo demonstrators   144

J. L. at age fifty-three   151
Stewart Culin, anthropologist   157
Roosevelt and Hubbell at the Snake Dance   162
Maynard Dixon   170
Charles F. Lummis   174
Lorenzo, Jr., and Roman   186
Navajo herder and sheep   191
Roman and tourist picnicking   200
Monnie during World War II   206
Lorenzo, Jr., in the rug room   209
Dorothy in trader's office   225
Dedication of Hubbell Trading Post National Historic Site   233

## Maps

Vicinity of Hubbell Trading Post   2
Building and grounds layout   4

# Acknowledgments

When I began researching Hubbell Trading Post for the National Park Service, I was just beginning my second year of graduate school. I wrote the report from which this book stemmed during a period of intellectual and professional growth, and I have many people to thank, not only for their assistance in this project, but for their mentorship. First, I wish to thank the Public History Program at Arizona State University for presenting me with the opportunity to pursue this project. Janelle Warren-Findley and Christine Szuter both provided excellent advice and assistance along the way. Linnéa Caproni Hallam, William Stoutamire, and William Kiser shared with me the particular experience of writing a Historic Resource Study while working on a PhD. I appreciate deeply the support of my friends and colleagues in the department. There are too many people who left an imprint on my life and scholarship during the years I worked on this project to mention each by name, but special thanks go to Linnéa, Meaghan Heisinger Siekman, and Thomas Walsh. Most of all, I thank Nancy Dallett, who saw me through from start to finish with wisdom and kindness. And heartfelt thanks go to James Nickerson and Kim Engel-Pearson for their excellent editing advice and assistance.

At Hubbell Trading Post National Historic Site, I want to thank the personnel who facilitated my visits and assisted me in innumerable ways as I researched this book, particularly Ed Chamberlin and Kathy Tabaha. At the National Park Service, my heartfelt thanks go to Regional Historian Bob Spude, who provided insightful feedback on my work and jumpstarted its publication, even after his retirement. I also want to thank his successor, Sam Tamburro, for his tireless efforts. Like all such projects, my work benefited from the generosity of archivists in libraries and special collections. I thank the many institutions in Arizona and New Mexico that made this work possible: Hubbell Trading Post; the Center for Southwest Research at the University of New Mexico; the Cline Library at Northern Arizona University; the New Mexico Commission of Public Records, State Records Center and Archives; the Arizona Historical Society; the Museum of Northern Arizona; Arizona State University Special Collections; and most especially the University of Arizona Special Collections Library. As I sifted through boxes of papers, I was constantly reminded that I followed a well-beaten path. I never met most of the researchers who went before me and made my work immeasurably easier, but I owe a debt of gratitude to all those who studied the Hubbells and left behind narratives, chronologies, deep insights, and stimulating analyses. For a place and a family as well loved and as thoroughly examined as Hubbell Trading Post and the Hubbells have been, the list is long indeed.

I wish to thank the editorial team at the University of Oklahoma Press, Charles E. Rankin, Steven B. Baker, and freelance copyeditor Rosanne Hallowell, for ushering me so pleasantly through the process of turning my report into a book. Any remaining errors are solely mine.

Finally, I give my deepest gratitude to my family and friends for their unflagging support, especially my mother, Joyce Cottam, for reading the manuscript and understanding what the Hubbells came to mean to me.

# Hubbell Trading Post

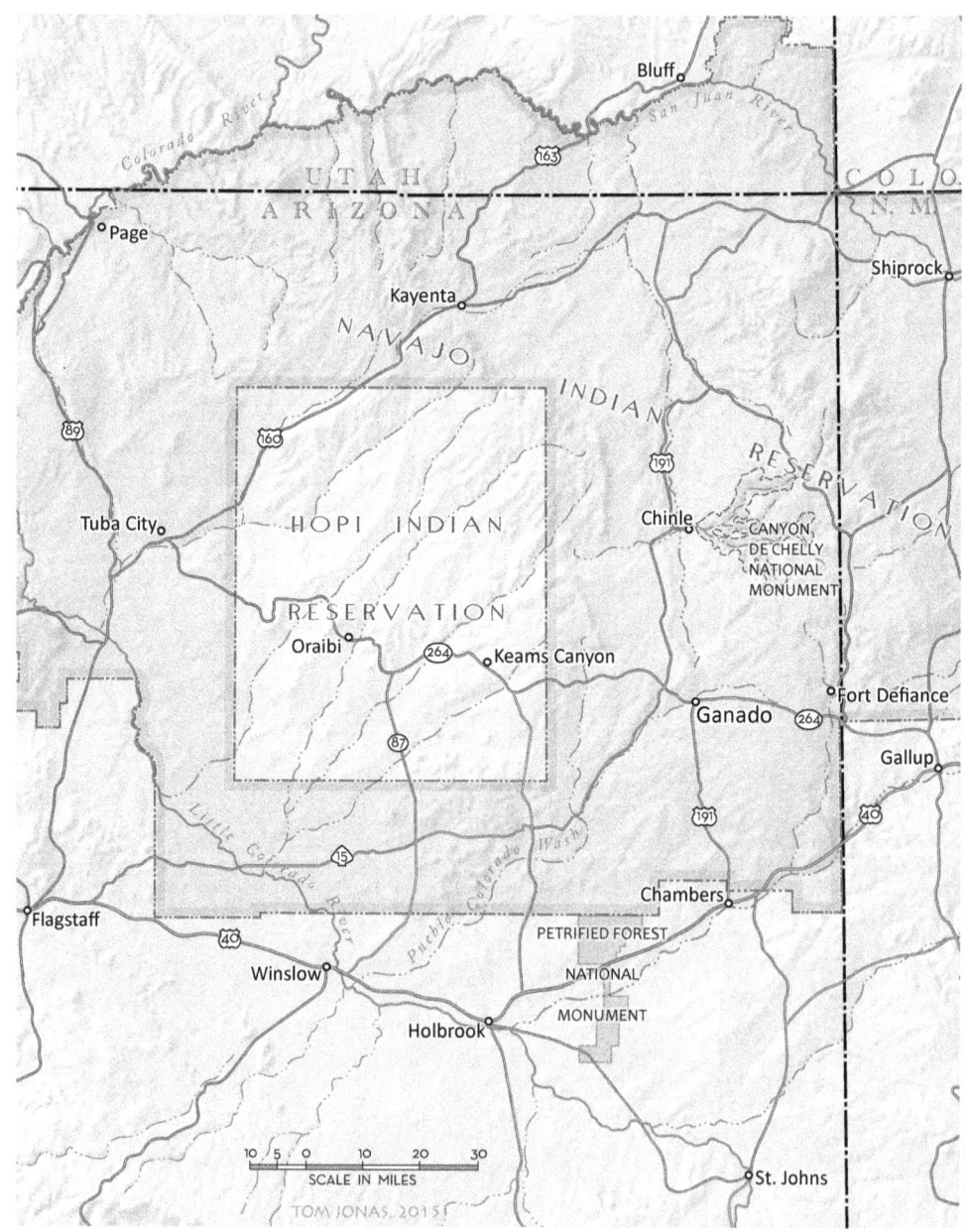

Northeastern Arizona and the Four Corners region. Map by Tom Jonas (based on Drawing No. 433/20,002, National Park Service, Technical Information Center). Copyright © 2015 by the University of Oklahoma Press.

# Introduction

In 1912, romance author Grace MacGowan Cooke spent a cold, sleeting afternoon sitting on a bale of blankets in the warehouse of an Indian trading post in Ganado, Arizona. She studied the half-Spanish, half-Yankee trader John Lorenzo Hubbell "covertly, as wielders of the pen have a trick of doing."[1] He sat behind his desk putting down figures while two Navajos and the trader's handsome young son, Roman, weighed, valued, and baled dozens of heavy wool blankets. Each blanket charmed her with its beauty, and the Navajos with their turquoise jewelry who strolled out of the freezing rain to stand in the warehouse and quietly watch added to the "riot of color."

Cooke had spent the winter living in the Hopi pueblo of Oraibi while she wrote a romance novel about the tempestuous relationship between an Indian trader and a spoiled socialite. All that winter, everyone she met told her that in neglecting to pass through Ganado, she had missed Navajo country's finest hospitality and its most interesting man. Charles F. Lummis, one of the Southwest's most noted devotees, told her that she had to visit Hubbell if only because "he was so magnificent a specimen of the western pathbreaker, a man who makes possible the civilization he rather shuns."

And so, as she prepared to leave the mesas and plateaus of northeastern Arizona, Cooke arranged to visit Hubbell Trading Post. As she approached it in one of Hubbell's wagons, she was welcomed, as many other tired pilgrims had been, by "a long, log adobe house, built in the unimposing Mexican style, sitting on the river bank with its store beside it." Inside, she found "a great assembly hall . . . of noble proportions, rough-ceiled to be sure, and with a big stone fireplace, but richly beautiful with its rug-covered floor, its walls a-tapestry of good paintings, admirably chosen photographs, and its

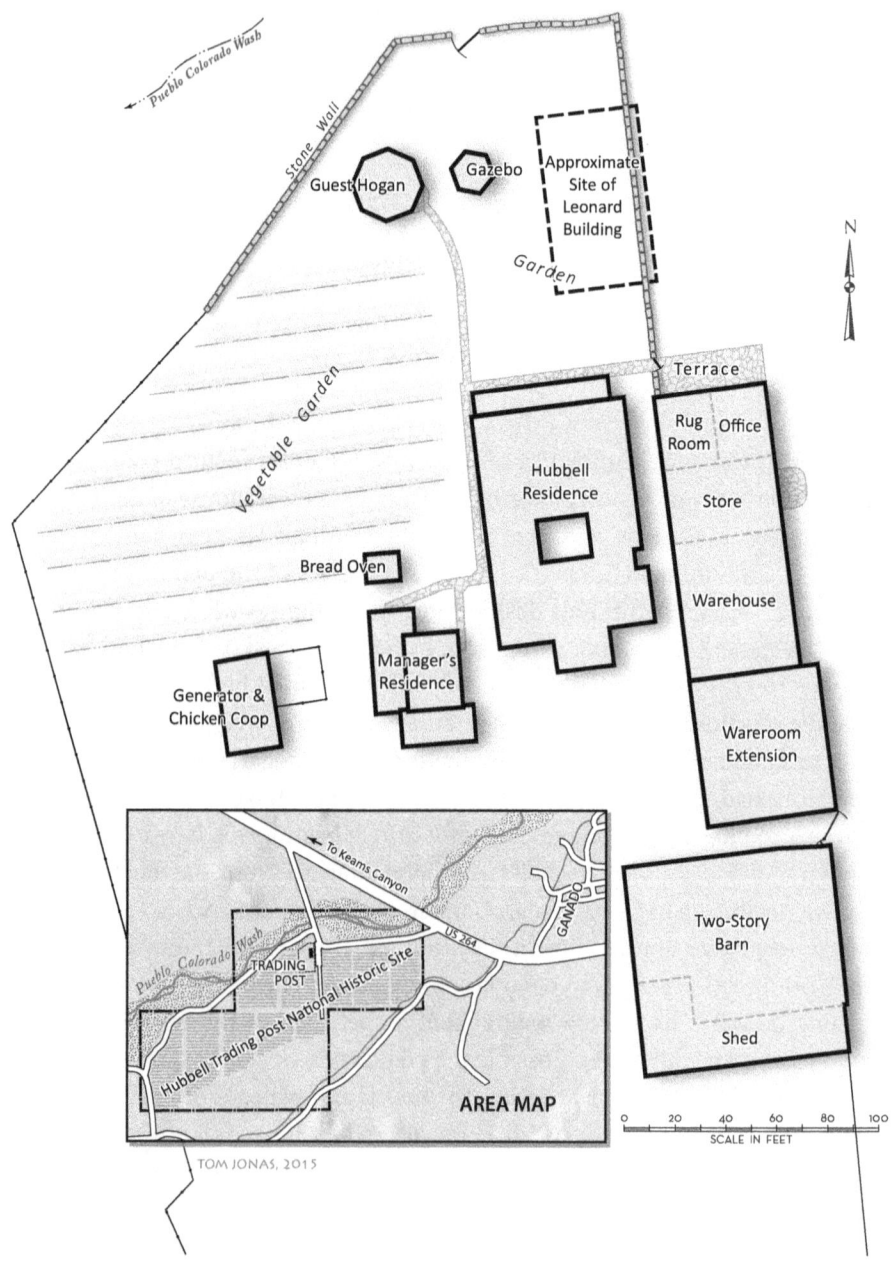

Buildings and grounds of Hubbell Trading Post. Map by Tom Jonas (based on Drawing No. 433/20,004, National Park Service, Technical Information Center). Copyright © 2015 by the University of Oklahoma Press.

ceiling a treasure of Indian baskets set in lines between the big beams." For three days, she forgot the hardships of her journey in the warm hospitality of the Hubbell home, spending hours upon hours admiring the "treasures of art, civilized and barbaric . . . beneath its roof" and watching Hubbell and his employees conduct the complex business of Indian trading. She enjoyed meals cooked over a bed of hot coals in the great fireplace, basking in the camaraderie that always garnished the Hubbell table. "What is it that gives the final exquisite flavor to a feast of this sort?" she wondered. "We all ate, the white people, the Indians, and the dog . . . and I think I never tasted food so delicious."

Her host she watched carefully, trying but failing to find in his Spanish generosity some trace of his Yankee father. She admired him, but was baffled by his complexity, his contradictions. When Cooke published her novel *The Joy Bringer*, she devoted a chapter to describing the trading post at Ganado, but Hubbell himself she did not attempt to recreate on the page. After all, she said, it was "only a fiction story" and she had already decided that Hubbell himself "was quite too romantic for any writer to put . . . in a book. One has to make up one's romance, and that of reality is apt to be voted quite too incredible by the reader."[2] Hubbell Trading Post would stand out brightly in her memory for the rest of her days, its proprietor a man too multifaceted even for stories.

John Lorenzo Hubbell was indeed a man of many guises. He had made his early reputation as the sheriff of Apache County, and many Arizonans knew him as a staunchly Republican politician, but his lasting fame came not from daring exploits or political influence, but rather, as historian Frank C. Lockwood notes, from his eminence as "a man of peace, a humanitarian, an able and honorable trader with the Indians."[3] His contemporaries and fellow Indian traders characterized him "as a brilliant, energetic, forceful man; always on his toes, ambitious to extend his control over the whole Navajo country, able to drive a sharp bargain, but never dishonest or oppressive."[4] Journalist and historian Charles Lummis perhaps said it best when he wrote:

> All along that strange, bald country are men worth knowing; for the frontier is the hardest test of manhood. It breaks the weaklings, and they slink off and fritter away. The strong man it makes a giant; and every man who has stood sentry in that land for a quarter of a century is worth knowing

and worth counting for friend. . . . But I believe not one of these grizzled veterans will grudge my estimate of Don Lorenzo as their dean. A frontier sheriff in the hard old times of Arizona and New Mexico; a political manager whose rival has never been known in the Territories; a handsome man, who looks old or young according to the activity of his razor; a mild blue-eyed person who no sane desperado would 'tackle;' the courtliest of men, the most generous of friends and foes, he has lived the paradoxes to the full.[5]

As the founder of Hubbell Trading Post, J. L. Hubbell is rightfully at the heart of any history of the homestead and business that would outlive him to become Hubbell Trading Post National Historic Site. It is, in fact, quite tempting to treat the trading post merely as a backdrop for the fascinating character of Don Lorenzo. But the story of Hubbell Trading Post, as an influence and an institution, extends beyond the reach of any one man, even as it extends far beyond the boundaries of a 160-acre ranch. It is the story not only of Don Lorenzo, but of the other people who called it home and spent their lives trying to hold it together: his children—Barbara, Adele, Lorenzo, Jr., and Roman—and their families, especially Roman's indomitable wife, Dorothy. It is the story of the people whose lives it profoundly touched and changed, and who, in turn, shaped its character: the Navajos and Hopis who traded there and the visitors who sheltered under its roof. It is the story of a trading empire that ceaselessly grew and shrunk, spreading the Hubbell influence across the Navajo Reservation, the trading post at Ganado its only constant, even when it seemed nearly forgotten.

This book covers the history of the trading post up to its designation as a national historic site in 1967. It is organized into nine chapters that move more or less chronologically through the site's history, with the exception of chapters 6 and 7, which deal with overarching themes that span the entire time period.

Chapter 1, "Drifting into Navajo Country," provides a broad overview of the interwoven histories of the Navajos and J. L. Hubbell's family. Between the sixteenth and eighteenth centuries, the Southwest became a hotly contested meeting ground of cultures. J. L. Hubbell, son of James L. Santiago Hubbell, an American soldier who had come to New Mexico in the Mexican-American War, and Juliana Gutiérrez, a daughter of one of New Mexico's most prominent Hispano families, was a product of that cultural meeting, as was the very practice of Navajo Indian trading. This chapter examines the violent forces that shaped Navajo culture in the nineteenth century, including the infamous exile at Bosque Redondo, which broke down the Navajo economy and provided a way for Indian traders to carve a niche for themselves.

Chapter 2, "Traders to the Navajos," takes us to the Pueblo Colorado Valley, where J. L. built his trading post. In this chapter, we meet the Navajo communities who called it home before the arrival of the first trader, as well as the men who pioneered the Indian trading business there. It examines the early partnership between J. L. Hubbell and C. N. Cotton, and follows J. L.'s business ventures in St. Johns, Arizona, his marriage to Lina Rubi, and his tenure as the sheriff of Apache County before he settled permanently in Ganado.

Chapter 3, "Laying the Foundations," takes a look at the early trading practices at the Hubbell Trading Post from 1878 to 1900. It examines the challenges of the seasonal trading cycle and the strategies Hubbell used to meet the peculiar demands of Navajo trading, including shipping and carrying the mail, the practice of taking pawn, and early farming activities. The chapter also chronicles the activities of the Hubbell family during the same time period, as well as the Navajo community at Hubbell Trading Post.

Chapter 4, "The Rise of an Empire," follows the expansion and evolution of the Hubbell Trading Post from 1900 to 1914. It examines J. L. Hubbell's career in Arizona politics and the contradictory role it played in the business—both as a platform from which Hubbell defended the rights of Hispanics and introduced water rights legislation that would benefit his claims on the Ganado homestead, and as a distraction that financially drained his business. The chapter also explores major changes that brought the Hubbell Trading Post to its zenith, including the development of irrigation and the coming of the automobile. It was during this time period that Hubbell also began to expand his reach on the Navajo Reservation by building up an empire of interconnected trading posts, one of the most important of which was his son Lorenzo, Jr.'s, first trading post at Keams Canyon.

Chapter 5, "Troubled Times," chronicles the time period from 1915 to 1929 that followed in the wake of J. L.'s failed bid for the United States Senate. The business continued to expand, contract, and evolve as global forces, from World War I to the Spanish Influenza, wreaked havoc on the Navajo economy and on the Hubbell family members' lives. This chapter also tells the story of the murder of J. L.'s brother Charlie, an incident that complicated the Hubbell family's relationship with the Navajos. In chapter 5 we also meet Dorothy Smith Hubbell, who came to the Hubbell Trading Post as a schoolteacher and later became its champion. The chapter closes with the death of J. L. Hubbell and leaves the trading post poised on the brink of change.

Chapter 6, "'No Misrepresentation, No Shams, and No Counterfeits,'" takes a step back in time to examine the role of Hubbell Trading Post in the development of Navajo weaving, the trade in Indian curios, and the rise of Southwestern tourism. It explores how the curio trade came to comprise one of the most important facets of the business, and attempts to gauge the impact J. L. and other traders had on Navajo weaving. It explores, too, the relationship J. L. built with the Fred Harvey Company, as well as the Hubbells' role in providing Navajo and Hopi demonstrators at events from world's fairs to local parades, and in supplying Native artifacts, both ancient and modern, to museum collections across America.

Chapter 7, "'Seekers of Beauty' and 'Adventurers into the Buried Long Ago,'" presents J. L. Hubbell in one of his most famous roles: as a host. It examines Hubbell Trading Post not as a business, but as a gathering place for the artists, writers, archaeologists, politicians, and tourists who flocked to Navajo country to experience its unparalleled landscapes and fascinating peoples. From Theodore Roosevelt to Maynard Dixon to E. A. Burbank, visitors found at Hubbell Trading Post a hospitable welcome and a trader overflowing with thrilling stories. This chapter also follows Lorenzo, Jr., and Roman as they carried on their father's tradition of hospitality after their father's death.

Chapter 8, "'The Worst They Ever Knew,'" picks up where chapter 6 ended: with the death of J. L. It analyzes the efforts of Lorenzo, Jr., Roman, and Dorothy to hold the family business together from 1930 to 1945 during the harsh years of the Great Depression, livestock reduction, and World War II. Lorenzo, Jr., took over management and ownership of the trading business, while Roman and Dorothy founded Roman Hubbell Navajo Tours. But the deaths first of Roman and Dorothy's son, Monnie, a born trader who would have inherited the trading post business, and then of Lorenzo, Jr., set the stage for desperate times to come.

Chapter 9, "A New Era," covers the period from 1945 to 1967, a time of massive change for the Hubbells, the Navajos, and the business of Indian trading. As modernization swept over the Navajo Reservation in the wake of World War II, it fundamentally altered the relationship between the Navajos and the traders. This chapter investigates the forces that led to Hubbell Trading Post's designation as a national historic site, including a devastating bankruptcy that left the Hubbell empire in ashes, and the death of Roman. It follows Dorothy's indefatigable efforts to preserve the Hubbell family legacy through years of congressional deliberation, and ends with the dedication of her one-time home as Hubbell Trading Post National Historic Site.

This book began its life as a report entitled "'The Hospitable Home of Lorenzo Hubbell': A Historic Resource Study of Hubbell Trading Post," commissioned by the National Park Service. Its purpose was to gather together and distill into a single narrative history the vast pool of knowledge on Hubbell Trading Post. The trading post and its proprietor have been much written about; the National Park Service has commissioned several historic reports on Hubbell Trading Post, and independent scholars have produced even more, with topics ranging from biography to irrigation and agriculture, weaving, and archaeology. Newspaper and magazine articles on the Hubbells and Navajo trading are more numerous still. In addition, the archival record on Hubbell Trading Post is startlingly voluminous, once preserved in barrels in the Hubbell barn and now housed in 574 boxes of letters, ledgers, and records at the University of Arizona Special Collections Library. With such a thorough primary and secondary record, I had to make difficult choices about what to include in the narrative, and I am convinced that the records still hold many other stories. Revised and shortened, this book represents my efforts to tell the overarching history of Hubbell Trading Post and the local and national forces that shaped it. Above all else, I have tried to tell a human story. It is my hope that the reader will come to see what the trading post meant to the Navajos, the Hubbell family, and their friends.

CHAPTER ONE

# Drifting into Navajo Country
## *Juan Lorenzo Hubbell and the Navajos*

In 1870, a handsome, bespectacled seventeen-year-old named Juan Lorenzo Hubbell invested his savings in a saddle horse and outfit and embarked alone on a journey that would eventually see him crowned the "King of Northern Arizona," owner of an Indian trading empire that bridged the gulf between the Navajos and the American consumer.[1] The short, barrel-chested young man had spent the previous year working as a clerk in the Albuquerque post office for the rather good wage of $40 a month. But Hubbell was, as noted by historian Frank McNitt, "a self-reliant fellow . . . ready to wrestle any man for fun or to fight in earnest if forced to."[2] In short, Hubbell found that "the indoor life of a postal clerk" failed to satisfy his "craving for romance and adventure."[3] He set off for Utah Territory "through little-known country and along very uncertain trails" that wandered through vast areas of desert reigned over by the Navajos.[4] He pressed through the sandy expanse of Navajo country to Kanab, a fledgling Mormon settlement perched on the knife-edge of failure and prosperity, where he found employment as a clerk at a trading post. For a few critical years, he learned the ropes of the trading business and the Navajo language, but Utah, for reasons more mythical than factual, disagreed with young Hubbell. It spat him back out into Navajo country, the stories say, with a couple of bullet holes in his body.

Many years later, an aging, white-haired Hubbell would enjoy long hours sitting on the porch of his trading post in Ganado, Arizona, spinning yarns for the travelers and tourists among whom he was something of a legend. Like most such stories, they grew taller in the telling, and the historical record offers few crumbs that can either contradict or corroborate them. The tale of his flight from Utah, a favorite of his admirers, took on many different contours. He evasively told one reporter, "Some parts of a story are best left untold, so it is enough for me to say that I became involved in difficulties."[5] To others he told a more embroidered tale—that the trouble began when he "started courting a girl up there."[6] Hubbell's neighbor, Gene Haldeman, recalled, "He liked her pretty well and decided he'd better lay off of that, and, so he was getting ready to go back towards Albuquerque, a bunch of hombres decided that he'd courted that girl just enough that he should marry her but he wasn't about to."[7] Humorously, the way Hubbell's own grandson heard it from one of the farmhands, he fled because "he got mixed up with one of the Mormon girls up there and then it seemed that the Mormon bishop wanted to have a word with him, and that he was going to [have to] marry all of the sisters."[8]

Before he could be "pronounced 'man and wives,'" J. L. packed his things and took off on horseback, with his pursuers not far behind. In the "rumpus" that followed, bullets flew and Hubbell escaped by the skin of his teeth with a wound in his left leg and another in his back.[9] He told his doctor (flourishing his scars for dramatic illustration) that he had waited in ambush and killed all seven of his pursuers in the gun battle that gave him his wounds.[10] To others, he said he simply took off his clothes and dove into the roaring Colorado River.[11]

"I wandered for days," he intoned, "scarcely knowing where I was or what actually happened."[12] Delirious, he staggered into a Paiute camp where he was nursed back to health, a rescue from "certain death" that forever disposed him kindly toward all Native Americans. Under the care of the Paiutes, the stories say, he was shortly on his feet again and headed south. He spent a golden summer at the Hopi pueblos, where he witnessed his first Snake Dance ceremony at a time when few outsiders had seen it, though it would later become one of the premier tourist attractions of northeastern Arizona.

"After nearly five years of wandering and the collection of experiences somewhat similar to those of Marco Polo," Hubbell reflected, "I drifted back into New Mexico again, and then into Navajo country." In 1876, he bought a trading post in the Pueblo Colorado Valley, a little speck of green in the desert with a shallow lake, a modest river, and a Navajo village. He arrived at a crucial time. Not long before, the Navajos had been rounded up by the US Army and forced onto a reservation in eastern New Mexico, far from their traditional homeland in the Four Corners region. The exile lasted only four years before the government acknowledged the project's failure and allowed the Navajos to return home, but it had a lasting and devastating effect on their economy, opening the door to a new system of trade. American entrepreneurs, Hubbell among them, moved into Navajo country on the heels of the returning Navajos, bringing with them an array of manufactured goods and working a dramatic economic transformation that would eventually tie Navajo-made arts and crafts into the national market.

Hubbell played a central role in that transformation. He is credited with being one of the first traders to see the market potential of Navajo rugs and silver jewelry at a time when the trade centered on wool, hides, and sheep. Through concerted advertising efforts which coincided with a cultural movement in which Americans became enamored of the "primitive," by the turn of the twentieth century, Hubbell had become one of the most well-known dealers in Navajo and Hopi products in the Southwest. George Wharton James, tireless promoter of Southwestern Indian arts and crafts, captured public sentiment toward Hubbell: "Few men have ever held so honored and rare a position in the esteem of the Navahos and in relation to the blanket industry as does John Lorenzo Hubbell. . . . That his name is synonymous with honorable and upright dealing goes without saying, for no man can stand as he does with the Navahos without being—as the Indians would say—'a walker in the beautiful way.'"[13]

Hubbell built up his fame on two other fronts: as a player in Arizona politics, and as "the most hospitable man in the world."[14] An avid Republican, Hubbell served terms in both the Arizona territorial and state legislatures, and in a dozen other small delegations and offices, most notably as the fabled sheriff of Apache County. His impact on Arizona politics was unremarkable, but his involvement helped spread his fame as an Indian trader and earned him connections in political circles across the country, especially those concerned with Native American rights. Meanwhile, the same cultural impulses that drove the market for Navajo arts and crafts beckoned travelers to Navajo country. At first, they were occasional scientists, artists, and writers traveling on horseback or by wagon, but as the years rolled on, the railroad and the automobile brought increasing numbers of tourists into the heart of Navajo country. In the absence of hotels, Hubbell flung open the doors of his trading post and stately home, surrounded by irrigated fields, herds of Navajo sheep, and the endless piñon-covered landscape. As he sheltered, fed, and guided visitors, he regaled them with tall tales until both he and his hospitality had become legendary. Even after Hubbell's death in 1930, his trading post remained closely associated with the Navajo Southwest. The Hubbell name was carried on by his two sons, who became as well-known in their day as their father had been in his: kindly Lorenzo, Jr., for his selfless hospitality, charming Roman for his exciting Navajo country tours, and both of them for their intimate knowledge of Navajo arts and culture. Theirs was a family inseparably connected to the Navajos.

Just as that connection persisted after J. L.'s death, its roots extended further into the past than J. L.'s first foray into northeastern Arizona in 1870. His family heritage was inseparably entangled with the history of Spanish, Mexican, and American conquest, his own life of trading, politics, and hospitality shaped by his upbringing in the tri-cultural Southwest. Even at seventeen, the venturesome and romantic Juan Lorenzo was nothing if not the product of his heritage. His mother was a daughter of Spanish dons, his father an adventuring son of Connecticut Yankees. Every branch of his family tree was heavy with politicians, soldiers, traders, landowners, and ranchers who earned and maintained power by their own sweat and blood, almost always in competition with the Southwest's indigenous peoples.

## Spaniards and Navajos

By all accounts, Juan Lorenzo's mother, Juliana Gutiérrez (sometimes affectionately called Julianita), was a remarkable woman, graceful in character and appearance. Family stories say she was a blue-eyed blonde, "her Castilian blood ... traceable in her sparkling beauty."[15] The descendent of some of the earliest of New Mexico's Spanish settlers, she was an heiress to a large parcel of land and a family legacy of wealth and influence. Her family had been in the New World since the 1500s, when Luis Baca crossed the Atlantic from Toledo, Spain, to settle in Mexico City, which was then rising from the ashes of the conquered Aztec city of Tenochitlán.[16] In 1600, his grandson, Captain Cristóbal Baca, took his family north into New Mexico to reinforce the fledgling Spanish colony of San Gabriel de los Caballeros under Juan de Oñate.[17] From the seventeenth century onward, the family left its mark on New Mexico, while the enchanted land in turn left its mark upon them. Of all the actions and conflicts that shaped the generations that followed, perhaps it is most important to understand that from the time they first set foot on New Mexican soil, the lives of Juliana's ancestors were inseparably entangled with the lives of the Native Americans. Every generation was involved at some level in the wrestle for New Mexico. The Baca family were among the Spanish settlers who fled the violence of the Pueblo Revolt of 1680, and they were among those who later returned to take back their *estancias* and retrench the Spanish foothold in the Southwest, acre by acre.[18]

At first, the Navajos, or the Diné (the People), as they call themselves, were somewhat removed from the upheavals brought by Hubbell's ancestors. When Spanish explorers penetrated the New World in the sunset years of the sixteenth century, they were enticed over the desert horizon by persistent rumors of gold, but when their forays into Navajo territory yielded no gleaming profit, they concentrated their efforts on settlements in the Rio Grande Valley.[19] Spanish explorer Francisco Vásquez de Coronado and his men encountered many sights that would later be called wondrous, including the Grand Canyon and the Hopi mesas, while traipsing about the Southwest in search of wealth.[20] But their enthusiasm waned when their search proved fruitless, and for forty years Spanish settlers largely ignored the region save for a few far-flung missions.

In 1583, Antonio de Espejo, "a fugitive fleeing a murder charge who financed an expedition to find two missing priests and thereby redeem his name," became the first European since Coronado to explore northeastern Arizona, and the first to record contact with the Navajos.[21] At the time of Espejo's expedition, Navajo culture had not yet coalesced into what it would be. Scholars argue that the Navajos, along with the Apaches, differ markedly from the Southwest's Pueblo cultures in language and custom, instead sharing linguistic traits with indigenous groups in western Canada, collectively known as Athabaskan- or Dene-speakers. Archaeologists posit that the Navajos migrated into the Southwest from the subarctic between 1000 and 1525 CE. Whether their route took them over the High Plains or along the backbone of the Rocky Mountains, the migration involved a journey of thousands of miles, hundreds of years, and significant cultural change. The Navajos are known for being ever ready to incorporate other peoples and traditions into their lives. Old ways were adapted or exchanged as the migrating Athabaskans encountered new climates, environments, and peoples.[22] As Peter Iverson argues, nearly every group with which the Diné came into contact, "people from Jemez Pueblo, San Felipe Pueblo, the Utes, the Chiricahua Apaches, the Zunis, other Puebloans, Paiutes, and even Spanish/Mexican groups were integrated in time into the Diné."[23] The extent and rate of that change is impossible to judge—but at the time of Espejo's expedition, they had not yet become the Apaches de Nabajó described by seventeenth century explorers, and even the Apaches de Nabajó were not yet the Navajos as Americans would know them.[24] The outlines of the expedition's impressions of the Navajos are faint, but they noted a few key characteristics: namely, that the Navajos were growing corn, raising livestock, and already burnishing a reputation as warriors.[25]

Espejo and his men clashed briefly with the Navajos, but it was the Pueblo peoples who bore the brunt of their violence. On his way back to San Bartolomé, "Espejo set out on a troublemaking journey among the pueblos, killing people who resisted . . . in any way and in one instance putting a village to the torch."[26] It was a portent of things to come. When the Spanish government sent Juan de Oñate to establish the first Spanish colonies in New Mexico in response to Espejo's reports, Oñate infamously subdued Acoma Pueblo by massacring several hundred Acomas and cutting off the feet of the survivors.[27] Unlike the stationary Pueblo peoples who were pounded by the iron fist of Spanish colonialism, however, the Navajos were mobile, still living "on the margins of the Spanish Empire in a rugged terrain that the Europeans found difficult to penetrate."[28]

However, European goods, primarily livestock, continued to flow north into Navajo hands. Recognizing the utility of sheep, goats, horses, and cattle, the Navajos readily appropriated them for their own use, even absorbing them into their cosmology. "Long ago," the stories go, "when the Holy People still roamed the earth, Changing Woman created livestock to reward the Hero Twins for ridding the world of evil."[29] Sheep became increasingly central to Navajo culture as they developed a seasonal economy centered on herding and began to weave wool textiles.[30] With the help of four-legged beasts, in the cradle of Dinétah in northwestern New Mexico, the birthplace of the Navajos, they became "the largest and most powerful Native community in the Southwest."[31]

As the Navajos' herds and flocks grew, livestock became a source of conflict between the Navajos and their neighbors. While the Navajos acquired many of their livestock through trade, others they obtained through raiding. Mounted, they became a force to be reckoned with in the Southwest, for their adaptability did not mean they made no distinction between themselves—the People—and others, especially enemy people, *anaii dineé*.[32] The Navajos

A Navajo boy and his dog herd sheep in the Pueblo Colorado Valley. Courtesy of the National Park Service, HUTR 05556.

were curious, enterprising, pragmatic, and expansionist. "Once the people acquired a few horses," Peter Iverson explains, "they wanted or needed more horses—and more land for them. Once they obtained a few sheep, they understood the benefits of having more—and the necessity of finding a place for them. Such an approach guaranteed that the Navajos would gain a reputation."[33] And gain a reputation they did—the Navajos were ever willing to trade with or fight against their neighbors, Native American or European, as best served their interests. They frequently clashed with the Comanches and Utes, each side taking horses, sheep, and even human captives from the other. With the arrival of the Spanish, slave raiding became an epidemic in the Southwest, and though they were removed from the frontier of Spanish settlement, "[t]he Navajos suffered more from Spanish slavery than any other Native group."[34] The Spanish indulgence in the slave trade dramatically increased Navajo raids, as they were motivated not by material gain, but by the attempt to retrieve slaves, especially captured women and children. The Navajos and the Spanish became locked in a seemingly endless cycle of raiding and retribution: the Navajos raided Spanish settlements, and in return the Spanish launched punitive invasions, "seizing Navajo horses; taking men, women, and children captive; killing others; and burning their cornfields."[35]

A few episodes of the centuries-long Navajo–Spanish feud are particularly worth noting here. Some individual Navajos participated in the Pueblo Revolt of 1680, when the Pueblos declared emphatically that they had had enough by violently ejecting the Spanish colonists from New Mexico. Twelve years later, the Navajos provided a refuge for fleeing Pueblo peoples during the Spanish Reconquest in 1692, an important moment in Navajo history, as the influx of Pueblo peoples helped shape Navajo culture.[36] War with the Spanish colonists continued more or less unabated from then on, with an interlude from about 1716 to 1774, during which the Navajos and the Spanish formed a fragile alliance while they fought a common enemy in the Utes. During that peace, Spanish settlers moved onto Navajo lands for the first time, and "the encroachment of thousands and thousands of Spanish sheep, and the lure that they held for young Diné seeking prestige and power, triggered a round of raiding."[37] In 1774, Navajos attacked the settlements and successfully drove out the colonists, but the victory was brief.[38] In 1805, Lieutenant Antonio Narbona led a retaliatory expedition against the Navajos, who retreated to Canyon de Chelly and Canyon del Muerto, where Narbona and his men massacred 155 Navajo men, women, and children, an episode that still haunts Navajo memory.[39] The Navajos, however, remained unsubdued and continued to test their might against the Spanish government until Mexico won its independence from Spain in 1821. The Mexican government had no better luck subduing the Navajos than the Spanish had—if anything, warfare and slave raiding increased under Mexican rule. Violence escalated in the 1820s and 1830s. Once Spain was ousted, lines of trade with the Anglo-Americans, once kept clamped tightly shut by the Spanish government, opened, flooding the territory with superior firearms that further fed the cycle of raiding.[40] It was a crucial period in Navajo history. Contact with the Spanish colonists and their livestock "fostered a metamorphosis from a relative small population almost invisible to Spanish observers to one of the most populous and powerful indigenous nations in North America."[41]

J. L. Hubbell's ancestors remained in the thick of the violence, benefitting from the Indians' losses. Among the company of men who invaded Canyon de Chelly with Antonio Narbona was Hubbell's great-grandfather, Lorenzo Antonio Gutiérrez.[42] He followed in the footsteps of his fathers, who had fought in exchange for land grants in the conquered territory. Each generation amassed property, including a tract of land in Pajarito, New Mexico, not far from Albuquerque, where Juan Lorenzo would one day be born.[43] They amassed wealth, too, as educated, successful businessmen married into the family. One of Hubbell's ancestors, Clemente Gutiérrez, became known by the regal name "King of the Chihuahua traders," with extensive business connections that allowed him to "virtually control New Mexico's export and import of goods vital to the . . . colonists."[44] The Gutiérrez family used their combined affluence and prestige to control local economics, politics, and even religion. For example, after campaigning against the Navajos, Lorenzo Antonio Gutiérrez served as the mayor of Albuquerque under Spanish rule and was made the first provincial governor of New Mexico after Mexican Independence.[45]

The Mexican-American War soon brought change to both the Gutiérrez family and the Navajos. James L. Hubbell, a young New Englander, came to New Mexico to fight and ended up marrying Lorenzo Antonio's granddaughter, Juliana. He was an unlikely but apt successor for the political, military, and economic heritage of a prominent Hispanic family, fitting in as if he had been born in the desert Southwest instead of the verdant East.[46] The Navajos, however, found that despite having been bombarded with change for centuries, Spanish and Mexican rule "could not prepare the Navajos for the kind of demands the Americans would make upon them beginning in the 1840s."[47] No longer would their isolation from Santa Fe and the colonial government keep them on the fringes of white interference. Once the United States took control of the Southwest, it entered into the process of exploration and military subjugation with single-minded vigor.

## *The American Period*

Tensions between the United States and Mexico had been simmering since 1836 when Sam Houston and his army of American settlers-turned-rebels won Texan independence from Mexico. The Mexicans feared the furor of Manifest Destiny that seemed to drive American settlers westward in an unstoppable wave that penetrated Mexican territory with a cheerful disregard for political borders. When the United States annexed Texas and initiated a failed attempt to buy California and New Mexico in 1845, tensions finally came to a head; President James K. Polk declared war on Mexico in May 1846 in what has been called "the most monumental land grab in North American history."[48]

The war that followed was relatively short. By September 1847 American troops had seized Mexico City, and by the following March, the Treaty of Guadalupe Hidalgo had been signed and ratified. In fact, James Lawrence Hubbell, who had mustered in to the army in Kansas and marched over the Santa Fe Trail to reinforce General Stephen W. Kearny's forces, found that by the time he got there, Santa Fe had already been bloodlessly captured.[49] James had grown up in Connecticut, with family roots sunk deep in the New England soil, but something about the promise of New Mexico as it became an American Territory enticed him to stay, as it did many American volunteers. "Presumably he fell in love with this strange land," one of his descendants speculated, "or perhaps it was the beautiful Juliana."[50] Historian Marc Simmons echoes those sentiments: "For a New Englander, the land and people were as foreign as anything that could be imagined. But since youth often responds to the adventuresome and exotic, Hubbell concluded to stay and make a new life for himself."[51]

Whatever the reason for his decision to remain, James fit into the New Mexico political and economic scene as if he had been born to it—and he was not alone. In the wake of the Mexican-American War, masses of Yankee traders flooded into Santa Fe to take advantage of the new markets opened up by the change in administration. They "married Hispanic or Indian women, and immersed themselves in the area's cultures."[52] In James's case, that embrace of Hispanic culture is symbolized by his change of name—he swapped James Lawrence for Santiago Lorenzo—and by his marriage on May 31, 1849, to the sixteen-year-old Juliana Gutiérrez, heiress to the 45,000-acre Pajarito land grant. James's brothers, John, Sidney, and Charles, soon joined him in New Mexico, followed in 1880 by their parents.[53]

James's—or rather, Santiago's—ready adaptation to Spanish culture served him well. Martha Blue writes, "James, who could move gracefully from 'good morning' to '*buenos días*' and from 'mister' to '*señor*' and back again, was heavily relied upon by his in-laws for his bilingual skills. These, coupled with his vigor in pursuing his various private endeavors—freighting and sheep-raising—rapidly carried him up the Southwest's ladder of success."[54] He became a prosperous trader, with "his 48-wagon freight lines to Kansas City, along with his cattle imports from Mexico . . . fast making him a wealthy man."[55]

The United States, meanwhile, found itself in possession of a territory about which it knew almost nothing, with Navajo country at its heart. At the close of the war, in return for $18,250,000 in cash payments, Mexico ceded to the United States an immense section of land, including all of present-day California, Nevada, and Utah, most of Arizona and New Mexico, and parts of Wyoming, Colorado, Kansas, and Oklahoma. California was the prize—and Arizona almost an afterthought. As anthropologist Thomas E. Sheridan states, "[M]ost Anglo pioneers and politicians considered it a wasteland, a desert, an Indian-infested obstacle between Santa Fe and San Diego."[56] The Americans could get very little information about the land or its people from the Spanish and Mexicans, who, despite having been in the area for hundreds of years, had scarcely a better notion of Navajo life and culture than the newcomers. The only reliable information Anglo-Americans received as they stood poised to penetrate the Southwest lay in three areas: trade, warfare, and the already famous Navajo blanket.[57]

A smattering of Anglo mountain men had encountered the Diné and visited Navajo lands in the decades leading up to the Mexican-American War, but after the war came an avalanche. The US government swiftly dispatched official parties of soldiers, surveyors, and explorers in the late 1840s and 1850s to map wagon and rail routes through this inconvenient new land they had acquired. It was a change in administration that the Navajos noticed immediately. In 1846, not long after seizing Santa Fe from the Mexicans, General Stephen W. Kearny, who saw the Navajos and New Mexico's other Native peoples as problems waiting to be solved, dispatched Colonel Alexander W. Doniphan into Navajo country to recover any goods that the Navajos may have stolen, and to secure a promise of future good conduct at whatever price was deemed necessary. On that expedition, Doniphan would procure the first peace treaty between the United States and the Navajos, opening an era of rocky relations.[58] Contact between Navajos and Americans increased in frequency when the California Gold Rush began with a bang in 1848, lighting a fire under Congress to build a rail route to connect the suddenly important hinterlands with the East. Congress passed a flurry of railroad legislation, authorizing three surveys to determine the most practicable route to the Pacific, one of which crossed through Navajo territory.[59]

One of the first of many American military expeditions to explore the Colorado Plateau was an 1849 expedition led by Colonel John M. Washington. James H. Simpson, a member of the corps, kept a journal recording his observations of the Navajos and the landscape in rich detail. Simpson described the desert country of the Colorado Plateau as "one extended *naked, barren* waste, sparsely covered with cedar and pine of a scrub growth, and thickly sprinkled with the wild sage . . . suggesting very appropriately the dead, lifeless color of the wild."[60] The Navajos, too, puzzled him, as he wondered how a people he saw as so poor could weave such beautiful blankets.[61] The expedition also included an artist, Richard Kern, whose (generally inaccurate) sketches and watercolors went forth with Simpson's written observations to become the first images of the Navajos and their land to enter the fertile American imagination.[62] Many other scientific, surveying, and military expeditions followed, blazing trails that became major thoroughfares of travel in Navajo country for many years. As the 1850s came to a close, more and more Anglo-Americans found their way into Navajo country.[63]

Together, these expeditions built a composite image of the Navajos and the Colorado Plateau in the American popular consciousness—an image that would affect military and assimilation policies involving the Navajos. At first, the image was flattering. "In the popular imagination, the Navajos were powerful, dominant, noble, aboriginal, and wealthy," magnificent weavers, and superior to both other American Indians and to Hispanics.[64] But during the 1850s and 1860s, the image transformed as the Navajos' military might was turned against the United States. Lieutenant Joseph Christmas Ives described the Navajos as "saucy, impertinent, merry, and generous," but where he saw liveliness, others saw a threat.[65] War colored Americans' impressions of the Navajos until the dominant image of the Navajos transformed into a caricature of marauders who raided for the sheer love of plunder. These images were black and white, with no subtlety to shade the complicated motives and history underlying Navajo raiding and reprisals.[66]

## *The Long Walk*

When the United States inherited Mexico's military troubles with the Navajos, it wasted no time in attempting to put an end to the generations-long raiding and slaving wars. Even before the Treaty of Guadalupe-Hidalgo had been signed, General Stephen Watts Kearny promised Santa Fe residents that the United States would "protect the persons and property of all quiet and peaceful inhabitants within its boundaries against their enemies: the Eutaws, the Navajoes, and others," a promise that was tantamount to a declaration of war on the Navajos.[67] The United States immediately dispatched military expeditions into Navajo lands to make seemingly endless treaties that were invariably broken before the ink had a chance to dry. Between 1846 and 1868, seven treaties were negotiated between the Navajos and the United States.[68]

When Colonel Alexander W. Doniphan negotiated the first of the treaties at Ojo del Oso—present-day Fort Wingate, near Gallup, New Mexico—he warned the Navajos that if they did not cease their attacks on New Mexican villages, the United States would retaliate. Navajo Zarcillos Largos expressed his outrage and confusion at such a proposal:

> Americans! You have a strange cause of war against the Navajos. We have waged war against the New Mexicans for several years. We have plundered their villages and killed many of their people, and made many prisoners. We have just cause for all this. You have lately commenced a war against the same people. You are powerful. You have great guns and many brave soldiers. You have therefore conquered them, the very thing we have been attempting to do for so many years. You now turn upon us for attempting to do what you have done yourselves. We cannot see why you have cause to quarrel with us for fighting the New Mexicans on the west while you do the same thing on the east. . . . This is our war. We have more right to complain of you for interfering in our war, than you have to quarrel with us for continuing a war we have begun long before you got here.[69]

The Navajos held little respect for this treaty or the ones that followed it. As Peter Iverson states, "They understood it for what it was: an arrangement negotiated in haste and signed under duress."[70] They continued in their efforts to retrieve the children they had lost to the New Mexican slave trade.

Consequently, many of the explorers who entered Navajo country did so on military errands in the project to pacify the Navajos. Colonel Washington's 1849 expedition was, in fact, for the purpose of signing yet another treaty—but a senseless fracas resulted in the death of Navajo headman Narbona, one of the Navajos' most prominent peace leaders, then a frail old man. Narbona's son-in-law, Manuelito, witnessed the old man's death and subsequent scalping by a New Mexico volunteer, an incident that deepened his distrust of Americans. Manuelito would become one of the Navajos' fiercest war leaders, joining with other Navajo headmen to launch a concerted resistance against American occupation.[71]

The treaty signed in the wake of the violence allowed the military to build forts on Navajo land, which "led to unremitting warfare and unimaginable suffering."[72] Fort Defiance was constructed in 1851 some thirty miles east of the Pueblo Colorado Valley. As Sheridan writes, "Fort Defiance lived up to its name—an isolated gesture of aggression against a people it could neither conquer nor control."[73] It became the center of increasing conflicts between the Navajos and the US Army, culminating in April 1860, when Manuelito and Barboncito, another prominent headman, led a thousand Navajo warriors in an attack against the fort in the early morning chill. They nearly succeeded in taking it, but were thwarted by the Americans' superior firepower. The event thoroughly convinced the New Mexicans that the Navajos were more dangerous than the US military was prepared to handle, and that it was time to take matters into their own hands.[74]

In the aftermath of the attack, companies of volunteer militia under the command of Manuel Chaves "scoured the Navajo country, killing any men they found and enslaving about a hundred women and children. The volunteers . . . destroyed Navajo cornfields and captured thousands of cattle, horses, and sheep."[75] But this was only a prelude to the sledgehammer blow that would cripple the Navajo resistance when Brigadier General James H. Carleton took command of the US military in New Mexico. "Lean, sharp-featured, and ramrod straight," Carleton was brought to New Mexico by the force of the Civil War—a war that would have far-reaching impacts for the Navajos.[76] When the Confederates took southern New Mexico and established the Confederate Territory of Arizona in 1861 (New Mexico Territory had previously included Arizona), the Union retaliated by sending a column of California Volunteers into Arizona under Carleton's command. The column pushed through Arizona into New Mexico, meeting little Confederate resistance, and by the summer of 1862, the Confederate threat in the Southwest had been all but eliminated.[77]

In August, Carleton succeeded Colonel Edward R. S. Canby as commander of the Department of New Mexico—and subsequently of the huge numbers of troops left idle in the wake of the Civil War, a military force larger than any New Mexico had ever seen. Carleton has been described as many things: "tough and efficient," an "uncompromising disciplinarian," "energetic, articulate," "aloof and imperious," and a "rabid unionist."[78] With the Confederate threat neutralized, Carleton brought his considerable energy and resources to bear on scouring New Mexico clean of the Indian threat. He "assumed the role of deliverer of the Southwest," swiftly implementing a program that "was harsh and simple: to kill or capture the Indians until they agreed to surrender and live on a single reservation, where they could be taught Christianity and agriculture."[79] He was convinced that the only way to defeat the Indians was to remove them to a remote reservation where they could be assimilated into American culture through schooling, agrarianism, and conversion to Christianity, ideas that had been gaining currency in American Indian affairs since the 1840s.[80]

With the increased military resources available to him at the close of the Civil War, and with the Utes as powerful allies, Carleton was able to subdue the Navajos where all of his predecessors—Spanish, Mexican, and American—had failed. Throughout the Navajos' vast territory, Carleton's commanders delivered an ultimatum: "Go to the Bosque Redondo, or we will pursue and destroy you. We will not make peace with you on any other terms."[81] And then they carried it out.[82] Santiago Hubbell, who had served in the Union Army in New Mexico during the Civil War, took part in the beginning phases of Carleton's plan.[83] He campaigned against the Mescalero Apaches, but resigned to pursue more lucrative business opportunities before the campaign turned its devastating force against the Navajos.[84]

Carleton's plan culminated in the brutal and much-remembered winter campaign of legendary mountain man Christopher "Kit" Carson in 1863.[85] Though Santiago watched from the sidelines, his brother Charles served under Carson as a Lieutenant in the First New Mexico Cavalry during the roundup. The Navajos held out against the army's attacks for months in the wake of the ultimatum, retreating into their mountain fastnesses as Carleton's men burned their crops, ate their livestock, and murdered or enslaved captives. But their resistance was shattered when Carson invaded the tribe's stronghold at Canyon de Chelly, the key to Navajo defenses. His indiscriminate warfare and scorched-earth policies wore the Navajos down during the harsh winter as they were unable to store food. Starving and desperate, they began to surrender at the close of 1863. The campaign against the Navajos went on for several more years under Carleton's direction as the army continued to ferret out fugitive bands of Navajos and force them to the reservation; war leader Manuelito eluded the authorities until 1866.[86]

The site chosen for the Navajos' incarceration was Fort Sumner, called Bosque Redondo by the Mexicans and Hwéeldi by the Navajos, located in eastern New Mexico along the Pecos River. The three-hundred-mile forced march from Diné Bikéyah, the Navajo homeland encircled by four sacred mountains, to Bosque Redondo was interminable and brutal. Known as the Long Walk, it haunts the stories of the Navajos. Navajo historian Jennifer Nez Denetdale writes: "Their remembrances tell of how their ancestors, in the face of starvation, death, and brutality, were forced to abandon the elders and pregnant women who could no longer keep pace with the group. Mothers killed their newborn infants because they did not want to see them suffer or because the children had been products of rape by the soldiers or New Mexican raiders. In the face of starvation, they attempted to eat the crow and coyote, only to find them inedible. The memories are filled with such anguish, pain, and humiliation that we cannot help but feel overwhelmed with sadness for our ancestors, who were forced to debase themselves in order to survive."[87]

Santiago's brother, Charles Hubbell, escorted a group of 1,073 Navajos from Fort Wingate to Fort Sumner in October 1864—53 of whom he lost to death or desertion, on top of another 164 he lost driving another group of surrendered Navajos to Fort Wingate "at a killing pace."[88] His brother Sidney, meanwhile, "cashed in . . . on the bonanza New Mexicans experienced in supplying Fort Sumner," and Santiago may have also reaped part of that financial harvest.[89] Later, when the Navajos were returning to their homeland after the ordeal of Bosque Redondo was finally over, they encountered a profit-hungry Santiago on the swollen banks of the Rio Puerco, where he ran a toll bridge. "Determined to take advantage of this windfall, Hubbell demanded five cents apiece for every man, woman, and child who crossed his bridge plus fees of twenty-five cents apiece for each horse and sheep."[90]

Once they reached Bosque Redondo, the Navajos found no relief, only misery. The land chosen for the Navajo farms was flat and barren, the water alkaline, shelter and firewood scarce, rations rancid, clothing threadbare. The deplorable conditions were made worse by extreme homesickness. Navajo headman Barboncito gave voice to the Navajos' yearning for their homeland. "I think now it is true what my forefathers told me about crossing the line of my own country," he said. "It seems that whatever we do here causes death . . . [T]he cries of the women cause the tears to roll down on to my moustache. I then think of my country."[91]

After four years of Navajo incarceration, even the US government could see that its plan to assimilate the Navajos had failed. As geologist and natural historian Donald L. Baars argues, "It became clear to everyone involved at Fort Sumner that *Diné* could not survive beyond the four sacred mountains—beyond *Diné Bikeyah*. Outside of these markers, set in stone by First Man and First Woman, nothing exists. The five-fingered people of the Fifth World were destined to inhabit this land of beauty. This is where the Holy People lived, where they created First Man and First Woman. . . . This is home to *Diné*."[92] The reservation was an unmitigated disaster. Eleven thousand Navajos went to Fort Sumner, and more than twenty-five hundred died there.[93]

In May 1868, the Navajos negotiated another treaty with the United States, but this one would be different—a cause for Navajo celebration. On June 1, 1868, Manuelito, Barboncito, and other Navajo leaders signed the treaty that would create for them a new reservation within their traditional homeland. The treaty stipulated that the process of Americanization would go on—churches, schools, and Indian agencies would be built—but the Navajos would be in their own country again. On June 18, more than eight thousand Navajos began the march home.[94] When they glimpsed the sacred mountain of the South, they "wept at the vision of that beautiful land formation, rising in grandeur, welcoming them home."[95]

The sad chapter of Bosque Redondo was finally closed, but the Navajos' troubles were not over. Exile permanently altered the Navajo economy. During the four years of incarceration and the brutal battles leading up to it, the Navajos' crops had withered and their herds of sheep, cattle, goats, and horses had dwindled to almost nothing. For a people who counted their wealth in flocks, the loss of the sheep was devastating. To help the Navajos through the winter of 1868–1869 and urge them toward self-sufficiency, the treaty promised annual distributions of goods for ten years, as well as 1,000,000 pounds of corn, 500 beef cattle, and 15,000 sheep and goats. The sheep, however, were not delivered until November of 1869; during the year in which they waited for the promised sheep, the Navajos worked diligently to reestablish themselves, but it was a struggle against early frosts and other hardships.[96]

Navajos under a juniper tree. Courtesy of the National Park Service, HUTR 11398.

The first years on the newly created Navajo Reservation were difficult. Without stores of food, the capricious northern Arizona weather wreaked havoc on the Navajo crops, pushing the Navajos to the brink of starvation and forcing continued dependence on government rations. Despite their hunger, the Navajos refused to butcher their sheep, and as a consequence, their herds thrived. By 1871, New Mexico's Indian Superintendent reported that the Navajo flocks had increased to 40,000 head. By 1878, the herds had grown to 500,000 head, and by 1883, to one million head. Although reservation agriculture remained marginal for many years, the Navajos' sheep were quickly reestablished as the hub of the Navajo economy.[97]

Although the Navajos returned to their former way of life as much as possible, some changes Bosque Redondo wrought would not be erased, but would open the door to the system of reservation trading. As Willow Powers writes, "The years at Fort Sumner, coupled with the need for rations when they returned home, had broken up the old ways and led to new habits. Now, the Navajos were familiar with and reliant on flour, lard, and other foods, and factory goods. These were at first essential, and then, increasingly, seen as convenient; and from this familiarity and need, trade was born. As people settled down and built homes, and returned to the patterns of herding and farming, a few traders came out onto the reservation to barter goods for wool and sheep. So begins the trader story."[98] While at Fort Sumner, the Navajos "were also quick to pick up the use of the new tools and the exchange of new goods—one or two Navajo smiths first learned their skills at Fort Sumner."[99] Silversmithing and weaving would also rise to prominence in the Navajo economy and culture in the wake of Bosque Redondo, forging another link to the American economy. These changes would prove immeasurably important to the story of the Navajos. They begat one of the most mythologized and romanticized of Southwestern figures—the Navajo trader. Enterprising individuals came onto the harsh and beautiful Colorado Plateau to fill the new demand for Anglo goods in the Navajo economy. One of those men would be a young New Mexican named Juan Lorenzo Hubbell.

## *Juan Lorenzo in Navajo Country*

On November 23, 1853, in the thriving Hispanic village of Pajarito, Juan Lorenzo Hubbell was born, the third of twelve children. As members of the wealthy *rico* class, Juan Lorenzo's family held economic and social sway over the *pobres* who maintained their households and ranches.[100] Juliana Gutiérrez Hubbell stood at the heart of the community, called "*mi mama* or *mi Tia Julianita,* 'my mother' or 'my Aunt Julianita,'" by the village's inhabitants, who looked to her for assistance and guidance while Santiago was away on matters of business and war.[101] Juan Lorenzo grew up speaking Spanish and playing under the watchful eye not only of his mother, but of the Hispanic and Native American village women who served as wet nurses and governesses to the Gutiérrez–Hubbell children.[102] It was a lively place, colorful and busy. As Hubbell's biographer imagines, "Within the adobe walls, dried anise and coriander hung from the *vigas* (roof beams) and scented the air; burros and roosters vied with each other at dawn and bullfrogs held forth at dusk; and alfalfa, chile peppers, corn, geraniums, and grapes colored the irrigated river lands."[103] It was an ideal place for an active childhood spent joining "in the sports and games of the Indian boys, and establish[ing] a

Hubbell-Gutiérrez family portrait. Standing, left to right: Charles Hubbell, J. Felipe Hubbell, Barbara Hubbell, Thomas Hubbell, and Frank A. Hubbell. Seated, left to right: Luisa Hubbell Thomas, Julianita Gutiérrez Hubbell, and Juan Lorenzo Hubbell. Courtesy of the National Park Service, HUTR 04711.

comradeship with them that stood him in good stead in his later dealings with the Indians."[104]

Though the outlines of Hubbell's childhood are faint, his family and the multicultural environment in which he was raised left indelible marks on his character and future endeavors. His parents, as members of the upper class, insisted on educating their son, even with the limited resources available in New Mexico in the nineteenth century. He learned at the knee of Spanish tutors until he was nine years old, at which time Santiago sent him to boarding school in Santa Fe.[105] He also undoubtedly learned the basics of business and ranching at an early age, and he worked for his father in varied enterprises as a young man.[106] His education would give him a taste for books and cultured company that he would carry with him his whole life, while being brought up on his family's vast landholdings and amidst all of its business ventures taught him to see livestock, homesteading, farming, and trading as sources of wealth and happiness.[107] His friends would later be fond of noting the gifts given Hubbell by each side of his family—that "with a combination of Yankee ingenuity and Spanish vitality and spirit of adventure, John Lorenzo Hubbell received as his birth right a place in life that afforded him the qualities necessary to carve out his own place in life."[108]

By 1873, three years after he left home as a seventeen-year-old, Juan Lorenzo found himself at Fort Defiance. Constructed to defeat the Navajos, the fort became the center of Navajo political activity after Bosque Redondo: it became the first Navajo Indian Agency when the treaty was signed in 1868, the location of the first day school for Navajo children in 1869, the home of the first mission in 1871, and the first hospital on the Navajo Reservation in 1897.[109] But in the early years, Fort Defiance was a wreck. One visitor described it as a huddle of "rude adobe buildings" that was "altogether unfit in its present state to serve as an Indian Agency," with quarters "unfit for cattle" and leaky roofs and floors—in short, "a disgrace."[110] But it was a bustling place where a keen young man like Hubbell might learn a great deal about the Navajos, trading, and politics.

Hubbell did not have to "[drift] about in the vicinity of the Navaho agency unattached and looking for a means to keep a full stomach" for long before his bilingualism landed him a job.[111] He worked as an interpreter at the agency through several significant episodes of upheaval, translating negotiations from English to Spanish, while another interpreter would translate from Spanish to Navajo, and back again. He was involved in the ousting of controversial Navajo Agent William F. M. Arny, who has been described as "a hypocritical rascal, a Bible-pounding moralist who plotted larceny."[112] Hubbell, along with his friend, Thomas Keam, took the Navajos' part in a fight to depose Arny after he schemed to "defraud the Navajos of the best part of their reservation."[113] He also served as an interpreter in a dispute between the Navajos and their Mormon neighbors that boiled over when three Navajos were killed in Utah.[114] The Navajos demanded reparations for the killings, while the Mormons insisted that non-Mormons had done the deed. Hubbell accompanied Navajo headman Ganado Mucho to investigate the murders and attempt to settle the dispute. The group rode north and carried messages to Mormon representative and mediator Jacob

Hamblin—but the dispute dragged on for years. Hubbell's opinion of the matter was never recorded, but given his later dislike of Mormons, it is easy to speculate that Hubbell sided with the Navajos. It also may have been on this assignment that he first met and befriended Ganado Mucho, who lived in the Pueblo Colorado Valley, a relationship that would prove important to the young man's future, as would his relationship with Thomas Keam, one of the most successful and powerful Indian traders on the reservation before 1900.[115]

By 1876, Hubbell's days as agency interpreter were over. He clerked at trader Henry Reed's store at Fort Wingate for a time, from which position he began to strike out on his own in business, entering into a contract to supply the Navajo agency with 100,000 pounds of corn, backed by Keam and Reed.[116] Some accounts say that Hubbell worked in Albuquerque after leaving the agency, and the chronology has been muddled by time, but "what we do know is that Hubbell clerked for traders to the Navajos, worked for the Bureau of Indian Affairs, and befriended key people in Navajo country during a tumultuous time."[117] By the time Hubbell left the agency and finished clerking at other men's trading posts, he had gathered a good deal of experience under his belt and seen broad areas of the Navajo Southwest. As Hubbell himself put it, "By that time, I had learned a great deal about the Indians and Indian trading, and was anxious to get into the business for myself."[118] In 1876, he found his way to Ganado, then still called Pueblo Colorado—the site of ancient ruins, modern hogans, and a couple of rickety trading posts—there to make his fortune.

CHAPTER TWO

# Traders to the Navajos
## Early Trading Posts in the Pueblo Colorado Valley

Not long after Juan Lorenzo Hubbell embarked on his trading venture with visions of fortune before his eyes, he found himself in a pickle. The year was 1878, and he was a newcomer in the Pueblo Colorado Valley, still distrusted by the Navajo community and learning the ropes of trading. The Navajos, "not reluctant to relieve themselves of undesirable non-Indians" and known for "testing the mettle of traders," decided to see how far they could push the young man.[1] As the story goes, a Navajo man entered Hubbell's trading post and demanded a sack of flour, though he had no money or trade goods to pay for it. Hubbell naturally refused to give it to him, so the Navajo man picked up the sack and strode out of the post. Standing dumbfounded behind the counter, Hubbell "realized that if I let him get away with it, every Indian in the country would storm the post to carry off anything they might lay hands upon. I'd have been financially ruined, and any further hope of doing business on peaceful terms would be gone forever. There was nothing to do but settle the matter then and there."[2]

Firm in his resolve, J. L. "bounced over the counter and overtook the Indian with the sack of flour as he got outside the door," only to discover that the Navajo was not alone. Seventy-five other Navajos stood outside the post to back up their companion's demands, amusedly wondering what the unarmed trader intended to do about it. "Well," J. L. joked, "it didn't take them long to find out. I grasped my Indian by the hair, and twisted him to the ground. Then I got him by one ear, marched him back into the post, and ordered him to deposit the sack of flour on the pile exactly where he'd found it." The Navajo man complied and meekly fled, but his companions were unsatisfied with the outcome, and a bigger, braver representative stepped forward to challenge the trader. By his account, the athletic adventurer wrestled his second opponent to the ground and twisted his ears, too, before hurling a challenge at the amazed onlookers: "Come on any of you who think you can steal from me. I'll twist the ears of any Indian who wants to try it." Hubbell admitted to "running a tremendous bluff. But, it worked successfully. I stood there eyeing the angry throng for several minutes, ready to begin twisting ears—and there were no ears to be twisted. One by one the Indians began slinking away. That lesson seemed to last. At least, I've gotten along for forty-eight years now without a repetition of any similar incident."[3]

Whether Hubbell actually managed to cow a group of seventy-five Navajos with a bit of ear twisting and a heavy dose of sheer bravado, or whether he was merely inflating his ego with a little hot air, the moral of Hubbell's tale was "that a white man must never let an Indian know that he has the slightest fear of a single Indian, or any hundred Indians. The slightest show of fear would put the white man on the defensive, and the Indians would literally have him 'on the run' from that very moment."[4]

Despite the humor of J. L.'s story, it illustrates the precariousness of his early situation in Navajo country. He was an intruder, an outsider in a close-knit community that had called the Pueblo Colorado Valley home for generations. Though he had friends among the Navajos from his days translating at Fort Defiance, including prominent headmen like Ganado Mucho, Many Horses, and Manuelito, many years would pass before he would become an accepted part of their community. In 1878, he was just another wet-behind-the-ears trader with no special significance and no lasting ties with the place that would later become synonymous with his name. In the 1870s and 1880s, the Pueblo Colorado Valley played host to a parade of traders while J. L. blew around the country like a tumbleweed.

## Navajos in the Pueblo Colorado Valley

When the first Anglo traders came to the Pueblo Colorado Valley, they were attracted by three key qualities that made it an ideal site for a successful trading post: water, proximity to transportation routes, and accessibility to Navajo communities.[5] The Pueblo Colorado Valley boasted a long-standing Navajo community, a lake and river, and an enviable position at a crossroads south of the reservation line. Archaeological evidence indicates that the valley had sheltered human societies for thousands of years.[6] The

Juan Lorenzo Hubbell as a young man, c. 1880. Courtesy of the National Park Service, HUTR 17469.

Ancestral Puebloans, architects of the great houses of Chaco Canyon, left ruins along the Pueblo Colorado Wash—Lók´aahnteel (Place of the Wide Reeds) and Kin Dah Łichíí (Red Upon the House), the latter giving the valley its Spanish name, Pueblo Colorado.[7] Traditional Navajo stories say that the Ancestral Puebloans deserted the ruins amidst a fury of destruction by supernatural fire and wind. In that time of calamity, they scattered to the pueblos where their descendants still live today, leaving the Pueblo Colorado Valley devoid of human habitation until the Navajos arrived.[8] Though Spanish explorers and missionaries likely passed through the valley on their way to the Hopi mesas, the Navajos did not migrate that far west until the mid- to late-eighteenth century, so there was little about the valley to excite comment in their records.[9] But as the Navajos expanded their territory, the Pueblo Colorado Valley became a center for Navajo settlement, "where there were hogans and cornfields and a place where dances were held."[10] By the time American explorer Lieutenant Joseph Christmas Ives passed through the valley in May 1858, he found it teeming with life. He described "a brilliant sheet of verdure dotted with clumps of cedars, and extending far to the north and south. Countless herds of horses and flocks of sheep were grazing upon the plain."[11] Ives and his party camped that night in the company of Navajos and Hopis, and when they moved on toward Fort Defiance, they followed a network of "well-beaten trails, and parties of Indians were constantly riding by."[12]

Oral histories of life in the Pueblo Colorado Valley tell of peaceful times punctuated by raids and military expeditions passing through in a hail of arrows or bullets.[13] Local legends tell of Jihaal (Sound of a Rattle), a skilled hunter and runner who fought in battles against the Apaches, Zunis, and Hopis, and who adroitly juggled the demands of his many wives living in the ancient ruins of the Pueblo Colorado.[14] As Mexican and American warfare against the Navajos intensified in the mid–nineteenth century, military expeditions often camped in the Pueblo Colorado Valley.[15] By the time Kit Carson began his campaign, the valley was known to be such a major locus of Navajo settlement that he was ordered to establish his army there. It was undoubtedly scoured during Carson's campaign, its inhabitants corralled and marched to Bosque Redondo.[16]

J. L.'s granddaughter, LaCharles Goodman Eckel, said the Navajos called the Pueblo Colorado Valley the "Mother of the Navajos."[17] It was a familiar and beloved place into which the Navajos settled when they returned from exile—regardless of reservation boundaries. In the early years after Bosque Redondo, the reservation borders were somewhat of a mystery, "laid out along lines of latitude and longitude" over a rugged land that had not yet been surveyed.[18] The Navajos and the Indian agents knew that the reservation stretched from the borders of Utah and Colorado on the north to Fort Defiance on the south, an "arbitrary description [that] ignored the natural geography and the customary uses the people made of the land."[19] Though the Pueblo Colorado Valley lay beyond the limits of the treaty reservation, there were no white settlers to challenge the Navajos' claim.[20] J. L. Hubbell's friend from Fort Defiance, Navajo headman Tótsohnii Hastiin (Man of the Big Water Clan), who was known by the Spanish name Ganado Mucho, settled back in with members of his clan.[21] Homes and farms reappeared in their old places like grass returning in the spring, and sheep once again thronged the waterways. The Pueblo Colorado Valley belonged to the Navajos, but they would not have the valley to themselves for long. Traders followed hard on their heels.

## Traders in Navajo Country

Trade between Native Americans and Europeans has a long, convoluted history wrapped in layers of hides, furs, slavery, and disease. From the shores of the gray Atlantic to the sands of the Pacific coast, Native Americans bartered the bounty of the wilderness with which they were intimately familiar to the Europeans—English, Dutch, French, Spanish, and Russian—for manufactured goods that were at first merely convenient, but later necessary for survival.[22] Because different governments established a patchwork of rules regulating Indian trade, and enforced them with varying degrees of enthusiasm, the nature of trade varied significantly from place to place.[23] In an effort to protect the tribes from dishonest traders, the young American government began regulating trade in 1790, requiring traders to post bond and apply for a license, and punishing unlicensed traders with fines and confiscation of goods.[24] But it would be a long time before American rules governed trade with the Navajos.

In the Southwest, the Spanish initially had far less interest in trade than in obtaining gold by whatever means necessary, but over time a broad spectrum of goods, including livestock, alcohol, firearms and other weapons, textiles, tobacco, and human captives passed from Spanish to Native American hands and back again.[25] Spanish trade with the Native peoples of the

Southwest was not tied to fixed trading posts; they sent traders out to visit particular tribes and established annual trade fairs.[26] The Spanish resolutely kept the Americans, whose eyes were fixed hungrily on Western markets, out of the Southwest by arresting any adventurers who managed to make it to Santa Fe and summarily confiscating their goods. But no sooner had Mexico gained its independence from Spain than trade barriers tumbled, and the Americans came pouring over the Santa Fe Trail with pack mules and wagons heavy with goods, a significant portion of which were "channeled immediately . . . into the rapidly expanding trade with the Indians."[27]

Over the next few decades after Mexican independence, trade in the Southwest expanded slowly as trappers and mountain men scoured the land for furs, their scattered and isolated forts doubling as supply depots and trading posts. After the Mexican American War, the market expanded more quickly as Yankee traders like Santiago Hubbell began launching operations in the Southwest—but few had penetrated Navajo country, and those who did failed to regard the Navajos, who were poor in furs but rich in sheep, as valuable trade partners. But by the 1850s a few entrepreneurs began to trade with the Navajos. James S. Calhoun, the first Indian agent appointed in New Mexico Territory, reported in 1852 that "[t]raders are now travelling alone, or in parties of two and three in every direction of [Navajo] Territory," leading strings of overloaded pack mules or struggling over the rough trails in wagons—but most of their names are lost.[28] Before the 1860s, trade with the Navajos was uncertain, irregular, amorphous, and disrupted by frequent warfare, but Bosque Redondo would change all of that profoundly.[29]

The Navajos, of course, maintained networks of trade with other Native American groups both before and after the arrival of the Europeans, with the Pueblo Colorado Valley serving as one locus of trade. Even with the influx of American goods in the middle of the nineteenth century, the Navajos remained relatively economically independent, just as, until the 1860s, they remained militarily independent. It was while they were immersed in the misery of Fort Sumner that most Navajos encountered their first licensed government-appointed traders, and where, separated from their farms, herds, and food stores, they became exposed to, and dependent upon, a broad range of manufactured American goods.[30] By the time they returned, their subsistence patterns had been so thoroughly disrupted that the reservation trading posts that cropped up to supply the new demand for American goods would engender a "profound alteration of the whole Navaho economic structure."[31]

The first stationary licensed traders in Navajo country operated at Fort Defiance beginning in 1868. But Fort Defiance was a long, hard journey away from home for many of the Navajos who lived in small clusters of hogans enfolded in the ridges and washes of Navajo country. In the 1870s, traders began to settle closer to their customers both on and off the reservation, some traveling with their wares and setting up temporary trading posts in tents, and others building more permanent structures of lumber, stone, and adobe. Many of those who settled in Navajo country and traded with the Navajos in those years, including Hubbell, did not consider trading their primary enterprise—they set up "trading ranches" to run cattle, often just outside the reservation so as to avoid jumping through the hoops of federal licensing.[32] Unlicensed traders on the reservation faced steep $500 fines, confiscation of goods, and even banishment from the reservation. For many, selling their wares just beyond the borders saved a world of trouble in negotiating the complex relationship between trader, Indians, and government, especially since many Navajos persisted in living outside reservation boundaries.[33]

These early traders concentrated their sporadic and uncertain trade on hides, pelts, livestock, and a few craft products until Navajo agent William Arny experimented in 1875 with shipping Navajo wool to Eastern woolen mills. That year, he shipped sixty thousand pounds of Navajo wool eastward by wagon—where it found a ready market. With this new promise of profit shining in their eyes there came an influx of traders, and by 1883, traders were purchasing and shipping more than a million pounds of Navajo wool annually.[34] Navajo wool as an export commodity had been discovered. Arny's "experiment was a success; the foundation of Navajo trading had been laid."[35] Existing trading ranches "metamorphosed into true trading posts, and would-be ranchers became the inadvertent owners of mercantile establishments," while new trading posts cropped up on the fringes of Navajo country like weeds.[36]

## Early Trading Posts in the Pueblo Colorado Valley

The early trading posts in the Pueblo Colorado Valley, little more than wooden shacks and mud-daubed hovels, have been obscured by time and memory. In the 1870s, ambitious men came and went, dabbling in the life of a trader here and there before disappearing from the scene to chase after other dreams, leaving only scant records behind.[37] Most of the men who rushed into Navajo country to begin the lonely life of a trader never planned to stay there, intending "to get rich quick by cornering the market for wool, blankets, or some other tempting product, then moving away to live the life of luxury among their own people."[38] Of those who traded among the Navajos in the 1870s and 1880s, few lasted longer than a scanty handful of months—or a few years at the utmost. According to David Brugge, the first non-Navajo to settle in the Pueblo Colorado Valley was Charles Hardison, "who had married a Navajo wife at Fort Sumner and began ranching as a member of the family near Kinlichee. For a few years he raised cattle there, but when his marriage did not last he moved away."[39] By 1871 the valley attracted its first trader, a man named Charles Crary, who worked with a partner called Mr. Stover. A second trader, William B. Leonard, and his partner, Barney Williams, arrived in 1875, and Hubbell followed shortly in 1876.[40] There were two trading posts in the valley during that time—one by Ganado Lake and one at the present site of Hubbell Trading Post. Historians disagree whether Crary built the post near the lake and sold it to Hubbell after Leonard built his more elaborate post a few miles downstream, or whether Hubbell built the little trading post by the lake.[41] In either case, the story goes that for his first two years in the Pueblo Colorado Valley, Hubbell traded near the lake until, in 1878, a Navajo suspected of witchcraft was killed in the doorway of his trading post, placing it off limits to his Navajo customers, who historically avoided the dead, believing "contact could cause illnesses and premature death."[42] Hubbell then bought Leonard's trading post while Leonard went on to become the post trader at Fort Defiance.[43]

But even that story, frequently repeated, casts a doubtful shadow. In 1878, a wave of terror and violence did indeed sweep through the Navajo community, culminating in the killing of at least forty suspected Navajo witches.[44] Attributing death, illness, and poverty to the widespread practice of witchcraft, Navajos accused several medicine men of burying others' belongings, a practice believed to cause the deaths of livestock and people.[45] In late May, Navajos in the Pueblo Colorado Valley killed suspected witch Hastiin Jéékha Díjólí (Little Deaf Man) and gathered their forces to go after another medicine man, Hastiin Biwosi, who lived near Canyon de Chelly. J. L.'s younger brother, Charlie, left at the trading post while J. L. was away on other business in Navajo City, sent a frantic letter by Navajo runner to Fort Defiance that puts to bed the oft-repeated tale that the witch was killed

The Leonard Trading Post, c. 1895. J. L. Hubbell stands under the tree; his friend, Many Horses, wears a serape; and Dahanna Nez (or Hastiin Nez) wears an apron. Courtesy of the National Park Service, HUTR 08632.

in front of the Hubbells' store.[46] "There is a big row going on here, among the Indians," Charlie wrote. "They just killed one of them and we are in danger of our lifes please send all the ammunition you have, and my rifle, a big crowd just passed here, and are going to fit themselves to go on a fight at Cañon de Chelle. They are going to start right away, and the Indians arrived here are expecting the Indians from Cañon de Chelle and have a big fight. If you do not want to trust the boy with the ammunition and gun send out a white man but do not fail to do it. The boy was killed in front of Hardison's house was beaten down with rocks, and pluged full of arrows, and they are going to kill Hombre and four others. They sent out courriers, all over the country to get their people together."[47]

Before Charlie's hasty message received a response, the assembling Navajos discovered by chance that Hastiin Biwosi was conducting a ceremony in nearby Cornfields. A group of at least fifty Navajos rode into Cornfields, found Hastiin Biwosi in a hogan, and tore it down. They shot him, dragged him out of the wreckage, and "stoned him so much that there was a great big pile of rocks and you couldn't recognize the body."[48] When they learned of it, the Navajos at Canyon de Chelly began to arm themselves to avenge his death. Charlie prepared to retreat to Fort Defiance, thinking it useless "to risk our lives when nothing can be gained by it."[49] Somehow, the situation diffused; by the time troops arrived from Fort Wingate in answer to Charlie's frantic calls for help and ammunition, they "found the settlers . . . entirely free of alarm and apprehensive of no danger, the excitement having wholly subsided."[50] Meanwhile, J. L. found himself embroiled in the conflict from where he was in Navajo City, New Mexico.[51] After six Navajos were killed in that region, he wrote to Fort Wingate for help at Manuelito's request.[52] He acted as interpreter when the army stepped in to rescue two or three accused witches other Navajos were holding captive. The accused received a reprimand and were set free after promising to give up witchcraft, and Navajo life apparently quieted back into its normal rhythms.[53]

The Navajo witch purge throws into sharp relief the fact that the position of a new trader on the Navajo Reservation was uncertain. J. L. later loved to tell stories of his early days in Ganado before he had won acceptance in the Navajo community. For instance, he told an unlikely yarn about how one day, while he was loading his wagon, a group of Navajos decided to kill him. They tied him up—to the wheel of the wagon or a mesquite tree, depending on whose version of the story we read—and took the trouble to draw him a picture in the sand of exactly what how they intended to kill him. Just as they were about to carry out their threat, either Manuelito or Ganado Mucho's son, Many Horses, rode into the camp, beating about with a club, and delivered the assembled Navajos a stern lecture about "how Hubbell was their best friend, had been just and fair to them, and had never lied to them . . . and that they ought to be ashamed to take advantage of him in the way they had."[54] With his life no longer threatened, J. L. apparently calmly went back to loading his wagon, unflappable and one step closer to acceptance in the Navajo community. He took another step in 1886 during a smallpox epidemic. Immune from his own childhood bout with the disease, J. L. "waded right in to help the Indians with their sick, their dead, and their dying. I vaccinated Indians by the hundreds, and buried dead Indians by the wagonload."[55] He said that they credited him "supernatural power" because he worked among them without coming down with the plague "against which all their chants and rituals had failed."[56] In those early years, the Navajos called him Nakeznilih (Man Wearing Glasses), and later they dubbed him Nakai Sání (Old Mexican).[57]

These years were a period of germination for Hubbell's trading philosophy and practice. The characters of the early traders came in as many colors as any other group of entrepreneurs—some earned the respect of the Navajos while others earned only reputations as "bad" traders.[58] What distinguished the former from the latter had much to do with the adaptability of the trader and the role that he was willing to play in the Navajo community beyond the pursuit of profit, for in the years after Bosque Redondo, "the trading post emerged as a focal point in the workings of Navajo life."[59] It was to the trading post the Navajos brought their sheep for shearing and their crafts for selling, in the bullpen that they bought food and supplies for their families, on the porch where they gambled and gathered. In the vast landscapes of Navajo country where official government presence was often hundreds of miles distant, the trader often became the most important, if not the only, white man in the Navajo community.[60] Hubbell's upbringing as part of the *patron* system in New Mexico fitted him uniquely for the odder aspects of a trader's life—settling disputes, burying the dead, making decisions about his customers' credit, writing letters for them, and a host of activities that fell far outside the traditional job description of a store owner. Hubbell put it this way: "Out here in this country the Indian trader is everything from merchant to father confessor, justice of the peace, judge, jury, court of appeals, chief medicine man, and *de facto* czar of the domain over which he presides," a role that he relished.[61] Though his relationship with the Navajos could today be considered paternalistic, it served to win him a place in their community and, over time, a reputation as one of the "good" traders.[62]

## C. N. Cotton and the Trading Post

As the snapshot of the Navajo witch purge suggests, in the early years, Hubbell was not always behind the counter of his own trading post. At first, he relied mostly on his brother, Charlie, to mind the business while he bounced around in Arizona and New Mexico pursuing other enterprises. But Charlie seems to have lacked the business acumen that J. L. needed if he planned to leave his store in someone else's hands for any length of time.

Charlie was shuffled around his brother's business operations for years, his position clearly that of an employee rather than an equal partner.[63] Hubbell increasingly relied on other associates to help run his trading post. Evidence from scattered visitors before 1900 paints a jumbled picture, with nearly every passer-by recording different owners and clerks. For example, in 1881, when scientist John G. Bourke passed through the Pueblo Colorado Valley on his way to the Hopi Snake Dance, he mentioned partaking of grand hospitality at the trading ranch—not of Hubbell, as we might expect from the simple narrative that he bought out Leonard in 1878, but of George "Barney" Williams and his partner, Mr. Webber. "[O]ur friend Mr. Hubbell," Bourke noted, joined the party a few days later.[64] Whether Williams and Webber operated another trading post located elsewhere in the valley near Kinlichee, or whether they were working for Leonard or Hubbell is uncertain—but in any case, in 1881 it was still quite possible for a traveler to pass through Ganado without associating it with Don Lorenzo Hubbell.[65] A few years later, in 1884, a traveler recorded Charlie trading from a tent at Washington Pass with a partner named Clark, while "Mssrs. Hubbell & Pillsbury" ran the trading ranch at Ganado.[66] In this jumble of passing references, we can only surmise that the restless young Hubbell was not yet ready to settle down in one place.

To that end, around 1884 Hubbell acquired himself a more permanent partner: Clinton Neal Cotton. Born in 1859, Cotton grew up on a farm in central Ohio. His father was an educator and a whiz at calculating columns of figures in his head, a skill he took on the road, giving demonstrations in rural communities. When Cotton lost his father, he left school at the age of eleven to help support his mother and siblings as a telegraph operator. For eleven years he supported them, and when their situation finally seemed secure, Cotton headed west. The 22-year-old landed in Albuquerque, where his telegraph operating skills secured him work with the Atlantic and Pacific Railroad. The job took him to lonely places at the end of the rail line in New Mexico, outposts like Guam and Fort Wingate. The solitude seemed to suit him. At Fort Wingate, he lived and worked in a boxcar with a rescued Newfoundland dog at his side. He returned to Ohio in 1882 just long enough to marry Mary Alice Crain. The two of them would spend their honeymoon in Cotton's boxcar and the rest of their lives in Navajo country.[67]

It was likely at Fort Wingate that Cotton first met Hubbell. The two of them, both with heads full of money-making schemes, probably exchanged dozens of ideas and entertained any number of business propositions. The one that stuck was a ten-year partnership in the trading business, which began officially on September 23, 1884, when Cotton bought half an interest in the Pueblo Colorado Store.[68] At that time, Hubbell was focusing most of his attention on business and politics in St. Johns, Arizona, and he would need a reliable partner to hold down the trading post. Cotton moved his wife and their infant son to Ganado and took up all of the day-to-day tasks of running a Navajo trading post far from the railroad.[69]

The two jacal structures that Hubbell bought from William Leonard were a haphazard affair, squatting low behind a picket fence and sprouting chimneys from the packed-earth roof in an irregular fashion that indicated the original structure from the 1870s had been added onto multiple times. One building doubled as living quarters and trading post, while the other served as an office, guest house, and storage.[70] The Leonard buildings were barely adequate, and Hubbell began construction on a new rug room and office in the summer of 1883, adding a store and wareroom in 1889, projects that Cotton must have supervised in his absence.[71]

On the inside, the trading post was probably arranged in the traditional pattern, though no descriptions or photographs of the interior of the Leonard buildings survive. In most trading posts, Navajo customers entered a main room called the bullpen, which held a wood-burning stove and enough room for the Navajos to gather and visit. Around the edges of the room in an L or U shape ran elevated counters, behind which the traders and all of their merchandise stood, well out of reach of the Navajos. Conflicts with the Navajos were not always solved with a little judicious ear-twisting, and many traders kept a gun within reach behind the counter. The arrangement was practical, but it also served to separate the trader from his customers and increase his power over the Navajos in the bullpen—a separation that probably went a long way toward making Cotton feel comfortable as a trader.[72]

The Navajos called Cotton Béésh Biwoo' (Metal Teeth) because of his gold dental work. His contemporaries described him as tall and big-boned, "a bluff and hearty man who spoke loudly and chomped on a big cigar."[73] His reputation among the Navajos and his business philosophy were of a different sort than J. L.'s. Teresa J. Wilkins notes, "Though he traded at the Ganado post for several years, he was not popular with the Navajos," who felt that he did not respect them.[74] Cotton was a rule-abider to a fault; he

The bullpen at Hubbell Trading Post. Courtesy of the National Park Service, HUTR 07071.

adhered strictly to trading regulations and, because the government hoped to convert the Navajos to Christianity, refused to do business on Sundays even though other traders opened their doors whenever their customers happened to show up. He also dealt only in cash, which did not suit the Navajos in the late nineteenth century. In short, Cotton "operated according to strict capitalist business standards of the day and had little time or patience for some of the trading activities that did not result in direct monetary gain."[75] To add to that, Cotton, unlike J. L., who tended to handle any conflicts himself, routinely took his problems with the Navajos to the Indian agent.[76] Whenever the Navajos stole from him or threatened him, he promptly demanded help from Fort Defiance.[77] However, Cotton was a capable businessman who kept tidy records and conducted his business correspondence neatly, despite his truncated education. The earliest surviving records at the trading post are mostly in his hand, for he kept neater records than either of the Hubbell brothers.

The firm Hubbell and Cotton lived a short life on paper. On June 22, 1885, J. L. wrote to inform his bank in Albuquerque that "I have this day sold out all my interest in the Pueblo Colorado store to C. N. Cotton."[78]

With those words there commenced a decade when Hubbell's trading post was known by travelers and government officials simply as "Cotton's."[79] What prompted the sudden action was a political mess in which Hubbell found himself deeply mired; cutting ties, at least officially, with the trading post was a last-ditch effort to save himself from being forcibly ousted from public office.

## St. Johns

During the late 1870s and 1880s, Hubbell poured most of his attention into business ventures and politics in the promising little town of St. Johns, Arizona.[80] Eight years before Hubbell opened a store there in 1878, St. Johns had been nothing more than a shack at a crossing of the Little Colorado River.[81] Now, it was the seat of Apache County with a predominantly Hispanic population of several hundred citizens, and the epicenter of enough economic, racial, and religious conflict to do justice to any western imagination. St. Johns had to deal with its share of outlaws and cattle thieves, and saw commonplace battles between small landholders and ranchers against the railroad and cattle companies. But the "classic struggle for political control of a community between 'oldtimers' and 'newcomers'" played out between the Hispanic residents of St. Johns and the Mormon settlers of nearby Springerville.[82] A rash of ballot-box stuffing and threatening went on in a battle for control over the county shrievalty, judiciary, and juries in St. Johns in the 1880s—and Hubbell was in the thick of it.[83]

Hubbell's economic interests in St. Johns were considerable. Over the course of a decade, he owned a store, a saloon, and a freighting company that handled goods, mail, and passengers. He also served on the Board of Jail Commissioners of Apache County and superintended the Arizona Co-operative Mercantile Institution.[84] He would keep up the same pattern of diversified economic interests throughout his life, but in St. Johns, he did not do it with any of the polish that marked his later efforts. When Mormon settler Joseph Fish visited St. Johns in early December 1879, before the strife started, he stayed the night at Hubbell's store in the absence of a hotel in town. He was singularly unimpressed by his host. Fish wrote in his diary, "At a late hour he gave us the keys and went off, and it was surmised by us that he had an engagement with one of the gentler sex of the Mexican race. He returned about daylight" as his guests fended for themselves at the scanty breakfast table.[85] The store and its proprietor, by Fish's description, fit the ramshackle frontier town perfectly: "The houses were all built close together and of the Mexican style having no floors, no windows, and flat roofs covered with dirt. There were two stores, two billiard halls, one saloon, and one monte bank, where most of the male population spent the greater part of their time and money."[86]

As a significant player in the local economy, Hubbell was also a key member of the "St. Johns Ring," an organization of about six prominent citizens, headed by Jewish merchant Solomon Barth, bent on consolidating political and economic power out of the hands of the Mormons.[87] The animosity between the two groups cropped up almost as soon as the first Mormons set foot in town to scout land for a settlement. The natural apprehensions of the town's residents, who "likely had heard that the group was extremely cohesive and feared that Mormons would vote together, establish their own stores, generally pose a challenge to traditional Christian community morals, and possibly even threaten the economic position of non-Mormons in the town," were exacerbated when Barth initially sold the Mormons a tract of land bordering the Hispanic part of town that most residents viewed as communal grazing property.[88] Playing on the resulting misunderstanding, the St. Johns Ring rallied the support of the town's Hispanic citizens against the Mormons. Tensions between the two groups mounted over the next several years, and Hubbell launched his career in politics by running for sheriff in 1884 on the anti-Mormon platform. Fish ranked him with the "rabid anti-Mormons" of St. Johns, Hubbell having apparently boasted "that he would fight them until Hell froze over and then give them a round on the ice."[89] He won the election, despite the powerful opposition of the Mormons' allies, the railroad and cattle companies, and began a term marked by partisanship and scandal, with his brothers, Tom, Frank, and Felipe, serving as his deputies.[90]

J. L. would later revel in telling tales of his days as sheriff, casting himself in a far more positive light than the facts merit. He depicted himself as a hero in a lawless territory that had "a great need for honest men in political affairs."[91] Hubbell later buried his differences with the Mormons, and so the villains in his stories usually took the familiar form of range-stealing Texas cattlemen who "opened bloody warfare upon all the poor, ignorant Mexicans, Indians, and Spanish-Americans who were owners of sheep."[92] With characteristic exaggeration, he claimed that when the Texans swept into town, "I was slated for killing for a period of nearly three years. . . . During the period of strife I'd been shot at from ambush no less than a dozen times, and my home had been converted into a veritable fort. For one solid year not a member of my family went to bed except behind doors and windows barricaded with mattresses or sand bags."[93] Many writers would retell Hubbell's stories of settling the range war between the sheepmen and the cattlemen, but none more dramatically than Hamlin Garland in his 1902 short story, "Delmar of Pima." The story gushes with romantic descriptions of "Delmar's" arresting grey-blue eyes and his astounding ability to quell hostile groups of armed cowboys with his mere presence. In a final showdown fit for any western, "Mounted on a fine black horse, and totally unarmed," Delmar triumphs over his foes, "one man against a hundred" while "the women moaned and prayed, and the men stood on the roofs of the houses watching."[94]

The truth of the matter, however, was that J. L.'s days as sheriff were less charmed than he liked to remember. With his interests divided between St. Johns and his trading post in Ganado, J. L.'s dedication to the office of sheriff suffered, giving his political enemies ample opportunity to work against him. In June 1885, the Board of Supervisors of Apache County held a special meeting at which M. V. Howard presented an affidavit with the following charges against Hubbell: "That he had failed to give a proper bond and that his bondsmen were insufficient; that he had absented himself from the county without permission for more than sixty days; that he refused to serve bench warrants issued by the county judge; that he refused to serve numerous subpoenas issued out of the county court; that he has refused to work in harmony with the District Attorney's office, and that he has been insulting to said officer and also to the Judge . . . of the county court, etc."[95] On the grounds that by spending long stretches of time at his trading post, which had by then been swallowed up by an expansion of the Navajo Reservation, Hubbell had in fact left Apache County and the Territory of Arizona altogether, the Board of Supervisors declared the office of sheriff vacant and appointed James E. Porter in his stead.[96] When he heard this news, J. L. swiftly sold his interest to Cotton and rushed to St. Johns to defend himself. His allies maintained that Hubbell was being targeted because, upon taking the oath of office, he had "indignantly refused to be used as a tool of the old clique of corruptionists, and the result was an early declaration of hostilities on their part," but the local newspapers had been complaining about Hubbell's absences and neglect for months.[97] Hubbell refused to turn the office over to Porter, and managed to obtain a ten-day reprieve, during which he hurried to the District Court in Prescott to secure an injunction, leaving his deputies in charge of defending the office "at all hazards."[98] The situation looked tense. "Mr. Hubbell's opponents have expressed a determination to disregard the mandates of any tribunal except the County Court, and declare that they will take the office by force," one newspaper wrote. "Should this be attempted there is no doubt but what a bloody conflict will take place, as both sides are armed to the teeth and dying for a chance to wipe out old scores with each other."[99] The matter, however, was eventually settled peacefully. Though "in disgrace," Hubbell kept the shrievalty, but was promptly defeated by Commodore Perry Owens 419 to 499 votes a few months later in the November 1885 elections.[100]

Politics and business were far from Hubbell's only interests in St. Johns. It was while he lived in the rowdy little town that he became involved with a young Mexican woman named Lina Rubi, who had not had good luck with men. Born to Cruz Rubi and Tafayo Reyes around 1861, the reputedly beautiful Lina found herself married to a man named Encarnacion Lucero when she was just eleven years old.[101] They lived together "as man and wife" for about a year and a half until the later part of 1874, when Lucero abandoned his bride after a night of drunken revelry.[102] Left alone with her parents, Lina eventually moved with them to St. Johns. She did not hear so much as a whisper about her absent husband until the spring of 1877, when Lucero suddenly showed up to reclaim her. She took him back, dutifully, and they lived together again for the short span of six weeks before he indulged in two weeks of round-the-clock gambling and drinking and disappeared for the last time.[103]

J. L. probably became involved with the abandoned Lina shortly after his arrival in St. Johns in 1878. Her first child, Adele, was born in 1880, three years after Lucero disappeared, and two after Hubbell arrived in town. Adele's baptismal records at St. John the Baptist list her father as "unknown," but it is not outside the realm of plausibility that Lina may have been the "one of the gentler sex of the Mexican race" with whom J. L. kept his appointment when Joseph Fish visited him in 1879—the same year, in fact, that J. L. would later remember (incorrectly) as the year he married Lina Rubi.[104] Two other children were born to Lina in the years before she filed for a divorce from Lucero: Barbara in 1881 and Lorenzo, Jr., in 1883. Lina filed for divorce in 1884, probably at J. L.'s insistence and certainly with his support, as some of the court records of the divorce are written in his hand. His signature appears as witness next to her mark—a simple "X."[105] Six years after the divorce, they finally married on July 27, 1891; their fourth and final child, Roman, was born three months later on October 13. By that time, Hubbell had determined to focus his attentions on the Ganado store and trade with the Navajos, leaving the political intrigues of St. Johns behind.

## *Troubles with the Land Title*

Though J. L. determined to move permanently to Ganado by the late 1880s, exactly when Cotton sold the trading post back to him is uncertain. As early as 1888, Cotton began to entertain the idea of starting a wholesale business in Gallup catering to reservation traders. He built a home and moved his wife and children there in November of that year, but he continued to help run the Pueblo Colorado store for several years after that.[106] Cotton's interests in the Ganado venture seemed to gradually fade, and there is no written evidence of a formal transfer of interests back to Hubbell—but most sources point to a date in the mid-1890s.[107] All evidence of Cotton's involvement had faded by 1890, save the occasional sheet of leftover letterhead.

The confused history of the ownership of the post is connected to disputes about the ownership of the land at Ganado and the changing boundaries of the Navajo Reservation. When J. L. purchased Leonard's trading post in 1878, the Pueblo Colorado Valley was still south of the reservation boundary and in the public domain, and Hubbell bought it without bothering to file for a homestead claim—in fact, he could not have filed a claim if he had wanted to, since the land had not been surveyed. When an executive order on January 6, 1880, pushed the boundary south by a mere six miles, swallowing up the Hubbell store, J. L. found himself in possession only of squatter's rights and on shaky legal footing.[108]

Despite this, neither Hubbell nor Cotton made any attempt to secure legal title to the land or water rights until 1890. Their inaction probably stemmed from the simple assumption that their physical occupation and improvement of the land would prove their right to it in the end. For years, Hubbell and Cotton seemed not to even realize that they needed to apply for a trader's license since their trading post had become part of the reservation. It was not until 1887 that Cotton applied for a license and acknowledged

The Hubbell family, c. 1893. J. L. and Lina sit on either end; Barbara and Adele stand in the rear; Lorenzo, Jr., sits between his parents, holding Roman's arms. Courtesy of the National Park Service, HUTR 04711.

that "I have nothing but a quit claim and that's no title. Land has never been surveyed."[109]

As land disputes began flaring up around railroad land grants, range wars, and, increasingly, conflicts between white settlers and Navajos in northern Arizona, Cotton took the first steps toward securing the title.[110] In

August 1890, he wrote the Commissioner of Indian Affairs asking that the homestead be excepted from the executive order that had expanded the reservation in 1880.[111] Cotton used both his credentials of having lived on the land continuously since 1884 and Hubbell's of having purchased it in 1878 to stake his claim, and the Navajo agent backed him up in his embellished declaration that he had been living in Ganado long before he had even set foot in Arizona.[112]

Despite Cotton's truth-stretching, the battle to secure the land title was long, and it resulted in added confusion as to the date of Cotton's transference of his interests in the Ganado store back to Hubbell.[113] At some point between 1892 and 1899, Cotton handed the fight off to Hubbell.[114] Congress finally granted J. L. the rights to the land on June 23, 1902, when it passed the bill titled "Adjustment of Rights of Settlers on the Navajo Indian Reservation, Arizona." Earlier versions of the bill had languished because of lack of support, concerns about the number of individuals who would be affected, and, in the usual manner of congressional action, objectionable provisions attached by the Senate at the last minute.[115] But through his connections with politicians, missionaries, and Indian agents, J. L. marshaled enough support for both his character and the quality of his business that members of Congress were persuaded that his cause was a matter of "justice," and that if he were allowed to remain on the reservation, he would "give the Indians in that part of the country a daily object lesson, in the way of farming and stock raising."[116] In Congress's eyes, J. L. was a force for the popular doctrine of assimilation, a boon to the Navajos rather than a detriment. Congress cleared the way for J. L. to keep his 160 acres, an island of private land in the Navajo Reservation. Trouble with surveying, however, kept the patent out of Hubbell's hands for another 15 years.[117] By the time the land was fully and legally his in 1917, Hubbell's trading post had blossomed from a couple of jacal huts to a full-fledged trading, farming, and freighting operation—the best known on the reservation.

CHAPTER THREE

## Laying the Foundations
### The Daily Business of the Hubbell Trading Post, 1878–1900

Six Navajos and nine horses jogged down the trail toward the Ganado trading post, among them a boy named Left Handed. Having been born in the spring of 1868 when the Navajos were jubilantly returning home, he was still too young to lift the heavy bundles of densely packed wool onto his packhorse by himself. He and his companions had spent the last few warm spring weeks planting corn in the damp earth with their families and shearing their sheep before making the two-and-a-half-day trek from Where the Grey Hill Comes Out to Ganado to sell their wool. On the journey, they spent two afternoons at watering holes, resting their sweaty horses, and two nights camped under the endless stars before they reached the trading post at noon on the third day.[1]

As soon as they crossed under the shade of the cottonwoods lining the wash and arrived in the dusty yard, a trading ritual began. The trading post was more than a *naalyéhé bá hooghan,* a house with things of value, where goods and money changed hands; it occupied a delicate cultural borderland where faux pas were almost inevitable and clashing values about the accumulation of property, profit, and sharing led to frequent misunderstandings.[2] But J. L. Hubbell forded the uncertain waters deftly, and as the trader and the Navajos grew used to one another, "Hubbell became a humane point of cultural adjustment between the Navajos and New Mexicans on one hand, and the aggressive Anglo society on the other."[3]

When he caught sight of the approaching Navajos, J. L. rushed out to meet them, delighted at the prospect of trade for his fledgling business and company to relieve the isolation. "Welcome, my sons-in-law," he greeted them, "Thank you all for coming to see me."[4] Like many Navajos, this group had come a long way to trade, as posts on the reservation were few and far between, so Hubbell invited them to feed and water their horses. He gave them wood for a fire, a bucket of water, a Dutch oven, and a pan of flour, salt and baking powder, inviting them to rest up in the shade—all gestures of generosity strongly emphasized in Navajo culture. The Navajos took their time, filling their stomachs and talking and laughing with the trader. Only when they were finished did Hubbell sit in front of them in the shade and say, "Any time now when you're ready you can take in the wool, and we'll start trading. I'll give you a good price for it. I'll treat you well." He continued, "I know you've come a long way. After you're through trading you can stay here tonight. You can spend a day or two or three or even four, because I like to have company all the time." The Navajos considered this offer. "We have lots of things to do at home," they said. "We don't want to eat up all your grub." Hubbell answered, "Well, I don't care about feeding you. I only care for friends, that's all. . . . But it's up to you. If you hurry home it's all right. I know you have many things to do." The Navajos decided to depart the following morning, and with that settled, the trading ritual went on.

Inside, a battle of wits began, with the Navajos trying to get the best of the trader, and the trader trying to balance generosity with a reasonable profit margin.[5] Hubbell expertly weighed the wool and evaluated the goods the Navajos brought in, taking into account the latest news about fluctuating market prices as he decided exactly how much he ought to pay—enough to encourage them to come back with their next load of wool, since the loyalty of a customer with a large herd could make the difference between a good wool season and bad one, but not so much that by the time he had paid the cost of shipping it he found himself broke.[6] Perhaps Hubbell and his customers haggled over the price a little before they agreed on an amount and the trader paid them. Sometimes he paid in cash or simply gave a written receipt for the value of goods to be taken out in trade in the store—but usually, he paid them in what was called "tin money."[7] On the reservation in the nineteenth century, hard cash was rare. Traders often minted their own tokens, called *seco* or "dry money" by the Navajos, feather-light chits of round or octagonal brass or aluminum stamped with the store name and denominations ranging from five cents to a dollar. Tin money was usually good only at the trading post of issue, which could tie a Navajo customer to a particular store, but it stimulated the cash-poor economy and circulated among the Navajos like currency, even showing up in mission collection plates.⁸ But the Navajos had not come to the trading post to walk away with a handful of tin money or even silver coin; Navajos generally did not accumulate reserves of cash, storing their wealth instead in sheep and silver jewelry. They came to the trading post for goods, so with the selling finished, they moved on to the buying.

In the bullpen, which "smelled of burning juniper and faintly musty wool," the Navajos lounged and visited with one another while they eyed the goods arrayed before them.⁹ They enjoyed a can of peaches or tomatoes, or rolled a cigarette from the concrete bowl of Bull Durham tobacco that Hubbell and almost every other trader kept on the counter. As he stood in the bullpen, the wide-eyed Navajo boy, Left Handed, looked upon shelves "full of groceries and dry goods . . . robes of all different colors and designs, and a big stack of leather of two colors and different sizes."¹⁰ Every article that the trader offered for sale lined the shelves or dangled from the rafters, in plain view, but out of reach.

When he had decided which goods he wanted or needed, a Navajo stepped up to the counter and pointed to them—with his lips, since pointing with a finger was considered bad manners among the Navajos.¹¹ Ensconced behind the counter, the trader fetched the goods and offered them up for closer inspection. J. L. described the transaction that typically followed: "If we assume, for instance, that the value of goods brought in by a certain Indian is $100, the Indian wants to see $100 in actual money laid out on the counter before him. He may then start in to do his own buying of the white man's wares, and if he buys a tin of sardines costing ten cents, he demands that the purchase be paid for then and there out of his money pile. That means that if he hands over a dollar he must receive ninety cents in change before he goes on making additional purchases of beans, flour, coffee, or whatever else he needs."¹² This slow ritual rolled forward, with the customer asking, "How much left?" between every purchase until the pile of money shrank and vanished.¹³

All of this transpired in a mixture of sign and Navajo. Most traders knew a little of the difficult Navajo language, at least a simplified jargon called "trader Navajo" or "Navvy" that sufficed in the bullpen.¹⁴ Even Hubbell, who spoke better Navajo than most traders, admitted that after fifty years of studying the language, "I am constantly learning new Navajo words that I've never heard before."¹⁵ However tenuous a trader's grasp of the language, "he or she would at least greet customers, shake hands, try to call them by a name—perhaps any name—laugh at jokes, tell stories," a friendly interaction that Hubbell excelled at.[16]

When the trading was finished, the Navajos departed to their homes with pack horses laden with goods. Often, when their homes were far away, they stayed the night (or, as Hubbell suggested, two or three or even four nights), eating dinner in the kitchen and camping in the yard or staying in the guest hogan specially built for their accommodation.[17] The Navajos in Left Handed's party stayed the night, as they knew their journey home would be long and hot. They ate breakfast at the trading post the following morning and then lounged around in the shade of the porch and the cottonwoods until the hot afternoon grew older and cooler. They rode off across the valley, driving their pack horses before them.[18] When he reached home, Left Handed displayed his wares proudly and told his family about the trip, about "Wearing Spectacles . . . how he'd joshed with the fellows, about the lunch he gave us and how he'd fed our horses in his pasture, about selling our wool and all about the trading that we did." Intrigued by Left Handed's description, the boy's father asked, "What kind of man are you talking about? Is he half Navaho? How is it that he talks just the way we do?" Left Handed answered, "I don't know anything about him, but they say he's a real Mexican, so I don't know where he picked up our language." The boy then told his father that the trader had asked him to bring the rest of their wool when they sheared their other sheep. Impressed with his son's account of this new trader, the old man agreed to let him take all their wool to Hubbell's trading post. In the delicate exchange of goods and values, Hubbell had negotiated the trading ritual well. He had made a few mistakes, broken a few rules of Navajo culture, but had smoothed the faux pas with his customary generosity and his language skills. He had gained another customer.[19]

## *Early Trade and Shipping at Hubbell Trading Post*

In the period between 1878 and 1900, when Left Handed made his visit, Hubbell's trading enterprise began to mature from uncertain infanthood to vigorous adolescence. It was a time in which Hubbell and Cotton laid the foundations for the many-faceted business that would flourish after the turn of the century. Together or separately, they began many tasks—attempting to secure the title to their land, improving their buildings and fencing their fields, establishing shipping networks and mail routes over treacherous trails, stimulating the trade in Navajo textiles, and opening branch stores across the reservation. It would be many years before their work came to full fruition, symbolized by the image of J. L. sitting at the head of his table, surrounded by his family and dozens of guests, the center of a web of influence. But in the beginning, the business and all its trappings were modest indeed.

In its first decades, "Indian trading was a lonely, male-oriented activity involving travel and much absence from family."[20] In Ganado, J. L. and his brother Charlie were miles away from family and friends, miles away, in fact, from any contact with the world beyond the sage-covered hills of Navajo country. Time passed slowly. Days might go by between customers or shipments of goods. Left Handed's account of J. L.'s enthusiasm upon his party's arrival reveals a man hungry for company and conversation of any kind. The mail arrived only once weekly, bringing news from Fort Defiance, Albuquerque, or New York.[21] The margins of the trading post's early account ledgers, which the bilingual brothers kept in a garbled mixture of English and Spanish, are filled with bored doodles and cluttered by sums and stains.[22] When shipments did arrive, they brought the barest staples, not luxuries. In the earliest surviving ledgers from 1879, Charlie and J. L. noted down in handwritten columns each wagonload of beans and barley, with potatoes, tobacco, corn, chili, a little canned fruit, and live beef cattle providing the only variety.[23] Within a few years, the range of goods J. L. offered expanded as the trading post became more embedded in Navajo life with the advent of the wool trade. By the time Cotton bought in as J. L.'s partner, the trading post carried nearly every kind of merchandise one would expect to find in a country store.[24] As Robert McPherson writes, "When people entered the bullpen, they saw brightly colored shirts and hats, bolts of cloth, cans of peaches, tomatoes, and milk, candy, and hardware items, but the staples of the trade were sacks of flour, Arbuckle coffee—either whole or ground—sugar, and baking powder. Packing crates served as shelves, seats, and storage bins and were also sold to the Navajo for similar uses in their hogan. Anything that enhanced life on the reservation and could be freighted in a wagon . . . went to the trading post for sale."[25]

Meanwhile, J. L. and Charlie shipped out heavy wagonloads of sheep pelts, goat skins, and wool.[26] Trading in remote Navajo country was a business venture inseparable from slow and costly freighting.[27] In the 1870s, most of the Hubbells' suppliers operated out of New Mexico under

Spanish surnames—undoubtedly they were men much like Hubbell's relatives, members of the wealthy classes engaged in the flourishing Southwestern trade. Before the Atlantic and Pacific Railway reached Albuquerque in 1880, west-bound freight traveled by rail only as far as Fort Dodge, Kansas, ox teams carrying it the rest of the way over the well-traveled Santa Fe Trail.[28] From there, Hubbell explained, it was "re-freighted by ox teams from Albuquerque here."[29] He added wryly, "We began to feel pretty close to the rest of the world when the railroad got into Albuquerque."[30] With no railway to glide across the distances, J. L.'s suppliers in New Mexico sent the goods he ordered over the 200 miles of intervening country by wagon, pack animals, or "on foot."[31] In the next few years, the railroad steamed closer to Ganado, reaching Gallup in 1881, then Holbrook and Winslow, and by August 1882 it had hurried on to Flagstaff. Each stop became a railhead that served Navajo country; Hubbell and Cotton typically used the railheads at Manuelito and Gallup, New Mexico, in the 1880s and 1890s.[32] They also expanded their business associates from the small Hispanic New Mexican firms Hubbell worked with in the 1870s to larger wholesalers based out of Albuquerque and Chicago.[33]

With closer railheads, shipping became a little swifter but was by no means reliable—it could, in fact, pose a major obstacle to the business. Ox teams plodded along at two miles per hour at top form. But the draft teams were often weakened by lack of feed, especially in years of drought or heavy winter snows.[34] In the unpredictable climate of Navajo country, "One year, the grasses withered and animals might die because there was no forage. The next year, winter storms or summer monsoons might sweep away teams and turn trails into muddy quagmires. Freighting was a hard way to make a living, and many freighters lost money along the way."[35] In the spring of 1886, for example, Cotton found himself unable to pay the bills because his teams were too weak to haul his freight to market. "My bull teams are slower than the second coming of our Savior," he complained to one of his creditors while 35,000 pounds of wool languished in the Ganado store room.[36] By 1900, Hubbell had given up on oxen as draft animals and shifted to the use of more efficient horse and mule teams, but in the meantime, the oxen's sluggish pace kept the traders scrambling to meet their obligations.[37]

Trading was, from the first day, a financial rollercoaster that soared and dipped in seasonal cycles and shuddered violently when the national economy declined. In one week, Cotton was certain "that he had enough wool to pay every cent he owed and have enough left over to take in the Albuquerque Territorial Fair," and in the next week he dejectedly noted, "I'm busted, as usual."[38] Young and entrepreneurial, Hubbell and Cotton both maintained perennially high hopes that their latest scheme—whether sheep-raising, the acquisition of a new store, or another freighting contract—would be the one to provide profits, but rare was the year when the business seemed not to suffer from a shortage of cash. Hubbell and Cotton wrote letters to creditors heavy with the refrain, "We regret to say we are unable to meet your bill promptly," and "We have been disappointed in money matters But think we can pay you all in the next ten days."[39]

The ordinary risks of business were compounded by the special circumstances of Navajo trading—namely, its chronic shortage of cash and its seasonality. The Navajo economy turned on a seasonal wheel based on stock raising, weaving, and piñon gathering. Long periods of time would pass in which the Navajos had no source of income. This required traders to extend credit and carry accounts, especially through the winters and summers when the Navajos needed to buy provisions to get them through to shearing time in November and May.[40] This seasonal cycle of want and plenty, coupled with the surfeit of cash on the reservation, led to an important system of trade among the Navajos: pawn. As William S. Kiser notes, "Pawn began as a nonchalant practice among Indian traders in the Navajo country, essentially just another component of a large and often complex trading business."[41] In times of need, Navajos pawned their silver and turquoise jewelry, concho belts, saddles, and even guns to the trader for small loans.[42] When they sheared their sheep, the Navajos would redeem their pawned valuables, which were kept for a certain amount of time, usually six months, in the "'pawn rooms'—a frontier version of a jewelry store—a room flashing with silver and glowing with red and pink coral and turquoise ropes of beads, all tagged, the room smelling of leather and metal, the pawn dangling from hooks on the walls, all waiting to be redeemed."[43] If the Navajos failed to redeem the pawn after six months, the trader might move it into a display case in the store to advertise it for thirty days before it became officially "dead" and eligible for sale.[44]

Hubbell, as well as some other traders, often hung on to pawn long after it was dead out of courtesy, based on an individual's record of dependability. Hubbell was even known to lend pawned jewelry back to its owner for special occasions.[45] Visiting artist Maynard Dixon dramatized Hubbell's

Navajos shearing sheep. Courtesy of the National Park Service, HUTR 06117.

attitude toward his pawn business in a short story called "Chindih" that he wrote in the early twentieth century:

> Like all Indian traders, the Old Man ran a "pawn shop" for the convenience of his customers. In a glass case in the store front were all kinds of Indian valuables—semi-sacred medicine bags, native wampum, silver and turquoise jewelry, harness, firearms. Some of the items fascinated me.
> "*Tukwi pesoh* for that squash blossom necklace there," I said.
> The Old Man pawed over the silver work, peering at the tags through his thick lenses. "Mmm—that was due last December," he said, running the fine necklace through his fingers. "I know that family. A lot of their sheep froze to death last winter. No, they'll redeem it sometime ... About that? Well, that string has been here two years. Belongs to Hosteen Tchaiyoni, the old scoundrel. But hell, no, I couldn't sell it. That man has confidence in me. He's my friend."
> I laughed. "This is part of your regular business, isn't it?"
> "Oh—well," said the Old Man. "Yes, you could call it that. But I don't figure to make much on it. . . . This one? Let's see. That fellow, he's no good. Gambled everything away. Yes, I'll sell you this one."[46]

The system "became an honored one" for both trader and Navajos, though abuses happened on both sides, and, as Hubbell said, pawn seldom resulted in much profit for the trader.[47] The trader walked a fine line between extending enough credit to his customers to get them through the lean months and going bankrupt.[48] With these complicated systems bridging the gaps between shearing time and stock-selling time, traders could expect their customers to pay off their accounts only twice a year in six-month intervals.[49] Because of this, business profits languished during the winters, and Hubbell and other traders required as much financial leeway from their suppliers as the Navajos required from the traders.[50]

Other peculiarities of Indian trading contributed to its instability. Hubbell always insisted that, although trading offered ample opportunity for exploitation of Navajo customers, "[t]he trader's margin between what he pays for the Indian's goods and what it will bring when shipped to the market is seldom more than that prevailing in other lines of legitimate business. The trader, too, takes all the risks of spoilage in hides, losses in shipping, fluctuation of market prices, and damage to goods in one form or another, the same as any other form of private business."[51] As anthropologist Teresa J. Wilkins argues, the trader's venture did in fact entail a significant amount of risk. Government trading licenses required a $10,000 bond, traders were required to maintain their own buildings and homes on land that they did not own (except in Hubbell's case), and establishment of inventory required a significant financial outlay. All of these factors "represented a considerable capital investment with little or no guarantee of quick return. A trader in the late nineteenth or early twentieth centuries was gambling that the return on wool would be fast and profitable enough to be worth the risk."[52] Traders also faced competition, which kept prices relatively controlled, since a Navajo who was unsatisfied with what a trader offered for wool could take his business elsewhere. Traders therefore guarded their territory jealously. When Cotton, for example, caught wind that someone else was attempting to secure a license to trade in the vicinity of Ganado, he hurried to rush his bond and license through before the interloper could. Though Cotton had secured a verbal promise from the Commissioner of Indian Affairs that the office would not grant a license to anyone within 30 miles of Ganado, in reality he was "at the mercy of the fort."[53] Too-close competition might lure customers away or further drive down prices, a prospect that made the businessman in Cotton squirm. As he wrote to Indian Agent John H.

Bowman in 1886, "I think you know me too well to think I am trading with the Navajos for their benefit exclusively. And when the time comes that I have to sell goods cheaper than I am now doing I will quit the business. So far I've been the last man to come down in prices."[54] Fluctuations in national and regional economies also had the power to drown a trading venture. Locally, extensive drought weakened the Navajo economy in the late 1880s and early 1890s, while on a national scale, the Panic of 1893 staggered businesses, factors that undoubtedly contributed to the slow pace of growth for the Ganado trading post in its early years.[55] In a business as unsteady and swiftly evolving as Indian trading was before 1900, there was no such thing as a typical year.

## *The Seeds of Empire: Trading Posts, Ranching, and Mail Contracts*

In the struggle to stay afloat financially in the chancy Indian trading business, many traders diversified their operations, mixing trade, freighting, ranching, and US government mail contracts to stabilize their revenue streams.[56] In the years before 1900, Hubbell and Cotton invested in a variety of schemes, laying the foundations upon which Hubbell's trading empire would later rest. One of the first steps they took, likely prompted by Lorenzo's past experience as a postal clerk, was to apply for contracts to carry the mail on the Navajo Reservation. Rural routes and post offices were often operated by private contractors for a modest salary. Hubbell won his first contract in 1883 to operate the route between the railhead and the Pueblo Colorado Valley, running the post office out of his trading post.[57] According to Lorenzo's granddaughter, LaCharles Eckel, it was the post office that finally gave Ganado its name. Regular confusion of the address Pueblo Colorado, Arizona, with the town of Pueblo, Colorado, necessitated a change; Lorenzo chose Ganado, in honor of his Navajo friend, Ganado Mucho.[58] Charlie, Cotton, and Hubbell juggled the title of postmaster between them for a few years, occasionally losing the contract for brief periods of time, but Hubbell eventually secured it once and for all, passing it on to his daughter, Barbara, who held it until she resigned her post in 1943.[59] Though the pay for operating contract routes and the postmaster's salary were slight, and Hubbell was constantly chastised by the postal service for late deliveries when the roads washed out, the mail contracts provided just enough steady income to help balance the fluctuations of the Navajo economy.[60]

Another strategy Hubbell and Cotton employed almost as soon as they entered into partnership together was to expand the reach of their business by opening additional trading posts across the reservation. Besides Hubbell's stores in Navajo City and St. Johns, Hubbell and Cotton had interests in at least three other trading posts in the mid-1880s: Chinle, Blue Canyon, and Sin Let Za He.[61] A trading post in Chinle at the heart of Navajo country was a particular wish of Cotton's, but he realized that dream only a short time in 1885 before he lost in the murky, partisan game of federal licensure and had to clear out.[62] The Blue Canyon store, located near the Hopi mesas, was similarly short-lived. It opened only long enough to do a brisk spring wool business before the Indian agent, suspecting that it was on reservation land, ordered the unlicensed and uninsured operation shut down.[63] Cotton opened another location at Sin Let Za He briefly in 1886, but it, too, vanished as quickly as it appeared.[64] Hubbell's younger brother Charlie was often the man behind the counter at these fleeting trading posts, shuffled around while Cotton maintained the trading post in Ganado and Hubbell politicked in St. Johns. In the 1890s, after Cotton relocated to Gallup, records were so poorly kept, and ownership interests even in the Ganado trading post so unclear, that it is impossible to tell if Hubbell attempted to open any other branch stores. It appears that for the next decade, the Ganado store stood alone as Hubbell focused on building up its infrastructure.

Hubbell, like many other traders in the early period, saw his property in Ganado as more than just a convenient location for a trading post. He recognized its potential as a "trading ranch," where farming and ranching activities would be just as important as trading.[65] From the beginning, livestock played a significant role in the business—which was unsurprising given the central role of sheep in Navajo life and Hubbell's background in a ranching family.[66] While trade in wool, not sheep, dominated the early market as the Navajos built up their herds and the nation built up its appetite for mutton, the sale of live sheep soon emerged as a major facet of the Navajo trading economy. Hubbell and Cotton began purchasing small numbers of sheep and goats in the late 1880s, but, like many other aspects of the business, the stock trade did not truly flourish until after the turn of the century.[67]

Though both partners were involved in the sheep business from the beginning of their venture, an irrigated farm at Ganado seems to have been Hubbell's particular ambition. As historian Charles Peterson states, "Cotton did not object to Hubbell's interest in farming or even to his long campaigns to develop an irrigation system and create a farming community at Ganado, but there was an instructive difference of style and motivation in the two. It was Cotton who left Ganado for Gallup, set up a successful wholesaling firm, and became a banker," while Hubbell, always the product of his cultural heritage, "saw livestock as a source of wealth and personal satisfaction," and made "homesteading and farm development [his] passions."[68]

J. L.'s dreams of homesteading found an ally in the Bureau of Indian Affairs (BIA), where assimilationist doctrines held sway. Indian Agent G. W. Hayzlett was convinced Hubbell could "give the Indians . . . a daily object lesson, in the way of farming," which BIA officials thought would help speed the Navajos' transition to Euro-American ways of life.[69] With the dry, unpredictable climate of Navajo country to contend with, the BIA and other agencies promoted irrigation as a way to develop the land and stabilize the Navajo economy. Irrigation fever swept through the West around the turn of the twentieth century, fueled by John Wesley Powell's surveys, and Hubbell was just as caught up in it as the next man.[70] In fact, together with H. F. Robinson of the Division of Indian Irrigation, he would later play a key role in the introduction of irrigation on the Navajo Reservation.[71] Extended drought in the late 1880s and 1890s prompted an irrigation survey of the reservation, including the Pueblo Colorado Valley. Lieutenant E. M. Suplee spent six days taking measurements and drawing maps of potential dams and irrigation works in the valley in 1892, giving Hubbell just the plan he needed to realize the agricultural potential of his land.[72] When he was elected to the Arizona Territorial House of Representatives that fall, Hubbell pushed through several water rights laws that indicated his growing interest in harnessing the Pueblo Colorado River. Work on the irrigation projects was still a decade in the future, but the 1890s saw the laying of the ideological foundation upon which the irrigation system would rest.[73]

Hubbell and Cotton, in the meantime, made significant improvements to their land. In 1883, gathering rocks from the surrounding hills, and, some say, nearby Ancestral Puebloan ruins, they constructed the office and rug room of the current trading post building.[74] A few years later, they raised the office roof and added the store and the wareroom, giving the trading post buildings the configuration that endures today.[75] They also built a mammoth two-story barn and a smaller manager's residence behind the trading post in the 1890s.[76] They erected wire and wood fences to corral their stock, cleared the juniper trees from the land, and dotted the yard with a well house, a watering trough, and sheds.[77] After Cotton left for Gallup, Hubbell began construction on a home for his wife and family, which he completed in stages between 1889 and 1910.[78] By the turn of the century Hubbell was ready to move his family permanently from St. Johns to Ganado, and finally transform his bachelor's enterprise into a family operation.

## Family and Employees at the Trading Post

Though in the first decades of the trading post the traders faced times of utter seclusion, they also enjoyed times when company crowded the bullpen and the family gathered near. Cotton, of course, had the companionship of his family while he lived at the trading post. From 1884 until 1888, Mary Alice Cotton, "pretty, vivacious, sometimes quick-tempered, and always well dressed," was mistress of Ganado, and her children played in the dusty yard under the juniper trees.[79] When the Cottons left Ganado for more comfortable accommodations in Gallup, Hubbell's young children soon filled the trading post air with high laughter in the summertime. But times of family togetherness were outweighed before 1900 by times of relative isolation, when company meant a table surrounded by Hispanic teamsters and perhaps the occasional writer or scientist traveling into Navajo country.[80]

Lorenzo's earliest companion at Ganado was, of course, his favorite younger brother, Charlie. Martha Blue has described Charlie as "J. L.'s perfect counterpoint: a drinker, unmarried, no known children, no known affaires, mostly a store employee or a manager in an outlying post, and no political or financial reputation or aspirations."[81] He was thin and frail, and the Navajos called him Ja' abaani (the Bat or Bat Ears).[82] He never seemed to have much of a financial interest in any of the businesses, and he suffered more from the isolation than his brother, who developed a friendship with the Navajos that eluded the less adaptable Charlie. But he was part of his brother's family scene, and the two kept each other company for many quiet years.

Charlie, however, was not Lorenzo's only relative to work in some capacity at the trading post. In fact, a great many of Hubbell's teamsters were related to him by blood or marriage. Freighting for the trading post required quite a bit of manpower, and Hubbell usually kept four or five regularly employed teamsters, most of whom were Hispanic relatives, though some were Anglo, like Joe Lee, or Navajo, like Joe Tippecanoe.[83] J. L. and Cotton also occasionally hired teamsters from Gallup for special jobs, or local Navajos who had their own teams, a practice that was encouraged by the Indian agents as a work opportunity that helped the Navajos pay off their store debts.[84] The teamsters could be a rowdy bunch, and "the Hubbell barn resound[ed] with the yells of . . . freighters and animal snorts and brays."[85] Cotton often complained to Hubbell about their carelessness and drunkenness, urging his former partner to discipline or fire them. But J. L. generally exercised great patience with their behavior, evidently feeling some kind of familial obligation that prevented him from throwing them out when he otherwise might have.[86]

Though the milieu of teamsters and Navajos sufficed for company in the 1870s and 1880s, J. L. soon began bringing his wife and children to the store for short periods of time. His oldest son, Lorenzo, Jr., was born on April 14, 1883, in St. Johns, joining his two older sisters, Adele and Barbara. Like his father, Lorenzo, Jr., spent his earliest years in the bosom of a Spanish community, and only later learned to speak English. Though J. L. would not marry Lina until 1891, he had begun taking the six-year-old Lorenzo, Jr., on trading expeditions to the Navajo Reservation by 1889.[87] These excursions delighted the boy, who felt at home in Navajo country in a way he did not in St. Johns. He would later remember, "When as a small boy my father would lose track of me for awhile, all he had to do was follow his nose to where horse meat was being roasted by the Navajo and there I was feasting with the best of them!"[88] All through the summers of his childhood, Lorencito, as his family affectionately called him, ran free at the trading post, learning the Navajo language and the tricks of the trade from his father and uncle. The indulgent Charlie taught him to trade red striped stick candy to the Navajos for small items; later, Lorenzo, Jr., graduated to trading in copper bracelets.[89] In the summer of 1892, J. L. took the boy to Canyon de Chelly on a two-month trading expedition. "Those two months sped by like magic. So many interesting things were to be seen by a small boy led by Indian companions," and in August, Lorenzo, Jr., saw his first Snake Dance, where he was "thrilled to see little boys his own age fondling live rattlers."[90]

After 1891, the rest of J. L.'s family began to spend summers at the trading post, too, although their visits were probably brief before the house was habitable. The children always returned to town—either St. Johns or later Albuquerque—for school. Although she herself probably could not read and write, Lina held her children's education as sacrosanct. When J. L., who neither drank alcohol nor used tobacco but nursed a ruinous gambling habit, lost $60,000 in a poker game, Lina, who normally faded into the domestic background, snapped at him in Spanish, "Well, Don Lorenzo! I think it is about time for you to choose between your penchant for gambling and the question of whether or not our children are to be educated ladies and gentlemen."[91] Stung by her rebuff, J. L. gave up gambling—and the children went to school: Notre Dame in Indiana for Lorenzo, Jr., and Roman, and St. Joseph's Academy in Prescott, Arizona, for Adele and Barbara.[92] Lorenzo, Jr., "never happy away from the desert and the Indians," protested violently at being sent to Notre Dame in 1897, but to no avail. He spent four years there, earning a commercial diploma, but "most of the time his mind was not occupied with Latin or literature. He was longing to be back in Arizona trading with the Indians, riding races with them, joining them in their holiday 'chicken pulls' and eating roast horse meat under the spiny juniper trees."[93] Lorenzo returned to Arizona in 1901, and a year later began his own trading operation at Keams Canyon under his father's guidance—no longer a child, but a young man ready to strike out on his own.

J. L.'s youngest son, Roman, was born on October 13, 1891, a few months after Lina and J. L. married. Soon the boy was making mischief at Ganado. The artist E. A. Burbank, who spent quite a bit of time at the trading post before the turn of the century, told Roman, "When I first met you you were a lively kid 5 years old, and we used to take long walks togeather [sic]. But you made it lively for that good father of yours."[94] Roman certainly did keep his father guessing, frequently exasperating the trader as sons often do. Significantly younger than the other children, Roman was more indulged—even spoiled—than his siblings, and as a consequence, wilder. Like his older brother, he would later be sent to Notre Dame in 1908, but even as he put his son on the train east, J. L. wondered if he was making a mistake. "The trouble is," he told Roman after the boy left the school in disgrace within a year, "that you think you can do as you please and have no idea of your duty. . . . I expect you home here soon, and hope that while you are in Albuquerque, you will behave yourself like a gentleman."[95] But before 1900 J. L.'s troubles with his youngest son were still in the future, and he had only to enjoy the handsome child's liveliness and sense of wonder.

The necessary separations between J. L. and his family during the winters were typical of traders' families who wanted their children educated.[96] Even after J. L. built the house in 1901, Lina spent much of her time living at the family's second home in Albuquerque. She did, however, spend some time at Ganado, teaching Hubbell's Navajo cook, Hastiin Ne'e'y, called Loco by the family, how to make her husband's favorite dishes of roast corn, pigeons and squab, turkey, pies, and roast lamb.[97] J. L.'s guests rarely mentioned her, but a few remarked upon her "rare Spanish courtesy . . . when she played hostess."[98] After the birth of her children, Lina became a portly woman; the Navajos called her Asdsa Tsoh (Large Woman) and spoke of her kindly.[99] Lorenzo, Jr., remembered her as a devoted mother, honest, firm, and wise, and her grandchildren would recall a fashionably dressed and generous woman ensconced in her favorite chair.[100] But because she did not write and therefore left behind no records, her imprint on Ganado is faint and lives only in the recorded memories of others.

## The Navajo Community at Hubbell Trading Post

Between 1878 and 1900, Hubbell went from an outsider the Navajos delighted in testing to an accepted and even respected part of the community. Martha Blue has compared J. L.'s reputation among the Navajos to a double-faced token: good on one side and bad on the other. However tall and magnificent Hubbell's legend grew over the years, the Navajos' stories remind us that he was only a man. Though the early days at the trading post may have been lonely, they were not as lonely as they might have been had not J. L.'s other vice been a weakness for women. "In Navajo culture," Blue explains, "a woman who has a child by a man married to someone else is called a 'stealing wife.' J. L. must have done a lot of stealing, as the careful records kept by Hubbell's friends, the Franciscans at St. Michaels Mission, record six Navajo women as J. L.'s Navajo wives," and seven births as his children.[101] Many of Hubbell's artist friends, more privy to his indiscretions than his wife probably was, joked in letters about "the fine little girls" and the "Navajo beauties."[102] Some Navajo women remembered avoiding the trading post as girls because of the way J. L. stared at them.[103] Thus, on the dark side of Hubbell's coin were his many unacknowledged Navajo children, as well as the low wages—usually in trade tokens—that he paid his many Navajo employees.[104]

Despite this, J. L. always insisted that there were more good traders than bad, and that he himself held fast to a commitment to helping the Navajos whenever he could. He was well aware of the trader's reputation for dishonesty, and refuted it vehemently. In 1931, historian C. C. Rister called the Indian trader of the Southwest "part of the jetsam of the turbulent sea of border life," a ruthless misfit unable to bear the restraints of civilization, who only made the "Indian problem" worse.[105] As J. L. told journalist J. E. Hogg, "There are black sheep among all herds."[106] He insisted that dishonest traders, though there had been a few, never lasted long. "I've been an Indian trader for fifty years, but I've dealt honestly with them. I've never taken a dollar from an Indian without giving the Indian value received, and I've often given the Indian what should have been my own legitimate margin of business profit just to help them when they needed it."[107] Hubbell once told one of his guests, who was writing a series of articles defending the reputation of Indian traders:

> No intelligent Indian trader desires to live among a community of Indian paupers.... The first duty of an Indian trader, in my belief, is to look after the material welfare of his neighbors; to advise them to produce that which their natural inclinations and talent best adapts them; to treat them honestly and insist on getting the same treatment from them; to practice honesty and enforce on the Indians the same policy by all legitimate means in his power; to find a market for their products and vigilantly watch that they keep improving in the production of same, and advise them which commands the best price. This requires patience, energy and unselfish interest in the Indian. This does not mean that the trader should forget that he is to see that he makes a fair profit for himself, for whatever would injure him would naturally injure those with whom he comes in contact.[108]

Hubbell's relationship with the Navajos was, indeed, complicated by conflicting cultural values, by his commonly held nineteenth century biases, and by the Navajos' "indifference, with an underlying current of hostility" toward non-Indians.[109] But, as the account of Left Handed demonstrates, the rifts between them were bridged by J. L.'s generosity and the efforts he consciously made to accommodate Navajo cultural traditions. He, like other traders, sometimes exploited the Navajos in some fashion or another, but he also "came nearer being part of the Indian community than other whites."[110] As Peterson argues, Hubbell fit readily within the Navajos' "well-established social-welfare customs, through which the *ricos* both exploited and supported the *pobres*. Wealthy Navajo stockmen kept property pretty well in their own hands but provided herding opportunities, and, in times of crisis, food and shelter for poor relatives and neighbors."[111] Many Navajos would remember Hubbell helping them with food and gifts of livestock in times of need. In fact, some Navajos moved to Ganado to be closer to the trading post to escape hunger and other hardships.[112] J. L. also readily filled the role of intermediary between "his" Navajos and the federal government, which relied on traders "to disseminate news of changes in federal policies, contact specific people in the community, help recruit students for the Indian schools, and support official programs."[113] He often read and wrote letters for Navajos and facilitated their employment off-reservation, as well as assisting in burials and community disputes.[114]

    J. L. further endeared himself to the Navajo community, and, not incidentally, increased the reach of his business, by providing ample opportunity for socializing around his trading post. He sold cards and provided space for the popular pastime of gambling, his Mexican and Anglo employees often joining the Navajos in the gambling hogan for a game of poker or rummy, or a stick dice or shoe game.[115] Hubbell also held Christmas celebrations where he gave gifts to the Navajos. But the highlight of Navajo social life at the trading post was the chicken pull, a forerunner of the Navajo rodeo, with horse races, footraces, and tugs-of-war.[116] Though the outlay of funds on Hubbell's part was significant—he had to feed the assembled Navajos and put up prizes for the contests—it served as an effective mechanism for stimulating trade.[117]

    Donald Sidney Hubbell, whose father was J. L.'s cousin, spent four years of his childhood living at the trading post between 1914 and 1917. He recalled a chicken pull he witnessed as a boy, describing a scene humming with excitement as nearly five hundred Navajos gathered at the trading post in anticipation of the event. The day's festivities began with J. L. and the Navajos giving "long tiresome speeches" praising one another before the horse races began.[118] Next came the chicken pull itself, an old Spanish sport. The boy explained, "To play this game, a rooster was buried in the ground with only his neck and head showing. About fifty Navajos then formed a circle around the rooster on their horses and starting at a mad gallop tried to grab the rooster's head and pull him out of his earthy nest. When after thirty minutes someone managed to make a grab he headed for the judges' box and received his prize unless some other Indian snatched the bird away

Oil painting by E. A. Burbank of Navajo men gambling in the Leonard building. Courtesy of the National Park Service, HUTR 05277.

from him."[119] The air was alive with heavy betting in cash, tin money, saddle blankets, jewelry, and buckskins.[120] After the games, Navajos, Mexicans, and Anglos alike settled in to feast on a whole beef and several sheep barbequed in a pit, drinking Arbuckle coffee and sopping up the juices with bread.[121] Events like these tied the Navajo community to the trading post not only economically, but socially. Whether Hubbell's family was near or far, whether the teamsters were yelling in the barn or off on the trail, the Navajos were a constant presence in Ganado.

In the coming years, the operation at Hubbell's trading post in Ganado would grow exponentially from an isolated huddle of low buildings, with a handful of teamsters joining the trader at the table, to an extensive network of trading posts operated by dozens of employees. The trading post also became a part of the lives of more and more Navajos as Hubbell encouraged

Navajos preparing for a horse race at Ganado, 1913. Photograph by Dane Coolidge. Courtesy of the National Park Service, HUTR 10619.

weaving and the curio trade, as he hired Navajos to build a dam at Ganado Lake and bring his 160 acres under cultivation, and as he employed more Navajo teams to haul his ever-increasing volume of freight.[122] Cooks, blacksmiths, bakers, maids, and laborers in the fields and in the gardens each added their voices to the growing din of life at the busy trading post.[123] J. L.'s children and grandchildren would soon be running underfoot, and an endless stream of visitors joined Hubbell in his newly built home to partake in what would be the heyday of the Hubbell Trading Post.

CHAPTER FOUR

## The Rise of an Empire
*Expansion and Evolution, 1900–1914*

As the twentieth century dawned on Ganado, the trading post and its proprietor stood poised to enter a new era. In 1901, J. L. finished construction on the grand hall and bedrooms of his house and threw the doors open to receive his family and guests. The last of C. N. Cotton's influence had faded, and the time had come for J. L. to build upon the foundations he and his partner had laid. He began purposefully expanding his business holdings, his shipping routes, his irrigation works, and his political influence. The tenor of his life began to mellow from the clash and fanfare of adventurous youth to the calmer, more measured tones of experience. In a 1902 letter to his cousin, Charles H. Hubbell, he indulged in a little reminiscing about his days as sheriff of Apache County. But those times lived only in fond, embellished memory. "I have quit all those foolishness [sic] long ago," he wrote decisively. "I am the oldest of the family, and am now forty nine years of age, and will soon have one foot in the grave."[1] But if he had one foot in the grave, the other tirelessly danced a political jig while his hands juggled the complicated demands of several trading posts spread out across Navajo country.

### A Second Generation of Hubbell Traders

Fortunately, as J. L. Hubbell's business interests multiplied and matured in the early years of the twentieth century, so did the Hubbell family. Both of J. L.'s daughters married in the first decade of the new century, and Roman soon followed, and though the Hubbell children all made forays into the wider world at one time or another, a magnetic pull seemed to draw them inexorably back to Ganado, where they began to take on more and more of the responsibility of running the business. When his children entered adulthood, J. L. gained the help of two Indian traders in his sons, a clerk in one of his sons-in-law, a housekeeper in one daughter, and a postmistress in the other, not to mention a handful of grandchildren.

Adele, nicknamed "Lala" by her family, was the first to marry. She met a young accountant, Forrest Miles Parker, while she was living in Albuquerque with her mother, and they were engaged by early February 1903.[2] Forrest was a native New Mexican whose parents had come to the territory from Kentucky and Ohio, and a graduate of the New Mexico Agricultural College. He was also an adept marksman, a skill that helped earn him J. L.'s approval. After his engagement to Adele, Forrest wrote a letter assuring his future father-in-law "that I consider it an honor that you can willingly trust me with your daughter and I will try to show my appreciation by being as good & kind to Adele as is in my power. I tell you I think well enough of her to do anything for her."[3] J. L. offered no objections, seeing Forrest as the sort of young man who could be quite useful in the running of his expanding business. "Here's a young fellow I can take out there to Ganado," he said, "he's adept with a gun, not that I want anybody killed, but I do like to have a man who somebody might fear."[4] With J. L.'s approval, Adele and Forrest were married in Albuquerque on September 30, 1903, and after a honeymoon in California, they settled in Ganado—Forrest to manage the books and Adele to oversee the house in her firm, meticulous way.[5]

Forrest's niece remembered him to be "a very charming man, a very kind man," and he was certainly well liked by J. L.'s employees and family, especially Lorenzo, Jr.[6] The move from Albuquerque to Ganado, however, was surely a shock to an educated man like Forrest, who was independent enough to clash with J. L. from time to time. When, one morning not long after he arrived at the trading post, Forrest showed up to work wearing a tie, J. L. told him to "take it off . . . because he was in Indian country now and the Navajos might grab him by the necktie and pull it tight."[7] Forrest adjusted, learning the trading business and becoming a valued employee, in high demand at the family's growing number of trading posts to straighten out the typically badly kept and baffling books.[8] Soon, children's cries and laughter filled the hall. Adele and Forrest became the parents of J. L.'s first grandchild, Lorenzo Hubbell Parker, nicknamed Hub, on May 9, 1906. Five years later, Forrest Miles Parker, Jr., called Mudgy or Mudge, was born on January 17, 1911.

Adele (right) and Barbara (left) before their marriages. Courtesy of the National Park Service, HUTR 04760.

J. L. acquired another son-in-law when his second daughter, Barbara, married Charles Q. Goodman, a Virginian who had come to Albuquerque to work as an accountant for the Southwestern Brewery & Ice Co. Like Forrest, Charles sent a humble letter to J. L. asking for his daughter's hand in marriage, acknowledging that he would not be able to "give her the home and luxuries she has been accustomed to."[9] The old trader gave his consent, and Barbara spent the summer juggling wedding preparations with her duties taking care of her mother and helping look after her younger brother, Roman. Always more practical than Adele, Barbara soon found she could not rely on her sister's help with the wedding plans since Adele had "such extravagant ideas that I think it best to do it myself."[10] The couple married in late October 1906, settling in a rented house in Albuquerque to be near her ailing mother. Though she now lived in her own house, Barbara continued to manage her mother's finances and monitor her health, sending updates to her father in Ganado and eating dinner at Lina's almost every night.[11]

Barbara and Charles, however, were married for scarcely two years before tragedy struck. On January 24, 1909, Charles was accidentally shot through the abdomen with a twelve-gauge shotgun by his close friend, Harry Benjamin, while hunting quail south of Albuquerque. The two had fired on a bunch of quail that flushed from cover, killing four before the rest of the birds scattered and ran along the ground with the two hunters pelting after them. Benjamin stumbled, his shotgun fired, and Charles fell. When he saw that he had shot his friend, Benjamin, "with rare nerve and presence of mind, in the face of the awful tragedy . . . picked up his wounded and bleeding companion, and with much difficulty carried him to a nearby house."[12] From there, he dispatched a messenger to J. L.'s brother, J. Felipe Hubbell, in Pajarito, which was not far the scene of the accident. Charles lay in agony for nearly two hours before the physician arrived from Albuquerque, and he died only an hour later. When she received the news, Barbara was so "completely prostrated by the terrible shock" that she required the care of a physician—for she was pregnant with Charles's and her first child.[13] In Gallup, J. L. heard the news of his son-in-law's death and hurried to Albuquerque to take over the funeral arrangements. Keenly feeling his daughter's loss, he wrote in a biting letter some months later to his friend, Ralph Cameron, that Charles "was accidentally killed by an idiot while out hunting. I generally call men idiots who handle carelessly enough to endanger human life."[14] Benjamin himself was devastated to have been the cause of his dear friend's death, and after carrying Charles to help, joined Barbara in a state of collapse. The newspaper article detailing the accident declared Charles to have been a "capable and valuable" employee, a man whose "winning personality had made him large numbers of friends in Albuquerque."[15]

Bereft of her husband, Barbara moved in with her mother. Her child was born on June 26, 1909, five months to the day after Charles's burial. Barbara had determined to name the child after its father, and when a daughter instead of a son wailed into life, she simply added the Spanish feminine "la" to the name: LaCharles.[16] She stayed with her mother in Albuquerque for about two years, and when Lina became too ill to run her home even with her daughter's assistance, the three of them moved to Ganado to shelter under the family wing. J. L. always paid special attention to Barbara after Charles's death, making it known that around the house she had "more rights than anybody else" and encouraging her to get out of the trading post once in a while, and he took Barbara and LaCharles with him on political trips.[17] Around the trading post, Barbara became known by the affectionate nickname Auntie Bob. LaCharles, meanwhile, had no shortage of father figures growing up at Ganado. "Forrest, Roman, and Lorenzo were fathers to me," she remembered. "So actually, I didn't miss my father. I never knew him or anything but I had three very loving 'fathers,' that's for sure."[18]

Meanwhile, J. L.'s youngest son, Roman, a full ten years Barbara's junior, caused a fair amount of trouble in his teenage years. Like Lorenzo, Roman was sent away to school at Notre Dame in 1908. Roman was partially deaf—the Navajos, in fact, would later call him Jai-kal (Deaf One)—and J. L. worried that Roman would not be able to hear the instructors.[19] But the school's president assured J. L. that Roman would not be inconvenienced if he were placed in the front of the class.[20] And indeed, it wasn't Roman's deafness that got him dismissed from the school before six months had gone by. As the school explained to J. L. after he had sent the boy home, "Roman's difficulty arose from a distorted sense of humor. He and another student were discovered moving about the dormitory . . . at night and they explained that their only object was to part the curtains around the beds of the other students so as to have a little fun in the morning when the boys woke up."[21] Roman was a practical joker, but "public disorders" were not tolerated by the school, and he was sent back to Ganado by the end of March 1909.[22] J. L. did not seem surprised by his son's dismissal, only disappointed. "As long as you think that there is nothing very wrong in what you do, so long will you continue to be in trouble," he told Roman. "That is rather hard to say, but the sooner you learn it the better. . . . You cannot lay the blame on any one, it is yourself alone to blame."[23] It would take more than a dismissal to squash Roman's carefree spirit, though. He began learning the life of an Indian trader, putting his restless energy to use in a constant quest for new business avenues. Lorenzo, Jr., thought Roman had "the makings of a good trader," but that he suffered from the weakness of carelessness with goods and softness toward the Indians even more than the rest of the family.[24] But by 1911, when Roman was just 20 years old and with very little experience, he was running the store at Ganado while his father was busy pursuing politics.

## Hubbell in Politics

For all that Hubbell complained of having one foot in the grave by the turn of the century, he loved politics and could not refrain from engaging in public debate, especially with Arizona Territory seeking statehood.[25] He was an opinionated man who had plans for his business and land that would be best fulfilled through direct political action. He also liked to win—and the worse the odds, the more he liked to beat them. As a Republican in a thoroughly Democratic territory, his odds were not good, and therefore politics was all the more tempting. Having acquired a taste for opposition in his days as sheriff, J. L. ran for and was elected to the Seventeenth Territorial Legislature of Arizona in 1893.[26] The *Arizona Republican* greeted his arrival in Phoenix with enthusiasm and a little humor: "Mr. Hubbell will occupy a prominent place in the council chamber, a place to which his natural abilities will lift him, assisted by the loneliness which will pervade the Republican side of the chamber."[27] As one of only four Republicans on the senate, J. L. introduced bills defending the rights of Hispanics, enthusiastically supported women's suffrage, and, most importantly for the fate of a little patch of 160 acres in Ganado, introduced water rights legislation that would later be of benefit as he secured the title to his land.[28] J. L. thrived on political discussion, and as he traveled to Phoenix or Washington, DC, he "abandoned his Ganado look—long, unkempt hair, raggedy beard, suspendered pants, and short-sleeved jacket—and emerged groomed for political battle. He was well read on issues of the day and smartly suited, hair clipped short and neatly parted and a mustache that copied Teddy Roosevelt's."[29]

Despite his love of politics, J. L. served only one term on the territorial legislature before returning to Ganado. As he told his cousin, "I find that business and politics do not work well together," and at the turn of the century, it was his business he wished to expand.[30] He remained politically active in Apache County and in the Republican Party, regularly attending conventions, but he seemed to have sworn off the heady draught of political office.[31] In 1908, he was considered a strong candidate for delegate to Congress, even attracting the support of Territorial Governor Joseph H. Kibbey, but he flatly refused to run and pled that he could not abandon his business interests, which needed his personal attention.³² But as the statehood question heated up, so did J. L.'s involvement, for though nearly everyone in Arizona could agree that statehood was desirable, they could not agree on the shape—political, cultural, and physical—the state ought to take. Those matters, predictably, were divided sharply along party lines, and they involved an issue guaranteed to bring Hubbell into the fight: disfranchisement of Hispanic voters.

In Washington, the Republican-dominated Senate feared that Arizona, as an overwhelmingly Democratic territory, would elect two Democratic senators if it achieved statehood. As a way to keep Republican control of Congress, they proposed that Arizona and New Mexico be admitted as one state, for New Mexico was as Republican as Arizona was Democratic, and more populous. J. L. reluctantly supported the measure as a better alternative than no statehood at all, but most "Arizonans reacted with an indignation that was as much racist as righteous," opposing joint statehood with a vigor that was called by one senator "a cry of a pure blooded white community against the domination of a mixed breed aggregation of citizens of New Mexico, who are Spanish, Indians, Greasers, Mexicans, and everything else."³³ In November 1906, New Mexico voted in favor of joint statehood, Arizona overwhelmingly against it, and the movement died.³⁴ "From then on," writes Tom Sheridan, "the battle was on to shape the kind of state Arizona would inevitably become."³⁵

As part of that shaping effort, in 1909 the Arizona legislature overrode the governor's veto to pass a literacy law known as the Educational Qualification Law, which prohibited anyone who could not read a section of the United States Constitution in English from voting, thereby disfranchising many Hispanic voters, who, not coincidentally, tended to vote Republican. The introduction of the bill lit a fire under Hubbell, who spent hours that year bent over his typewriter churning out letters of opposition.³⁶ "Can you imagine," he wrote in outrage to one university professor, "the conditions that will exist in this Co. in particular, when men who were born in this Terr., born American citizens, perfectly honest a majority of them Tax Payers, who were not at fault that they were born in communities where nothing but Spanish was spoken, not any less loyal to the American Gov. which they proved on many an occasion, their being deprived of the right of suffrage."³⁷ The outlook was grim, and the death of Hubbell's son-in-law that winter forestalled his efforts to defeat it. Once he returned home from overseeing Charles's funeral in Albuquerque, however, he seemed energized by the terrible odds. As he wrote to his close friend and political ally, Ralph Cameron, who was then serving as the delegate from Arizona Territory to the United States Congress, "I am getting old and if this bill passes I will yet live in spite of it to see this County Rep. again. I shall not get discouraged at the outlook, but rather gird my loins again and imagine that I am 25 years old, when I commenced the fight before."[38]

The bill passed, and, true to his word, Hubbell did not give up the fight, especially when it became one of the key issues standing between Arizona and statehood. Two versions of the bill that would allow New Mexico and Arizona to become states vied for supremacy in Congress: one that retained the educational qualification and one that struck it down. Hubbell and prominent Arizona lawyer Robert E. Morrison traveled to Washington in order to testify against it before the Senate in February 1910.[39] Those in support of the educational qualification argued that very few genuine citizens were disfranchised by the law, the real purpose of which was to prevent Mexican migrant workers from slipping across the border to vote. Hubbell, however, argued that in Apache County alone, 250 Hispanic voters would be disfranchised, and more than 1,800 statewide, while Morrison warned of possible abuses of the law.[40] On June 16, the Senate vote was cast along strict party lines, the Republicans voting against the educational qualification with 42 votes, and the Democrats voting for it with only 19 votes. Under pressure from President William Howard Taft, the House reluctantly followed suit, and on June 20, 1910, Taft signed the enabling act to admit Arizona and New Mexico as separate states free from the educational qualification.[41]

Having accomplished his goal, Hubbell returned to Arizona, but he did not retreat from politics. He ran for the position of delegate from Apache County to Arizona's constitutional convention, but lost because he neglected to "do any electioneering."[42] He spent that year and the following year as chairman of Arizona's Republican Central Committee, working to elect Republicans to office and urging the repeal of other discriminatory laws against Hispanics.[43] In 1911, he faced Democrat Fred T. Coulter in a seemingly hopeless race for the Apache County seat in the first state senate.[44] As Hubbell told his friend David K. Udall, "It will be a great source of humiliation to me to see in this campaign, the most important to every Republican, that Apache County should go democratic. I would rather lose personally myself than to have any of the balance of the ticket defeated."[45] Hubbell and

President William Howard Taft signing Arizona into statehood, 1912. J. L. stands directly behind Taft. Courtesy of the National Park Service, HUTR 04717.

a few other Republicans triumphed by a narrow margin.[46] When President Taft finally signed the proclamation admitting Arizona as the forty-eighth state on February 14, 1912, Hubbell stood right behind him in a crowd of politicians, satisfied and victorious.

As a senator, Hubbell spent long periods of time away from his business and family, absences that troubled him even as he relished his political involvement. The first state legislature had a staggering list of things to accomplish, which necessitated three additional special legislative sessions that kept J. L. away from Ganado for months on end in 1912 and 1913.[47] In early 1913, Lorenzo, Jr., wrote to J. L.'s friend, Maynard Dixon, that his father had just gone to Washington again, and he did not know when to expect his return. "In the last two years," he wrote, "he has been home only about two months in all that time."[48]

J. L. vacillated between guilt at his neglect and surety that his absence would inflict no great harm on the business. One week in 1912, he wrote to Roman regretfully, "I have neglected attending to anything else here and I feel kind of guilty that I attended more to politics than I do to our business."[49] Days later, he wrote cheerfully to Lorenzo, "I don't think the trade will have been affected very much by my absence and I know very well if I had been at home I would have been trusting the Indians too much, which is my great failing."[50] The following week he confessed glumly to his friend Charles F. Lummis, "I have been neglecting my own business for so long that it is really getting dangerous for me to stay away."[51]

As the senate sessions dragged on, J. L. yearned toward home more and more. With the still unproven and very young Roman in charge at Ganado, and with Lina having recently moved there with Barbara and LaCharles, J. L. asked his family and employees to write him twice a week to keep him abreast of business developments, and at least once a week to apprise him of his wife's health.[52] He asked Lorenzo to keep an eye on Roman, "who is rather young for such a large business as we do. It is best to give the boy an opportunity to show what he is made out of, although a nineteen year old boy is rather of an optimistic turn of mind and may make some mistakes but it is best for him to make mistakes than to put a man in charge who could not conduct the business with as much interest as he will."[53] J. L. wrote letters full of advice to his sons and employees often, but the business did suffer in his absence. Hubbell's sons quarreled with C. N. Cotton, who had become one of their main suppliers, some Navajos refused to sell their wool to anyone but J. L., and the supply of stock and cash at the trading posts dwindled.[54] At the same time, the first fifteen years of the new century saw significant changes to the business and massive improvements on the Ganado land, developments that required J. L.'s guiding hand. The years of J. L.'s most intense political involvement were also some of the most significant in the trading post's evolution.

## *The Birth of a Trading Empire*

When Hubbell first entered into the business of Indian trading in the 1870s and 1880s, he opened trading posts in locations scattered across the reservation in Arizona and New Mexico, all the while pursuing business interests in St. Johns as if he had not yet settled on Ganado as his home and center of operations. But by 1890 Hubbell committed himself to Ganado, spending the next decade focusing on foundational work for future development while he abandoned his other interests.[55] Around 1900 he began to expand his business again, purchasing or building additional trading posts. As David Brugge rightly notes, owing to the irregular nature of the business records, "It is not possible to date all of the posts that were owned, nor to be certain in some cases whether Don Lorenzo or Lorenzo, Jr., was the owner. There is even some confusion as to the location of certain posts. One store was at a place called Mud Springs, a mysterious name that does not seem to have survived in common usage."[56] Records indicate that between 1900 and 1914, J. L. and Lorenzo, Jr., operated trading posts at Mud Springs, Cornfields, Oraibi, Steamboat Canyon (also known as Sheep Springs), Black Mountain, Keams Canyon, and Cedar Springs, as well as a store just upstream from the Ganado trading post called the Dam Store and a wholesale house in Gallup.[57] The purchase of these additional trading posts signaled a change in the business of Indian trading, once a relatively simple operation based on the exchange of basic manufactured goods and foodstuffs for wool and livestock, now transforming into a flourishing trade in Native American arts and crafts.[58] The Keams Canyon and Oraibi posts in particular reflected the growing importance of the curio trade in the Hubbell business as American tourism and fascination with Native Americans stimulated the market demand for blankets, baskets, jewelry, and other Navajo and Hopi products.[59] The expansion from one trading post at Ganado to a network of trading posts would precipitate other changes in the scope and character of the Hubbell family business, especially the role of J. L.'s children in its administration, changes aptly illustrated by the 1902 acquisition of Lorenzo, Jr.'s, first trading post at Keams Canyon.

In a canyon thirteen miles east of the Hopis' First Mesa, Thomas V. Keam founded a trading post in 1875. Keam was as famous and influential in his day, among both Hopis and Euro-Americans, as Hubbell was in his.[60] After decades of trading with the Hopis and working tirelessly with the government to establish a school at Keams Canyon, Keam's health began to fail him. His doctors diagnosed him with a heart condition, angina pectoris, and ordered him to a lower elevation. In May 1902, with the pain pressing into the left side of his chest, Keam abandoned his trading post. From Albuquerque, he sold it to Hubbell, who bought it for his eldest son. Like an exile coming home, Lorenzo, Jr., had just returned from school at Notre

Dame and was ready to begin the life of an Indian trader that he had longed for since his childhood.[61] The trading post at Keams Canyon, called the Tusayan Trading Post, provided the perfect opportunity for the nineteen-year-old Lorenzo, Jr., to test his skills. It was a secure trading post with a solid building and an established customer base, far enough away from his father that Lorenzo could learn to stand on his own feet, but close enough for ready advice and assistance if he should need it.

By mid-May, Lorenzo, Jr., was on his own at Keams Canyon, writing letters to his father on his predecessor's stationery, with Keam's name carefully crossed out and his own written in. In the early years, Lorenzo relied on the advice of his father, but never depended upon him completely. A month after he began trading at Keams Canyon, Lorenzo expressed sentiments typical of his relationship with J. L. "You ought to come out to see me," he wrote, "although really, it would not be a set back if you wouldn't. But when you are at your leisure, I wish you would come out and see how the business is running."[62] J. L., meanwhile, wrote his son letters peppered with advice on how much to pay for wool and lambs, where to ship his goods, which buildings to invest in, and how to treat his customers. J. L. had been in the trade so long that he when he wrote his son a warning not to buy too many blankets because there would be a surplus that year that would drag down the market, his only reason was the simple declaration, "I can feel it coming."[63]

At first trade was slow, but Lorenzo was "not discouraged, as I should not expect to do a good business right at the start," especially since his customers had been used to trading with Keam for twenty years.[64] Like his father in the early days at Ganado, Lorenzo ran into some troubles with the Hopis and the Navajos as they tested him and entangled him in their disputes—and like his father, with time he grew to become a fixture in the local community.[65] As Lorenzo wrote determinedly to his father after a scant week on the job, "You need not worry about me having trouble with the Indians and even if I did, I should be able to take care of myself," and indeed, over the years, Lorenzo would become at Keams Canyon what his father was at Ganado.[66] The Navajos called him Nakai Tso (Big Mexican), a name that perfectly captured his Spanish-American upbringing and his portliness. Lorenzo was a gentle man, a little unsure of himself, but unfailingly friendly. One of his friends remembered that "If he accepted a man as a real friend it took up to six hours to say hello and goodbye to him! He was just that kind of person."[67]

Lorenzo, Jr., at Keams Canyon, sitting in front of his collection of Hopi katsinas, c. 1904. Courtesy of the National Park Service, HUTR 04697.

Lorenzo quickly learned the ropes of trading, building on his childhood foundations. At Keams Canyon, he bought his first Navajo blanket: "I remember distinctly that it was an old diamond and lightning design without a border, and I bought it from The Man Who Doesn't Talk."[68] That blanket probably ended up in the wagonload of five bales of blankets and a sack full of baskets that Lorenzo, Jr., sent to the home business on May 25, 1902, the first of many shipments of goods to pass from Keams through Ganado on the way to market.[69] Lorenzo's location near the Hopi mesas meant that he had far more Hopi customers than his father did, and he supplied J. L.'s flowering curio trade with Hopi arts and crafts he would buy on special trips to the Hopi villages. But in other ways, the trading post echoed the familiar pattern at Ganado. Lorenzo became involved in all the many aspects of trade his father pursued—sheep, wool, piñons, curios, freighting, and carrying the mail—in a complicated relationship with his father's business that makes it nearly impossible to disentangle where one ended and the other began.[70] J. L. ordered goods for Lorenzo and shipped them to him, and sometimes requested that Lorenzo send him goods he found himself short of, as well as wool, rugs, and curios—all on a system of credit. Lorenzo kept his own accounts and owned several trading posts separately from his father—in fact, many of the trading posts attributed to J. L. were actually owned by Lorenzo—but the two operations loaned one another money so often and were so connected by ties both financial and personal that Lorenzo would never achieve the degree of separateness that an unrelated competitor would have. Lorenzo's trading posts at Keams, Cedar Springs, and Gallup were just as connected to the Ganado business as J. L.'s trading posts at Oraibi, Cornfields, and Steamboat Canyon, and all were joined together by a network of freight and mail lines, a rotating supply of employees, and the same cycles of fortune and misfortune, profit and debt, that ruled the life of an Indian trader.

## Freight, Mail, and the Coming of the Automobile

The growing empire of Hubbell-owned trading posts spreading out over the Navajo landscape led to significant expansion of the family's freighting and mail-carrying activities into more remote parts of the reservation.[71] The distances between the Hubbells' trading posts were "not remarkable but were still imposing," for the railroad never did get any closer than Gallup,

Holbrook, and Winslow, while the volume of trade conducted at the trading posts increased as the years went by. The longest leg of the journey from trading post to railhead was the sixty miles from Gallup to Ganado. From there, Cornfields was a mere five miles away, and the Dam Store was only three miles. Keams Canyon, however, lay about forty miles to the west of Ganado, and Oraibi was another thirty miles beyond that. Other trading posts, including Cedar Springs, Piñon, and Black Mountain, were even farther away.

Though Lorenzo, Jr., cultivated a wholesale relationship with the Babbitt Brothers of Flagstaff, and maintained some of his own freighting teams that ran between his posts and the railheads at Holbrook and Winslow, a good deal of freighting between his posts and his father's still went on. The mammoth task of hauling supplies, wool, hides, hay, and curios between the Ganado post and the outlying posts, and between Ganado and Gallup kept freight wagons on the trails almost constantly. A year's shipment of wool alone, some 100,000 pounds in a good year, required at least 45 wagons to get it from Ganado to Gallup. Hides and pelts, pine nuts, blankets, curio items, and passengers kept the wagons full and rolling. The Hubbells also won government contracts hauling hay, grain, lumber, concrete, and other supplies to outlying Indian agencies and government schools. Their most important shipping contracts for the government stemmed from water and livestock development on the reservation. Hubbell even began supplying saddle horses, light rigs, and freight wagons hired by the day to survey crews and engineers.

In the early years of the twentieth century, the roads in Navajo country were still as bad as they ever were. Spring rains continued to wash out trails and strand travelers. Even the introduction of the automobile into J. L.'s freighting fleet in 1912 failed to overcome the challenges Navajo country posed—in fact, they provided ample fodder for humorous anecdotes as J. L. and various travelers joined "the league of stranded motorists."[72] Though cars shortened the two-day trip between Gallup and Ganado to a journey of a few hours in good weather, clear skies and dry roads could not be counted on, especially in the spring, which was one of the busiest freight times.[73] Despite its unreliability, the Hubbells greeted the advent of the automobile with enthusiasm; a Franciscan father at St. Michaels noted that in 1917 there were only a handful of cars on the reservation, and all of them "belonged to the Hubbells, the agency superintendent, Sam Day, and Chee Dodge."[74]

Miles Parker, LaCharles Goodman, Hubbell Parker, Forrest Parker, Dollie Williams, Charlotte Chain, and Adele Parker pile in and on an automobile, c. 1915. Courtesy of the National Park Service, HUTR 04777.

Roman, for one, was thoroughly convinced of the car's virtues: "They are very easy to handel [sic]," he wrote to his cousin, "you can learn how to operate and take care of one inside of a day. I have been carrying the mail with the cars and I find that they are cheaper than horses and I am making money by using them."[75]

The Hubbells started carrying the mail between Keams Canyon and Ganado and Ganado and St. Michaels by automobile by September 1912, but despite its greater speed and economy, the car simply could not completely replace the wagon on the reservation.[76] Where Cotton once could not get his goods to market because his bull teams were too weak to make the journey, now a simple mechanical breakdown could scuttle an automobile and throw off the freighting schedule. In February 1913, for example, the Hubbells had to revert to carrying the mail by horseback and wagon when Lorenzo's car stripped a gear and a storm delivered a heavy load of eight inches of snow that choked the roads for weeks. The mail delivery was delayed and the Hubbells did not find much sympathy from the Postal Service, which failed to grasp just how unpredictable the conditions of Navajo roads were; they preferred a fixed schedule based on either automobile travel times or wagon travel times, not both. In the wake of the delays that spring, J. L. asked for a more flexible delivery schedule "because the conditions of the roads, during the rainy season, make it impossible to carry the mail by automobile, and I am then obliged to substitute horses and buckboards."[77] When the Postal Service answered his request with a flat refusal, J. L. wrote in exasperation, "The conditions of the roads . . . are not well understood in your office or the proposition made that we run automobiles at a specified time would be utterly impossible. For you cannot tell when a road would be impassable."[78]

Joe Schmedding, a trader who bought Keams Canyon trading post from Lorenzo, Jr., in 1918, described the Hubbells' freight roads and the conditions that often crippled motorized transport in his autobiography. He, his wife, and their baby boy made the journey to their new home in the winter in the Hubbells' freight and mail wagons. They traveled over the well-worn road between Gallup and Ganado in an open buckboard behind two horses, spent the night as Hubbell's guests, and finished their journey on one of the Hubbell mail wagons, a buckboard drawn by four horses and driven by a Navajo teamster. Schmedding described the exhausting journey: "Throughout the long day it had snowed intermittently, and a cold wind swept across the mesa lands. Occasionally, and for all too brief moments, we would enjoy the shelter of some dunelike rises, or have a bit of protection when crossing smaller canyons and arroyos . . . but as soon as we got into the open again, the numbing cold penetrated the blankets and robes wrapped around us. . . . [A]s the afternoon wore on, [the horses] tired from the exertion of breaking through the many breast-high snowdrifts that the wind had piled in our path. Several times during the last two hours of the trip we found ourselves straying away from the snow-obliterated trail, and had to grasp the headstall of one of the leading horses and pull the team back onto the almost invisible roadway."[79] The mail stage reached Keams Canyon in the dark after a solid day of traveling with a change of fresh horses at Steamboat Canyon. The frozen travelers stumbled into their new home while Lorenzo, Jr., and Elias Armijo unloaded the mail and baggage. A journey that would have taken a day in an automobile took three miserable days in a wagon. The conditions of the roads made travel and freighting exclusively by car impossible through the 1920s, when roads began to improve.[80]

The Hubbells staffed their trading posts and manned their vehicles with an endlessly rotating supply of employees, many of whom were relatives, some of whom lasted only a short while, and some of whom became regular fixtures in the family business. David Brugge states that both Lorenzo, Jr., and J. L. "were able to command a loyalty in their workers that exceeded that of a normal employer-employee relationship," a fortunate trait given the isolated nature of trading and the hardships and dangers of freighting on the reservation.[81] The daughter of Jot Barnett Stiles, one of Lorenzo's employees at Piñon, remembered, "The roads were very poor. Our only contact . . . was with Lorenzo Hubbell and he was at Oraibi. . . . And of course we didn't get any mail, much," and had neither radio nor telephone.[82] The mail stage and the freight wagons, even slowed by heavy snows and drifting sand, were often the traders' only link with the outside world.[83] Some of the Hubbell trading posts were even more isolated than most, making their staffing difficult. When Lorenzo, Jr., bought Cedar Springs, J. L. told him that "I believe a good business can be developed there, but only a good man can do it."[84] Unfortunately, a good man for the job was hard to find, and even harder to convince to stay at a trading post so lonely that clerks pleaded for company in their correspondence with Ganado. Andy Romero worked at Cedar Springs for a time in 1912, but was too lonesome and left, and another clerk, Simeon Schwemberger, who worked there in 1913, begged his employers for a magazine or a newspaper—anything to keep him occupied during the long, lonesome evenings.[85] And so the Hubbell employees shifted from location to location as the family bought and sold trading posts and as former employees moved on, lured away by greener pastures.

## Irrigating the Homestead

J. L.'s dreams of creating an irrigated farm at Ganado also began to take shape around the turn of the century. Having pushed through important foundational laws while serving in the Territorial House of Representatives beginning in the fall of 1892, and having finally received some confirmation that he would be able to retain claim to his homestead, J. L. began the work of developing an irrigation system in 1902. As Charles Peterson writes,

"Using Indian labor (sometimes as many as fifty outfits), store credit, and supplies freighted over the rough miles from Gallup, New Mexico, Hubbell cut a canal several miles from the Rio Pueblo Colorado, built trestles and flumes, and at the head of his place scooped out an impounding reservoir."[86] Navajo workers terraced his fields and built five laterals and more than a hundred masonry head gates; by 1905, they had brought large portions of Hubbell's 160-acre homestead under cultivation and harvested the first crops of hay and rye.

J. L. did not have long to bask in the fruits of his achievement; he found out all too soon that the harsh realities of the climate, already a bane to his freighting and mail operations, made irrigation a constant and costly struggle against fickle weather and rapid erosion. His low earthen and brush dam washed out frequently, and "each succeeding round of repairs was more difficult" than the last.[87] Even before his increasingly complicated irrigation works were finished, J. L. saw that the labor and financial outlay required to build and maintain such a system were beyond him alone, and by 1903, he began a vigorous campaign to involve the government in turning the shallow Ganado Lake into a larger reservoir. Using the full force of his political and personal connections, he lobbied for his reservoir, exploiting the "interest that Navajo agents and the Indian Irrigation Service had entertained since the early 1890s to develop a reservoir at a point near his diversion dam where backwater from the Rio Pueblo Colorado floods formed the thin sheet of water and marshes around which cattle gathered."[88]

As in the matter of the Ganado homestead claim, the wheels of government turned ponderously. Eager to move forward, Hubbell at one point offered to build the dam himself, but when H. F. Robinson, who would become J. L.'s friend and tireless advocate of the Ganado Irrigation Project, took over as the Indian Irrigation Service superintendent in 1907, he steered the matter back toward government construction. But still, it was not until August 1912, when J. L. was serving on the Arizona State Senate, that the Indian Appropriation Act containing the funding for the Ganado Irrigation Project finally passed. When it at last looked as if he would get the money and government assistance he needed, J. L. wrote a triumphant letter to Lorenzo, Jr.: "The appropriation for the Ganado Reservoir has passed the House and it is sure to pass the Senate, so at last after many years, my dream has come true and under adverse circumstances and with an opposition that no one thought could be overcome. This will show you through life that what you always want, if it is right, persist in it and you will accomplish anything you start to do but first be right, then go ahead."[89] J. L.'s excitement was understandable, given that his dam and irrigation works had cost him between $4,000 and $25,000.[90] With the Indian Irrigation Service coming in to take the project out of his hands, Hubbell could step down from his position as the prime mover; in effect, he simply traded his ditch for a water right and turned his attention to finding other ways of profiting from the project, including freighting building materials for the dam from Gallup.[91]

Construction on the Ganado Irrigation Project began in 1913, and as soon as it was underway, J. L. opened a branch store on the construction site near the location of his first trading post in the Pueblo Colorado Valley. The store was called the Dam Store, and operated whenever there were enough construction crews and freighters on the project to turn a profit by supplying oats and hay for the stock animals as well as food and clothing for the workers.[92] "Not surprisingly," Peterson notes, "the store absorbed most of what the Navajos were paid. Of course, the dam store was set up to exploit crews working on the government project, but employees on Hubbell's own project were caught even more closely in the web of credit and tin money that prevailed on the reservation generally."[93]

Extreme weather plagued the Indian Irrigation Service even more fiercely than it had Hubbell. What seemed at the outset "a fairly straightforward proposition" turned into "an unremitting battle that drew on for four decades."[94] During construction, major flash floods regularly wreaked havoc on the irrigation works; in 1914 a flash flood turned a flume into an unsalvageable wreck of metal; in 1916 a series of floods crippled the whole works, necessitating a complete overhaul of the system; in 1917 "ice blew against the 'outlet tower' of the headgate, literally ripping out the entire works and toppling it over"; and in 1923 a series of furious storms wrecked the works in nearly every possible way.[95] Though the main period of construction lasted less than a decade, work on the Ganado Irrigation Project never really finished. If repairs, enlargements, and technical improvements were not continuously underway, they were badly needed.

Work on the dam, however, did reach points of stability. Ultimately, the dam enabled the irrigation of more than 700 acres, including Hubbell's land and land at the nearby Presbyterian Mission, which the missionaries used to teach modern farming methods.[96] Other land brought under irrigation by the project was allotted in twenty-acre plots to the Navajos for cultivating squash, melons, corn, hay, oats, and vegetables.[97] The success of the farms, both Hubbell's and the Navajos', varied from year to year with drought and flood, for irrigation was an imperfect management tool, not a miracle. The farms had considerable success in the 1920s, but the Ganado Irrigation Project drew fewer federal funds as the years went by and other projects that would benefit larger numbers of Navajos caught the eye of the Bureau of Indian Affairs. The project entered "a period of slow collapse as funds and energy necessary to continue the fight were shifted elsewhere and as Indian policy and national interests changed."[98]

## The Trouble with Politics

During the early twentieth century, the trading business rode its ups and downs as before. The Panic of 1907, which caused banks to fail across the country, began to affect the Hubbell business in December of that year. J. L. wrote to a friend, "I hope times are better with you. Here it is just commencing to get hard. I have no Blankets to speak of in stock, but am commencing to get them in faster than I want to see them come. There is no doubt that we are going to be up against it this winter."[99] But by 1909 the outlook was sunny, and after a wet spring Hubbell declared, "Business has never been better with us."[100] But even in times of prosperity, running a trading post was always something of a guessing game. "Business has been rushing this spring," J. L. told his brother, "but do not know whether there will be any money in it or not. Have quite a bunch of wool on hand and am paying I guess what it is worth."[101] A booming business also meant increased difficulties in keeping the trading posts supplied with goods, and J. L. struggled to collect money owed him even as he struggled to pay his own bills. In March 1909, even amidst the hope of a wet spring, a good crop, and a bustling trade, J. L. wrote to Lorenzo, "I am getting a little afraid of the trust business. The scrubs do not owe me anything, but the big bugs owe me too-much and I am getting afraid. They all paid last year, but what will they do this year."[102]

The uncertainties of Indian trading were exacerbated further by J. L.'s heavy involvement in politics. His absences from the trading post increasingly caused problems in his family and in the business. In 1910, Forrest and Adele left the trading post for several years, depriving the trading post of its best bookkeeper while Forrest worked for the Southwestern Drug Company in Clovis, New Mexico.[103] Left in charge of the Ganado post without Forrest's aid, Roman, only nineteen years old, found himself simultaneously overwhelmed by the magnitude and complexity of the business, and chafing under J. L.'s continued oversight from afar. Roman "often questioned his father's trading practices," balking against having to sell wool to Cotton merely because J. L.'s friendship demanded it, and flatly arguing against his father's insistence on lowering prices to benefit the Navajos, for example.[104]

J. L. did not seem able to delegate power to his sons or employees, yet was frequently absent during the busiest times of the trading post's seasonal cycles. Beginning in 1911, when J. L.'s absences became the rule rather than the exception, the business truly began to suffer, for "not only was the trader physically gone, he was also depleting the company's cash reserves."[105] J. L. even began borrowing large sums of money from Lorenzo, who in turn had to ask Roman to send him money to keep the trading post at Keams Canyon stocked in cash.[106] But Roman had no cash to send—none of the trading posts did. In a voice that echoed the plight of clerks at other Hubbell posts, Charlie complained from Oraibi, "I have not a cent in the house and am having a hell of time to keep up with the trade."[107] Without cash, Charlie could not buy anything from the Navajos; wool season came and went and competitors' stores, stocked with fresh goods and cash, drew the business away from the Hubbells, with their bare shelves and empty registers.[108] In May 1913, Lorenzo, Jr., wrote a pleading letter to his father, who was ensconced in a seemingly never-ending special legislative session in Phoenix: "We have been in hopes, that you would be home, by this time; it is a great inconvenience without you, every once in a while, business deals come up, that its [sic]very hard for Roman or I, as to what is best to do. Cotton has been pressing Roman every little chance he gets, and Roman, is getting so, that he is mighty timid, and the business, will naturally suffer, as he has to run, the business, on such a low stock of goods. . . . Wool is going down, every few days, its [sic] awfully hard to do business this spring. A new store has started at Tse-la-ni, near Salt Water, north of here, naturally he has a fresh stock of goods, and paying cash, and that is his bonus. I wish you write, papa, or better still if it is possible, for you to come home, come."[109] Heeding his son's desperate call for help, J. L. returned to Ganado a few weeks later, but by the time he arrived, Roman had fled.

Though taking over the business at such a young age surely matured Roman, he still displayed the same impulsiveness that had given his father

Roman and Alma at a Navajo Squaw Dance, c. 1916. Courtesy of the National Park Service, HUTR 04976.

gray hairs in years past. In the fall of 1912, while his father was busy politicking, Roman eloped with a beautiful young woman who had come to Arizona to see the Hopi Snake Dance: Alma Juliette Dorr of New York.[110] After a few weeks of ushering her and a handful of other tourists around Navajo country, Roman was smitten, while Alma was surely intrigued by Roman's mystique as an Indian trader. At Oraibi, Navajo medicine man and family friend Miguelito married the young lovers in a ceremony that captured the romantic imaginations of everyone who heard of it. According to the stories that circulated in the newspapers, Roman rode some 60 miles to procure enough cornmeal to make the wedding cake, "the eating of which by the young couple constituted the marriage ceremony."[111] Roman and Alma then rushed to Pasadena, California, where they were married again, this time by a Catholic priest.

How Alma's parents took the news that their daughter had married an Indian trader and intended to take up residence on the Navajo Reservation is unknown. But when he returned to Ganado in late September, J. L. wrote to reassure his son that he and his new bride would be welcome there.[112] Roman and Alma returned to Ganado for a few months, but they did not stay for long. "Whether or not motivated by the overbearing demands of trading with a shortage of money under his father's written directions, sometime between the end of April and the first of June 1913, Roman took his pregnant wife and bolted from the Ganado post. They gypsied across the Southwest," down to Mexico to look for work, to El Paso, Texas, then on to Clifton, Arizona, where Roman found temporary employment with the Shannon Copper Company.[113] When Roman lost his job at the copper company, Lorenzo wrote a letter to his father stating that Roman "is now in Douglass, doing nothing. I guess he is up against it; he drew a draft on me for twenty five dollars."[114] But even unemployment seemed not a hardship enough to drive Roman back to Ganado. In September he wrote a bitter letter to his father, asking, "By the way who is now taking care of the books? I hope that you now have someone that can keep them straight . . . a first class bookkeeper can be had for $75 a month room and board to keep the books straight. . . . By the way, I have this craw in my gut or my throat. Did you get someone as dumb as me to take over, someone drunk enough to do that thankless job?"[115]

Hard on the heels of Roman's defection came another family crisis: the death of J. L.'s wife, Lina. Her health had been failing for years—while still in Albuquerque, Barbara sent her to Faywood Hot Springs for three weeks in an attempt to improve her health, but when she returned, Lina was, if anything, more tired than before.[116] In early 1911, they sold her home and she moved to Ganado with her daughter and granddaughter. But life at Ganado was still too much for her. In October of that year, Lorenzo, Jr., wrote to Roman to ask him to bring Lina to Keams Canyon. "It will help her to be here," he wrote, "she'll rest better, and there'll be nothing to worry her."[117]

At Keams Canyon, she had the company of an adoring son and visits from her other children and grandchildren, but very seldom did she enjoy the companionship of her husband. J. L. evidently considered taking Lina with him to Phoenix, but the doctors warned him not to take her to such a low altitude on account of her asthma. All he could do was ask for weekly updates on her health and send messages of love through his children.[118] "I suppose your mother is with you still," J. L. wrote to Lorenzo in May 1913. "If she is give her my love and hope that she doesn't think I have entirely deserted Ganado but tell her I will come back as usual, even at the eleventh hour."[119] Lina lived with Lorenzo for the last two years of her life; she died of vascular heart disease at Keams Canyon on July 13, 1913. Her family buried her on a hill overlooking the Ganado trading ranch and marked the spot with a tall sandstone grave marker.[120] When they read the news in the papers, J. L.'s friends in politics sent condolence letters, but if he confided his feelings to any of them, they have been lost. Perhaps Lorenzo, who spent the most time with his mother in her last years, felt her loss most keenly. When she lay slowly dying, she gave Lorenzo a gold brooch she had worn as a young woman, a gift he would treasure; she would remain his "ideal all through life; for her honesty, her firmness, and wisdom."[121]

When J. L. returned home from Phoenix in March 1913, his family life was a shambles and his business was limping. He turned to one of the only friends he knew who would and could lend him enough money to save his business: Henry Chee Dodge, a wealthy Navajo stockman. Dodge lent him $32,000, secured with a mortgage on the Ganado property, including its water rights and "the entire stock of goods of every description."[122] Between the money he spent on politics, the irrigation system, and the expansion of his trading empire, J. L.'s "reach had come to exceed his grasp."[123] Sobered, J. L. declared, "I am through with all politics till 1916."[124] But like a gambler unable to stay away from the cards, J. L. was back in the game within a year, this time campaigning as the Republican candidate for the United States Senate.

The campaign further strained the business's already crippled finances. Forrest and Adele returned to the trading post to handle the business correspondence while J. L. was out campaigning. In the fall of that year, Forrest wrote dozens of letters to people who owed the trading post money, asking them to pay their bills as "we are very much in need of funds."[125] Forrest confessed the desperateness of their situation to C. N. Cotton when the trading post's former owner wrote to collect on a bill. Forrest asked Cotton to destroy the letter so none of his clerks would see it, admitting that their bank account showed less than $500. He wrote, "The lord knows and so do you that I would like to send you a wagon load of money if I could, and you know just as well that I cannot. I wish to say that I have . . . fought to get enough money to load our team and this dam money is all I have to go on.

Everybody who owes us hang back. I have, however, collected one or two accounts which I did through the help of a collection agency. You can see by this to what extremes I have gone to get money. As I have written you before, I will pay you for all goods I order and if I can will send you money to reduce the account. I need cash here to buy sheep with but cannot order it. This is another handicap for me which is only one of the many I have when Mr. Hubbell is away."[126] The clerks and family labored diligently, but their hands were tied. J. L. had evidently not learned to delegate authority any better—he still insisted on handling the blanket trade himself, which meant all orders for curios had to be delayed until after the election.[127]

In this race, more than any of the others, J. L. had little hope of prevailing.[128] In the spring of 1912, not long after J. L.'s election to the state senate, a decisive split opened up in the Republican Party when Theodore Roosevelt challenged his own hand-picked successor, William H. Taft, for the presidency.[129] Roosevelt ran as a Progressive candidate, and the split reverberated all the way down to the level of local politics in Arizona.[130] With the Progressive Party drawing votes away from the Republicans, the elections in 1912 went decisively to the Democrats, and the outlook seemed no better in the next election. Hubbell spent much of his campaign time in 1914 traveling around the state trying to heal the rift, knowing that if the vote was split, they had not a prayer of defeating the Democrats. The Progressives, however, stood firm in their resolved separateness, and the Republicans seemed to taste their loss long before the vote was cast.[131] Even J. L., normally fired by unfavorable odds, acknowledged his likely defeat at a subdued Republican political rally. While hoping and fighting, as ever, for a Republican government, he assured his audience in his political speeches that "he would not be heartbroken should his advice be neglected by the voters. He would still preserve an unsullied faith in the wisdom of the majority."[132] The majority spoke, and it spoke Democratic. J. L.'s opponent, incumbent Marcus A. Smith, raked in 25,790 votes, leaving J. L. with a paltry 9,178.[133]

Badly beaten and financially strapped, J. L. returned home to Ganado. "The defeat struck the sixty-one-year-old Hubbell a bitter personal blow. His post-election correspondence withered" and he never again held major public office.[134] Though he and his trading empire would both rebound and enjoy times of prosperity in the future, the year 1914 marked the beginning of a decline. It was a harbinger of troubled times.

CHAPTER FIVE

# Troubled Times
## *Changing Fortunes, 1915–1929*

In the aftermath of Hubbell's failed bid for the Senate, the family struggled to make the business profitable again, but the Hubbell Trading Post was headed for tribulation. Moments of contentment occasionally relieved the grind of unpaid debts—prodigals Roman and Alma returned home with their toddling son to run J. L.'s new wholesale business and garage in Gallup, where their second son was born in early 1917, and in some brief seasons the trading posts all seemed miraculously profitable. When Hubbell limped home in 1915, he and Forrest wrote stacks of letters to their debtors, pleading for the payment of outstanding bills, but it was a thankless task that bore little fruit. All they could do was sell trading posts, the only asset they seemed to have in excess. By 1916, the Hubbells owned trading posts in thirteen locations, the newest of which—Nazlini, Piñon, Piñon Springs, and Chinle—they had acquired in 1915 and 1916, even as existing posts languished for lack of cash.[1] But for the following four years, they sold posts, using the profits from Sheep Springs and Chinle to pay off part of the mortgage to Chee Dodge.[2] In early 1918, Lorenzo, Jr., even sold Keams Canyon and all its contents, including stock, pawn, and Lorenzo's personal collection of thousands of pieces of hand-painted Hopi pottery, in order to satisfy J. L.'s substantial debt to Cotton.[3] After sixteen years at Keams Canyon, Lorenzo introduced the local Hopis and Navajos to the new trader, Joe Schmedding, and moved to one of his father's trading posts at Kykotsmovi, near the Hopi village of Oraibi.[4] The sale of Sheep Springs, Chinle, and Keams Canyon might have stabilized the business if not for a quick succession of personal and financial blows that kept the Hubbells and their business staggering.

## World War I in Navajo Country

When the First World War began half a world away from Arizona, it sent ripples even into the remote reaches of the Navajo Reservation. Anthropologists Garrick Bailey and Roberta Glenn Bailey state that the "Navajos took very little part in World War I, which they considered a white man's problem. Like other reservation tribes, they were not citizens of the United States, so they could not be drafted; unlike members of other tribes, few Navajos volunteered," no more, in fact, than a dozen.[5] The war's impact, however, reverberated through Navajo life in other ways, most profoundly economically. The price of wool, mutton, lambs, and cattle rose dramatically in 1914 after the war broke out in Europe, and they continued to climb until they peaked in 1918.[6] With the Navajos' goods in such high demand, the war drew them more fully than ever into the cash economy first introduced by the traders at Bosque Redondo.[7]

The increased price of Navajo goods, however, did not necessarily translate into high profits for either the Navajos or the traders: "While Navajo goods commanded high prices, so did the products that Navajos bought. The consumer price index rose 50 percent between 1914 and 1918."[8] That meant that, though traders could sell Navajo goods on the national market for much higher prices, they also paid more for goods to stock their shelves. Even after the war ended and the price of Navajo goods fell, inflation continued. Not only did the Hubbells and other traders have to pay more for consumer goods, they had to cope with the problems of running a store during rationing, submitting special requests to receive sugar, flour, and other staples, and then having to limit the amount of each sold per person per month, a difficult task in any country store and a phenomenal one in the trading post with its unique business model and haphazard record-keeping.[9]

Unlike the Navajos, the Hubbell men faced the threat of being drafted from the desert and the scent of piñon to the muddy, reeking trenches on the front. None of the Hubbell men seemed reluctant to fight, though Forrest was the most likely to be drafted since Roman had a wife and child and was partially deaf, and Lorenzo, Jr., was portly enough that the family did not expect him to pass his physical.[10] Forrest determined he would volunteer in the hopes of getting an officer's position since "[a]nything is better than being drafted."[11] J. L. vacillated between urging Forrest to "get a crack at the Kaiser first hand" and worrying about him since he had already lost one son-in-law to a bullet. Forrest wrote to Lorenzo, Jr., that with J. L.'s "fighting blood he would rather see me right up at the front. He is wishing that he had nothing to prevent him from going. Adele and Barbara look at it in the most sensible way. Naturally they do not like it but they think it is the proper thing to do."[12] The Hubbells all seemed to share the opinion that too many people shied away from their duty. In August 1918, Forrest left for Wichita and Chicago to try to get into the army as an officer, though he found it more difficult than he had imagined since the officer training camps were open only to men already enlisted. In early October, Lorenzo, Jr.'s, draft questionnaire arrived in the mail, and he did not claim an exemption, which he might have gotten for his health or his occupation. A few days later, he noticed in the paper that his serial number would be one of the first called if he passed his physical. Instantly he began planning what he would do with his trading posts should he be called. He wrote to his employee and fast friend, Thomas Edward "Ed" Thacker, that if he passed his physical he would sell three of his trading posts—Black Mountain, Oraibi, and Cedar Springs, where his uncle Charlie worked—leaving only the Piñon post in Ed Thacker's care for the duration.[13] But Lorenzo never had to implement his scheme. The armistice ending the war was signed in November 1918, scarcely a month after Lorenzo sent in his registration, putting an end to both his and Forrest's military plans and keeping all of the Hubbell men at home.

## *Influenza Pandemic*

No sooner had the war ended, however, than the Spanish Influenza pandemic of 1918–1919 extended its pestilential reach to the Navajo Reservation. The pandemic swept across oceans and continents that fall and winter, killing more than 21 million people worldwide, including half a million Americans.[14] The virus struck especially hard among Native Americans, particularly the Navajos, who lacked access to health care, and whose cultural practices, "such as exposing the very ill to the elements rather than allowing them to die in the family dwelling, seeking the ministrations of itinerant 'singers' who carried the infection about with them, and assembling family members and neighbors in ceremonial 'sings,'" increased mortality rates dramatically.[15] When the disease reached the Navajos in October 1918, public places surrounding the reservation were closed in an attempt to keep it from spreading, but to no avail; about 150 Navajo workers employed in the construction gangs of the Durango–Silverton highway in southern Colorado carried the virus home with them when they fled the infected work camps.[16] In the winter that followed, an estimated 10 to 15 percent of Navajos—more than two thousand individuals—died in what has been called "the worst calamity to befall the Navajo tribe since their incarceration at Fort Sumner."[17]

Rose Mitchell, a Navajo woman, poignantly described the devastating influenza as it swept through the Chinle area. "It was in the fall; the crops had ripened and we were almost done harvesting them, drying some for our winter use, and putting some into storage for the next year . . . when the sickness started," she wrote. "It started spreading across the reservation almost overnight and lots and lots of people died from it. People would feel fine during the day, get sick in the night, and by morning, they'd have all passed away. It was like that. It killed whole families overnight; up to about twenty people in a family would die in one night. It seemed to really hit the young children; little children all over the area were dying day and night, night after night. People died right and left. No one knew what it was. . . . no one knew what to do about it."[18] With entire families stricken overnight, sometimes there was no one left with the strength to bury the dead or care for the ill, which left many to die of pneumonia or starvation.[19] Herds of livestock belonging to sick or perished Navajo families were also left "wandering over the hills at the mercy of the wolves."[20]

Traders and their families were not immune to the influenza's effects, and the Hubbell family suffered its share of loss. Though little record of the epidemic's course at the Ganado trading post survives, Lorenzo, Jr.'s, letters from Oraibi paint a picture of a business hobbled by stricken employees. On October 9, Lorenzo, Jr., wrote to Ed Thacker that "the Spanish Influenza is around here to beat the band. . . . Both the Dr. and his wife are down, Mrs. Griffith, Marks and his wife, and about 60 other cases. Alice seems to have a touch of it too."[21] A grim correspondence between Lorenzo and Thacker followed, each letter containing a list of the sick, the dead, and even some who had been driven insane by the disease.[22] Then Ed fell ill and spent weeks in delirium, asking for Lorenzo, who dared not visit or even write for fear of making his friend fret over the neglected state of the business.[23] After a month's convalescence under the watchful eye of his wife, Ethel, Ed finally recovered enough to pick up a pen. "Well," he wrote to his friend, "I

Alma Dorr Hubbell holding baby John shortly before her death in 1918. Courtesy of the National Park Service, HUTR 07074.

am up and look like hell but feel pretty fair."[24] Relieved, Lorenzo told Ed not to worry about the business until he was fully recovered. "Though we will not get along as well, without your help, we can go on till you feel, like going back. . . . You have been a faithful employee of mine for years, but more than that you have been a faithful friend," he wrote.[25]

Though Lorenzo did not sicken, his sister, Barbara, did. She caught the virus while visiting her late husband's parents in Virginia, and returned to Ganado ill. LaCharles remembered that she "was one of the few [who] got lucky and didn't die of it."[26] Roman's fragile wife, Alma, however, was not so fortunate. Already prone to sickness, Alma died quite suddenly at their home in Gallup at the beginning of the epidemic on October 22, 1918 "after an illness of pneumonia superintended by Spanish Influenza."[27] Roman was visiting one of the outlying posts when she passed away. Someone—probably an employee—rushed the news to him by automobile as far as Ganado, and then another 40 miles on J. L.'s fastest horse, which is said to have died of the strain a few days later.[28] Alma left behind two young children, five-year-old Roman Dorr (called Monnie) and seven-month-old John Lorenzo (usually called John, but sometimes called Jack). The death announcement in the *Gallup Independent* extended sympathy to the bereft of "this most estimable and lovable woman. . . . She was always kindly sympathetic and her smile was a benediction, lavishing them freely on all those afflicted or in distress."[29] Reeling from his wife's premature death, Roman evidently spent the next few years gambling and otherwise living the life of "a playboy" in Gallup, while his two boys spent most of their time at Ganado under the watchful eye of the family.[30]

### The Murder of Charlie Hubbell

The Hubbells would receive no reprieve. Just as Navajo country emerged from the dark winter of the epidemic, J. L. received the chilling news that his brother, Charlie, had been murdered by Navajos, burned along with Cedar Springs Trading Post. On March 22, 1919, trader William F. Williams and his family were woken in the middle of the night by Little Gambler, a Navajo man, pounding on the door of their trading post at Leupp. The family stumbled outside to see that "the whole northern part of the valley was brilliant in reflected light as huge red flames licked into the sky." Billie, the trader's daughter, remembered, "It was ten miles away, yet those leaping tongues of fire seemed so near that I imagined I could feel their heat. . . . Mother and I watched the fire. The sky was partly cloudy, with broken rifts showing the moon. The wind blew unusually strong, as it always does on the Arizona desert in March. The fire would burst into tremendous vividness as the wind caught points of flame, curling them into weird and eerie shapes. Then there'd be a lull and the north would become as dark as the rest of the night."[31] By the time Williams and Little Gambler arrived on the scene, only the chimney remained standing. The metal stove and iron bedstead protruded from the smoldering ashes, twisted and tortured by the heat.

Charlie's body, burned beyond recognition, lay in the ruins, kept silent company by the blackened bones of his dog and four five-gallon kerosene cans.[32]

The following days passed in a confusion of rumor and revenge as the story unfolded and the suspected murderers, two young Navajo brothers, were chased down. The news of Charlie's death spread rapidly across the reservation and into the surrounding towns. When he heard it, Ed Thacker fired off a letter to Lorenzo, Jr., begging for news and hoping that Charlie was merely missing, not dead. "Please let us know all you can about the matter as I am very anxious to hear," he wrote. "Charlie and I have been friends for years and there is not a man that I would do a favor for any quicker than I would for Charlie. . . . Lorenzo, it hurts me as much as if it were my own brother that was dead and I hope that it is not true."[33] But Charlie *was* dead; by March 25 the Associated Press had reported that "the charred body of Charles Hubbell was found lying beside the cash register in the ruins of a fire which destroyed the trading post. . . . It is believed he was robbed and murdered by Indians and the post set on fire to hide the crime."[34] An avalanche of articles across the country reported facts and speculation with equally lurid zeal under sensational headlines: "Brother of Senator Is Burned to Death"; "Indian Slayer of White Barricaded"; "Navajo Slayers Standing at Bay—Ex-Senator of Arizona to Join Posse"; "One of Slayers of Trader Hubbell Very Valuable Navajo Medicine Man; Tribesmen Plead for Clemency."[35]

When members of the Hubbell family heard about Charlie's death, they rushed to Cedar Springs. Lorenzo, Jr., arrived early in the morning on March 24, two days after the murder, to find his uncle's body, identifiable only by its frail form, still lying in the ashes. J. L. and Roman arrived on the scene shortly thereafter. Meanwhile, the sheriff and several Navajos from the vicinity tracked the murderers northeast across the reservation. When the trail went cold, J. L., Roman, and Lorenzo buried Charlie in Winslow and went home.[36] But none of them dropped the matter. When the suspects had still not been apprehended after eight days, Lorenzo, Jr., began calling in favors. He told Hopi Superintendent Leo Crane that "I have every Indian that I can see interested in the case. . . . I tell the Indians, that I have never asked them for a favor but I do now, and expect it."[37] He wrote to his Navajo friends, Hastiin Nez and Adakai, "You have been my friends for many years, I have helped you many times, now I want you to help me."[38] He offered a $200 reward for any information leading to the identification of the murders, and to pay everyone trailing them. "I have many Navajo friends," he said, "and I am sure that when a crime like this is committed, that they are all against it, and will do all in their power to punish the murderers."[39]

Two Navajo trackers soon found the suspects holed up in a cave 55 miles northeast of Cedar Springs, having left the goods they stole from the trading post at their father's home. They were 22-year-old Adeltoni Bigue No. 1 and 19-year-old Adeltoni Bigue No. 2, sons of a Navajo medicine man. Trapped and determined not to be taken alive, the brothers evidently confessed to the crime and waited for the "desperate fight" that would come with the arrival of the heavily armed sheriff's posse that was gathering in Winslow.[40] J. L. joined the posse, but before they could get to the Navajos' mountain hideout, two Navajo policemen had arrested the brothers peacefully.

Once it was determined that Charlie had been murdered off the reservation in Coconino County, the brothers were taken to Flagstaff for trial. Lorenzo, Jr., testified, single-mindedly bent on exacting the severest punishment for the murder of the beloved uncle who had indulgently taught him the ropes of trading when he was a small boy at Ganado.[41] During the trial, conflicting stories emerged from the two brothers and from the prosecution. The Navajos claimed that Charlie's dog bit one of them while they were arguing over the price of a cookie. Charlie would not give the brothers change, insisting that they trade the balance. And then, rather than tie up the dog and pay for the damage, as the Navajos demanded, Charlie, apparently at the end of his frayed rope, "told them to get out or he'd kill them."[42] The elder Adeltoni brother and Charlie reached for Charlie's gun on the store counter at the same time, but the boy was faster. Adeltoni Bigue No. 1 said that Charlie then ran into his bedroom and came out with another gun that he kept near his bedside. Charlie fired at the Navajos and the elder brother fired back. The bullet struck Charlie in the head and the two young men doused the counters in oil, set fire to the trading post to cover their tracks, and fled. The county attorney refuted the self-defense story, arguing that Charlie's gun—the one he had reportedly retrieved from his bedroom and fired twice—was found outside the store with five loaded cartridges, one empty chamber, and no exploded shells, proving that Charlie had not shot at the two Navajos. "Besides," the attorney argued, Charlie "was a frail man weighing only 103 pounds, and he was 63 years old, opposed to men with the drop on him, who, under such circumstances were in a position of advantage that required no defense of their own lives."[43]

Whether the two Navajos had shot Charlie in self-defense or not, public sentiment was against them. Charlie was not the first white trader to be murdered by Navajos. Before 1900, such incidents were rare, but between 1901 and 1934, with the rising consumption of alcohol on the reservation, Navajos killed twenty traders. According to Frank McNitt, the murders generally followed the pattern of Charlie's death quite closely: the traders were killed when alone after sunset, and then robbed, their posts burned to destroy any evidence.[44] The *Coconino Sun* reported that in Charlie's case, "It was generally felt that the extreme penalty was justified and that nothing short of it would serve as a restraint upon the aborigines against future crimes of the very same nature. In fact, there are many who openly say that they believe failure to assess the extreme penalty in such cases operates virtually as an encouragement of these semi-savages in showing more openly their contempt of the law and its penalties."[45]

In the end, the jury convicted the elder brother of murder in the first degree, sentencing him to life in prison rather than the requested death penalty. The younger brother was convicted of murder in the second degree and received 15 to 20 years, a lighter sentence because of his age and his brother's confession that he was the one who had killed Charlie.[46] The Hubbells and their friends, who had hoped the two Navajos would "stretch hemp for it," were bitterly disappointed.[47] "It's too bad, but some people don't believe in hanging, though their own mothers were killed in cold blood," Lorenzo, Jr., wrote in frustration to Ed Thacker.[48]

The trading post at Cedar Springs had been Lorenzo's, and its loss must have delivered a significant financial injury. He wrote to his bank, "You no doubt have heard of the terrible murder of my uncle Charles, it was one of the worst crimes, that a person can imagine. The store building, and property that was burned, was mine, same was not insured."[49] But even worse was the emotional blow. As he stood in the ashes, it was not the uninsured goods Lorenzo wept over, and it was not financial failure that made him unable to "think of starting a store there any more, at least for some time."[50] He "felt it was his fault. He'd suggested building the post and staked his uncle to it. He said he never should have allowed the old man to live there alone."[51] Though Charlie was a chronically lonely alcoholic who never did get along with the Navajos as well as his brother, and who "picked up official complaints as wool picks up burrs," he was well liked, even by the government officials who had to sort out those complaints.[52] His years at Cedar Springs were among the most isolated of his life. Cedar Springs did not even get regular mail, and Charlie's piercingly lonely letters to his brother begged him or Lorenzo to send some newspapers. "[B]y god," he wrote, "it is six months since you or him have sent me a paper. You know I have nobody here to talk to. I am like a hermit and I would like to hear from the outside world once in a while."[53] But such isolation was part of a trader's life, "the possibility of sudden, violent death" a calculated risk.[54] Though they carried their grief close to their hearts, the Hubbells went on trading.[55] But Charlie's death "shattered what was left of the Hubbells' seeming invulnerability to misfortune."[56]

## The Trading Empire in the 1920s

Following the tragedies of the late 1910s, the decade of the 1920s began badly for the beleaguered Hubbells. After Charlie's death, J. L. suffered recurring bouts of incapacitating illness, while Lorenzo, Jr., lapsed periodically into depression.[57] Even the land suffered. Drought parched Arizona from 1918 to 1921, followed by years of violent summer storms that eroded deep cuts into the soil, while the Navajos' huge herds of sheep began to denude the range in a grim prelude to the stock reduction programs that would come in the 1930s.[58] Prices for wool and sheep, driven up by the war, plummeted in its wake, while prices for consumer goods remained high. The Hubbells scraped together what money they could to buy sheep, but the range was so bad and the animals so scrawny that they fetched only a fraction of what they had in more prosperous days.[59] At the same time, the Navajo economy was changing again, the blanket trade eclipsing the wool trade, and old customs that had kept traders on their feet, like the use of tin money, broke down as the Navajos began to demand cash that could be spent anywhere.[60] In the 1920s, J. L. borrowed tens of thousands of dollars from Chee Dodge, taking out multiple mortgages on the Ganado property to secure loans on which he struggled even to pay the interest while bills piled up precariously.[61]

Both Roman and J. L. borrowed heavily from Lorenzo, Jr., whose keen sense of family obligation kept him sending money even when he had little himself. As he told Roman, "I am most anxious to do all I can to help you as long as I am doing well; I have already advanced my father $3000.00 this year, and also paid his bill in Winslow, on Feb 26th, amounting to $817.79."[62]

A year later, when Forrest asked him for yet another $3,000, Lorenzo sent the check, but enclosed a note imploring his family to stop: "How much more do you need, my goodness it is getting beyond my capacity."[63] To make matters worse, in 1927 competition finally came to break the Hubbell monopoly on Ganado trade when Albert H. Lee opened the Ganado Trading Post a stone's throw away. J. L.'s nephew George, who was managing the post at Piñon, thought that even the Navajos' loyalty to the Hubbells could not save the old trading post unless the family made some changes in how they ran the business.[64] All in all, they were lean years for the Hubbells, who tried, as Lorenzo, Jr., put it, to "do with as little as possible, and slave and save for a couple of years, and see if we cannot get our heads out of water; we must all be economical, and do without all unnecessaries, its [sic] only he, that can save, that can expect to have anything."[65]

The Hubbells' attempts to be frugal, however, did not seem to extend to the purchase of yet more trading posts and business ventures. In 1920, J. L. moved into Roman and Alma's old home in Gallup to operate the wholesale branch of the business that he had opened there in 1914. Roman took over management of the Ganado post.[66] Forrest, possibly because of personality conflicts with Roman, moved to Oraibi to work for Lorenzo, Jr., as soon as Roman took over. Lorenzo, understanding the conflict that could come when two men both tried to do the trading, let Forrest take over all the buying at Oraibi so he could concentrate on building up his curio business.[67] The two of them began hatching schemes, and by the spring of 1921, had made a trip to California to take scope of the market for Navajo blankets. They rented a storefront in Long Beach, and Forrest stayed there to manage the latest branch of the Hubbell business: a curio shop. Lorenzo had his share of doubts about the venture, especially since he and Forrest both lacked experience outside the peculiar business of Indian trading, but he put everything he had into it. "I have confidence that Forrest will do alright," Lorenzo told his skeptical father; "he is alone and no one over him, and that ought to bring him out."[68]

They called the business the Arizona Navajo Indian Rug Co., plastering signs on the windows that boasted "Hubbell Quality Navajo Indian Rugs, Hopi basketry and pottery, Direct from our reservation stores," while Forrest advertised and put up curio displays in hotel lobbies.[69] The business did well at first, and Adele brought their oldest son Hub and their niece LaCharles to join Forrest in California. But they quickly found that customers in

California did not care as much for quality, authentic Navajo rugs as they did for certain patterns and sizes at cheap prices.[70] By early fall, the business began to flounder. Lorenzo's debts mounted and the stock of goods at the Oraibi store suffered as the Long Beach venture siphoned away its resources. Forrest even ordered Gila monsters to put in the windows to attract attention, but the desperate move proved fruitless.[71] Against Lorenzo's better judgment, he and Forrest entered a partnership with a group of California businessmen in an effort to save their scheme, but the relationship soured, and in the end they pulled out at a significant loss.[72]

Leaving Long Beach, Forrest and Adele moved to Phoenix, where Forrest got a job as a salesman for the Joannes Brothers Company, a grocery supplier, and enrolled Hub and LaCharles in school.[73] He evidently did well enough as a salesman, but the pull of the Hubbell family and business drew him and his wife back. In 1926, Lorenzo asked him to come work for him as a salesman for the wholesale business he had bought from Hubert Richardson in Winslow in 1924.[74] Forrest felt a little trepidation because of past failures. "It has seemed in the past that I could not produce for you like I can for other people," he wrote apologetically to Lorenzo.[75] But Forrest was beginning to feel his age, and Adele longed for a home of her own; here was the perfect opportunity for them to settle down within reach of the family. Forrest resigned his position at the grocery, convinced anew that a partnership with Lorenzo would "be the means of my future success."[76] For three years, Forrest and Adele lived in Winslow, overseeing the wholesale business, but Forrest and Lorenzo's working relationship rapidly deteriorated, terminating abruptly and unpleasantly when Forrest quit and took a job with another grocery company in El Paso, Texas, in June 1929.[77]

While Forrest was working in Winslow, Lorenzo took the opportunity to give the curio trade in California another try, sending a longtime employee, H. C. "Dad" Hibben, to scout out a location in September 1926. Hibben selected a little one-story building across the street from the Egyptian Theater, and, given free reign by Lorenzo, commenced to ordering jewelry cases, fixtures, pottery shelves, an electric sign, and stationery for the new store, wrapping himself up in a Pendleton blanket to drum up business.[78] But the Hollywood venture seemed doomed to follow the stunted footsteps of its predecessor in Long Beach. Hibben nervously watched crowds of curious people come into the store every day, only to see them leave again empty handed. Following the time-honored Hubbell tradition of trying to conquer hard times by buying more stores, they opened a second location a mile away from the first.[79] The second business failed too, and by the end of 1928, Hibben accepted a job with another trader in order to start paying off his debts.[80] The Hollywood stores closed their doors, and Lorenzo put to rest his dream of a California curio outlet. In the meantime, the Hubbells bought or sold nearly a dozen other businesses in the 1920s, ranging from traditional trading posts, to a lodge in Marble Canyon meant to attract tourists, to Lorenzo, Jr.'s, wholesale house in Winslow.[81] Despite the decade's financial struggles, the family entered the 1930s with 10 trading posts in operation, though each seemed to hang by a thread.

### *The Farm at Its Peak*

While other aspects of the family business struggled weakly through the 1920s, the farm at Ganado entered its glory days. With the Ganado Dam project completed—as much as it was ever completed—water rushed down the irrigation ditches into the parched fields, and the costly labor of decades finally began to bear fruit for the farmers of Ganado, Navajo and Anglo alike.[82] Roman took over the role of overseeing the farm with enthusiasm, and by 1926 he had every acre of fenced land on the property under cultivation.[83] The Hubbells also owned and cultivated several other farms in New Mexico and Arizona, including fruit ranches in Farmington and a bean farm at Piñon Springs, used to help supply the trading posts.[84]

Roman planted his fields primarily in alfalfa, a hardy crop well suited to the extremes of the climate of northeastern Arizona. Two or three times a year, up to thirty Navajo laborers, paid $1.50 per day, brought in the harvest, which was used to feed the fifty or sixty horses and mules that still ran the freight and mail stages. Roman also sold hay a bale or two at a time to Navajos, and to the Hopi Agency and the government school at Keams Canyon. The Hubbells also planted corn, rye, oats, and potatoes from time to time, as well as melons, garden crops, and a few fruit trees.[85] The image of the trading post with its high counters and colorful merchandise so saturates the fabric of Ganado memory that its role as a farm and homestead is often forgotten. In the memory of those who lived there, however, the sweet smell of hay and the clucking of chickens mingles with the scent of piñon and tobacco and the shouts of the teamsters: "On the farm we raised corn. . . . We planted sweet potatoes, peanuts and garden crops. . . . We had all kinds of vegetable kale, rhubarb. We always had a couple of milk cows and made our own butter. . . . We had lots of watermelons, pumpkins, banana melons, cantaloupes, and similar things. . . . The big iron kettle by the guest hogan was used to render lard. The pigs would always get out. We had chickens. We found eggs in the hay. We also had turkeys, guinea hens and peacocks."[86]

Though the responsibility of overseeing the farm when it reached its peak in the 1920s seemed to fall mostly to Roman, J. L. took pleasure in its success, too. The farm was, after all, his dream.[87] He did not allow his many responsibilities in Gallup and at the other trading posts or his failing health to prevent him from keeping an appreciative eye on the farm. "He spent a lot of time just walking over the farms, just walking over the alfalfa beds to see how the alfalfa was growing in each bed, where it might need something. . . . He was careful about that."[88] His "affinity for land . . . stirred deeply" when he saw his 160 acres bearing fruit.[89]

With the fields planted, the Ganado homestead began to take on a more cultivated look, and a more modern one as farm machinery grumbled along in the fields, plowing and harvesting.[90] It became less a fortress in the wilderness and more a country home as ripples of modernization spread to the reservation after the war, telephones and electricity following in the wake of the automobile. In the 1920s, the Hubbells installed an electric light plant, replacing the old kerosene lamps in the house and trading post with the glow of electricity, plumbed the house with running water, and put telephones in the grand hall and the trader's office.[91] New buildings cropped up on the Ganado property, including two guest hogans for Navajo customers, a water tower, and large corrals across the wash to pen up the sheep and cattle, as the barn and yard began to fill up with metal farm machinery and cars as well as wagons and horses.[92] In 1923 the Hubbells tore down the Leonard building, the last relic of the trading post as it had once been, and replaced it with a flower garden bordered by pieces of petrified wood.[93] Lorenzo described the curious mix of modern and traditional that prevailed in Navajo country in those days. "Everything here has been more or less modernized, better roads, less horses and more autos; but right here at Oraibi the same old houses store and all are just the same, Indians come in on burros, a horseback and on wagons, and a good many of them afoot, but at that there is not a hungry indian on the reservation, they are ten times in better shape than when you left the country," he observed. "Conditions are changing so that I will have to modernize my business, and no doubt when I do I'll have my office about ten miles away in some old adobe shack, where the mice can come through the floor, and the spiders will have a chance to live."[94]

With the conditions of the roads slowly improving, especially as the BIA built bridges over troublesome washes, cars increasingly replaced wagons on the freight and mail runs. In 1925, Lorenzo said he had not had to send a team to the railroad for over a year.[95] The postal contracts became an even more crucial part of the business in the 1920s than they had been before, the additional income from half a dozen routes and Barbara's modest salary as postmistress helping to get the family through lean times in the other branches of the business.[96] Lorenzo urged Roman to sacrifice anything he had to get the mail contracts. "Remember," he advised, "that it's a four year job, and it's a great help to you and whatever you get from the government is pay for transporting your own goods, which otherwise would come out of your business."[97]

The 1920s were also active years in the sheep and goat trade, though not necessarily profitable ones. "Competition and concern for the good will of the Indians kept pressure on all of them to price competitively," and to keep buying sheep even when cash was short.[98] Buying the sheep Navajos brought in to the trading post to weigh and sell required massive lots of up to $1,000 in silver dollars, cash that was hard to come by for the financially struggling Hubbells; usually, they secured loans from their banks, but in the 1920s the banks were more cautious than usual about lending.[99] But without the sheep trade, the business would die as Navajo customers took their animals and their trade elsewhere, and each year the Hubbells somehow scraped together enough money to buy stock. As Lorenzo wrote to his friend, Ed Thacker, "I want to do as well by the Indians as I possibly can, but we must work and handle our sheep with the greatest possible economy, as every cent with us counts. I am not in a very good shape to buy stock, but we must and do the best we can with what we have."[100]

The same paradoxical relationship between productivity and profit was true of the Hubbell farm. Though the 1920s saw plentiful crops, "there is little to indicate that the Hubbell farm ever turned a profit or that it was even essential that it do so."[101] It served mostly as a support service, providing feed for the draft animals and the huge herds of sheep gathered in from the outlying posts in November every year before being driven to the railhead at Gallup.[102] The sheep herds sometimes pastured on the Hubbell ranch for days or even weeks while they awaited buyers or shipment dates, feeding on the uncut alfalfa that sprang up along fence lines and in the fields after the last harvest.[103] Lorenzo called the hay farm a "business getter," implying that the hay itself, like sheep, was not in itself always profitable, but helped drum up business and stave off the additional cost of importing feed.[104] In any case, both the farm and the sheep trade were "part of the mystique and part of a setting carefully staged by John Lorenzo"—part of the essence of Ganado.[105]

## "Moments of Happiness and Moments of Sorrow"

When Lorenzo, Jr.'s, dear friend and employee, Ed Thacker, passed away of heart failure while dipping sheep in October 1923, Lorenzo summed up the difficult years of the Hubbells' lives poignantly. "The loss of Ed to me from every angle is more keenly felt as the days drag by," Lorenzo wrote to another friend. "Ed was closer to me than any one, and its [sic] for me to adjust myself to be without him, but such is life, it is made of moments of happiness and moments of sorrow."[106] Amidst all the misfortunes that followed in the wake of J. L.'s political campaigns, both financial and personal, there shone glimmers of ordinary happiness. Along with the excitement of long-awaited developments on the farm, the Hubbell family enjoyed their share of small personal joys that made the financial strain and the loss of loved ones bearable. As Lorenzo said in a letter to an old friend, "I . . . am plugging along in the same old way, doing much of nothing, but ignorance is bliss, and being so am fairly well pleased with my misfortunes."[107]

If ignorance was bliss, the Hubbell grandchildren—Hub, LaCharles, Miles, Monnie, and John—were the happiest of the Hubbell family. Blithely unaware of the financial troubles that plagued the adults of the family, they had the whole ranch, except the strictly off-limits store, as a playground. If they were reading *Treasure Island,* the barn became a ship in their young imaginations, and their laughter and shouts rang out from the loft.[108] They kept a veritable menagerie of pets: dogs of every shape and size, cats, turtles, canaries, guppies, guinea pigs, rats, eaglets, a badger, a bobcat, a crow named Jimmy, Powhaton the sheep, and a monkey called Eva.[109] The grandchildren also enjoyed the adoring company of their grandfather whenever he could spare the time; he sat them on his left and right hands at dinner, relegating even his most esteemed guests to positions further down the table. J. L. would pick up the children, set them on his shoulders, and gallop up and down the great hall. "My grandfather was an absolute delight!" LaCharles remembered. "I think he really loved his grandchildren," but he also kept them in line with stern looks and sterner lectures.[110] The children knew what J. L. expected of them and rushed to deliver it. When the bell woke them at six in the morning, the children scrambled to be washed, dressed, and sitting at the table in time for breakfast at 6:30 or risked the wrath of their Papa, who would not tolerate tardiness.[111] Hub remembered J. L. rising long before the sun and rousting the children along with him; the mornings were the grandchildren's time to be with J. L. before the demands of the day took him into the bullpen, the warehouse, or the fields, or to some other trading post.[112] The grandchildren, eager and excited about the world around them, could not help but infect the adults of the Hubbell family with some of their joy. Lorenzo, Jr., in particular adored his nieces and nephews, who took trips to Oraibi to visit him and sent him birthday cards.

With all those grandchildren running around the ranch, sometimes joined by their cousins, including Donald Sidney Hubbell, George Hubbell, and Rafael Armijo, and with the family's traditional dedication to education, the Hubbells brought private teachers to the trading post. Every year, another young woman came to Ganado to teach the Hubbell children, among them Miss Barnart, Miss Mitchell, Miss Rogers, and Miss Charlotte Chain.[113] But in 1920, faced with a shortage of teachers in the wake of the war, Barbara could not find a soul to take the position and was going to have to either teach the children herself or send them away to school.[114]

Meanwhile, in Connersville, Indiana, a twenty-one-year-old school teacher named Dorothy E. Smith wrote to the Albert Teachers Agency in Chicago to apply for a teaching position in Portland, Oregon. Her father was about to sell out his general store and move the family to the Northwest, and Dorothy, with two years of public school teaching under her belt, intended to move with them. Her father's plan fell through, but Dorothy's name had already gone out on the agency's listings; she began receiving letters from every corner of the country. One of them was from a Mrs. Barbara H. Goodman.[115] "I am very anxious to secure a teacher for three very much alive youngsters," Dorothy read. The letter outlined the children's ages, the school and living facilities, and directions for travel, concluding charmingly, "I am sure you will consider it quite an experience to be in the 'Wild and Wooly.'"[116] Intrigued by the possibility of going farther from home than she had ever been before, to a place unlike anything she had

Hubbell, LaCharles, and Miles with their pets, c. 1915. Courtesy of the National Park Service, HUTR 07262.

known, Dorothy accepted, despite the vocal objections of her parents, who wanted her closer to home.[117]

Dorothy arrived in Gallup in October 1920, where J. L. met her, escorted her to her rooms at the El Navajo hotel, and thoroughly won her over with his gallant behavior and twinkling charm. Roman arrived in Gallup on business the next day and Dorothy rode back to Ganado with him, crossing the desert miles toward her future home.[118] "I knew nothing about the West," she remembered. "The place was so wild and strange, I thought I was in a foreign country. . . . There were piñon pines, junipers, and empty spaces."[119] They arrived at the trading post at dusk, and Dorothy sat down to her first dinner in the hall of the Hubbell home, brightened by gas lamps and the intriguing conversation of visiting archaeologist Earl Morris.[120] But she felt surrounded by strangeness. "I didn't know anybody," she said. "I didn't know a Hopi from a Mexican from a Navajo. And when I went to bed I didn't see any lock on the door. I had to do something. So I took a chair and I propped it under the doorknob."[121] She woke the next morning to the eerie screeches of the peacocks, and during the first session of school that day, a parade of hooting, masked *Yeis,* dancers representing Navajo deities, came prancing and leaping through, demanding food for the *Yeibichai* ceremony. "It was just as strange as anything," she remembered.[122]

Dorothy taught LaCharles, Monnie, and John until the eighth grade, and Rafael Armijo, a cousin whose father worked in the store, from 1920 to 1921.[123] They used a room of the Hubbell home as a classroom, with blackboards and maps hung on the walls, school desks, and a curriculum approved by the state. Their education included the usual English, writing, and mathematics, but it also included days off to attend Navajo ceremonies, and a little school newspaper, called *Rajolaro*, about the daily goings-on at the trading post, from the first two letters of each of the students' names.[124] From the first time they saw Dorothy, the children were "impressed with her poise and her graciousness."[125] Three-year-old John breathed out a sigh of wonder over "the new lady," and before long, Dorothy became known respectfully around the trading post as "Lady."[126] With Barbara as her guide, Dorothy watched the goings on of the trading post, the ranch, and Navajo life with great interest. But there was something—someone—else that she was watching with great interest; at the end of her first school year at the trading post, she eloped with Roman.

As soon as wool season was over in July 1921, Roman loaded Dorothy into the car and told the family he was driving her to the train station in Gallup so she could go home and see her family for the summer. But they kept on driving straight to Albuquerque, where a minister of the Christian church to which Dorothy belonged married them.[127] A few weeks after the wedding, Roman wrote to Forrest, who was then in Long Beach, "Suppose it was rather a surprise for you to hear that I married the other day. But you can never tell what is coming from one day to the next. Was sure a lucky shot to be able to fool Dorothy."[128] But if the two of them expected anyone else in the family to be shocked or surprised at their elopement, they were disappointed. The romance had not escaped the notice of Barbara or J. L., who watched with tacit approval, for Dorothy was of a much more stable, capable character than Alma had ever been.[129] It was not until after the wedding that J. L. told Dorothy, "You know, when I met you at the station when you came, I just said to myself, 'Goodbye Roman.'"[130] But J. L. would not lose Roman this time—he would gain a daughter-in-law, and more than that, the future caretaker of his beloved trading ranch, the one who would outlive all of his children, and see it turned into a National Historic Site. The Navajos called her Asdaáán Nééz (Tall Woman)—she who had once been

Roman and Dorothy standing in front of the barn, c. 1935. Courtesy of the National Park Service, HUTR 04984.

so frightened of the Indians that she shoved a chair under her bedroom door knob.[131] "When I married Roman," she said, "my fears vanished, and I became one of the family, unafraid, and determined to live the frontier life I had so willingly chosen."[132]

Barbara, too, remarried. Having "remained single till LaCharles had been given every opportunity for an education," she married A. B. Myers, an engineer on the Ganado Irrigation Project, the autumn of 1926.[133] The family seemed to approve of Myers—Lorenzo called him "a mighty fine fellow," but for some reason, the marriage lasted for less than two years before ending in divorce.[134] The marriage, however brief, indicates the social connectedness of the Ganado homestead and the community development that went on around it in the early decades of the twentieth century. Construction and maintenance of the dam brought Anglo neighbors to a place that had once been quite isolated. The Hubbells also socialized regularly with people at the Presbyterian Mission. Though they were Catholic, Barbara and Adele would walk the mile or so from the trading post to the mission to play on the "old fashioned, wheezy organ" for Sunday services each week.[135] In the 1920s, "the many activities that the Mission engaged in boomed and bloomed: buildings seemed to spring up over night and became alive with activities" as the church was joined by a school and then a hospital.[136] As it grew, the mission brought new people to Ganado—missionaries, teachers, nurses, and physicians, many of whom became close friends with the Hubbell family.[137] Together with the parade of visitors to Navajo country who stayed as guests in the Hubbell home, the family never wanted for company—the trading post had changed from the isolated outpost of the early days to the center of a community.

## On Hubbell Hill

Running beneath the high squeal of children's voices, warm visits from new neighbors and friends, and the excitement of development, deeper than the rumble of financial troubles and unexpected tragedies, was the fact that the 1920s were the last decade of the life of John Lorenzo Hubbell. For one with such a romantic, tempestuous youth, J. L. faded from life slowly and gently. By 1921, the man who had only a few years before been a significant political force in the state had become "the Grand Old Man of Apache County," sitting "with snow white hair and mustache, and the air of a real Spanish 'cavallero'" in the lobbies of hotels at political conventions, telling anecdotes and jokes with a twinkle in his blue eyes.[138] J. L. suffered through several serious illnesses in the 1920s, but he refused to stay down in bed or in one place for very long, still coordinating the freight lines from his Gallup office and making frequent visits to Ganado. His children worried about him. Lorenzo confessed to his friend, "I tell you Ed, it certainly scares me, when my father gets a spell, he gets so sick."[139] Lorenzo made visits to Gallup to see his father whenever he became "dangerously ill," but J. L. always seemed to have recovered by the time his son arrived.[140] He continued life much as he always had, albeit at a slower pace with a good deal less haring off to Washington or Phoenix on political business. Then, in early 1929, J. L. finally became ill enough that he had to abandon the business at Gallup.[141] He spent the last two years of his life at the Ganado homestead, his dream made reality, dozing off in a wheelchair, telling stories and reminiscing, when he could catch his wheezing breath, about the famous and important people who had been his guests. He still tried to get around, taking walks around the property, perhaps down to check on the irrigation ditches or to pick a melon as he used to do, but his family would have to take his wheelchair out to bring him back when his frail legs could carry him no farther.

Slowly, the vitality drained away from J. L. and the pounds withered on his once barrel-chested frame. Dorothy remembered, "For the last several months he wouldn't go to bed. They said he couldn't breathe, and he'd sit up in a chair all night. And we took turns sitting up with him . . . in a chair by the fireplace."[142] Clarence G. Salsbury, a physician at the Presbyterian hospital, tended J. L. in his last days, listening to his old friend's stories. "It was distressing," he said, "when I came to treat Don Lorenzo, to see how little I could do. The strains of an incredibly active life and the infirmities of age were too much."[143]

J. L. passed away at the age of 76 on November 11, 1930. The feelings of those closest to him at his death are lost. Those were words spoken at his bedside in the darkness, not written in letters or newspaper articles. But those who received the news of his passing from the frozen lips of freight and mail drivers, J. L.'s friends and relatives employed in the outlying posts, sent in letters expressing their loss. J. L.'s nephew George and his wife Madge wrote to Lorenzo of their mingled sadness and relief at the passing of the old trader, whose "last year of life was full of agony and suffering. . . . [H]e was a thoughtful, kind and generous friend, and I shall never forget the

J. L. sits in his wheelchair outside the Hubbell home with his grandson, Jack, and pets Jimmy and Eva. Courtesy of the National Park Service, HUTR 04974.

many times his generosity and thoughtfulness helped us in our struggle."[144] Tommy Hubbell, another of J. L.'s nephews, wrote that "Papa was the only father that I really remember of ever having."[145]

J. L. was buried on top of Hubbell Hill "in the kind of weather he liked so well, sleet and snow; there he rests leaving a memory of his kind deeds, that will never be forgotten."[146] One of the local newspapers published an account of the "simple Catholic ceremony" with which "Don Lorenzo Hubbell was buried on Hubbell hill in Ganado at 2 o'clock yesterday afternoon between the graves of Lina Rubic [sic] Hubbell, his wife, and Chief Many Horses, great Navajo ruler. Snow fell upon the bared heads of more than 100 friends of Don Lorenzo, the most noted of Navajo Indian traders and friend to everyone, as the body was lowered into the grave. The Rev. Jerome Hesse, O.F.M., superior, who came from St. Michael's mission to administer the last rites of the Roman Catholic church, led these friends in prayer during the service at the grave.... Then, as the snows formed a blanket of warmth over the grave of Don Lorenzo, they departed."[147]

The news of Hubbell's death spread through another community with much greater drama—a dispersed community of writers, artists, scientists, and politicians who had been J. L.'s friends and guests at the Hubbell Trading Post. More fantastic accounts of his funeral would be circulated by their pens, the requiem high mass at St. Michael's drowned out by the mournful, perhaps imagined, pulse of Navajo drums: "Drums of the Navajos beat the funeral dirge, and the voices of a thousand bronzed shepherds of the Arizona hills chanted the Indian songs of the dead, as the body . . . was carried up the ruby colored Hubbell hill at Ganado."[148] In the imaginations of his guests, and from thence to the printed pages of magazines and books, the legend of John Lorenzo Hubbell would never die.

CHAPTER SIX

# "No Misrepresentations, No Shams, and No Counterfeits"
## Tourism and the Curio Trade

When J. L. Hubbell passed away, a chorus of newspaper articles eulogized the life of "the last and greatest of the Patriarchs and Princes of the Frontier," but most of them did not remember him as an underdog politician or a businessman struggling to make ends meet when the price of wool hit rock bottom and winter storms erased the roads.[1] They remembered him for the role he had played in transforming Navajo country into a tourist mecca, heralding him as "a charming host, a dispenser of hospitality and information."[2] They regaled him as the savior of Southwestern Indian arts and crafts, the man who ushered the Navajo blanket out of obscurity and into the homes of thousands of Americans and the collections of dozens of museums. "J. Lorenzo Hubbell," wrote Charles Lummis, one of the Southwest's most ardent promoters, "did more to save and rehabilitate this noble art-craft [weaving] than all government, philanthropic and other influences and agencies put together."[3] Herman Schweizer, the heart and soul of the Fred Harvey Company's Indian Department, similarly declared, "There is no doubt that Mr. Hubbell was the greatest Indian Trader, and did more in a practical way to promote the sale of their products than anyone else."[4] They called him the "father of the Navajo rug trade," painting him in the soft, heavenly glow of sainthood.[5]

Men like Lummis and Schweizer trumpeted the beneficence of J. L.'s influence with the characteristic blindness of boosters, for though he figured prominently in the commercialization of Indian arts and crafts—more prominently, perhaps, than any other trader—it should come as no surprise that in this, as in every other aspect of his business, his motives were not purely philanthropic. J. L. *was* a businessman struggling to make ends meet, and in carefully cultivating a market for Indian products, he reaped a profitable harvest that became the single most important facet of the Hubbell Trading Post business in the twentieth century. J. L. was among the first traders to directly market Navajo products off the reservation, creating what came to be known as the trade in "curiosities" or "curios," Indian products that fed Anglo consumers' fascination for the novel, the rare, and the exotic.[6] They "ran the gamut from cheap gew-gaws to one-of-a-kind museum pieces," including katsinas, basketry, pottery, jewelry, silverware, and, chief among them, the Navajo rug.[7]

As the twentieth century turned, traders stood at a confluence of forces that transformed the Southwest and primed eastern markets for the consumption of Indian-made goods. Between 1890 and 1920, many Americans became disenchanted with their new industrial way of life and enthralled by "primitive" Indians; the railroad thrust its way through New Mexico and Arizona, shortening once-formidable distances, while unprecedented economic affluence drew masses of people to the rails; and, as advertising and consumerism ascended in American culture, Southwestern tourism blossomed and handmade Indian curios became coveted commodities. J. L. Hubbell and his sons were perfectly positioned to hasten the transformation, hosting visitors, peddling curios, and convincing their Navajo neighbors to demonstrate their artistic skills for white audiences from San Diego to New York. They helped to sell, in short, the *idea* of the Southwest as a "strange enchanted land," shifting "the stereotype of the Navajos decisively and quickly . . . from that of 'savage' plunderers to 'primitive' artists."[8]

## Hubbell, Cotton, and Navajo Weaving

Long before railroads and automobiles carried tourists into Navajo country and away again laden with bright memories and souvenirs, long even before young J. L. Hubbell first crossed Diné Bikéyah alone on horseback, Navajo women sat at their looms and wove the designs passed down to them by their mothers.[9] Using wool from their own treasured herds of sheep, which they carded, cleaned, spun, and dyed with sage brush and sumac, piñon pitch and prickly pear, they wove blankets and clothing for their families and for trade.[10] As sheep became the center of Navajo life, weaving became the heart of the Navajo economy, and "by the early nineteenth century, Navajo blankets were prized within a wide regional market for their quality—so tightly woven they were waterproof—and their beauty."[11] Scholars generally suppose that the Navajos learned weaving from Pueblo peoples who took refuge with them during the Pueblo Revolt of 1680 and the Spanish Reconquest.[12] Navajos, however, "believe that weaving was taught to them by the Holy People who walked Mother Earth at the dawn of mankind. . . . The Navajo brought it with them to this world, they took it with them to Bosque Redondo, they have it with them today."[13] By the time American explorers encountered the Navajos, they had more than earned their reputation as skillful weavers; whatever else the Americans thought of the people they met in the deserts and canyons, they could not help but admire the quality of their textiles.[14]

The American conquest of the Southwest—military, economic, and cultural—affected weaving as it affected other areas of Navajo life, and by the close of the nineteenth century, outside pressures had transformed Navajo weaving from a home industry to a commercial product coveted nationwide.[15] At the crux of the shift were the Indian traders, exerting their influence on Navajos and Anglos alike in order to make the trade in curios, especially textiles, the backbone of their businesses. In the 1870s and 1880s, blankets were little more than dead weight, for there was no ready market of eager easterners hoping to decorate the parlors of their Victorian homes with authentic Indian products. At the same time, the Navajos' incarceration at Bosque Redondo and the subsequent establishment of trading posts had destroyed the traditional market for their textiles, as Navajos and other Southwestern Indians adopted Anglo-style clothing and cheaper factory-made Pendleton blankets.[16] Traders who bought the products of Navajo looms had to find a market for them elsewhere or cut off the blanket trade altogether in order to turn a profit.

At the little trading post in the Pueblo Colorado Valley, Hubbell and Cotton bought only a few Navajo blankets at first, focusing their buying power on wool, skins, and livestock. According to George Wharton James, Hubbell and Cotton purchased only three or four hundred pounds of common blankets in 1884, which probably amounted to only a few dozen blankets, but that was a few dozen more than they could sell.[17] While J. L. divided his attentions between St. Johns and the reservation, Cotton launched a campaign to find a market for the Navajo blankets piling up at the trading post. He did not advertise them to wealthy collectors, but rather to suppliers at mining camps and Indian reservations as durable, waterproof blankets

A Navajo woman weaving under a juniper tree. Courtesy of the National Park Service, HUTR 05552.

that would "out wear any American blanket manufactured" for only $3.00 apiece.[18] He said not a word about the blankets' beauty.[19]

Cotton had some success selling blankets to mining camps and other reservations, but not enough to use up his supply.[20] If he was going to realize the potential for profit that he could see in his mind's eye, he was going to have to cast his net wider. His descriptions to buyers became more and more detailed as he and other traders exerted all of their influence "in adapting Navajo weaving to the tastes of the Anglo buying public" by introducing new commercial dyes and yarns to the Navajos, and new uses for Navajo textiles to Anglo buyers.[21] Cotton, in fact, is credited with the idea of selling Navajo blankets, originally woven for clothing, as rugs—an idea that "revolutionized the trade and greatly increased the potential market for Navajo blankets."[22] By late 1887, he was writing to buyers in New York City, calling attention "to Navajo Indian Blankets which can be used for rugs, curtains they are very pretty and much sought after by people in Washington and elsewhere where known."[23] He described the "fine blankets . . . made of scarlet yarn with very unique and pretty designs in yellow, green, blue, white, and black," and the months it took "to make one as each thread has to be put through the loom by hand."[24] Cotton still sold coarse blankets woven of the Navajos' "own native wool" to miners and cattlemen, but he had turned his efforts to cultivating buyers among the easterners to whom he was already selling petrified wood, garnets, piñon nuts, and whatever other lucrative curiosities Navajo country had to offer.[25] When he moved his business to Gallup, handing the Ganado post back over to Hubbell, Cotton kept on executing his scheme, printing circulars and mailing them to merchants in cities across the country.[26]

Cotton's circulars went out just as upper- and middle-class Americans became mired in a deep cultural crisis. The previous decades had seen sweeping changes in the United States as advances in technology and industrialization revolutionized American life: railroads crossed even the most forbidding landscapes, and machines distanced Americans from their own labor. The whole nation was flooded with "anxiety over the fate of the 'American character' and public concern with immigration, industrialization, labor unrest, and the disquieting effects of world war."[27] In the face of such rapid and comprehensive change, Americans felt increasingly powerless, isolated from nature, and trapped by meaningless daily drudgery. Fearing that "machine-aged technology would erode the human spirit,"

America's scholars, artists, and intellectual leaders searched for personal fulfillment in "real" experiences and objects.[28] Their search for authenticity soon focused on Native Americans, whom they swiftly mythologized as colorful relics of a spiritual, authentic past doomed to vanish.[29] Across the nation, hearts cried out with John Collier, "We—I mean our white world in this country—are a shattered race—physically, religiously, socially and esthetically shattered, dismembered, directionless. . . . But let us examine with a wondering and tender concern, and with some awe, these Indian communities which by virtue of historical accidents and of their own unyielding wills are even today the expressions, even today the harborers, of a great age of integrated, inwardly-seeking life and art. . . . Our understanding of art, of work, of pleasure, of the values of life, and even our world-view, may be somewhat influenced if we will pay attention to them."[30] By buying Indian-made products, American consumers attempted to create for themselves a small pocket of the real in a modern world, as if mere proximity to Indian art would elevate them to a higher plane.[31] Their hopes for the future of America also settled on the West, and "essays, travel guides, promotional pamphlets, and popular fiction, all promoted an image of the desert Southwest as the last resort of American exceptionalism, a final haven for the regeneration of the nation's Anglo-Saxon heritage."[32]

Cotton, Hubbell, and other traders like J. B. Moore and Richard Wetherill knew and even sympathized with the sentiments of the anti-modernist Arts and Crafts Movement, which was born out of this crisis in American culture. With the help of writers like Charles Lummis and George Wharton James, they capitalized on popular sentiment to develop eastern markets for Navajo products. As Bsumek writes, "To increase sales of Navajo-made rugs and jewelry, traders realized that products had to make their way into the stockrooms of curio chops, ethnic-art dealers, and department stores across the country. To achieve this goal, the traders used the same marketing approaches that larger companies used: advertising. They advertised in regional and national newspapers and in widely circulated magazines and gazettes. They mailed out their own sales circulars to potential customers and retailers. They publicized their shops, themselves, and the behavior of the Indians with whom they worked. They paid to be mentioned in books as reliable dealers of Navajo textiles. In all these venues, they emphasized the ways in which their businesses were unique in the American marketplace."[33] Cotton issued a catalog in 1896, its pages resounding with romantic descriptions of "simple and primitive" Navajo weavers, the "mythologic symbolism [that] seems to be instinctive with the Navajos," and the "beauty and attractiveness" of the patterns, no two of which were ever the same.[34] As anthropologist Teresa Wilkins states, "Cotton marketed the idealized Navajo weaver as a savage person of 'unrestrained freedom' whose designs teemed with the influences of the natural environment of which she was such an integral part."[35]

In 1902, Hubbell followed Cotton's lead and issued his own mail-order catalog featuring not only Navajo blankets, but also jewelry and silverware, as well as Hopi basketry, pottery, and katsinas. He commissioned his friend H. G. Maratta, a graphic artist from Chicago, to design and print it.[36] J. L., too, played to anti-modernist sensibilities by emphasizing the rarity and great antiquity of truly genuine Navajo blankets, tracing their reputation for "richness, beauty, and durability" back to the "first white occupation of the Southwest."[37] He cautioned consumers against unscrupulous dealers who took advantage of easterners' ignorance and positioned himself as a champion of authenticity: "Cheap and gaudy blankets, loosely put together—made here, there and everywhere—have been sold at fabulous prices. Unless one has given study to the matter, it is easy to be deceived. I point to my long residence and my extended references in this country as guaranty [sic] of my sincerity and honesty. I have been at the greatest pains to perpetuate the old patterns, colors and weaves, now so rapidly passing out of existence even in the memory of the best weavers. I have even at times unraveled some of the old genuine Navajo blankets to show these modern weavers how the pattern was made. I can guarantee the reproduction of these antique patterns.... no misrepresentations, no shams and no counterfeits."[38]

Such language was calculated to appeal to the hunger of the antimodernists, and indeed, the blanket and curio trade exploded around the turn of the century as the catalogs and other forms of advertisement went into circulation. "The impact was obvious," McPherson writes.[39] "In 1899, the weaving trade amounted to only $50,000 reservation-wide; fifteen years later it had skyrocketed to $700,000, and by 1923, a variety of blankets were available from the Sears and Roebuck catalog."[40] Hubbell's shipments of rugs doubled from 14,000 pounds to 28,000 pounds within a year of publishing his catalog, and he soon sold curios to authorized dealers in dozens of cities.[41] Overnight, it seemed, an "Indian decorating craze" swept the country.[42] No longer did the traders advertise Navajo textiles simply as warm, durable bed or saddle blankets, but as parlor and dining room rugs, table runners, portieres (Victorian-era curtains for interior doors), couch covers, pillow tops, and auto robes.[43] Indian curios—even entire Indian Rooms—became essential elements "in every tastefully decorated Victorian home."[44]

As demand rose, curios soon became a cornerstone of the Indian trading business. J. L. called the rug business his "good business," for not only did it eclipse every other part of his trade in sheer volume, it provided the trading post with a crutch that helped it hobble through the very worst of times.[45] Although the "rug business experienced the rise and fall of sales, complaints and compliments from customers, and advertising expenditures common to other businesses," it often compensated for fluctuations in the seasonal cycles of Indian trading.[46] Whereas the wool trade brought in income only every six months, blanket sales provided year-round income and kept the business going when the wool market plummeted.[47] As anthropologist Kathy M'Closkey states, "blankets became the 'currency' by which Hubbell (and other traders) paid creditors" in the cash-poor business of Indian Trading.[48] In the period just after World War I, for example, when the price of wool dropped from forty-five cents per pound to seventeen cents per pound, blanket sales increased dramatically, since the Navajos could get more money for their wool in the form of a finished blanket than they could for the raw product.[49] During the Great Depression, when the price of wool languished at a meager eight cents per pound, the Hubbells used their rug inventory to buy potatoes, seed, and other supplies, as well as to pay off outstanding accounts with suppliers.[50] Even in less extreme times, Hubbell often paid off his overdue accounts with Cotton by means of huge shipments of Navajo blankets.[51] As Wilkins states, "Had Hubbell continued to market only wool" when the markets turned sour, as they did so many times, "he would have lost his shirt. . . . Instead, his empire expanded significantly after the turn of the century. And it was marketing Indian 'curios' (especially the Navajo blanket) that enhanced his fame, expanded his influence, and augmented his bank balance."[52]

The curio trade, however, did not always carry the Hubbells through financial difficulties unscathed. Sometimes, when markets slumped and the business struggled, the Hubbells could not buy all the blankets they needed to survive—they either lacked the cash to pay for them, or, in some years, found blankets simply "scarce as hens teeth."[53] And when the blanket trade faltered, it crippled the rest of the business: "Without rugs, Hubbell was unable to pay down his accounts with his creditors. Therefore, he could not order in any goods. Without goods, weavers will not weave for trade. It was a vicious circle."[54] J. L.'s stubborn insistence on handling the trade of old blankets personally added to the family's financial quandary during his lengthy political engagements, and in 1916, when the business was at one of its lowest points following J. L.'s senate campaign, Forrest was forced to turn away potential buyers. "Nearly every stock of good blankets on the reservation were completely sold out," he told one customer.[55] Just when they needed blanket sales to help them climb out of the hole J. L.'s politicking had dug, they could not afford to buy so much as a pound. At other times, the Hubbells bought far more blankets than they thought they could sell in an effort to keep the Navajos trading even when the rug market was down.[56]

Despite the occasional difficult year, the curio trade was one of the Hubbell's most lucrative and dependable. They sold to hundreds of curio shops nationwide, and boasted a reputation as the dealers with the highest quality Navajo rugs and the widest variety of Native products on the reservation, since, "[H]aving seven stores scattered over the reservation, [we] are in a position to get a greater variety of patterns than any other dealer."[57] J. L. was a well-liked and knowledgeable trader, which meant he commanded a huge share of the Navajo trade, and when Lorenzo, Jr., took over the trading post at Keams Canyon, he secured a hefty slice of the Hopi trade, too.[58] By the turn of the century, J. L. boasted confidently that he had the best Navajo blankets and curios available. "It is very customary for men to brag about their ability to do better than others by you," he wrote to a customer, "But I assure you that when I say that I have the very best and the best assortment of Navajo Blankets placed in the market, that is something that does not bear contradiction."[59]

## Hubbell's Influence on Navajo Textiles

In his classic study of Navajo weaving, George Wharton James wrote that "it would be as impossible to write truthfully and comprehensively of the history of the Navaho blanket and leave out Mr. Hubbell's relation to it, as it would be to give the history of the phonograph and leave out the name of Edison."[60] James, of course, exaggerates, for even the legendary J. L. Hubbell cannot be credited with the invention of the art, nor did he so easily outweigh the quiet influence of thousands of Navajo weavers. But he did unquestionably exert all his influence as a major buyer of Navajo textiles to shape the development of Navajo weaving as it entered its commercial phase.[61] As in everything else, J. L. nursed strong opinions about Navajo weaving. Aesthetically, he preferred that Navajo textiles remain as close to their roots as possible—as he put it in his catalog, he sought the "antique" and "genuine" over the "cheap and gaudy."[62] He favored traditional colors achieved with natural dyes over the brighter hues that appeared after the introduction of Germantown yarns and commercial aniline dyes, to which he objected strongly, with the sole exception of red.[63] J. L. also resisted the use of cotton warp and other innovations that he thought reduced the quality of Navajo weaving, even when they saved the weavers time and money.[64] Buyers in New York might not know the difference, he thought, but if badly made blankets flooded the market, the whole business would suffer.[65] He valued above all else antique and old-style blankets, collecting them and encouraging Navajo weavers to make new blankets based on the old patterns.[66]

J. L., however, was also a businessman who paid close attention the tastes of his customers, for no matter how "authentic" a blanket might be, if the design failed to appeal to Euro-American aesthetic sensibilities, he could not sell it. Even if J. L. had personally preferred brightly colored rugs, his customers did not. As he told one buyer, "I have made a specialty of the old styles that contain only the four standard colors Navajo Blue, Blk [black], Red and white. Also the old style grey Bkts. I get a few of the very bright ones but have found that the taste of my . . . customers is turning to the darker colors."[67] As Liz Bauer explains, "Aesthetically, the eye-dazzlers that were being woven during the late 1800s were unacceptable to Anglos. Light colors and busy optical rugs did not fit into the interior decoration of many of the homes of the period."[68] In this case, Anglo preferences conformed to Navajo weaving's traditional forms, but sometimes the tastes of customers led J. L. to encourage innovations that took weaving away from its roots. Navajo patterns, for example, did not originally feature borders, but Hubbell and other traders encouraged weavers to add them into their designs because they sold more readily.[69] Though personally committed to reproducing the old patterns, Hubbell tried to accommodate the colors, patterns, and sizes his customers suggested in their letters, and as a result, new patterns emerged that combined elements from both traditional and nontraditional styles, including oriental influences.[70] Other traders did the same, and soon characteristic styles emerged around specific trading posts; around Hubbell

Trading Post, the regional style became known as the Ganado Red.[71] Hubbell's other innovation was in commissioning weavers to produce rugs large enough to cover entire floors, extending extra credit to finance them since most weavers could not afford to wait for payment when they could finish a smaller rug much more quickly.[72]

As a way of mediating between his customers and his weavers, J. L. commissioned several artists, including Elbridge Ayer Burbank, Bertha Little, H. G. Maratta, and Herbert B. Tschudy (Herbert B. Judy) to make over a hundred small oil paintings of blanket designs, which he used as models to show the weavers.[73] The little paintings, ranging in size from five-by-seven to twelve inches square, hung on the wall behind J. L.'s desk in a colorful hodgepodge of crooked rows. George Wharton James described the paintings as follows: "In his office at Ganado, Arizona, John Lorenzo Hubbell has scores of blanket designs, painted in oil, hung upon the walls, and they present a most surprising and wonderful combination. These are designs that have been found to be pleasing to purchasers, and when a special order for a blanket of a certain design comes in, the weaver is shown the picture of the one desired. She studies it a while, takes the wool provided, or herself prepares it, and then, with such slight variations as she is sure to introduce, goes ahead and makes her blanket."[74] Navajo weavers seldom followed J. L.'s instructions exactly, or copied in every detail the patterns he showed them in the paintings. "Though weavers were concerned with the serious business of earning a livelihood by making a marketable product, they also asserted their own ideas about weaving," echoing, rather than imitating, the patterns in the paintings.[75] Hubbell and Cotton both always cautioned their buyers that they could not get exact duplicates of the rugs featured in their catalogs since no two blankets were ever woven exactly alike.[76] The old patterns Hubbell wanted the weavers to imitate were already part of the Navajos' "cultural repertoires," and they introduced changes freely.[77] They even altered oriental patterns, "attack[ing] these intricate, bordered alien designs with the same appetite for improvisation, innovation, and variety as they once brought to their experiments with the Pueblo stripe and the Hispanic serrated diamond."[78]

James and other connoisseurs of Navajo weaving generally portrayed J. L. as a prescient visionary who "saw the art deteriorate, and then set himself to work to stem the tide of ignorance and carelessness which bid fair speedily to wreck what his far-seeing vision knew might be a means of great

J. L.'s office, with oil paintings of Navajo rugs, 1906. Courtesy of the National Park Service, HUTR 04272.

wealth to an industrious and struggling people."[79] And that is certainly how J. L. presented himself in his catalog and in his business letters. However, as M'Closkey reminds us, "What Hubbell and his contemporaries *wrote* about Navajo textiles in catalogues and memoirs and how they actually *treated* them are dramatically different."[80] When J. L. advised his brother Charlie in 1912 to buy only the finest blankets, profits motivated him as much as, if not more than, any altruistic desire to improve Navajo weaving as an art. "Navajo blankets are going to be a drag in the market, except the very fine blankets, but medium grades and common blankets you have to buy cheap for we will lose money on them," he wrote.[81] And though Lorenzo, Jr., once told his father, "I believe in handling the blankets, placques, baskets, and pottery at any cost," and "I am willing to sacrifice the little profit I make, to preserve it," Navajo women actually received very little for their products.[82] A three-foot-by-five-foot rug could take between 150 and 250 hours to weave—hundreds more if the weaver had to shear, wash, card, spin, and dye her own yarn. With blankets as large as five feet by seven feet retailing for astonishingly low prices—as little as $3.00 in 1885 when the blanket trade was still aimed at mining camps, increasing to around $15.00 in 1901 when the tourist trade started to blossom, but still only $65.00 as late as 1955—the weavers made literally pennies per hour.[83] But Navajo weavers were not paid by the hour, but by the pound, and in order to make a profit, traders bought textiles for far less than they sold them. Hubbell generally paid his weavers between twenty-five cents and thirty cents per pound, regardless of quality, and sold them at nearly a 100 percent markup.[84]

Nevertheless, the Hubbells' sincerity in wanting to help the Navajos cannot be discounted completely. Naturally, they kept their eyes on profits as much as they did the well-being of the Navajos, because they firmly believed that the two were inseparably connected. "Treat yourself and your customers right," Lorenzo once wrote to Roman, "what is fair to them is fair to you."[85] In December 1940, when blanket prices slumped even lower than they were when Hubbell issued his catalog in 1902, Lorenzo, Jr., wrote to one of his buyers explaining why his prices were a little higher than those of his competitors: "I am in hopes that you are having good luck with the Navajo Rugs, as its [sic] such a help to us and these primitive people in obtaining an income from these hand made rugs, the only small permanent income they have, the Lord knows its [sic] not much."[86]

## The Birth of Tourism in Navajo Country

The antimodernist movement and the rise of Indian-made products on the market in the decades flanking the turn of the century went hand in hand with the development of another phenomenon: the birth of American tourism. By the early 1870s, the "celebration of dramatic western scenery by scientific surveyors, artists, photographers, sportsmen, publicizers, and adventurous travelers had become commonplace," but only a very few individuals had the fortitude and the funds necessary see wonders of the Southwest first hand.[87] Not until the arrival of the railroad were tourists able to travel en masse for the first time, and even then it took at least a decade for the Southwest's businessmen to fully recognize and capitalize on the possibilities of transforming Arizona into the "Grand Canyon State."[88] In the 1880s, the Santa Fe Railroad's main revenue had come from shipping. But the economic depression of the 1890s—the same depression that helped prompt the revival in Navajo weaving—devastated the railroad financially; when the railroad reorganized, it turned to the travel and tourist industry for sustenance. The Santa Fe spent millions of dollars on a massive and revolutionary advertising campaign that dramatized the scenery of the Southwest and romanticized Native American life, casting Indians as "premodern actors in a modern drama."[89] The railroads capitalized on the growing fascination with the Southwest in their advertising to lure tourists in increasingly great flocks.[90] Through their pioneering "promotional efforts, the passenger departments of the major western railroads helped reimagine the West, transforming it from a desert wasteland to a tourist wonderland, rivaling, if not surpassing, the most famous tourist destinations in Europe."[91]

The Hubbells had a vested interest in the success of tourism. They understood that the popularity of Navajo arts and crafts "stemmed from the tourist trade, which in turn grew out of efforts by scholars, artists . . . authors . . . and tourist-industry executives," and the Hubbells gladly did their part "to feed the growing craze for all things 'primitive.'"[92] The Hubbells were chief among the "network of curio entrepreneurs [who] played a major role in shaping the public's conception of the Southwestern United States," turning their Indian trading businesses into "a publicity vehicle promoting an entire region of the country."[93] But the catalogues and advertisements the traders issued on their own were only a drop in the bucket when compared with the efforts of the passenger departments of railroads and their subsidiaries, most importantly the Fred Harvey Company. Hubbell formed an early partnership with the Harvey Company, making "certain that a wide range of Navajo-made goods were available, accessible, and affordable," and supplying the Indian demonstrators who were the keystone of the company's advertising strategy.[94] In fruitful cooperation with the Harvey Company, the Hubbell Trading Post played a cardinal role in the promotion of Navajo country as a "wonderland of the pictorial in geography and in humanity."[95]

## Hubbell Trading Post and the Fred Harvey Company

The Fred Harvey Company was founded by an English immigrant, Frederick Henry Harvey, who climbed his way out of obscurity working as a restaurant dishwasher to preeminence as "the legendary 'Civilizer of the West,'" the creator of America's first chain of restaurants and railroad hotels.[96] Scholars have characterized Harvey as "the epitome of the Victorian era's self-made man, an entrepreneur who developed a distinctive niche in the growing consumer economy."[97] At a time when the food offered on the new railways of the West was so notoriously abysmal that travelers packed their own meals to avoid eating from the moldy menu, Harvey struck a deal with the Atchison, Topeka, & Santa Fe Railway to provide food service to its passengers. The Santa Fe realized "that travelers could be enticed to see 'primitives' but did not want to be treated like them."[98] Harvey opened his first restaurant at the rail depot in Topeka, Kansas, and the business soon blossomed into a hospitality empire founded on good food, comfort, and polite service. By the time Harvey passed away in 1901, his business included twenty-six restaurants, sixteen hotels with restaurants, and twenty dining cars.[99] His son, Ford Harvey, took over the business, and, with the help of his younger brother Byron, his sister Minnie, and her husband John Frederick Huckel, he led it—and thousands of Americans—"away from its midwestern roots to focus on the Southwest."[100] In the twentieth century, the Fred Harvey Company did more than make travelers comfortable as they endured rail trips across Arizona and New Mexico: it transformed the Southwest into a romantic and desirable destination, the antidote to the overcivilized East.

In 1887, Herman Schweizer, a German immigrant, began managing the Harvey lunch room in Coolidge, New Mexico, when he was only 16 years old. Like Hubbell, Schweizer was a young adventurer who had traveled around the West on his own as a young boy. He began buying Navajo jewelry and blankets and selling them to travelers. "In his free time, he rode horseback across the adjacent reservation lands and became acquainted with local people, Native American craftsmen, and Anglo traders," creating a network of friendships and mastering "the art of intriguing train travelers with Native American arts and crafts."[101] Schweizer's work came to the attention of Minnie Harvey Huckel, who had proposed the idea of integrating an ethnographic museum and curio shop into the design of the Fred Harvey Company's new Southwestern-themed Alvarado Hotel in Albuquerque. Minnie had cultivated an interest in the Southwest and become "an ardent student and discriminating collector of Native American arts and crafts."[102] She suggested putting Schweizer in charge of the museum, and together, Schweizer, Minnie, and Huckel formed the new Fred Harvey Indian Department and "established The Alvarado Hotel complex as the heart of the Southwest in the minds of tourists."[103] When the hotel opened in 1902, tourists stepped off the train in Albuquerque into a passageway that led directly to the hotel, with impressive architecture evoking both Pueblo and Spanish heritage, by way of the Indian Building. Inside, tourists encountered a museum and gift shop filled with "the finest old Navajo blankets ever woven," and Indian artisans, "undisturbed by the eager gaze of the tourist," demonstrating their techniques and skills.[104] It was through Schweizer's contacts on the reservation among Indians and traders—among them Hubbell—that the Fred Harvey Company was able to secure both goods and demonstrators.[105]

J. L. began selling blankets and curios to Schweizer and the Fred Harvey Company around the turn of the century, and when Lorenzo, Jr., took over Keams Canyon, he assumed Thomas Keam's role as the Fred Harvey Company's supplier of Hopi goods.[106] During the decades-long business relationship, J. L. "supplied the Harvey Company with more Native art and craftwork than any other single source," his access to the best blankets and curios available making him "nearly indispensable to the Harvey staff working in the Southwest."[107] Huge amounts of the Hubbells' blanket inventory went to the Fred Harvey Company. J. L. told Schweizer in 1902 that he "would like to give you the first show at all the good Bkts that I get. . . . When I do not send them to you, and sell them to some one else I feel almost like I have not treated you right. . . . I will have to acknowledge that so far you have been my best customer and will do anything in reason to please you."[108] Some years, in fact, Hubbell could not scrape together enough blankets to sell to his other buyers by the time he finished selling them to the Harvey Company, which was also his largest wholesale account for Navajo silver and jewelry.[109]

Though it lasted for half a century, the relationship between Hubbell Trading Post and the Harvey Company was not always rosy. J. L.'s habitually shoddy paperwork led him into a long series of conflicts with the Harvey Company's accounting department, which demanded itemized invoices that J. L. customarily ignored or forgot. But Schweizer realized how critical J. L. was to the success of the company's operations in the Southwest, and "when Ford pressured them to drop Hubbell as a supplier . . . Schweizer went to great lengths to smooth things over so they could continue to work with him."[110] Dorothy Hubbell remembered Schweizer as "a very friendly person who was all business. . . . He seemed to be very knowledgeable as to rugs," she said, "and he'd know what a good rug was."[111] Though J. L. was "very fond of Mr. Schweizer," the balding German was one of his toughest customers.[112] "Repeatedly, he rejected half a lot of jewelry or blankets, reasoning that the quality was poor and he would not stock poor quality

J. L. buying blankets from a Navajo weaver. Courtesy of the National Park Service, HUTR 02165.

merchandise in Harvey establishments. His letters were critical and to the point."[113] He complained when J. L.'s prices were higher than other traders', or when the sizes, patterns, or colors did not suit him.[114] But by the same token, Schweizer considered his business relationship with Hubbell "really more like a partnership than merely the question of buying goods, and I have always considered Mr. Hubbell part of the family."[115] Although he complained, he bought J. L.'s rugs, even when they cost more than his competitors'. As he explained it to Lorenzo, Jr., "[O]ur arrangement was to mutual advantage. . . . Many times I could have bought blankets for a great deal less, but I gave your father the preference as he was depending on me the same as I was depending on him when the market was short."[116] His loyalty was difficult to maintain when the Hubbells' business slowed and the family lacked the cash to buy rugs, and misunderstandings abounded in a business relationship complicated by friendship, with Schweizer as much as it ever did with Cotton. On one occasion, the hot-headed Forrest complained to Lorenzo that when he saw Schweizer in California, Schweizer "never came near me. He shows the kind of bird he is. We should let him go to ——. He will buy nothing from us that he can get elsewhere. . . . I feel like giving him a dam good cussing the next time I do see him."[117] Lorenzo, Jr., however, like his father, was a bit steadier and learned to roll with Schweizer's criticisms, and the relationship between the Fred Harvey Company and the Hubbell Trading Post continued well after J. L.'s death.[118]

## *The Harvey Company and Navajo Demonstrators*

The Hubbells supplied the Harvey Company not only with blankets and curios, but with a steady stream of Navajo and Hopi demonstrators to enchant and entice tourists at the Alvarado Hotel in Albuquerque, the La Fonda Hotel in Santa Fe, and the Hopi House at the El Tovar Hotel on the south rim of the Grand Canyon. Schweizer and Huckel painstakingly created idyllic scenes of domestic and artistic life at their destinations, populating mock pueblos and hogans with silversmiths, weavers, and picturesque children, while carefully concealing any signs that the Navajos were anything but a pure and primitive society.[119] Tourists fresh off the train watched the demonstrators with keen interest, snapping photographs and buying their wares, convinced that here at last was the elusive authenticity they had been searching for.

The Fred Harvey Company evidently paid the demonstrators well enough to gain the approval of the Indian Agency and to persuade artisans and their families to leave home for months at a stretch, but problems inevitably arose when demonstrators wanted to go home for cultural "reasons that mystified the Harvey people."[120] After all, it would not do "to have Albuquerque out of Indians" and tourists "going to the Hopi House . . . asking where the Hopi Indians are."[121] Demonstrators went home for any number of reasons—"to plant their corn, check in with family and friends, attend ceremonies, take care of business, because they just wanted to, or, in the case of one man called the 'Old Silversmith,' because 'people are bothering too much trying to take his picture'"—and the Harvey Company constantly scrambled to keep its sites populated with demonstrators.[122] On one occasion in 1905, when only two Navajos remained at the Grand Canyon, Schweizer begged J. L. to "get some Indians to the Canyon at once."[123]

Huckel and Schweizer wrote of the demonstrators in the same tone they used to discuss blankets—ordering silversmiths, "squaws," and children in the same manner they might order blankets in grey or red, and sending back the "unsatisfactory" ones as they might send back a blanket too loosely woven.[124] When a Navajo silversmith named Taos caused some trouble for Huckel by selling his wares to other Indians and directly to tourists in Albuquerque, threatening the Harvey Company's monopoly on Indian-made products, Huckel sent him home. He asked Hubbell to send him a replacement, as if J. L. might have a spare lying about the house somewhere. "A silversmith is quite an attraction, and . . . I would like to have another," Huckel wrote.[125] The process of finding Indians who met the Harvey Company's expectations and who could leave their homes for long periods of time, as well as explaining to them the rules and living arrangements they would encounter, was very human and personal, however, and the Hubbells under took it with care, if not altruism. While they were away from their homes, the demonstrators relied on J. L. to send supplies, check on their families, and settle disputes. Huckel realized that he alone could not convince the Indians to come work for him, despite the pay, and even Lorenzo, Jr., when he was a young trader in his first few years at Keams Canyon, struggled to persuade the Hopis to leave their crops without the added influence of his father.[126] Martha Blue states that "[i]t was only J. L.'s standing and quarter of a century in the Navajo and Hopi communities that enabled the Fred Harvey Company to carry off such a vast and regular display of Navajos and Hopis."[127]

The arrangement between the Fred Harvey Company and the Hubbell Trading Post proved mutually beneficial. J. L. supplied demonstrators, and in return billed the Harvey Company for the provisions and wool he supplied them, but the greatest payment came in the form of a vastly expanded market for Native products.[128] Both companies, however, harbored motives beyond profit. Huckel was convinced that the demonstrations benefited not only the Santa Fe Railway, the tourists, and both companies' curio businesses, but also the Hopi and Navajo craftspeople by creating a market for their goods; and indeed, many Indian artisans who would later achieve fame worked at some point for the Fred Harvey Company, including San Ildefonso Pueblo potter Maria Martinez and her husband Julian, Hopi-Tewa potter Nampeyo, and Navajo weaver Elle of Ganado.[129] And as Blue states, "These people, and their extended families, were closer to J. L.'s heart than were the fortunes of the Fred Harvey Company."[130]

## Marketing Indians at Fairs, Exhibitions, and Museums

In promoting the Southwest by populating mock villages with Indian craftspeople, the Harvey Company followed tried and true techniques first developed at the spectacularly popular world's fairs, beginning with London's 1851 Crystal Palace Exhibition.[131] As Nancy Parezo and Don Fowler write, "From then until 1915 world's fairs sprang up like mushrooms to celebrate the heyday of European and American industrialism and imperialism. In Europe international exhibitions became grandiose stages on which nations bragged about their industrial, financial, technical, intellectual, social, and scientific 'progress,' their ability to extract raw materials from their colonies, and their success in 'civilizing' their colonial subjects."[132] By the late nineteenth century, "displayed people, billed as 'savages' from Africa or Polynesia, who could be gawked at for a fee" had become a mainstay of world's fairs, and visitors thronged by the thousands to ogle sideshows and anthropological displays that reinforced "stereotypical images of colonized 'native' peoples."[133] As the world's fair tradition blossomed in the United States in the 1880s and 1890s, Native Americans were counted among the "exotic" peoples of the world, and a "long line of Southwestern Indians [found] themselves willingly or unwilling on exhibit."[134]

As well-known suppliers of Indian demonstrators, the Hubbells played roles ranging from negligible to pivotal in providing Navajos and Hopis and their products to world's fairs, traveling exhibitions, and museum collections. Before the twentieth century, J. L.'s influence was small; he played only a minor role in the hugely influential 1893 Chicago World's Columbian Exposition, popularly known as the Chicago World's Fair, especially compared to other Indian traders, such as Thomas Keam and the Wetherills, who supplied major anthropological exhibits. While Arizona's various economic and political interests squabbled over how best to present their territory to the expectant eyes of the world, J. L. was busy running for the territorial legislature, his attention bent on passing water rights legislation that would help him secure title to his homestead. His involvement at the Chicago World's Fair seemed almost an afterthought. The trader had begun carting loads of blankets around with him for display, sale, and promotion in his political travels as early as 1890, and when it came time to send the Arizona exhibits to Chicago in early 1893, he happened to have with him in Phoenix a load of seven suitable Navajo blankets.[135] The *Arizona Weekly Republican* supposed that "Mr. Hubbell will either take them to the world's fair or send them as part of the Arizona exhibit."[136] Whether he did so is a matter of speculation, but his blankets may well have been among the "unique exhibition of native crafts and artwork" put together by the Arizona lady managers in the Women's Building, or among those displayed at several anthropology exhibits featuring Navajo demonstrators living in "authentic" Indian villages.[137] At the Chicago World's Fair, dazzled by spectacles of every kind, many Americans encountered their first "real" Navajo weaver "toiling at her rude loom and the Navajo girl twisting wool on the rude hand-spindle as she watches her sheep."[138]

Ten years later, St. Louis commemorated the one hundredth anniversary of Thomas Jefferson's three-cents-an-acre real estate deal at the 1904 Louisiana Purchase Exposition. Glowing from the success of the Indian Building at the newly opened Alvarado in Albuquerque, the Fred Harvey Company created an award-winning exhibit of Indian arts and crafts at the request of the Territory of New Mexico, further fueling consumers' desire to purchase Indian curios in "ethnology-crazed America."[139] Members of the exhibit team traveled to the Hopi pueblos and Canyon de Chelly in November 1903 on a collecting trip, their route taking them through Ganado on the way home.[140] With J. L.'s stock of Navajo blankets and curios piled up in the rug room and adorning the walls of his home, and with his relationship with the Fred Harvey Company already well established, it seems likely that they purchased at least some of the objects in the Harvey Company's eye-catching display from Hubbell. But J. L. was also involved more directly. Indian Exhibit Superintendent Samuel M. McCowan asked him to supply blankets for the exposition's anthropology displays, and demonstrators to staff his "thorough, realistic Navaho exhibit of home life and native industries."[141] He asked J. L. to send a family of silversmiths and weavers, explaining, "They can work a few hours each day, or all day, as they desire. Booths are prepared in this building for these workers, and besides the Navahos we will have Pueblo pottery makers, Pima, Apache and other basket workers, Sioux stone workers, Chippewa bead workers, etc., etc. There will be some two or three hundred old Indians from various tribes in the country. These

Navajo demonstrators Jim Smith, Little Singer, Hastiin Gani's wife, Elizabeth Smith, and Charley Smith in front of a large loom, c. 1936. Courtesy of the National Park Service, HUTR 09476.

Indians, of course, will all live in realistic fashion and in homes as near like their native homes as it is possible to construct for them."[142] McCowan invited Hubbell to come along with the Navajos to the fair, expenses paid, and J. L. may well have joined the nineteen million Americans who visited the Louisiana Purchase Exposition. Decades later, his daughter-in-law Dorothy remembered hearing the old trader talk about the fair as one of the first places he had exhibited Indian products.[143]

Southwestern Indians again went to the fair in 1915 when San Diego and San Francisco—neither city willing to grant the honor of hosting to the other—celebrated the opening of the Panama Canal with the Panama–California Exposition and the Panama–Pacific International Exhibition. The Fred Harvey Company seized the opportunity to advertise the Southwest with glee, creating elaborate exhibits at both fairs with replica pueblos, hogans, and panoramas of the Grand Canyon "assembled from adobe on location, cholla, cactus, sagebrush, and yucca, as well as willow, cedar posts, and sandstone imported from Arizona and New Mexico."[144] Schweizer began coordinating Indian demonstrators with J. L. in 1914, asking the trader to find ten families to staff the California exhibits on top of the usual rotation of demonstrators at Harvey hotels.[145] The proposition became even more complicated when Schweizer asked Hubbell to supply ponies, burros, sheep, and goats to complete the scene. Hubbell dragged himself out of his sickbed in a Christmas blizzard in order to ensure that Schweizer's livestock arrived on time, an act of dedication that left a lasting impression.[146] The Fred Harvey Company made a lot of money selling curios at the fair, and the Santa Fe Railway happily cashed in on fares as tourists flocked to San Diego and San Francisco—and from thence, tantalized by glimpses of the staged Southwest, into Arizona and New Mexico for the real thing.

It seemed that wherever tourists found Navajos on display in the early twentieth century, the Hubbells were responsible. They supplied three families of Indians for a Fred Harvey exhibit in Chicago's Coliseum in 1909, a handful more to one of his guests who wanted to include Navajos in a small exhibition in Columbus, Ohio, in 1919, and even a few for Hollywood actor Harry Carey's California ranch.[147] The Hubbells sent exhibits or Indian craftspeople to at least two other world's fairs—the Century of Progress Exposition in Chicago in 1933 and the unofficial Fort Worth Frontier Centennial Exposition in 1936.[148]

Roman and Lorenzo, Jr., were just as enthusiastic about exhibiting Indian products as their father was. Lorenzo amassed a significant collection of Hopi products during his life as a trader, which he lent freely for exhibits. He sent Hopi and Navajo curios to the National Educational Association in Washington, DC, in 1924; to the Carson Indian Agency in Nevada in 1927; and to Mary-Russell Ferrell Colton's Hopi Craftsmen Exhibition in 1930.[149] Lorenzo felt a commitment to maintaining high-quality craftsmanship and combatting commercial knock-offs, and many of the exhibits to which he contributed aimed to do just that. He supported the American Federation of Arts' traveling Indian Arts and Crafts exhibit, a "selected group of articles in which standards of native craftsmanship are being maintained," which toured the country from 1931 to 1934.[150] Lorenzo thought the American Federation of Arts was "doing wonderful work," and hoped "that the

American people will be aroused to a greater interest in Indian Arts."[151] The same commitment led to his later involvement with the government's Indian Arts and Crafts Board.[152] Roman, too, felt committed to preserving Indian art, and used his knowledge of and connections with the Navajo artistic community to recommend sand painters and weavers to decorate day schools, community centers, and hospitals with Native arts and crafts for the government's Public Works of Art project during the Great Depression. When John Collier wrote to ask Roman for a list of artists, Collier admitted that "It is only thru such agencies as yours that we can reach the best artists and craftsmen and establish our contact with this group of Indians."[153]

The Hubbells not only supplied Navajo and Hopi demonstrators and curios to large-scale exhibits far and wide, but also created more than a few exhibits of their own in local and state fairs. Because of his political connections, J. L. was appointed to the Board of Fair Commissioners as the representative for Apache County in 1905 for Arizona's first annual Territorial Fair, and he served as Apache County Fair Commissioner for the first Arizona State Fair in 1912, too.[154] His early involvement established a family tradition. The Hubbells always set up a booth with "especially nice things, maybe special pottery and baskets and such," winning first prize for their exhibit in 1924.[155] They were also involved heavily in the Gallup Inter-Tribal Indian Ceremonial Association, which held "a stupendous Indian Pageant" and exposition yearly to "bring the Indians of New Mexico and Arizona before the public so that their products, crafts, and work may . . . prove to the people back east that this part of the United States contains places of greater scenic and historical interest than any other spot in the world."[156] The Inter-Tribal Indian Ceremonial grew over the years to become a vastly popular event, billed as "the most fascinating event in America," and the Hubbells participated year after year.[157] They also exhibited at the Navajo Tribal Fair, sent exhibits to chambers of commerce in multiple Arizona counties, and created parade floats in the backs of freight trucks displaying baskets, rugs, and pottery.[158]

The Hubbells helped take the show on the road in 1948 when Roman joined a group of Navajos and Hopis in flying across the country to "tell the people of the East about our State," and to "show the largest and most sensational exhibit" at the International Travel and Vacation Exhibition in New York City's Grand Central Station.[159] The Arizona Unlimited exhibit launched with an "all night pow-wow" in Winslow before the Indian demonstrators, Roman, and the other Arizona boosters boarded a plane for New York with stops in Oklahoma City, Chicago, Pittsburgh, and Washington, DC.[160] The promoters, dressed in western clothes, disembarked for ceremonies, meeting mayors and bearing gifts of boxed desert cacti and citrus fruit and handing out thousands of copies of *Arizona Highways* magazine. At Grand Central in New York, they built a replica Indian trading post out of old lumber, complete with shelves, counter, and pawn racks, while Roman displayed the family's prized "world's largest Navajo rug."[161] The Navajos—a silversmith, a sand painter, a medicine man, a chanter, and a weaver—met New York City mayor William O'Dwyer, toured an exhibit of William R. Leigh's paintings of American Indians, and gazed out upon the New York City skyline.[162] The promoters tempted New Yorkers with advertisements in the *New York Times*, on the radio, and even on television. In the end, Angus Macpherson, one of the event's organizers, thanked Roman for his personal and financial sacrifice, and told him that "[t]he exhibit of the Lorenzo Hubbell Company and the Winslow Chamber of Commerce was the feature of the travel show and the focal attraction of our trip across the country."[163]

During the time world's fairs and the railways began using Navajo and Hopi demonstrators to sell curios and the Southwest as a tourist destination, museums also began collecting the products of the "vanishing Indians," and the Hubbells contributed to some of the greatest museum collections in the country. Some of their contributions were through the Fred Harvey Company and other dealers who bought curios from the Hubbells and then sold or donated them to museums.[164] But the Hubbells also directly provided assistance to museum anthropologists on collecting trips to Navajo country, and donated or sold curios to several museum collections.[165] Between 1902 and 1910, for example, J. L. provided blankets and curios to Stewart Culin, curator of Ethnology at the Brooklyn Institute of Arts and Sciences—today the Brooklyn Museum.[166] J. L. arranged Culin's first collecting trip to the Navajo Reservation, on which the curator "collected a wide array of Indian-made goods—including prayer sticks, buckskin costumes, jewelry, and rugs—which he used in a display of 'traditional' Indian culture in the Brooklyn Museum."[167] J. L. contributed twenty ceremonial masks to the Field Museum of Natural History in 1910, and Lorenzo, Jr., later assisted bronze sculptor Malvina Hoffman in "gathering types" for her "Hall of the Races of Mankind" exhibit at the Field Museum.[168] J. L. sold a collection of ancient pottery he scavenged from the ruins at Canyon de Chelly and elsewhere to George G. Heye, a wealthy collector who had one of the best private ethnology and archaeology collections in the United States.[169] Heye's collection would later become the core of the National Museum of the American Indian.[170] All across the country, visitors to America's new scientific museums looked at tableaus of Navajo and Hopi life and displays of their products enshrined in glass cases. In many cases, they gazed upon objects that had passed from the hands of their makers to the Hubbells before finally coming to rest in the museums' marble halls. As Joseph Emerson Smith declared, "The most representative and valuable collections of baskets, pottery, rugs, blankets, and other Indian handcraft in the Smithsonian Institution, in Washington, and at the Brooklyn Museum, were presented by Lorenzo Hubbell. Objects beyond price, since they were the work of the old people and are no longer made, are included in these donations, the cream of years of collecting."[171]

## "The Most Hospitable Man in the World"

The Hubbells played yet another role in the development of tourism in northeastern Arizona—as hosts and guides, first to the artists and scientists who popularized Navajo country, and then to the tourists who came in their wake. In the early twentieth century, tourism and the curio trade both entered a golden age, and tourists began to ramble over the desert hills and forest plateaus in ever greater numbers. In 1895, photographer Adam Clark Vroman watched the Hopi Snake Dance in the company of some sixty other Euro-Americans; thirty years later, writer D. H. Lawrence and arts patron Mabel Dodge Luhan traveled to Hotevilla to witness the same ceremony, and found the Hopi village besieged by eight hundred cars and three thousand tourists.[172] In the days when the Navajo Reservation was a fortress protected by near-impassable roads, J. L. absolutely delighted in playing the gracious host to the intrepid visitors who came to his door. They slept in his spare rooms and guest hogans, and when those spaces filled, on piles of Navajo blankets on the floor of his home and even on the trading post counters.[173] "In a region known for its easy hospitality, the Hubbell home at Ganado became famous as a free haven for literally hundreds of visitors, from lonely lost souls of no rank or name to President Theodore Roosevelt" and everyone in between.[174] And when the automobile came rumbling and sputtering into the Navajo Southwest, Roman put on his cowboy hat and cheerfully played tour guide while Lorenzo, Jr., sold bowls of steaming stew to Snake Dance pilgrims and opened his doors to visitors at Oraibi. His guests remembered J. L. Hubbell as "the most hospitable man in the world," and his sons were not far behind him.[175]

CHAPTER SEVEN

# "Seekers of Beauty" and "Adventures into the Buried Long Ago"

*Visitors to the Post*

In the summer of 1899, American writer Hamlin Garland journeyed into Navajo country in search of two things: literary inspiration and Indian curios for his bride-to-be, Zulime Taft. Having been deemed too much underfoot of the wedding plans and chased out of Chicago by Zulime and her sister, Garland traveled west, leaving behind the smoke-belching train in Gallup and carrying on by horseback to the Navajo Agency at Fort Defiance. There he found a young Navajo to lead him over plateau and valley to his "real objective . . . the home of a famous Indian trader named Hubbell, whose store was known to me as a center of Navajo life."[1] His guide left him a half-day's distance from the trading post, and Garland picked his own meandering way to J. L.'s door, drinking in the bright colors and angled forms of "this strange landscape."[2] As his eyes swept over the cedars and pines and naked valleys, he felt himself caught up in a rush of romanticism. In words that echoed the sentiments of a generation of Americans captivated by the Southwest, he wrote, "As I rode on alone, the peace, the poetry, the suggestive charm of that silent, lonely, radiant land took hold upon me with compelling power. Here in the midst of busy, commonplace America it lay, a section of the Polished Stone Age, retaining the most distinctive customs, songs and dances of the past. Here was a people going about its immemorial pursuits, undisturbed by the railway and the telephone. . . . Late in the afternoon (I loitered luxuriously) I came to the summit of a long ridge which overlooked a broad, curving valley, at the far-away western rim of which a slender line of water gleamed. How beautiful it all was, but how empty!"[3]

Garland dropped down into that lonely valley and rode up to Hubbell's trading post, "a long, low, mud-walled building" where he "was met by the trader, a bush-bearded, middle-aged man with piercing gray eyes and sturdy, upright figure. This was Lorenzo Hubbell, one of the best-known citizens of New Mexico, living here alone, a day's ride from a white settler."[4] J. L., "hairy and spectacled" in his role of Indian trader rather than trimmed and polished in his political guise, welcomed the writer's company gladly, especially since Lina and the children were away in Albuquerque, as they so often were before he finished building the house.[5] Garland and J. L. spent a few long

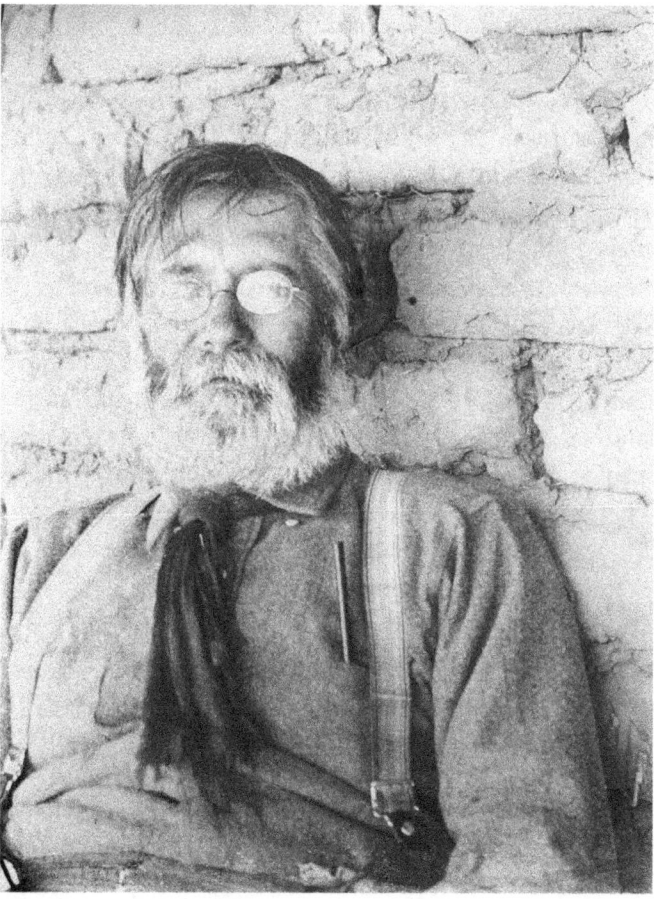

J. L. in his Indian trader guise at age fifty-three. Courtesy of the National Park Service, HUTR 05433.

days in the intimacy of one another's company, the writer scribbling down pages of notes on the trading post and the Navajos, and the trader spinning yarns about his younger, wilder days.[6] When it came time for Garland to depart, J. L. loaded him down with a gift of Hopi jars for Zulime, that Garland might take back to her "some part of the poetry of this land and its people."[7] Then, as quietly as he had come, the writer disappeared down to the trail to Fort Defiance, leaving J. L. to the business of Indian trading and the usual company of his customers and freighters.

Hamlin Garland was one of hundreds of travelers to come to the Navajo Southwest in search of authenticity and a connection to the landscape who found in Hubbell a gracious host and valuable guide. As enthusiasm for all things Indian swept the nation in the late nineteenth and early twentieth centuries, "Anglo-American artists, writers, intellectuals, scholars, archaeologists, and tourists descended, almost locustlike, on the Southwest," and from the late 1880s until his death in 1930, J. L., following in the footsteps of other traders, offered himself as their guide, host, and facilitator.[8] They went anywhere they thought they might find timelessness and drama, and though the whole of the Southwest beckoned them, Canyon de Chelly and the Hopi mesas drew "seekers of beauty and the adventurers into the buried long ago" like a siren's song.[9] As the wave of visitors broke over Navajo country, Hubbell's ranch, once an obscure outpost, became one of the most famous landmarks for weary travelers in Northeastern Arizona, not only because it lay square in the path to two of the region's most popular destinations, but because its proprietor made himself indispensable to visitors.

## *Hospitality and the Hubbell Business*

In a time and a place where travelers sorely needed hospitality, J. L. Hubbell provided it lavishly. If an artist hoped to capture the mystery of Canyon de Chelly, if an anthropologist wished to witness the spectacle of the Hopi Snake Dance, or if a writer desired to dramatize the customs of the "vanishing" Indians, he would face a good deal of hard traveling over rough trails, not to mention cultural barriers he had little hope of overcoming without the help of an experienced intermediary. The railroad spit out its passengers in towns to the south of Navajo country, and decent roads north would be a long time in coming. If there was a sight commoner than sheep and sagebrush in those days, it was a wagon or automobile mired in a muddy wash, and the unfortunate travelers frequently found themselves being dug out by the same bearded, bespectacled man who greeted Garland.[10] In Hubbell, they found a man whose connections with the local Navajo community were paralleled by none. At his home in Ganado they entered a haven of old Spanish hospitality in what was for many of them a rugged wilderness. Paintings covered every inch of wall, Navajo rugs softened the wooden floors, and Hopi baskets hung from the ceiling. J. L.'s home was "a showplace, a well-set stage upon which he could royally entertain guests from all walks of life with food, drink, good conversation, and music."[11] He sat at the head of the dining table that became the symbol of his generosity, surrounded by a museum of Indian curios, with the Navajos themselves camped outside, and supplied an endless array of captivating tales.

J. L.'s guests, it seems, could not help feeling awed in the genial company of the "last patriarch of the Western frontier" who seemed to fit so perfectly all their hopes and expectations of a picturesque Indian trader.[12] His hospitality appealed to their romantic visions of Hispanic culture. One visitor remarked that travelers could find at Hubbell Trading Post "a type of the old-time baronial Spanish hospitality, when no door was locked and every comer was welcomed to the festive board, and if you expressed admiration for a jewel, or silver-work, or old mantilla, it was presented to you by the lord of the manor with the simple and absolutely sincere words, 'It is yours.'"[13] J. L. often boasted that he "never charged anyone for a meal or a night's lodging," even though the hordes of visitors kept a Navajo cook, a Mexican baker, and two Hopi housemaids busy to the tune of "tens of thousands of dollars" over the years.[14] Many of his guests speculated that his generosity was at the root of his financial woes later in his life, but that his pride prevented him from accepting a dime in payment. "In fact," wrote author Agnes C. Laut, "if you offered money for the kindness you received, it would be regarded as an insult."[15] J. L., who wanted not only to *be* a generous man, but to be *known* as one, told Dane Coolidge a story that would become a favorite of writers for illustrating the trader's hospitality—and its limits:

> His great adobe house was open to all who came, and he told me that only once in forty years had he turned a man away from his door. That was when an Englishman, after being told that he was welcome and to be sure and stay longer the next time, had left two dollars on the bureau of his room, in payment for what he had received. That night in a terrible

storm there was a knock at the door. It was the Englishman, who had been turned back by a devastating flood, but J. L. Hubbell closed his door.

"No," he said. "You have insulted me, sir, by daring to offer to pay me." He drove him out into the storm and that was the last of him.[16]

Although he prided himself on never charging his guests for food or lodging, Hubbell gladly accepted their curio business. The artist Maynard Dixon reported that when he offered payment for his hospitality, Hubbell answered, "No, sir, not a cent. I don't run a hotel. I'm in the blanket business. I'm the mildest mannered man that ever scuttled a ship or cut a throat. If you want to spend your money just come over in the blanket room with me and watch me knock your eye out."[17] The trader also had no objection to making money renting wagons, horses, automobiles, and guides to travelers. Hubbell did not distinguish between famous politicians and traveling salesmen around his democratic table, but he did distinguish between friends (or friends-of-friends) and gawking, green tourists. The former he personally conducted around Navajo country, often on his own dime, and the latter he charged up to thirty dollars a day for a wagon and team or a car and a guide.[18]

Perhaps more valuable than any monetary windfall Hubbell collected from the Navajo country tourism boom were the rewards of friendship and fame. Every visitor was a prize to him; he was widely read and enjoyed the company of intelligent and adventurous guests. He doubly treasured his visitors who wielded influence. He counted among his guests the Southwest's leading anthropologists and scientists, among them Adolph Bandelier and Byron Cummings; a long list of state and national politicians from Carl Hayden to John Collier to Theodore Roosevelt; writers from every corner of the country, including western novelists Zane Grey and Dane Coolidge; tireless promoters of the Southwest like Charles F. Lummis and George Wharton James; and artists, among them E. A. Burbank, Maynard Dixon, and Edward S. Curtis, who left with him an impressive collection of paintings, drawings, and photographs.[19] Many of the Southwest's most influential people at one time or another sheltered under Hubbell's roof, and though his impact on their lives and work is not always easy to gauge, many of them credited him with the success of their projects.

The friendship of such luminaries may have been payment enough for J. L., but these visitors rewarded him further by turning him into the most famous trader on the reservation, thanking him for his assistance and retelling his fabulous stories in articles, novels, and hometown newspapers. When Hamlin Garland left Arizona he had gotten from Hubbell and the trading post exactly what he had come for, and more. Within a year of his departure, he published two short stories of Navajo life based on his notes, and in 1902, he added to that a story dramatizing J. L.'s glory days as sheriff of Apache County in a *McClure's Magazine* article entitled "Delmar of Pima."[20] Sitting an evening by his fireplace, J. L. must have felt a flush of pleasure to read about the half-Spanish "Delmar" defeating the oppressive cowmen with nothing more deadly than a "keen, hawk-like stare" and his wits.[21] As the years went by, the busy writer regularly sent his old host autographed copies of more than a half-dozen of his books, and J. L. slid them onto shelves crowded with other works bearing signatures and personal inscriptions, each one representing a visit, a friendship, a debt repaid in glowing praise. With every visitor who slept under the solid wood beams of his roof, the legend of J. L. Hubbell grew. He played well the role of host that earned him the honorific "Don Lorenzo," assured that his "reputation for princely hospitality was no less distinctive than was his fame as an Indian trader."[22]

## Anthropologists among the Navajos

Among the earliest of the Anglo intellectuals to venture into Navajo country were anthropologists and archaeologists. As soon as the railroad reached New Mexico and Arizona in the 1880s, they converged on the Southwest with cameras and pencils poised, "determined to salvage information about a culture that many Americans believed would disappear through the 'progress' of civilization."[23] Descriptions of ancient ruins and modern Native Americans alike (usually brief and disparaging) had trickled out in the published reports of military expeditions for decades, but not until the anthropological disciplines began to develop, rising on the same tide as America's museums and world's fairs, did the Southwest become a paradise for scientists.[24] Native Americans held a special fascination for anthropologists, who at the time believed that all cultures the world over were separated merely by a degree of civilization, and that in so-called "primitive" cultures they could behold previous incarnations of their own. They held absolute faith in the power of science as "an agent of social reform" and trusted that "by observing civilization at earlier stages of its evolution they could understand the nature of progress and use this knowledge to further the nation's progress" and solve, once and for all, the perennial "Indian problem."[25] The Native Americans of the Southwest intrigued them most particularly, for "the combination of an open, unspoiled landscape and a settled, agrarian, highly developed Native American population made for a timeless, edenic image that contrasted sharply with the unhealthy, aggressive, industrial culture of the eastern and midwestern United States. As such, the region became the focus of economic and aesthetic as well as anthropological interest—places and peoples to be discovered, enjoyed, exploited, marketed, represented, and studied."[26]

As anthropologists and archaeologists came to the Navajo Southwest, Indian traders, isolated as they were, sometimes hundreds of miles from the government agent and the nearest railroad station, "became the only educated, reliable source of information on the region."[27] Visiting scientists depended upon them heavily as guides, interpreters, provisioners, and hosts.[28] Traders, standing with one foot in the white world and one foot in the Indian world, introduced scientists to their indigenous informants and smoothed the way for inquisitive scholars to quietly invade Indian lives, sometimes even gaining access to ceremonies that would otherwise be forbidden them.[29] Hubbell's friend Thomas Keam, with his trading post ideally located near the Hopi mesas, was the first Indian trader to play a critical role in fostering Southwestern anthropology, ushering pioneering soldier–anthropologist John Gregory Bourke to the Snake Dance in 1881, and thereafter working closely with the Southwest's anthropological luminaries.[30] He helped so many scientists gain access to the Hopis that "by the mid-1880s Keams Canyon had become the nominal field headquarters for the Bureau of Ethnology scientists working in northeastern Arizona."[31]

Until the 1890s, Hubbell's obligations in St. Johns prevented him from cultivating the close relationships with visiting scientists that Keam enjoyed. Even then, Ganado, unlike Keams Canyon, had no spectacular ruins or canyons just beyond its doorstep, making it less useful as a base of operations, but that did not prevent J. L. from becoming the scientists' friend and benefactor. And after Keam sold his trading post to the Hubbells in 1902, Lorenzo, Jr., assumed Keam's role as intermediary to the Hopis and facilitator of tourism to the increasingly popular Snake Dance, further tightening the bonds between the Hubbell name and Navajo country. "Practically

Stewart Culin, anthropologist from the Brooklyn Museum, poses in front of a Navajo rug. Courtesy of the National Park Service, HUTR 05312.

every scientist who has delved into the prehistoric life in Colorado, New Mexico, and Arizona has been Lorenzo Hubbell's guest," newspaper man Joseph Emerson Smith later wrote. "The late Dr. J. Walter Fewkes and Dr. Stewart Culin, the latter curator of the Brooklyn museum; Dr. Sylvanus G. Morley, now having charge of the extensive Chichen Itza restorations, in Mexico; Dr. Edgar L. Hewett, were lifelong friends," while "the immortal Adolf Bandelier, ragged and bearded, a small gray-brown burro carrying his water jugs, blankets and provisions, was a frequent guest while wandering from pueblo to pueblo during his years of studying and writing about the southwestern Indians."[32] Hubbell made himself indispensable by outfitting their expeditions with wagons, supplies, guides, and laborers and by arranging meetings with key figures in the Navajo community, taking real pleasure in personally showing visitors around the land he called home.[33]

Whatever expense of time or money it may have cost the Hubbell family to play host, J. L. deemed it worthwhile. In facilitating the work of scientists as they collected specimens for museums, Hubbell and the other traders knew they were stimulating the commercial market for Indian curios.[34] Playing host also gave the Hubbells ample opportunity to bend the ears of scientists and prominent policy makers about issues affecting the Navajos. To that end, J. L. took a personal interest in anthropology, archaeology, and ethnography, filling his shelves with the publications of his friends and investing in memberships to the American Anthropological Association and other scholarly organizations headed by his guests. What's more, J. L.'s scientist friends helped spread his fame as an Indian trader and as a man who could show a traveler in Navajo country the best and most intimate look into Indian life. They lauded him in their reports and among their friends, expanding his network of visitors still further. Frank M. Palmer, director of the Southwest Society, articulated the feelings of many a scientist upon experiencing the hospitality of J. L. He attributed the success of his 1906 expedition to Canyon de Chelly

> to the courtesy and public spirit of the last patriarch of the Western frontier, Don Lorenzo Hubbell. The sudden hyphenation between the Age of Stone and the Age of Electricity brought out extraordinary types. It was a wonderful opportunity, but it took men of depth and breadth and elasticity to meet it. It found such men. The weaklings who tried, sank. The strong men who tried—they grew giants. Of what a man can do in this curious relation, as an intermediary between the new and the old,

between the patriarchal and the commercial, I have never known so extraordinary an example. Every man who has stood sentry there for twenty years is worth knowing, worth earning for a friend: but I believe not one of these gray pioneers will grudge my estimate of Don Lorenzo as their Dean. Every scientist, artist, writer, globe-trotter, Indian or tramp that ever passed his way is his particular debtor.[35]

Although J. L. was not as close to the region's most alluring attractions as some other traders were, he still became a gateway, his name the token that granted outsiders entry into Navajo life.

## *A Presidential Guest and Other Political Visitors*

Among the Hubbells' friends were eastern scientist Dr. Harold S. Colton and his artist wife, Mary-Russell Ferrell Colton. J. L. made arrangements in 1913 for the couple to make a trip to see Canyon de Chelly, Navajo country, and the Snake Dance. The trip "left an indelible impression on Harold and Mary-Russell," who sketched and photographed and bought souvenirs, becoming entranced with the place, like so many others had.[36] Later, when he and his wife had returned to the east, Harold would write to J. L., "Arizona you see is always before us."[37] The first trip led to many more, and finally to the Coltons' decision to move to Flagstaff, where they co-founded the Museum of Northern Arizona and launched the Hopi Craftsman Exhibition. But in 1913, they were only two more pilgrims in a sea of visitors, and they had either the great misfortune or the great pleasure of arriving in Ganado at the same time as one of J. L.'s most illustrious guests, one who commanded enough respect to spur J. L. into supplying *his* party with the horses and equipment he had set aside for the Coltons, leaving the doctor and the artist "with an improvised and inferior set. . . . The price of anonymity!"[38]

J. L. seemed to delight in nothing more than luring his political friends to Navajo country where he could entertain them royally at Ganado and perhaps sway them on policy issues. He used his connections freely to promote the Navajos' cause, especially when that cause aligned with his own, though his views on Indian Affairs were a quixotic blend of nineteenth century paternalism and real friendship.[39] When historian Frank McNitt asked Dorothy Hubbell who among the politicians had been to the Ganado trading post, she exclaimed, "All of them! All of them! During his campaign time they all came . . . Democrats and Republicans."[40] Among the Hubbell family's guests were dozens of Arizona politicians, including senators Ralph Cameron and Carl Hayden, as well as Arizona's first governor, George W. P. Hunt. Prominent among the Hubbells' friends at the national level were John Collier of the Bureau of Indian Affairs and Harold Ickes, the Secretary of the Interior.

But the crowning jewel in J. L.'s collection of political guests was President Theodore Roosevelt. J. L. claimed to have "been personally acquainted with every president from Grover Cleveland to Warren G. Harding" and that "Theodore Roosevelt was one of my best friends."[41] But his acquaintance with the other men of the Oval Office was tenuous, and Roosevelt was the only one he succeeded in bringing under his roof.[42] J. L. and Roosevelt disagreed on many political points, most notably Roosevelt's disastrous split of the Republican Party. When Roosevelt challenged Taft, J. L. told Charles Lummis that he would support Roosevelt if he should win the Republican nomination, but that he believed it would be "one of those things that I would have to account for in the next world to my detriment if it was not for the fact that in choosing between him and a democrat the Lord himself may forgive me the smaller sin for having failed to commit the bigger one."[43] Roosevelt lost the election, but because of the split vote, so did Taft, and J. L. must have harbored a smoldering resentment toward Roosevelt for handing the presidency to a Democrat.

But J. L. put aside any differences when, in May 1913, he received a letter from Nicholas Roosevelt, an old friend and Theodore Roosevelt's cousin. "The time has come," Nicholas wrote, that "Colonel Roosevelt is at last definitely coming out to the Snake Dance, and is in fact going to make an extended tour of Arizona. . . . I am writing you this as I wish to know whether you are willing to bury political differences, and if you want to outfit us with a wagon and team, and a man to drive it who is willing to cook."[44] The chance of having a presidential guest was too great an opportunity for J. L. to hold on to any political grudges, and he fired off a response to Nicholas with outfitting costs and itinerary suggestions, with Ganado, of course, a key destination. By summer, the former president and his party, including Roosevelt's two sons, Archie and Quentin, were hunting on the north rim of the Grand Canyon, with Navajo country their next stop. In early August, Hubbell sent two wagons and drivers—one of them his own Navajo cook, Loco—to meet the party at Lee's Ferry and drive them across the reservation, with as many interesting stops along the way as he could engineer, to the Hopi village of Walpi, where the Snake Dance would be held. J. L. joined them there, at last "meeting Colonel Roosevelt man to man."[45]

J. L. used all his influence among the Hopis to give Roosevelt a princely time, even gaining his guest admittance into sacred ceremonies normally off limits to tourists. Roosevelt, a world traveler and prolific writer, watched and listened eagerly that he might publish an account in *The Outlook* later that year.[46] He wrote, "Thanks to Mr. Hubbell, and to the fact that I was an ex-President, we were admitted to the sacred kiva—the one-roomed temple-house which I had already visited—while the snake priests performed the ceremony of washing the snakes. Very few white men have ever seen this ceremony. The sight was the most interesting of our entire trip."[47]

White visitors packed the streets and roofs of Walpi, craning their necks to see the Snake Dance and catch a glimpse of Roosevelt. For "the news, 'Roosevelt is coming,' seemed to flash across the desert in all directions. It tingled in our ears with the fresh arrival of every white visitor speeding in from the nearest railway station to combine a glimpse of the great ex-President with the sight of the Hopi ceremony."[48] J. L. and Roosevelt sat together on the ground to watch the dance, their backs against an adobe wall, with Harold and Mary-Russell Ferrell Colton sitting on the roof above them, their feet dangling over Roosevelt's head.[49] J. L. later recalled, "I still have a mental picture of him, clad in a pair of old shoes, a flannel shirt, two-gallon hat, and his corduroy trousers stuffed into canvas leggings that laced down the sides. He watched the dance from a sitting position in the sand, with his back against an old adobe wall, and raising himself on his hands occasionally so he might see better during some of the most interesting moments of this strange spectacle."[50]

When the Snake Dance was over, J. L., the Roosevelts, and a few other distinguished guests, including Arizona's Governor Hunt, "motored across the desert . . . to his house and store at Ganado."[51] Roosevelt stayed at Ganado for one full day. J. L. liked to stretch the visit out in his memory, telling Hogg that Roosevelt "came to Ganado in 1912 and spent a week as a guest in my house. After we'd spent several evenings discussing politics, Indian affairs, and various other subjects, Mr. Roosevelt said to me: 'Mr. Hubbell, you're a strenuous man!' 'Maybe so,' I replied. 'But if I am, I'm only following in your footsteps!'"[52] J. L.'s grandson, Hubbell Parker, remembered the pair of them arguing about politics that day "like they were mad at each other. It was very vociferous, that argument. But they were just good friends . . . oh,

President Theodore Roosevelt and J. L. at the Hopi Snake Dance, 1913. Courtesy of the National Park Service, HUTR 02124.

they'd cool off by the next morning, they'd never know they'd had an argument."[53] What Barbara must have felt at playing hostess for the former president while her father had a shouting match with him is a mystery, but she earned Roosevelt's warm thanks.[54] Meanwhile, the Coltons camped across the wash, kept from the Hubbell home by the presence of a former president who had taken their wagon, but not forgotten by their host. J. L. rose early in the morning and walked down to their encampment for breakfast and a little grousing about Roosevelt's betrayal of the Republican party.[55]

Of J. L., Roosevelt wrote, "Mr. Hubbell is an Indian trader. His Ganado house, right out in the bare desert, is very comfortable and very attractive, and he treats all comers with an open-handed hospitality inherited from pioneer days. He has great influence among the Navajos, and his services to them have been of much value. Every ounce of his influence has been successfully exerted to put a stop to gambling and drinking; his business has been so managed as to be an important factor in the material and moral betterment of the Indians with whom he has dealt. And he has been the able champion of their rights wherever these rights have been menaced from any outside force."[56] This was high praise indeed from the former president, and J. L. would forever wear Roosevelt's visit like a badge of honor. As Martha Blue states, "Roosevelt seems to have validated J. L.'s view of himself as a national figure, an active man, and a risktaker. That Roosevelt, so well traveled and versed in the world's exotica, viewed his Arizona sojourn as adventurous and thrilling reinforced J. L.'s self-image."[57] When Roosevelt left and Ganado settled back down from the uproar of hosting such a famous visitor, J. L. wrote in great satisfaction to Roman that Roosevelt "was pleased with his trip, and with the men that I gave . . . I also had good luck and got him in to see the washing of The Snakes. It was a great sight and he was very much impressed. His trip was a very successful one from every standpoint."[58]

## Seekers of Beauty: Artists at Hubbell Trading Post

The cultures and landscapes of the Southwest soon attracted artists as much as scientists. With its "broad expanses of 'empty' space, angular mesas, vivid and bold colors, and intense light that flattens forms," the desert landscape seemed perfectly fitted to the modern art movement that blossomed in America in the young decades of the twentieth century.[59] Drawn to Native American and Hispanic cultures, artists converged on Taos and Santa Fe with their brushes, pencils, and camera lenses in search of authenticity and inspiration. They "created the first images of the land and its native peoples seen by thousands of Americans."[60] Those images carried in their lines and colors a message—a myth. The artists made "the West look like a time-less, sepia-toned or strangely colored dreamworld that was closed off, distinct, and isolated from the 'outside world,' or from time itself."[61]

J. L. Hubbell was a rather unlikely man to develop an art collecting hobby, a pastime usually reserved for the very wealthy, but as artists tramped all over Navajo country, he collected their works piece by piece over the years. Artists who stayed in his house often expressed their appreciation by giving him paintings. Despite his own near-constant financial struggles, the trader also often bought art from his friends. But most often, he "financed his burgeoning collection by weaving a complicated system of barter with the artists. Artists became blanket brokers, trading and buying blankets and other crafts from him, most often on credit. In this way, the artists—like customers and laborers—became part of Hubbell's web."[62] Hubbell's art collection soon grew so large that his daughters had to hang his trove of Hopi baskets from the ceiling to make more room on the walls for the paintings, including a handsome portrait of Don Lorenzo himself in point of pride above the fireplace.[63] One of his artist friends once joked to J. L. that with his walls now "fairly covered with paintings, you can now have recourse to your floor space for the disposal of such canvases, drawings, and general fine art as your pet weakness may in future lead you to accumulate."[64] Each of those paintings seemed to have a story behind it—a visit to Navajo country, a friendship, a memory. In 1910, Taos artist Frank P. Sauerwein, who decorated his home with curios supplied by Hubbell, sent J. L. a painting of three Navajos fleeing across the desert before an oncoming storm. He told J. L., "I prefer to think that Ganado lies just this side of the canvas, where I have seen all alike, red man and white, made welcome from the storm and stress of the outer world."[65] Even when it did not grace the canvas, the trading post, it seemed, was always there.

If the walls were papered in art, the rooms seemed perpetually full of artists. One guest joked that only ill health kept him from Ganado, and if it were not for that, J. L. "would have found me taking all sorts of advantage of your hospitality, until you would have Ganado fortified like a Gibraltar against painters and their scurvy tribe."[66] To the Hubbell family, the artists seemed part of the natural bustle of trading post life. Some stayed only briefly, but others became close personal friends of the family, returning time after time. One sculptor, Frederick Allen Williams, stayed for nine or ten months, earning the playful and familiar nickname Fritzie. Dorothy remembered that they "made up one room [in the Leonard building] for Fritzie as his studio, because he had all this clay and water and it was messy and we didn't want it to get in the house."[67] Another artist, Mahonri Young, earned the unshakeable affection of the Hubbell grandchildren by letting them watch him paint. LaCharles remembered crying out, "But, Mr. Young, the horse has a fly on him!" and the artist would oblige her by putting a fly on the horse.⁶⁸ When she contracted the measles, he came to visit her at the side of her big brass bed in the Hubbell home. She asked him, "What does an elephant look like?" and he drew her an elephant. "What does a lion look like?" and he drew her a lion. "I had a whole stack of his drawings... All the animals I could think of."⁶⁹

### E. A. Burbank: Dangling Eye

Among all the artists who visited Hubbell Trading Post, none were quite so familiar as Elbridge Ayer Burbank. Born in 1858 in Harvard, Illinois, E. A. Burbank spent his early artistic career, after training in Chicago and Munich, painting portraits of African Americans, sometimes humorous or sentimental in tone and quite popular with white audiences, though today they often strike modern viewers as "patronizing and even racist."⁷⁰ But Burbank's uncle, Edward E. Ayer, soon set him on a new course that would earn him a reputation as one of the foremost painters of Native American life. Ayer, having made a fortune selling lumber to the transcontinental railway companies, and possessed of a keen interest in Native Americans born of his travels in the West, began investing in the preservation of "vanishing" Indian cultures, building himself a private collection of materials documenting Native American and European encounters.⁷¹ As a founding member and the first president of Chicago's Field Museum of Natural History, Ayer encouraged Chicago artists and literary men, including Herman A. MacNeil, Hamlin Garland, and Charles Francis Browne, in their "desire to study Indian life firsthand while this was still possible."⁷²

In 1897, Ayer commissioned his nephew to paint a life portrait of the iconic Chiricahua Apache resistance leader, Geronimo, who was then an old man and a prisoner at Fort Sill, Oklahoma. Burbank packed up the tools of his trade and headed west, as many of his artist friends in Chicago had done before him. At Fort Sill, he painted Geronimo many times, painstakingly capturing every wrinkle and every mole in an effort to portray the old warrior's character.⁷³ Burbank and Geronimo became friends after a fashion, and Burbank spent months at the fort painting Apaches, Comanches, and Kiowas, as what was meant to be a short summer outing to fulfill a commission turned into a lifelong pursuit. Burbank wrote his uncle that he "had never been so taken with a subject as I am with these Indians," and that he had, on the eve of his fortieth year, finally found his life's work.[74] Now motivated, like his uncle, "by the popular belief that traditional American Indian cultures were being lost," as well as more practical financial incentives, Burbank set out to paint every Indian tribe in America.[75] He fell short of this lofty goal, but not by far. For nearly twenty years, this "would-be artist-ethnologist" traveled extensively in the West, producing nearly 1,000 oil portraits and 1,200 red Conte crayon drawings of American Indians, a collection of ethnographic portraits so vast it is rivaled only by the work of George Catlin.[76] In fact, George Wharton James saw Burbank as Catlin's successor, urging Burbank to "not allow himself to be lured back into civilization to take up less important labor. May he continue and complete the work accomplished by Catlin for art and ethnology!"[77] Burbank's work proved highly popular. He exhibited and sold his paintings and drawings in Chicago and at world's fairs, and soon reproductions began to appear in calendars, newspapers, and Western travel literature, while prestigious institutions like the Field Museum and the Smithsonian Institution acquired his works for their ethnographic collections.[78] By 1900, Charles Lummis heralded Burbank as a "master of Indian faces" and proclaimed that "no one has at all rivaled Burbank as a historical painter of Indians. . . . one of the least hackneyed, most picturesque and most important fields possible to American art. And he has proved, very emphatically, his entire competence to dominate it."[79] Part of what endeared Burbank to the likes of James and Lummis was that, rather than painting anonymous ethnic "types," or dressing his subjects in fanciful and inaccurate costumes, as many painters of American Indians tended to do, Burbank painted individuals, and his paintings were direct and straightforward, not obscured by hazy romanticism.[80] "The result," art historian Bill Mercer states, "is that Burbank painted people who happened to be American Indian rather than American Indians who happened to be people."[81]

Burbank first heard of J. L. Hubbell when he arrived in Gallup in search of Navajos to paint in the fall of 1897, not long after he left Fort Sill.[82] Hubbell's old partner Cotton pointed the artist toward Ganado, pressed a safety razor into his hand, and asked Burbank to tell Hubbell to shave himself. When Burbank arrived at Ganado, he "found Hubbell looking like a wild man with a beard hanging to his belt."[83] In typical fashion, the trader invited the artist to stay free of charge, but refused to shave. Burbank stayed—the first of many visits, some of them stretching out months at a time—and eased his conscience by giving his host dozens of pictures and copying rug designs for him.[84] He set up a studio in the Leonard building, where, because of J. L.'s connections in the local community, he "had no trouble in getting the Navajos to pose."[85] In fact, his first sitter was J. L.'s good friend, Many Horses, wearing his colorful costume as a Navajo headman. Many Horses reportedly liked Burbank's portrait so much that he asked if he might come back the next day to pose for another picture. Burbank recalled, "Imagine my consternation when Many-Horses appeared again in his Navajo costume, but in addition he was wearing a tall stovepipe hat which had been presented to him by a tourist. I urged him to take the hat off, explaining that no one would want a picture of an Indian in such a garb. Many-Horses was terribly disappointed. He left the studio completely crushed. In a short time he was back. This time he had the plug hat decorated with eagle feathers. I decided that such perseverance should be rewarded. So I painted him, plug hat and all. Much to my surprise, Mr. Hubbell was delighted with the portrait and bought it. He had a cut made of the picture and used it on his stationery."[86]

J. L. extended to Burbank a standing invitation to come to Ganado anytime and with anyone he chose, and over the next two decades, Burbank stayed with the Hubbells so often that he seemed almost a part of the family, even working as a clerk in the trading post.[87] "He stayed there for weeks and weeks, and month after month," Hubbell Parker recalled. "Every year he would come out there, he'd stay nearly all summer."[88] The Navajos called him Náá'hadaa'dił (Dangling Eye) or Hastiin Naaltsoos Yik'ndaa'anilí (A Man Who Puts You on a Piece of Paper.)[89] Hubbell bought Burbank's Indian portraits by the dozen. He regarded Burbank as "the best Ind[ian] Painter in existence," and the artist's work came to comprise nearly a third of his entire art collection.[90]

Burbank made short trips east to sell paintings and hold exhibitions, but whenever he was away his heart yearned toward the West. "I want to get out West soon as I can," he once wrote to J. L. "I love the life. I cannot stand civilization and I would rather live on a ranch like yours than to live in New York City. Where you are you are living . . . like a King. You don't know your good luck."[91] The artist suffered bouts of depression, occasionally buckling under the pressure of financial and social stress. Burbank "would go through periods of intense activity followed by comparative paralysis," especially after his divorce from his first wife.[92] After her second abortion,

Burbank fled "out West where I belong."⁹³ It was his haven, and the hospitality of Hubbell and Thomas Keam offered him an escape from the things that sent him careening into depression. "Both men gave him free private lodging and board, allowing him to come and go as he pleased without the slightest restriction or expectation."⁹⁴ In the West, the square-jawed, mustachioed Burbank abandoned his high, starched white collars for plaid flannel and scuffed boots, and left his cares tucked away in his city clothes.

Burbank's success began to decline after 1905, as the most famous Native Americans died and the Indian wars faded from popular memory. Even the continued purchases of his work by Hubbell and Ayer could not rescue him. Never good at managing his money, Burbank's finances worsened and he suffered more frequent breakdowns. In 1916, his second wife left him, and in 1917, the artist suffered a nervous collapse. He took refuge at the Napa State Hospital in California, where he lived for two decades, copying his own drawings for the Huntington Library for $7.50 each.⁹⁵ Burbank left the hospital in 1934 and lived at the Manx Hotel in San Francisco until he was struck and killed by a cable car in 1949. Before his death, he carried on correspondence with the Hubbell family and wrote a book about his travels with the Indians. When he read it, Roman told him it brought "back the very many pleasant memories when you stayed at Ganado," memories that, along with hundreds of Indian portraits capturing faces both familiar and faraway, were Burbank's legacy at Ganado.⁹⁶

## *Maynard Dixon: Hooked Nose Man*

A second artist with deep ties to Hubbell Trading Post was Maynard Dixon, a slender, thin-faced man with "deep blue eyes . . . dark straight hair cascading toward one eye, a rakish mustache, a slightly hooked nose, and long, slim, facile hands."⁹⁷ Dixon was one of those questing souls who felt an immediate connection with Navajo land when he first saw it. "So long had I dreamed of it," he wrote, "that when I came there it was not strange to me. Its sun was my sun, its ground my ground."⁹⁸ Dixon traveled extensively in the Southwest after a sickly childhood in Fresno, California spent sketching everything around him and devouring stories about the Civil War, the Gold Rush, and Indian battles. When he was sixteen, he boldly sent two of his sketchbooks to the famous Western artist Frederic Remington, whose warm encouragement set Dixon on the path that would lead him to become "one of America's foremost illustrators of western life," with drawings appearing in nearly every leading magazine of the time and in the books of authors such as Jack London, John Muir, Mary Austin, and Dane Coolidge.[99] Though Dixon is most famous as a painter of the West, he also loved to tell stories. Donald J. Hagerty writes, "From 1900 to his death in 1946, Maynard Dixon roamed the American West's plains, mesas, and deserts—by foot, horseback, buckboard, and, ultimately, the dreaded automobile—drawing, painting, and expressing his creative personality in poems, essays, and letters in a quest to uncover the region's spirit."[100]

Dixon first visited Arizona in 1900, and Ganado in 1902 while on a trip to paint Canyon de Chelly and the Hopis with fellow artist Frederick Monsen. Pushed in that direction by several of their mutual friends, they stopped by Hubbell's newly built home and ended up staying for more than two months, sketching and painting the Navajos in the surrounding hills or in the "dark, smoky, tobacco- and pinyon-smelling" interior of the trading post.[101] Dixon spent hours in Hubbell's rug room, looking through boldly patterned Navajo textiles, and exploring "Hubbell's combination office, museum, bedroom, arsenal, and picture gallery, where Hubbell stored the most outstanding weaving."[102] He excitedly sent a letter to his friend, Charles Lummis, crowing, "Señor Hubbell has invited me to stay here with him and paint the Navajoes . . . the Navajoes are all right to paint,—if you nail them to a post and have somebody hold a gun to 'em while you do it."[103] Over time, Dixon began to grasp the basics of the Navajo language, and he grew to be such a familiar sight around the trading post that the Navajos granted him a nickname, as they had Burbank. They called him Bit-tsin-Nez (Hooked Nose Man).[104]

Dixon left Ganado in early November that year, "his bags stuffed with drawings, pastels, and a few small oil sketches, visual memories of the Navajo and their country," and his imagination equally stuffed with Hubbell's adventure stories.[105] He would visit again many times, spending the long days at Ganado on the receiving end of Hubbell's "endless flow of droll anecdotes."[106] He scribbled Hubbell's stories on scraps of paper, mingled freely with descriptions of the Navajo landscape, and with these notes and his own personal experiences at the trading post as material, Dixon wrote stories and articles to remember his time in Ganado.[107]

In his stories, Dixon saturates the pages with sumptuous descriptions of the landscape and the trading post, where "the yellow light of the afternoon

Maynard Dixon in front of a Navajo blanket, c. 1900. Courtesy of the National Park Service, HUTR 04842.

sun cut level across the flat and glared upon the grouped ponies, brightened the blankets and glinted on the silver and turquoise worn by the Navajos who lingered by the trading post door."[108] Desert country offered Dixon the redemptive qualities of a "sanctuary from pressures of an urban civilization and direct experience activating the creative drive."[109] For Dixon, Hubbell seemed to symbolize the nostalgic, authentic West that had captured his imagination as a child. He wrote that Navajo country was home to "*real* trading posts—not small town stores transplanted. Ganado was a solid mud-and-stone bastion—almost a fort—with barred windows and heavy double doors and ready firearms in every room."[110] Dixon portrayed Hubbell in his stories as a sort of benevolent dictator, his employees and son-in-law obeying his commands without question—they simply "didn't argue with the Old Man."[111] The young artist seemed to see J. L. as a source of wisdom, almost a mentor. During one of his stays, when Forrest reportedly complained over having to bury a dead Navajo girl, J. L. solemnly explained, "You see, this is a lonesome place. We help these people sometimes. *Es costumbre*—the custom of the country, you might say. And this family—well, they are friends of mine. They are afraid now, like children." Hubbell finished:

> Nada es verdad ni mentira
> En este mundo traidor;
> Todo es segun el color
> Del cristal con que se mira.[112]

The words seemed to soak into Dixon's mind as J. L. drifted out of the room: "Nothing is true or false / In this traitor world; / Everything partakes of the color / Of the crystal through which it is seen."[113]

So powerful was Dixon's attachment of his memory of Navajo country to Hubbell that, when the 1906 earthquake and fire consumed his studio in San Francisco, and he was forced to flee with only what he could carry in his arms, he left his paintings to the flames but rescued all but one of the Navajo blankets Hubbell had given him.[114] The day after the fire he drew a cartoon of himself fleeing the burning studio burdened with papers and canvases, rolled-up Navajo rugs draped wildly over his shoulder.[115] Dixon wrote to Hubbell immediately after the fire with a tone of forced cheerfulness, calling the fire a "little warm spell," and assuring Hubbell, "The pictures can be repainted some day."[116] But as the weeks dragged by, his optimism flagged. With his studio destroyed, he confessed to Hubbell, "Do you know, Ganado seems more like home to me now than any other spot! We are both really homesick for it.... I tell you, querido Viejo, we will be mighty glad to see you."[117]

Dixon maintained a correspondence with Hubbell for years, writing his letters in the gregarious, unguarded language of friendship, greeting Hubbell as *Querido Patron*, Dear Boss.[118] The correspondence came to an end when Roman wrote to Dixon in November 1930 to inform him of his father's death. Dixon could not attend his friend's funeral, but "his thoughts must have returned to the old days when, as a young man, he had come into Navajo country and been befriended by Hubbell, who encouraged him to seek his spirit and dreams in this red-earth country."[119] He was one of the many artists who found themselves in J. L.'s debt—not merely for a roof to cover their heads while in Navajo country, but for introducing them to the Navajos, for lifelong friendship, and sharing and fostering their own love of the landscape. Frank P. Sauerwein spoke in the voice of dozens of other artists when he wrote to J. L., "I do not for many days at a time forget that a Ganado exists, that by the cooperation of gods and men and nation it is fitted to be precisely what it is, what I know we all think of it: a painter's Mecca."[120]

### *Literary Pilgrims to the Southwest*

Hamlin Garland was far from the only literary pilgrim to make his way to the Navajo Southwest and to Hubbell Trading Post in search of inspiration, for along with artists came wielders of the pen. Legions of writers saw in the Southwest a remedy for the ills plaguing the East, and they "who feared that machine-age technology would erode the human spirit" found in the desert a place of refuge.[121] They joined the artists in Taos and Santa Fe, equally entranced by the landscape and by Indian and Hispanic cultures, and from this fascination sprang a unique Southwestern regional literature.[122] A great many pilgrims to the Southwest felt an intense connection to it, and none were in a better position to articulate it than the writers. D. H. Lawrence, an English novelist who joined for a time the creative colony at Taos, once wrote that "different places on the face of the earth have different vital effluence, different vibration, different chemical exhalation, different polarity with different stars: call it what you like. But the spirit of place is a great reality."[123] They rushed into the Southwest in search of that spirit, and in narrating their encounters, created a "region of the imagination."[124] With the drama and vivid imagery of their words, the writers created an enduring picture of the desert Southwest in the imaginations of Americans far away in towering cities and green parklands.

Among Hubbell's guests were some of the Southwest's most ardent lovers. Ernest Thompson Seton, author, wildlife artist, and one of the founding pioneers of the Boy Scouts of America, visited Hubbell Trading Post regularly. What Dorothy later remembered about him was that "[h]e was very much interested in the countryside and there wasn't a time that he came that he didn't say, 'I want to go up in the hayloft.' And then he'd go up in the hayloft where he could see all around, see the country, and he thought it was beautiful."[125] They were guests in love with the things Hubbell Trading Post offered them, perhaps none of them more than Charles F. Lummis, who would become the principle inventor of the myth of the Southwest.[126] Lummis found "in this lonely country" a place to dedicate his life to—for, as he put it, "There is something about this strange enchanted land which works on human nature."[127]

## Charles Fletcher Lummis

Charles Lummis was a small but flamboyant man, "hyperbolic, self-aggrandizing, and relentlessly enthusiastic in his promotional writing."[128] For over 40 years, he trumpeted the virtues of the Southwest on every corner and wrote enough booster literature to fill a library, becoming the universally acknowledged champion of the Southwest. The "scholar-entrepreneur" would be a journalist, editor, historian, photographer, amateur ethnologist and archaeologist, museum founder, art patron, poet, sculptor, folklorist, and, above all, writer during his lifetime, and he did it all with a flair that was at once intriguing and outrageous.[129] As a student at Harvard, he "devoted his college career largely to poetry, athletics, and poker," not to mention women, "although he did learn something about natural history and archaeology."[130] Lummis never graduated—he contracted "brain fever," perhaps a symptom of failing grades, and withdrew, retreating to the home of his first wife's parents in Chillicothe, Ohio. There, he dug about in archaeological ruins, became the editor and "one-man news staff" of the *Scioto Gazette,* a little local weekly newspaper, and looked about eagerly for ways fulfill his dreams of adventure.[131]

In 1884, Lummis presented Colonel Harrison Gray Otis, owner of the *Los Angeles Times,* with a proposition: the young writer would walk from Cincinnati, Ohio, to Los Angeles, California, writing weekly travelogues as he went, and upon arrival would become the paper's new city editor.[132] Otis, impressed by Lummis's spirit, agreed, and the writer packed his things and left Ohio dressed in an eye-dazzling costume of knickerbockers and red knee-high stockings, "as if he were headed to a picnic in the Tyrolean Alps."[133] On his 112-day, 3,507-mile trip, Lummis passed through Santa Fe (where he traded his knickers for a pair of buckskin leggings), Albuquerque,

Charles F. Lummis in 1917. Lummis sent this photograph to J. L. with the inscription "To J. Lorenzo Hubbell, Last Prince of the Frontier." Courtesy of the National Park Service, HUTR 04714.

several Pueblo communities, and Navajo country.[134] He stayed with locals when he could, and between the New Mexican hospitality that swiftly eroded his preexisting prejudices against Hispanics, and the magnificent landscape, Lummis fell ardently and irrevocably in love with the Southwest. It became his refuge from stress and responsibility, and he devoted himself to the cause of promoting it. He soon became editor of the promotional and literary magazine *Land of Sunshine,* which he later renamed *Out West,* and for twelve years, he used it as the platform from which he trumpeted the Southwest as "a veritable Eden . . . a place in which gentle and wise natural women and men—both Indian and Hispanic—live idyllic, gracious, and dignified, if poor, lives in an enchanting desert landscape."[135]

Lummis appears to have first met J. L. Hubbell in August 1890, making him one of Hubbell's earliest guests.[136] Lummis, who always had an eye for the romantic, was quite taken with J. L., whom he dubbed "the last of the Patriarchs—a Prince of the old Frontier."[137] The two men, one the gateway to Navajo country and the other the voice of the Southwest, shared many acquaintances and interests, especially as Lummis became involved in Indian rights issues and formed the Sequoya League, an organization to promote justice for California's indigenous peoples.[138] As both could boast of daring escapes and bullet wounds, the two became fast friends, keeping up a lively correspondence throughout their lives. J. L. supported Lummis in his many schemes, joining Lummis's Southwest Society of the Archaeological Institute of America and the Sequoya League, as well as serving as an organizer for Lummis's Southwest Museum, while Lummis regarded J. L. as the most "fascinating narrator" of Western tales, kept him well supplied with autographed books with fond inscriptions, and sent travelers to his door—Lummis, in fact, introduced Hubbell to John Collier and Maynard Dixon.[139] After that initial meeting in 1890, Lummis visited Ganado several times, including a memorable trip in 1906 in which he was accompanied by his illegitimate but favorite daughter, Bertha, and his secretary, Gertrude Redit, who later became his second wife. Lummis published an ode to J. L. in *Out West* in 1907, praising the Ganado homestead as "one of the few places left in all the West where the storied hospitality of Spanish America is still unspoiled and uncrippled."[140] Lummis was a regular guest at Ganado until his death in 1928. He sat at the table in his trademark corduroy suit and red bandana, reminiscing with the Hubbell family about old times even as his own life crumbled around his ears as his womanizing, drinking, and combative nature finally caught up with him.[141]

## George Wharton James

J. L. Hubbell, always the politician, also maintained a friendship with Lummis's nemesis, the Southwest's second great promoter, George Wharton James. The two writers shared enough wild eccentricities "to make southern

California, as often happens with literary turf, too small for both."[142] Born in 1858 in Lincolnshire, England, to a working-class family, James was "bright, obedient, but high-strung"; he suffered from respiratory problems, "neurotic tics," and morbid fears of heights, blood, drunkenness, and eternal damnation, but he was driven, introspective, and relentlessly active.[143] The details of his early life are scarce, but by 1881 James had donned the frock of an itinerant Methodist minister, crossed an ocean and a continent, and began preaching in the saloons and mining camps of western Nevada. Much like Lummis, James seemed to pick up interests and causes wherever he went—in Nevada, James taught music lessons and gave secular lectures while studying phrenology and natural history, and in California, he became involved in literary and reform circles. In the late 1880s, however, James's climb toward success turned into an uncontrolled spiral as he suffered through an extremely public and ruinous divorce in which his wife, no more stable than James himself, accused him of brutality, incest, and adultery. The press seized upon the sensationalism of the case, heedless of evidence, and "James ended up divorced, disgraced, and all but forced to resign from the ministry," even though he was later cleared of all charges.[144] Temporarily ruined, in debt, and on the verge of collapse, James took refuge in Arizona and New Mexico. There, in the desert among the Indians, he was "born again," and the gospel he would preach from then on was the gospel of the Southwest to the tune of more than 40 books and hundreds of articles and pamphlets.[145]

In the Southwest, James acquired an intense interest in Indian crafts, especially basketry and Navajo weaving, which is likely what brought him to J. L.'s door. The two had met by 1903, and over the course of their friendship, they exchanged scarcely a letter that failed to refer to Navajo weaving. James considered J. L. the ultimate authority on the subject, sending him blankets from time to time for authentication and making a special trip to Ganado for J. L.'s "kind and generous assistance" with his book, *Indian Blankets and Their Makers*.[146] The two men worked out a mutually beneficial relationship in which J. L. lent James a selection of blankets, a painting from his collection, and a loom for illustrating the book, and paid the author $150.00, while James peppered the text with references to J. L.'s influence and included a page on the trader in his chapter "Reliable Dealers in Navaho Blankets," all in the hopes that the book, backed by James' scholarly authority, would "help push the trade along."[147]

On one occasion, James was traveling with a friend "into the heart of Navaho Country."[148] The two drove their wagon leisurely and sumptuously, "enjoying the delightfully bracing air of the plateau, and of the pines, pinions, and cedars."[149] As evening fell, they approached Ganado on a straight stretch of road lined on both sides by barbed wire, anticipating the welcome that awaited them "in the hospitable home of Lorenzo Hubbell, that genial and royal host, at whose table every reputable traveler of the past thirty years has been made welcome."[150] But a sudden problem with the wagon whipped the horses into a frenzy of kicking and plunging that erased any contented thoughts as the wagon careened down the barbed-wire lane like a drunk. Confronted with the possibility of an unpleasant meeting with the fence, James abandoned ship, and with the help of some Navajos who had come running to his aid, managed to calm the horses and get the harness readjusted. He and his companion "drove to the store as gently as though there had been no such excitement," and James spent a good ten days as Hubbell's guest.[151] When he left, Hubbell sent him to Chinle and Canyon de Chelly with a buckboard and an experienced Navajo driver.[152]

## Dane Coolidge

The Southwest's eccentric cadre of promotional writers was joined at Hubbell's table by some of the West's greatest novelists. Owen Wister, Zane Grey, and Grace MacGowan Cooke all came under the Hubbell roof, but only one author, Dane Coolidge, wrote a western where the main character was modeled after Don Lorenzo himself. Coolidge, born in 1873, grew up on a citrus ranch in Riverside, California, where he nurtured an interest in biology. While in college, he spent his summers traveling widely in Baja California, Nevada, Arizona, and northern Mexico collecting specimens for natural history collections. He was a "skilled hunter, trapper, amateur taxidermist, and self-trained naturalist."[153] After dropping out of Harvard, Coolidge returned to the West and spent the next twelve years in "intellectual and equestrian vagabonding" in Arizona until he married Mary Roberts, a sociologist with whom he would later collaborate on several books about the Navajos.[154]

Coolidge was not just a naturalist—he was also "devoted to literature."[155] Along with Zane Grey and Eugene Manlove Rhodes, he contributed to the rise of the western as a literary genre, writing "stories that focus on strong heroic characters and simplistic frontier myths."[156] Coolidge, however, tried to reconcile fact and myth in his writing; he worried about portraying the West accurately, but his flair for the dramatic "caused him to drift towards 'horse operas.'"[157] Despite this, his work was often more intellectual and complex than that of his competitors, and he balanced his fiction with nonfiction essays about the people he met in the West, published in *Texas Cowboys, Arizona Cowboys,* and *Old California Cowboys,* in which J. L. makes his appearance.[158]

Coolidge visited Ganado in 1913, though whether he had been to the trading post at any time before then is unknown.[159] Like Garland, Coolidge found Hubbell to be a storehouse of western stories. He kept a clippings file of material he gathered while traveling in Arizona, and he must have listened in rapture as J. L. shared tales of his days as sheriff embroiled in the conflicts between the sheepmen and the cattlemen in St. Johns.[160] Nearly a decade after his visit, Coolidge published a novel which he said was based on J. L. Hubbell: *Lorenzo the Magnificent.* The story follows gracious Spanish gentleman Don Lorenzo De Vega in his battle against Texas cattlemen who attempt to wrest his land from him. De Vega is no mirror image of J. L., but echoes of the trader's personality and the bustling atmosphere of the trading post shine through in the text. When the Texans first arrive on his land, De Vega treats them with hospitality that those familiar with Hubbell and his stories would recognize immediately. At the first Texan's arrival, De Vega invites him in and declares, "I have lived here for twenty years and no one has paid me yet. That is, with one exception—and he is the only man that I ever turned away from my door. It is the custom of my people and all are welcome to Su Casa, which is the name I give my poor home. It means in Spanish: 'Your house.'"[161] When *Lorenzo the Magnificent* was published in 1925, Coolidge stopped by Ganado to give his friend a signed copy. He wrote on the inside of the red cover, "To J. L. Hubbell, 'Lorenzo Magnifico,' whose old-time hospitality at Ganado stands out like an island in a land being submerged by a commercialism which counts the cost even of friendship—From his friend, Dane Coolidge."[162]

Because of his dedication to authenticity—or perhaps because his acquaintance with Hubbell dated from a later period in the trader's life when financial storms had fallen heavily—Coolidge's depictions of Hubbell's hospitality contain a sadder note than almost any of the descriptions by others who remarked upon it. In *Lorenzo the Magnificent,* the generosity of the old Spanish gentleman was almost his downfall as unscrupulous men took advantage of him. In *Old California Cowboys,* Coolidge mourned the passing of the frontier and the hospitality that characterized it with a heavy heart—he knew J. L. in the period when the trading post was sinking deeper and deeper into debt, and recounted sadly Lorenzo, Jr., selling Keams Canyon to settle his father's debts. Though Coolidge himself had "enjoyed very much your open-hearted hospitality," Coolidge's outlook for his friend was bleak.[163] "That was the old Spanish *caballero,* still living in the past, thinking nothing of money and everything of friends—his religion, hospitality," he wrote. "But these ways cannot last much longer. The Mexican people are not geared up to meet the tempo of this barbed-wire and gasoline age."[164] In his eyes, the generous ways of Don Lorenzo, like the frontier West itself, were doomed to perish.

## A Tradition of Hospitality

So it was, with friends such as these, that when "death, slipping through the strange shadow-land of Northern Arizona," finally found Don Lorenzo in November 1930, the news of his passing traveled far and fast.[165] Elegies in newspapers and journals marked the life and death of the old trader as his friends, no strangers to the written word, took up the pen in his honor. In Colorado, Joseph Emerson Smith, archaeologist, editor of the *Denver Post,* and once a guest at Ganado, wrote a long obituary that began with the grim pronouncement, "Lorenzo Hubbell is dead." Smith continued, "This news, coming out of Navajo land, will bring a pause and a shadow in studios of painters in New York, Paris, Rome. Archaeologists and ethnologists in the jungles of Yucatan, the plains of Assyria, and the steppes of the Gobi desert, will find themselves transported in memory away from their excavations, to the sun-swept trading post in Arizona. To the seekers of beauty and the adventurers in to the buried long-ago, J. Lorenzo Hubbell, 'patriarch and prince of the frontier,' was friend and host."[166] Condolences poured in to Lorenzo, Jr., Roman, Adele, and Barbara from every corner of the country, each echoing the sentiments of artist Harold Harrington Betts, who wrote, "I always remember him as the generous, kind-hearted and most interesting man I have ever met. I am proud that I knew him, and will always treasure the good stories he used to tell while sitting around the fireplace at Ganado."[167]

J. L.'s death, however, did not terminate the relationship between the Hubbell family and the Southwest's pilgrims. Barbara remained the indomitable hostess of Ganado as her brothers, perhaps even more steeped in Navajo culture than their father had been, carried on the tradition of hospitality, introducing new generations of anthropologists and artists to the Diné and their homeland. In 1931, Henry Fountain Ashurst, a senator from Arizona and Chairman of the Committee of Indian Affairs, arrived on the Navajo Reservation to hold hearings, and his path took him to Ganado. There, he found a scene so like what visitors who had preceded him had found—it was almost as if Don Lorenzo still presided at the head of the table. He was looking at some sand paintings with the Navajos when "a bell sounded; it was the call to dinner with the Hubbells who came to the table *en famille* and the grand-mother was waited upon first; age is honored in this house of courtesy and chivalry. The meal was served in the large hall of the Hubbell home, and among other viands was savory Angora kid flesh. On the walls of the home are many paintings, pastels, drawings, and etchings, together with a valuable collection of old blankets representing many tribes, some of them prehistoric."[168] Dinner was followed by a Navajo dance around an enormous bonfire. Though J. L. now rested on top of Hubbell Hill with Lina and Many Horses, travelers still found the welcome of days past from his children. When visitors arrived in Ganado seeking his help, Roman was in his element. He "never cared so much about trading with the Navajo as he did exploring their beautiful country and taking visitors to the hidden away spots no casual traveler could find."[169]

Roman and Lorenzo, Jr., both had a more nuanced understanding of Navajo culture than their father had, a change reflected in the approach of a new generation of anthropologists who came to study the Navajos in the 1930s. In the 1920s, under the leadership of Franz Boas, who is known as the "father" of modern American anthropology, anthropologists began to reject the evolutionary framework that had dominated the field since the nineteenth century. Rather than denigrating Native cultures as "uncivilized" compared to Western culture, Boas and his followers argued that anthropologists should judge each culture on its own terms, an approach known as cultural relativism.[170] Among these new anthropologists were two women, Gladys Amanda Reichard and Laura Adams Armer, who would credit the success of their work to the Hubbell family just as surely as any of J. L.'s friends had done in earlier days.

Gladys Reichard, the most important woman anthropologist to study the Navajos between 1930 and 1960, was one Boas's most devoted students.[171]

Reichard first visited Ganado in 1923 with Pliny Earle Goddard, fellow anthropologist and curator of ethnology at the American Museum of Natural History.[172] The two returned to the reservation in 1924 and 1925, making summer field trips to study Navajo genealogies, clans, and folklore, and Reichard published several books from their field research. Her research soon took her away from the Southwest, but in 1930, two years after Goddard died suddenly in Reichard's home, throwing her personal and professional life at Barnard College into turmoil and scandal, she returned to the Navajo Reservation, ready to make a "break with her past" and try something new.[173] She returned with the intention of doing something few anthropologists of the time did: live with a Navajo family to learn the language and the art of weaving.

At first, Reichard had a difficult time convincing anyone to help her as they all seemed to think the rough living unsuitable for an Anglo woman. Finally, she went to Ganado with Ann Axtell Morris, another archaeologist, to seek Roman's help. She went to the right place. Within a few days, Roman had taken her to live with Miguelito (also called Red Point) and his family—his wife, Maria Antonia, and his two married daughters, Marie and Altnaba.[174] Roman chose well. He had known Miguelito and his family for many years; in fact, Miguelito had performed Roman's marriage to his first wife, Alma. Miguelito was a Navajo singer with a wealth of cultural knowledge, and the entire family had worked for the Fred Harvey Company as demonstrators, exhibiting at the world's fairs in San Francisco and San Diego in 1915.[175] Marie was to become Reichard's teacher, and in the years she spent living with them, Reichard grew close to both Miguelito's family and the Hubbells. Living with a Navajo family allowed her to see the culture, especially women's culture, from the inside, a place of sympathy and understanding rarely achieved by anthropologists observing from the outside.

Words failed her when she tried to express her gratitude to the Hubbell family. When Roman set her up with Miguelito's family, she wrote, "he put the stamp of success on my project."[176] She also offered a special thanks to the women of the trading post. "My thanks to Mrs. Goodman, Mrs. Parker, Mrs. Hubbell, and their children are of the kind of the lone stranger must have mentally accorded to the Good Samaritan when he came to."[177] In a letter to her sponsor and friend, Elsie Clews Parsons, Reichard wrote, "There are times when the language has me stopped. At such times I go to Hubbell's, stay overnight, get mail, food, etc. & start fresh & early the next morning."[178] She would maintain close friendships with Lala, Auntie Bob, and Lady for the rest of her life, visiting nearly every summer and spending holidays with the family.[179] Reichard published three books based on her work in the early 1930s—*Spider Woman,* a personal memoir of her time with Miguelito's family, *Navajo Shepherd and Weaver,* a technical exegesis on Navajo weaving, and *Dezba: Woman of the Desert,* a novel of Navajo life based on her experiences.[180]

While Roman helped Reichard, Lorenzo, Jr., took Laura Adams Armer under his wing. Armer, a white-haired woman who always wore turquoise earrings, was a novelist, ethnographer, and artist who first came to the Southwest in 1923 to paint and study Navajo and Hopi mythology.[181] After she met Lorenzo, Jr., he became her benefactor. When she wanted a Navajo to make a sand painting on the floor of the little museum of Indian art she built in her studio in Oraibi, she turned to Lorenzo. "When I spoke to Mr. Hubbell about it, he said, 'You ask for the moon,'" she recalled. But Lorenzo added, "'If anyone can get it for you, I can.'" Lorenzo convinced Ashi, a Navajo man, to make a sand painting for Armer as she watched in interested reverence. When Armer desired to live at lonely Blue Canyon, away from Anglo influences, to get a clearer picture of Navajo life, Lorenzo left her there with instructions to introduce herself to any strange Navajos as his friend. "Say to him, '*Na Kai Tso, bi kis,*'" and the Navajos, he said, would welcome her. And as she listened to old Navajo medicine men spin their legends for her, "Mr. Hubbell translated with rare understanding."

The two became friends—Lorenzo helped Armer gain entry into Navajo culture because he believed in her methods and ability to sympathetically and accurately portray Navajo life. He introduced her to the rest of the family in 1927 after he and Armer had together hatched a plan to make a film of the Navajo Mountain Chant. As he told Roman, "[I]f you would like the sand-paintings and legends worked out properly I believe she is the person to do it."[182] And so Roman helped her film "the first Native American motion picture directed in an Indian language—Navajo."[183] With two cameramen and their assistants, and "with the cooperation of the Hubbell family, the only white people who could obtain permission from the Navahos to allow their sacred ceremonies to be photographed," Armer captured on film the beauty of the Navajos silhouetted against the sky, riding across the desert, and performing their sacred ceremonies.[184] Armer showed the film, *The Mountain Chant,* at the American Museum of Natural History in the fall of 1928, where Gladys Reichard saw it and praised it as "extremely well done not only from an artistic, but more especially from a scientific point of view."[185] Armer would go on to write several novels for young adults portraying Navajo life more deeply than other writers had yet done. Her novel *Waterless Mountain* won the Newberry Medal; she dedicated it "To Lorenzo Hubbell, whose faith inspired this book."[186] Even after Don Lorenzo's death, the Hubbells still had "the open sesame to all which lies hidden in Navaho land."[187]

## On the Edge of Change

The Hubbells at Ganado held on to their family tradition of hospitality as long as they could, but the changes that swept the nation in the twentieth century began to seep in. Even rugged Navajo country could not keep at bay the advance of pavement and mile-eating automobiles forever, and soon the hardships that once necessitated a good host were overcome by speed, guidebooks, and hotels. Perhaps nothing better encapsulates the creeping changes than Dorothy's memories of Ferdinand Burgdorff, one of the artists who knew and loved the trading post. "Burgdorff told me that he came here first in 1900 and Mr. Hubbell let him have a wagon and horse and he went to Chinle to sketch," she remembered. "He came the last time after 1957. He put his easel right by the gas pump. I had to ask him to move it so that cars could get to the pump."[188] In sixty years, Burgdorff had gone from traveling across Navajo country in a wagon when he was probably the only visitor for miles in any direction on the road to Chinle, to having to move his easel so tourists could fill up their thirsty cars.

In the wake of J. L.'s death in 1930, the changes came fast and hard, weakening the family's hold on Ganado as it had been—the Great Depression, the Second World War, and a transportation revolution that brought more and more tourists to Navajo country with no need for traders' aid, and brought fundamental changes to the nature of Indian trading. The changes would leave those long familiar with Ganado gasping in their wake, cut off from the life they had once known. Their thoughts must have echoed those of Louise Swinnerton, who had stayed with Lorenzo, Jr., at Oraibi, when she wrote years later in a haze of remembrance: "Thank God for memory. No one can take that away from us, can they?"[189]

CHAPTER EIGHT

# "The Worst They Ever Knew"
## The Great Depression and World War II, 1930–1945

In September 1930, after the yearly crowds of Snake Dance pilgrims had gone home again with eyes brightened by memories, as summer slipped into autumn and J. L. Hubbell's legendary vitality faded in his final illness, Lorenzo, Jr., telephoned Roman in Ganado to discuss their father's debts. The two of them tried to comprehend J. L.'s incomprehensible finances—mortgages, interest, accounts, wages, leases, real estate holdings—and the more they learned, the grimmer the future looked. J. L. owed his own son $46,129, and there were three mortgages on the Ganado property totaling $30,000, not to mention innumerable smaller debts.[1] Although Roman and Lorenzo had taken on increasing amounts of responsibility in their father's business, first as J. L.'s politics claimed his attentions and later as his health began to fail, they would soon have all of it under circumstances they would not have chosen. Just before his death, the old trader handed over the entire business in equal shares to his four children under the Bulk Sales Act; it would continue to operate as a corporation under the name J. L. Hubbell Trading Post, with Lorenzo, Jr., acting as manager.[2] Before the snow covered their father's grave that November, the family shouldered the burden of a slowly dying business. Forrest left his job with the grocery company in Texas, and he and Adele returned to Ganado so he could turn his attention to the company's books while Roman and Dorothy managed the operations at the wholesale house in Gallup, and Lorenzo scurried back and forth between Oraibi and Winslow. Lorenzo worked frantically to collect on accounts while simultaneously running his own separate business, and the family assured him, "We are all hitting the ball and you may rest easy that we are going to try to do our bit as best we know how . . . everything is going to work out fine."³ In some other year, it might have. But the long years of the Great Depression had barely begun. The Hubbells were about to face the most difficult decade they had yet seen.

National markets crashed spectacularly in October 1929, and the effects began to reach the Navajos by the spring of 1930, when the price of wool dropped more than ten cents per pound. By the fall, Navajo lambs were fetching only half of what they had a year before, while markets for Navajo rugs and curios, once on fire with the high ideals of antimodernism, shriveled in the cold new reality of the Depression.⁴ By the time Roman and Lorenzo took up their father's mantle, the Depression had set in like a bad winter storm. Across the reservation, trade faltered as the Navajos, already impoverished, labored under the unrelenting weight of the reduced economy. Roman put it simply: "The Indians don't have much to sell."⁵ At all of the family's posts, the wool trade slowed to a trickle, and prices fell so low—lower than they had been since 1869—that it broke Lorenzo's heart to have to buy any at all.⁶ As he sat one spring day writing a letter to his cousin, George Hubbell, he looked out the window to see two wagons loaded with ten bags of wool pulling up to the Oraibi trading post. The sight weighed on his beleaguered conscience, and he wrote, "We have paid more than the market warrants but it cannot be helped, and could not have been avoided, I just cannot see how wool is so cheap, I am ashamed to buy it, knowing that in reality they are not getting paid what is just, and at the same time we are helpless to do anything about it."⁷ The traders' burdens were not so light that they could carry the Navajos' more than a few staggering steps. As historian Donald L. Parman writes, "Even the most sympathetic traders could do little to counter the Navajos' plight. The posts continued to accept the Indians' pawn. When that was exhausted, the Navajos began to spend the dimes and quarters that they normally used as buttons. Low wool prices compelled many Navajo women to increase rug weaving, but traders could not find outlets in an already sluggish market. In truth, the traders themselves often faced bankruptcy. Their prosperity was directly linked with the Navajos' sale of wool, lambs, and rugs; both struggled to survive the financial depression."⁸

Meanwhile, the banks, made cautious by disaster, refused to extend Lorenzo, Jr., any more credit. As he fell more and more behind every day, he confessed to Roman that his credit was "badly punctured now, and without some care it will be completely ruined."⁹ When the local banks turned him

Lorenzo, Jr., and Roman at a Navajo Conference at Keams Canyon, 1934. Courtesy of the National Park Service, HUTR 11594.

away, Lorenzo tried to secure a loan from the Federal Reserve Bank, explaining the dire situation in which he and the Indians found themselves—without credit, Lorenzo could not buy the sheep, and he had "hundreds of families of Indians depending on my organization for the handling of their stock and they are unable to sell."[10] The loan was denied. The Hubbells could only reduce their merchandise to the barest of staples—flour, sugar, coffee, and baking powder—and even then, there were times when the shelves were "clean of almost everything."[11] Lorenzo reluctantly cut the salaries of his employees.[12] He tried to get his creditors to take blankets in payment as many of them had done in the past, confessing that "all of the business we are doing is on a barter basis," but his creditors had no use for Navajo blankets when they had their own debts nipping at their heels.[13] To make matters worse at Ganado, J. L., the Navajos' familiar trader for more than fifty years, was gone. Many Navajos had become accustomed to trading with Roman, but trading had never been Roman's passion, and when he was away on other business, the trade at Ganado was "practically nil."[14] The view from Hubbell Trading Post was bleak.

## The Big Snow

As they adjusted to life without their father, the Hubbells kept reminding one another in a hopeful refrain that hard times had fallen before, and they had always managed to come out on top by tightening their belts and redoubling their efforts. "Work and Economy is what we must adhere to," Lorenzo told Roman, while Roman in turn assured his brother that "there is no doubt that all your effort will bear fruit. Times are hard now but they will all adjust themselves. We all have to have a little patience."[15] In 1931, the brothers hatched an optimistic plan to relieve some of the burden of debt. With Roman in charge, they attempted to increase their sheep trade dramatically, establishing a commission firm and making contacts in Kansas and Missouri to feed the stock. Leaving the Ganado trading post in the care of longtime Navajo employee Joe Tippecanoe and Roman's oldest son, Monnie, "Roman worked the reservation heavily the late summer and fall of that year, traveling from hogan to hogan, collecting debts and dickering for lambs."[16] He bought more than 10,000 lambs, a brisk buying year that promised a healthy profit. But back east, the firms with whom the Hubbells had contracted to sell the lambs stalled as markets continued to collapse all around them. Winter came early that year, and the lambs, unable to reach adequate feed beneath the early snow, lost weight rapidly as Roman waited to load them on the railroad.

And then "the most disastrous freeze-up old traders claimed they could remember" hit.[17] Snow fell layer upon layer until the land, "from mountain peak to sandy wash was buried beneath a wintry blanket" and starving sheep huddled together against the cold.[18] Navajos dug deep trenches through the snow to the juniper trees to feed the weakening sheep on twigs and bark, but the animals died by the dozens and were buried under the snow. Hungry coyotes and wolves dug through the crystalized white crust to reach the carcasses, and great mobs of hoarsely screaming crows descended to fight over the remains.[19] By the time spring arrived, dead sheep littered the range, and all the Navajos could salvage was the wool clipped from their rotten carcasses. "By summer the stench of dead wool surrounded every trading post on the reservation" as Navajos sold the rancid clippings to the traders at a discounted price.[20]

Meanwhile, Navajos who had been on the mesa tops gathering piñons when the snow hit began to straggle into towns and trading posts. Lorenzo, Jr., was in Winslow when the storms struck, and with him was anthropologist Laura Adams Armer, who had been working on her second book on the Navajos. She waited with Lorenzo and watched the trail for her Navajo friends. They came slowly, cold and bedraggled. One Navajo woman returned on foot with her family, thin and frostbitten, having killed her two ponies to feed her children and burned the wagon for heat—but she clung to hope because she had gathered nine sacks of piñons. Armer's heart beat fast as the woman turned trustingly to Lorenzo for trade. "I knew that hundreds of sheep were starving," she remembered. "Sheep which Mr. Hubbell had bought and paid for were unable to reach the grass buried beneath the snow. I knew that the trader could not give the woman what she needed. In that winter of 1931, he had been taxed to the limit of his resources by low market prices of wool, mutton and pinyons. I knew that he had no flour to sell the Navajos, for the wholesalers could no longer give credit."[21] But Lorenzo tried, nevertheless. That night, after he had done what he could for the beleaguered Navajos, Armer bought him dinner, for, he confessed, he had not a cent left in his pocket.[22]

In the days that followed, Lorenzo and Roman used all their political connections to try to convince the government to send emergency feed for the starving sheep—theirs and the Navajos'. They wrote to their friend John Collier, then executive secretary of the American Indian Defense Association and a fierce critic of the Bureau of Indian Affairs, to beg him to do whatever was necessary to help the Navajos.[23] Congress had allotted a mere $2,500 for relief, and Roman estimated they would need at least $200,000 to save *half* of the Navajos' sheep. He and Henry Dodge wired letters to Senators Wheeler, Frazier, Ashurst, and Bratton, who agreed to try to spur the glacial wheels of Congress. After another storm hit in January, Collier finally managed to drum up some aid, and the Indian agents distributed hay and feed cakes for the sheep, and a little food, clothing, and shoes for the Navajos.[24] Many of the sheep survived, but sheep dip counts the following summer revealed that the Navajos had lost 13 percent of their herds—some two hundred thousand head.[25]

For the Hubbells as well as the Navajos, the winter of 1931–1932 "was a bitter time. As many as fifty sheep died each day. Only their pelts could be salvaged. Prospects of lifting the mortgage gave way to deepened debt. When the storm finally lifted, Roman found himself facing a tough winter with thousands of sheep for which he had neither markets nor range."[26] He grazed the remaining lambs on the reservation on an expired permit while the Indian agent turned a blind eye in sympathy, but by the end of March, he had to get them off. The loss was staggering. In the best of times, stock-buying was a "hair-whitening gamble in which estimating numbers, competition, pricing, weather conditions, disease, failing markets and snafus along the way created great tensions," and in 1931, it was a gamble the Hubbells lost badly.[27]

## Livestock Reduction and the Navajo New Deal

John Collier's role in saving the herds that winter helped earned him the support of the Navajos and the Hubbells when it came time for President Franklin D. Roosevelt to appoint a new Commissioner of Indian Affairs in 1933. Collier had been the BIA's fiercest critic, and the Indians saw him as a man who would fight with energy and conviction on their behalf, whose "past record has established the fact that he is courageous, capable and honest, and deeply interested in the problems of the American Indian."[28] When Collier arrived on the Navajo Reservation after his appointment, he was heralded as "the 'Plumed Knight' of the Indian cause."[29] His appointment represented a significant step away from the assimilationist programs that had dominated Indian Affairs for decades. He championed the Indian Reorganization Act, which gave tribes the opportunity to develop their own governments, constitutions, and political systems, and implemented several programs meant to improve the economic conditions on reservations. On a personal level, he, like many of the Hubbells' other friends, saw traditional Navajo culture as a purer way of life, free from the corruption that marked modern American society. Collier "cared deeply about the fate of the Navajos," a care that ironically would lead him to implement a program that would turn his name into an epithet among them: the livestock reduction program.[30]

In the 1920s and 1930s, conservationists became alarmed by the state of the environment in northeastern Arizona. Navajo country had fallen into a pattern of severe drought and intense summer storms since the 1870s. Plants withered, the ground dried, and when the rain came pouring down in sheets as thunder growled in the skies, the water cut deep arroyos into the earth, carrying away the soil and scarring the face of the land. Meanwhile, the Navajos' vast herds of sheep voraciously stripped the land of its native plants, exposing the ground to the wind and rain and encouraging the spread of invasive plant species. The Depression only exacerbated the problem. With prices for lambs and wool so low, many Navajos could not sell their sheep, which increased the size of their herds.[31] By the 1930s, nearly a million sheep and goats grazed on the Navajo Reservation, and the cumulative damages of climate change and overgrazing had crippled the land's ability to regenerate. There simply was not enough forage left to sustain the herds. If something was not done, Collier believed, the livestock would starve and so would the Navajos.[32]

Collier and the conservationists concluded that the government must reduce the number of livestock on the Navajo Reservation dramatically to protect the range from further damage. They acted quickly. In their minds, rescuing the range was a matter of simple arithmetic, and they did not have the time to wait for the Navajos to comprehend their cold logic, though their actions "violated some of [the Navajos'] most important customs and patterns of life."[33] Despite his deep sense of responsibility toward and respect for the Navajos, Collier did not truly understand the significance of livestock to the Navajo economy, but more importantly, to Navajo culture:

Navajo herder and sheep on a hillside, c. 1910. Courtesy of the National Park Service, HUTR 11399.

"Grass was grass. Sheep were sheep. Soil erosion was soil erosion. Or so they assumed."[34]

Reduction commenced in 1933. Over the next three years, federal officials removed some 166,225 sheep and 164,716 goats from the Navajo Reservation.[35] Officials cut herd sizes "across the board," leaving "small herders without sufficient livestock to meet their subsistence needs, while those with large livestock holdings were relatively unaffected."[36] Reduction also disproportionately hurt Navajo women, who traditionally owned the herds.[37] Even worse than the simple fact of reduction, however, was the way in which it was implemented. Mired in the middle of the Depression and with the range depleted, government officials knew they would never be able to get the livestock from the remoter parts of the reservation to the railhead in any condition to sell for enough money to make it worth their while. So they would simply "seize the animals, take them over a hill or down into a canyon or into a corral, and shoot them and leave them to rot."[38] Episodes of slaughter stand out in Navajo collective memory like nightmares, and piles of bleached bones still testify to the brutality of reduction. One Navajo likened the trauma of stock reduction to "another Hwéeldi, Long Walk."[39]

Hubbell Trading Post was one of the many locations where such slaughters took place. Dorothy remembered "how the Indians would bring in their goats to be counted and killed" by a government representative left at the post to undertake the grim task.[40] "My only general impression is their bitterness," she recalled.[41] The government officials responsible for reduction may not have understood the importance of livestock in Navajo life, but the Hubbells certainly did. Lorenzo and Roman wrote Collier frequent letters in which they tried to steer conservation efforts away from reduction and toward irrigation and reforestation, provided that "the poor Indians who had no stock or any means of support" be employed on the projects.[42] Roman repeatedly proposed an exchange of one young ewe for two goats, since goats were harder on the range, a plan he said the Navajos accepted. "It will give them something upon which they can continue to live," he argued, "less stock but better stock which seems to be what the forestry service, erosion control service and others who think the range is overstocked, advocate."[43] On another occasion, Lorenzo, Jr., tried to explain to Collier the "inopportune" program's disproportionate ill effects on small herders.[44] "Now remember," he wrote, "the only large income is from sheep, sale of wool, sale of lambs, and sale of Navajo blankets . . . and it is the only industry that they can follow at the present time."[45] As traders whose economic well-being was tied directly to the Navajos', the Hubbells were also aware of the negative effects reduction would have on their business: "For the traders, the ultimate source of their income—the sheep herds—were being attacked by the government."[46] For one thing, stock reduction would damage the family's curio business. Fewer sheep meant less wool for weaving, but the program also replaced traditional Navajo breeds with sheep that produced wool ill-suited to weaving. Lorenzo would later explain to one of his customers in the 1940s, "Due to the reduction of sheep on the Navajo Reservation it is becoming more difficult to procure wool of sufficient quantity and quality to weave into rugs and saddle blankets, and the price has risen accordingly."[47] But the Hubbells' advice seemed to have little effect, and stock reduction moved forward with brutal single-mindedness.

Stock reduction thoroughly poisoned the Navajos against Collier. And because the program was carried out under the banner of the Indian New Deal, the Navajos rejected other federal programs that might have helped them, including the Indian Reorganization Act.[48] The Hubbells warned Collier about this, too, their letters getting more explicit as reduction continued.

"If any further reduction takes place before this . . . bill is voted upon by the Navajos," Roman told Collier, "I am sure this bill will be defeated."[49] And it was defeated, to Collier's great disappointment. The simple fact was, "To the Navajos, the Stock Reduction Program was the most tangible, most detrimental, and most hated aspect of the New Deal, and the only one most Navajos saw."[50] Other programs focused on providing wage-work on public works or conservation projects aimed at further developing irrigation resources on the reservation, and the Indian Civilian Conservation Corps (CCC-ID) and the Works Progress Administration (WPA) hired Navajos to build schools, roads, and bridges. However, as Roman repeatedly explained to Collier, individual Navajos who suffered from stock reduction had no guarantee of employment on these projects.[51] As David Brugge argues, "the New Deal projects intended to provide the income to offset the loss of livestock were slow to materialize and were temporary palliatives, at best."[52]

A 1934 incident in which a bitter fight erupted between Navajos and the BIA over work on the Ganado Irrigation Project illustrates the scarcity of the promised wage-work during the Depression. Floods in 1931 once again destroyed the diversion works, necessitating extensive repairs, and when rumors spread through the local community that the BIA would use mechanized equipment manned by Anglos for the project when the Navajos were desperate for work, the Indians protested. As the trader in charge at Ganado at the time, Forrest found himself in the thick of the debate. He and Navajos Yazzie Holmes and David Hubbard called meetings with the local Navajo community and filed adamant protests, earning the "scathing . . . denunciation" of the BIA, but winning a few hasty promises that Navajo trucks and drivers would be used for the project.[53] In the end, although the BIA did indeed hire Navajo drivers, they replaced the Navajos' older trucks with more modern vehicles, and the project, completed in 1935 and 1936, did not prove to be the significant source of employment Forrest and the Navajos had hoped it would be.[54] Other CCC-ID projects on the dam proved just as disappointing. In the early 1940s, local Navajos employed by the government worked on the project, and the Hubbells won a contract to sell them corn for their horses. But the project only employed thirty Navajos—the sale of the corn and the extra trade generated by the project "gave the Hubbells a piece of the action, but it was a far cry" from the old days when work on the irrigation project propelled the Hubbell ranch into its glory days.[55] At the end of the day, the New Deal projects seemed a paltry compensation for the horrors of stock reduction, the full effects of which would not be felt until after the Second World War, "when soldiers returned to a reservation with severely diminished economic opportunity."[56]

## Staying Afloat during the Depression

For the next decade, Roman and Lorenzo fought to keep intact a business that had never been terribly stable in the best of times. They continued to lean on Henry Dodge to secure loans the bank would no longer grant them. In January 1931, with years of economic turmoil still ahead, their total indebtedness to Dodge reached $40,000, an amount they could not even afford to pay interest on.[57] Dodge understood their position, and did not press too hard for payments as the Hubbells chipped away at their debt with agonizing slowness, but other lenders were less understanding.[58] Even as the Hubbells tried frantically to collect on overdue accounts, their creditors began to sue them.[59] Time-honored systems of pawn and credit that had been the backbone of Navajo Indian trading broke down as the Hubbells found themselves unable to extend credit to all but the most reliable of their customers. As Lorenzo remarked, "The Indian Trading business is getting to be very hard.... Trusting Indians without security is getting more and more dangerous."[60] They, like other traders who had extended credit to the Navajos far beyond their capacity in the early years of the Depression, had to cut them off in the wake of the 1931–1932 winter storms.[61]

The Depression was like a heavy boot heel on the backs of the Hubbells' necks, grinding their faces into the ground. Finances weighed so heavily on Lorenzo's spirits as the years trudged on that his solemn yet optimistic refrain, that things would get better if only the family could work harder, gave way to a grim lament: "Business is not easy, never was, and never will be."[62] A man known for his generosity, who sincerely believed his business lay in helping the Navajos and Hopis, began to question the foundations of his life. He confessed to one of his employees, a woman who would later become his wife, that the business was beginning to overwhelm him. In a letter that expresses the agony of a warm, personable man forced to abandon his liberality, Lorenzo wrote, "Business is getting more complicated, as there is so much more detail than formerly, and while my interests in life have been to serve the many, the situation has changed, as the demands are too great. Had I worked more efficiently dear I would not be writing like this, but having so many places to look after, and having a full job at Oraibi, it has just been more than I could attend to. I am not so fond of business sweetheart, but I like the human aspect of it, when it gets cold I desire to move away from it. While I complain and may know the cause of this condition, which could have been corrected, I only blame myself for it for not being a little more selfish."[63]

Although Lorenzo had been accustomed to running multiple trading posts, after his father's death he sometimes had to juggle a dozen at a time. During the first half of the Depression, as in years past, the Hubbells seemed to cling to their belief that the answer to their financial troubles was to open *more* trading posts and other subsidiary businesses. During the 1930s, the family reopened the Dam Store when work on the irrigation works and the reservoir recommenced, and Lorenzo bought as many as five other trading posts.[64] In a move that betrayed his financial desperation, he also opened in Winslow the Pronto Service Station and a liquor store called the Pioneer.[65]

As the Depression dragged on, the burdens of sustaining so many businesses became impossible to carry. The family opened their last new trading post in 1935, and began to sell any post they could find a buyer for, triggering a slow erosion of the Hubbell empire that would continue unabated until only the trading post at Ganado remained. Other businesses Lorenzo simply closed. For example, knowing almost nothing about the liquor business, Lorenzo left the management of the Pioneer up to his employees, "and before I knew it, a lot of money was lost, and had accumulated a lot of bills that were unpaid."[66] After an abortive attempt to sell it in 1937, he just closed it down in 1938; it was so unprofitable that he declared "there is no use keeping it open any longer."[67] He closed down the Pronto Service Station, too, when it failed to turn a profit. As he explained to one of his banks, even when the trading posts had what would have been a good year, "with so many debts, and interests to pay, its [sic] hard to make any headway," and since "buyers with money are scarce," sometimes his only option was to close the doors, lock up, and walk away.[68] The strategy worked—at least a little. Helen Corcoran, who ran Lorenzo's Winslow wholesale store for many years, wrote to him in 1940, after a solid decade of the direst conditions, "I never dreamed you would be able to demolish the accounts payable the way you have. I think the places that were costing you money that you have closed have helped a lot."[69] If nothing else, closing the trading posts at least kept them from sinking Lorenzo still further into debt.

## *The Family and the Old Ganado Homestead*

The ravages of the 1930s did not leave the old Ganado homestead unchanged. Without the magnetic presence of J. L. Hubbell, family members and guests alike drifted quietly away from its warm halls. Once the vibrant heart of the Hubbell empire, the trading post at Ganado subsided as the family dispersed. Lorenzo returned to Oraibi, and seemed to take with him the vitality and diversity that had once been the earmark of Ganado. Anthropologist Edward T. Hall frequently visited both Ganado and Oraibi during the 1930s, and while he praised the comfort and style of a dinner elegantly served on china plates by Navajo girls under Barbara's watchful eye at Ganado, "the conversation," he said, "lacked Oraibi's spontaneity and sparkle."[70] It was at Oraibi that the traveler could find seated around the table "Lorenzo's truck drivers, an occasional Navajo headman, a government stockman, visiting scientists from Europe, an Eastern writer who was a household name, occasionally the commissioner of Indian Affairs . . . or the wife of the Secretary of the Interior."[71]

Roman and Dorothy, too, left the old homestead, and moved to Gallup to run the wholesale business and put Monnie and John through high school. A few years later, Forrest took a job with the Office of Indian Affairs, and he and Adele left Ganado once again to live first in Window Rock and then in Phoenix. Roman traveled from Gallup to Ganado frequently to manage the farm and handle business matters, but his absences were long and frequent. And so the heart of the Hubbell empire split in two, one half drifting south to Gallup, and the other north to Oraibi, and for the first time since C. N. Cotton left, the store was entirely in the hands of a series of hired clerks.[72] Barbara, now in her fifties, was the only one of J. L. and Lina's children left in the Hubbell family home. She who had been the quiet but capable mistress of Ganado since her husband's death became its "chief presence," managing the post office and hosting the occasional guest as she had always done.[73] But her health began to flag in the 1930s as Parkinson's disease crept up on her, and she entertained less frequently. With finances as troubled as they were, and with guests so few, the Hubbells hired fewer maids and cooks. The house emptied.[74]

Though the Hubbell home contained only the echoes of livelier times, and the mortgages grew heavier each year, "the old homestead, even when occupied by hired help, had an emotional value far beyond what it represented as an investment. So, despite the Depression, construction at Ganado continued."[75] In 1934, Roman began building, as a memorial to his father, a modern stone guest hogan with electricity and plumbing, and the Hubbells made improvements to several other outbuildings on the ranch.[76] Roman also kept the farm plowed and planted in oats and alfalfa. Although the drought did not completely spare Ganado farms, irrigation took the edge off their suffering, and during the Depression years, the Ganado Irrigation Project was among the most productive on the reservation.[77] In 1937, Roman managed to grow enough alfalfa that the Hubbells did not have to buy any feed for their teams.[78] The sheep and wool business, however, stayed rocky throughout the decade—the same year that Roman's alfalfa crop proved so bounteous was also "the least that Ganado ever bought in wool."[79]

Away from Ganado, the Hubbell family grew. LaCharles, who had graduated from El Paso High School in 1926 and enrolled in college in Tucson as an anthropology student in 1927, brought her husband-to-be home to Ganado for the first time in 1930, not long before her grandfather passed away. His name was Edwin B. Eckel, a graduate student in geology at the University of Arizona. LaCharles and Ed graduated in the same year—he took a job in Colorado, and LaCharles went home to Ganado and her mother until the spring of 1931, when Ed and LaCharles were married at the old Hubbell family home.[80] In a rare moment, the whole clan gathered together, looking unusually sharp in dresses and suits with carnations in their buttonholes, and LaCharles was married surrounded by the uncles who had been like fathers to her. The newlyweds departed for their honeymoon, and then went to live in Colorado, where the first of J. L. Hubbell's great-grandchildren was born in early 1932.[81] Roman's oldest son, Monnie, married not long after LaCharles, in October 1933. Following in the impulsive footsteps of his father, he eloped with his high school sweetheart, Dorothy Ketner, so no wedding reunited the family in the Hubbell home.[82]

Even Lorenzo, Jr., a bachelor in his fifties, found a brief but brilliant romance during the Depression's dark years. In August 1934, he began "seriously keeping company" with one of the clerks in his Winslow wholesale house, though, as he wrote to her, "it was years before that our hearts had had their understanding."[83] Her name was Flora Sandoval, a woman twenty years his junior with a young daughter. The two of them spent a few stolen hours together on Sunday nights when Lorenzo went to Winslow for business, and during the week they sent each other passionate love letters written in an intimate blend of Spanish and English. Lorenzo, as one of his friends once remarked, "like many oldtime Hispanic males, put women on a pedestal," and he seemed to worship his "Florita."[84] He confessed to her in words uncharacteristically open for such a quiet, private man, "No matter where you are, *olvidarte no puedo,* the memory of our association will be remembered, as the most beautiful, the finest, and the best that Lorencito has ever had. . . . My days will be happy ones when I know yours are, and this will be until this body of mine is turned to ashes."[85]

Their relationship, however, was tempestuous, for Flora was emotional and impulsive, and Lorenzo's financial situation repeatedly delayed their marriage. Her letters were encouraging and sentimental one week, ringing with indignation the next, and then soothingly apologetic. She once threatened to leave Winslow with her daughter because she could not get along with another of Lorenzo's employees, a woman she called a "jealous 'cat.'"[86] When Lorenzo failed to fire the offending employee, Flora dramatically announced, "I am leaving, even tho I love you and it breaks my heart to part, for you have meant more to me than I can ever express. Goodbye dear in case I do not see you again."[87] Lorenzo managed somehow to smooth it over, but the two of them also faced the violent opposition of Flora's mother, which did not make their relationship any easier. Finally, after two years of turbulent courtship, the two were married in Oraibi on August 10, 1936, a momentous occasion which Lorenzo characteristically announced to the rest of the family after the fact in a brief letter.[88] Their marriage did not last—before two years had passed, Florita suddenly left Oraibi and Lorenzo. The Hubbells never spoke much of Lorenzo's marriage; LaCharles simply called it "a disaster, but those things happen."[89]

About the time Lorenzo's marriage ended, Adele suffered a diabetic attack that left her hospitalized and with a constant pain in her left hand and arm. Forrest wired the Hubbells from Phoenix with the news that the physician did not expect her to live longer than six months—though she would, in fact, live for two more years.[90] When she was able, Adele returned to Ganado wait out her last illness in the comfort of the family home under the care of her sister. Forrest reluctantly returned to Phoenix, knowing that "I must hang onto my job . . . I must keep on the pay roll," and fairly begged Roman and Dorothy to take care of her in his absence.[91] "Roman," he wrote, "I left Ganado, broken hearted this morning. My own life depends on doing what I can to make Lala's last days, weeks, months or years easy for her and happy."[92] Adele's illness was not an easy one, and she spent her last three months bedridden. When it became apparent that the end of Lala's struggle was finally near, Forrest returned to Ganado. Adele passed away on July 3, 1939, at age 59 and was buried alongside her parents on Hubbell Hill—a scene that would grow more and more familiar in the coming years.[93] Her friends, whether local missionaries or famous artists, remembered her "as a generous and gracious hostess."[94] She was the first of J. L. and Lina's children to pass away.

## *"Off the Beaten Paths"*

All through the personal and financial tragedies of the 1930s, Roman kept searching, as he always had, for new directions in which to take the family business. Edward T. Hall, a frequent visitor and family friend, recalled, "Roman was always full of ideas for making money, and Lorenzo, if he was quick enough, would squelch these schemes with the cold light of reality. I used to listen to him on the Oraibi end of the telephone while Roman was explaining something to him. Then there would be a short silence, which was not caused by the primitive line with its crackles and pops; it was tension. Lorenzo would shout with a combination of love and exasperation in his voice, 'My God, Roman. We can't do that. We haven't got the *money!*' The Depression was far from over, and Lorenzo was fighting other battles to keep his business alive."[95] As manager, Lorenzo, Jr., had the power to quash Roman's ideas when he felt they did not serve the interests of the business, and he was inclined to act cautiously after their disastrous sheep scheme in 1931. But Roman had always been a dreamer, and the brothers seemed to disagree on business matters so often that in December 1938, Dorothy and Roman sold their shares of the J. L. Hubbell Trading Post to Lorenzo in exchange for $5,000 worth of rugs and blankets.[96] With his interest in the Ganado business officially terminated, Roman, who "never cared so much about trading with the Navajos as he did exploring their beautiful country and taking visitors to the hidden away spots no casual traveler could find," turned his passion and what remained of his own financial capital to bringing to fruition a longtime dream of his: Roman Hubbell Navajo Tours.[97]

Roman had begun seriously to hatch his plan in 1937, and scarcely a year later he was ready and waiting, with two Buick sedans with his logo, the Navajo symbol Conveyance of the Gods, emblazoned on the side, to

Roman and tourist Ann Knock having a picnic in Monument Valley, c. 1938. Courtesy of the National Park Service, HUTR 23083.

shuttle tourists over the country. Roman had been unofficially taking visitors around northeastern Arizona since the 1910s—not only his father's friends, who received the treatment courtesy of the Hubbell hospitality, but also paying tourists.[98] Meanwhile, the Fred Harvey Company and the Santa Fe Railway launched their own motorized "Indian Detours" in 1926, offering "specialized automobile tours of the Southwest through which privileged visitors could travel through '200,000 miles of matchless virgin territory.'"[99] The Indian Detours capitalized on the same surge in interest in the Southwest that gave Ganado its golden age, taking Kodak-wielding tourists to the Pueblos and the Snake Dance in unprecedented numbers.[100] Led by its trademark female couriers bedecked in Navajo turquoise and silver concho belts and accompanied by cowboy drivers, the Indian Detours promised unparalleled access to Indian communities and remote areas formerly available only to intrepid travelers willing to brave a little discomfort. "Those who are passing on into the setting sun made the Southwest safe for you and for us," a 1930 brochure told potential visitors. "The railroad gave it gateways. Now the Harveycar has let down the last barriers of time and distance, of discomfort and inconvenience, until the Southwest's heart is no longer for the pioneer alone."[101]

The service Roman began to offer in 1938 closely paralleled in form and rhetoric the Harvey Company's Indian Detours. Like the Detours, Roman Hubbell Navajo Tours took care of passengers' transportation, meals, and lodging so that they need worry about nothing beyond taking in with wide eyes the experiences the Southwest had to offer them—for a fee.[102]

Roman offered fully customizable trips from Gallup to any place in Arizona or New Mexico, though he concentrated his tours around what he called the "Seven Great Wonders of the Southwest," which consisted of Canyon de Chelly; the Hopi Mesas; Zuni Village, the Ice Caves, and El Morro; Acoma Village; Chaco Canyon; the Petrified Forest and the Painted Desert; and the Aztec Ruins.[103] In words that echoed the high ideals and appeals to authenticity of the Indian Detours, Roman's brochure proclaimed, "Almost all of its most interesting spots lie off the beaten path, back in the real unspoiled primitive wilderness, untouched by modern life, unseen by more than a handful of white people. Until now there has been no way for the stranger to get into this vast back country."[104] Roman, no doubt, had in mind destinations and experiences a little more remote and intimate than those frequented by Harveycars. As a lifelong resident of Navajo country, he offered an experience that the couriers of the Indian Detours, no matter how well-trained, simply could not match. As Roman's brochures made no hesitation of boasting, "Since 1873 the Hubbell family has worked and traded with the Indians, learning to know their language and customs, visiting far corners of their country. This trading post of Don Lorenzo Hubbell is famous throughout two states, and a son of Don Lorenzo operates this new and unique way to see this country that so few white people have ever seen. . . . Knowing the country and the Indian tribes intimately (Roman Hubbell has been initiated into Navajo ceremonies and speaks their language), we hear by grapevine telegraph of strange ceremonial dances—and on such occasions can show our guests such weird ceremonies as the Yei-bei-chai, the Night chant, the Fire Dance, or the amusing Squaw Dance."[105] With Roman frequently acting as a guide—in the beginning, he and Dorothy were the only guides—and later hiring other drivers with an intimate understanding of the country who often spoke Spanish and Navajo, including Sam Day,

Milton Wetherill, and Shine Smith, guests were guaranteed an insider's perspective.[106] As Roman told the director of the Automobile Club of New York, "On account of the good will our natives have for the Roman Hubbell Navajo Tours, we are able to visit their homes and are accorded a sincere welcome."[107] Though he charged his customers, Roman carefully carried forward the family tradition of hospitality with his easy manners. One of his customers wrote, "We felt as guests or as part of the family, never as tourists. This made the experience twice as delightful."[108]

Roman and Dorothy poured their energies into drumming up publicity for their new business, sending brochures and information to travel agencies and automobile clubs all over the country.[109] They paid for advertisements, and enlisted the formidable help of their many friends who made their living by the pen to write newspaper and magazine articles and radio broadcasts that evoked the mystery of the Southwest and convinced readers and listeners that Roman's tours were the best gateway to that strange world.[110] They also relied heavily upon word-of-mouth advertising from their guests, who were often more than happy to provide it. After James Welsh, a writer and photographer for the Automobile Club of Michigan and *Detroit Motor News*, had taken one of Roman's tours, he unleashed a barrage of publicity for Roman. "Since returning home," Welsh wrote, "I have made 28 talks—luncheon clubs, etc.—and have done a good job of setting you up as the one authority on that section of the country, and have personally suggested to a number of prospective vacationists that they contact you before they start westward."[111] He also wrote articles and radio broadcasts, sending Roman copies of each one. "With all that grand publicity," Roman wrote in thanks, "I am going about with a chest about to burst!"[112] Another guest, Mrs. E. B. Kellam, wrote a two-page poem about her trip with Roman, which she sent to a hundred of her friends:

> It is hard to tell of the marvels
>     I saw in the space of a week
> As I traveled thru OUR Arizona,
>     A wonderland if you but seek!
> If pleasure bent, don't drive your *own* car
>     Just wire to Gallup, Roman Hubbell,
> *His* tours, *his* drivers, and *his* cars
>     Will save you, I know, Much, Much trouble![113]

The Tours made little profit in their first year, and Roman, who had been roaming around Navajo country with guests in tow unfettered for decades, found that he had staggering interstate business licensing hurdles to clear, and that some places, including Canyon de Chelly, which had become a National Monument in 1931, were now closed to him by regulation.[114] The Tours, however, served as "a necessary supplement to the declining revenues of the trading enterprise and the consistent losses of the farm as the Great Depression sapped the nation's economy."[115] Some of their most lucrative work was not in transporting tourists, but in shuttling crews and actors for movies being filmed in the country around Gallup.[116] But with the avalanche of publicity that Roman's friends unleashed, in the following years the Tours began to take off, and Roman was hopeful that the war in Europe—the chaos having not yet spread to the United States—would drive Americans tourists, barred from their customary European pleasure grounds, to look to the Southwest.[117]

Roman's hope was short-lived, however. Days after the Japanese attack on Pearl Harbor on December 7, 1941, a woman who had heard of Roman's tours from her friends and from a radio program, confessed in her letter of inquiry that her plans seemed to have been formed "in the distant past, what with the excitement of the war."[118] Wartime measures soon put a stop to Roman's tours. After the United States entered the war, the Office of Defense Transportation prohibited sightseeing services for the duration to save fuel, tires, and parts for the war effort.[119] Only the mail and freight lines were deemed necessary and allowed to remain open. Roman always intended to start the tours again as soon as the war ended, but by then the Hubbell family had suffered its own greatest losses, and he and Dorothy reluctantly sold the business in 1945 to a Gallup freighting company, Cresto Transfer.[120]

## *The Second World War*

As the United States watched war rage in Europe, the whole country seemed to vibrate with tension. The Hubbells, their minds already burdened with debts, read the newspapers and remembered the hard times that the First World War had already brought them. "Germany is doing the very thing she did before, fighting outside of her own country," Lorenzo wrote to his cousins, Tom and Nell, in the spring of 1940. "If this war lasts," he speculated grimly, "we will be in it."[121] Lorenzo was in as much debt as ever, and he was crippled by serious illness and constant worry. As the war loomed closer, shortages of goods began to cause further problems. As Helen Corcoran wrote, "Goods are getting more difficult to get all of the time. . . . We are going to know that there is a war alright."[122] For Indian traders and curio dealers, business in 1941 was "the worst they ever knew."[123]

When the bombing of Pearl Harbor finally broke the tension and secured the entrance of the United States into the Second World War, it wrought changes in Navajo country "so broad and deep that they shook the traditional pattern of living to its very foundations."[124] Within the first year of the war, over 1,400 Navajos joined the army, many as volunteers; over 3,600 Navajos would serve over the course of the war.[125] As Peter Iverson notes, "Even though Arizona, New Mexico, and Utah had denied the right to vote to residents of Indian reservations, these men and women reaffirmed their loyal duties to the Navajo Nation and to the United States and their commitment to fight to defend both homelands. They shared other Americans' anger at what had happened in Hawaii and they wanted to do their part to protect the sacred mountains."[126] Many young Navajos who stayed home took jobs at ordnance depots near Flagstaff and Gallup, earning wages that they could not hope to match herding and farming. During the war, ten thousand Navajos worked in war-related industries, with another two thousand working on the railroads.[127]

For the Hubbells, the war meant fewer Navajos trading at their posts, a shortage of labor, and rationing. Sugar, coffee, meat, gasoline, processed foods, shoes—everything, it seemed, that a trading post needed to stock its shelves—was subject to rationing.[128] Blackouts plunged the desert into darkness.[129] The curio trade ground to a halt. The business received orders for blankets occasionally, but the Hubbells were forced to tell customers they could not fill them. Stock reduction, combined with the ready availability of wage work on government projects, meant that fewer Navajo women were weaving—and when they did weave, they were increasingly likely to sell their rugs in town for a better price than the traders could give them.[130] The Hubbells also struggled to keep their posts staffed as the draft swept away the nation's young men. Roman asked the draft board for deferments for several of his clerks, trying to convey the clerks' importance to "civilian needs on the reservation."[131] He tried to explain that he could not simply hire new clerks, but would have to close the stores, "for in order to take care of the needs of the Indians it takes a long time to know them."[132]

Closing the stores, he argued, would hurt the local economy as well as the Hubbell business.[133]

The draft claimed not only the Hubbell's employees, but their children as well, and they frequently found themselves wishing "they could come give us a hand. But then everyone else is in the same boat."[134] Both of Roman and Dorothy's boys served—Monnie at the beginning of the war, and John later after initially being rejected by the Selective Service because he was underweight—and Ed spent the war years in the European theater.[135] Despite their belief in the necessity of the war effort, the absence of loved ones weighed heavily on the family. Barbara, suffering through the increasing pain and weakness of Parkinson's, would sit next the radio and weep as the news croaked its harsh pronouncements.[136] With Ed gone, LaCharles, too, struggled to keep her spirits up, knowing that "the news is so terrible from the Western Front."[137] On New Year's Eve, 1944, she glumly confessed to Dorothy and Roman, "I can't see anything much to celebrate—except to be darn thankful this year is over and done with and hope that this next year will be easier to take. I don't think any year could be much worse than 1944 was."[138]

While Ed was in Europe and help on the reservation was difficult to come by, LaCharles answered Roman's repeated pleas to "come out and give us a hand" at Ganado.[139] She took her three young boys to "get some life" at the old homestead—what she called "coming home"—and worked in the store under the tutelage of one of the Hubbells' longtime Navajo employees, Joe Tippecanoe, while her children played in the barn as she had done as a girl.[140] Having a Hubbell in charge after Ganado had been in the hands of hired help for so many years eased all their minds. Roman was even willing to acquiesce whenever LaCharles, who was burning a "short fuse," fired the occasional clerk.[141] Having sent the latest offender packing, she would simply pick up the phone and "call Roman and say, 'I fired so and so,' and he'd say, 'Well, I'll send somebody out.'"[142] LaCharles found joy in the work of Indian trading, perhaps because of its familiarity. "I loved doing the books," she remembered, "I loved buying the sheep and getting them delivered and stuff like that. I did it because I really liked it."[143]

In 1944, news reached the Hubbells of a tragedy that would have a devastating impact on the fate of the Hubbell Trading Post: the death of Roman Dorr Hubbell. Monnie spent most of the war in the Pacific, particularly Australia, with the 7th Cavalry. There were several Navajos in his group,

Monnie standing in a trench during World War II. Courtesy of the National Park Service, HUTR 04981.

and they often banded together to remember the smell of rain on the desert, the flash of sunlight on a concho belt, the puffy white clouds of sheep moving down a hillside. Dorothy later recalled that after the war, "a Navajo came into the store in Winslow and asked if I were Captain Roman Hubbell's mother. I said, 'Yes.' He told me that while they were in Australia I had sent a box of pinons to Monnie and he invited some of the Navajo in to share them. They sat all night in his tent eating pinons and talking about Arizona."[144] She remembered that because he spoke Navajo so well, Monnie worked from time to time with the Navajo Code Talkers, a group of Navajo men who used their language to develop an unbreakable code that would play an integral part in the war. Philip Johnston, a missionary's son who had grown up in Navajo country, proposed and set in motion the program, based on the use of Choctaw codes in World War I.[145] "I knew Johnston," Dorothy remembered. "When Monnie was killed overseas he sent me a letter" and later "a copy of the report he had written about the Navajo code program."[146]

After six days of costly fighting, Monnie was killed on Manus Island on March 24, 1944, by heavy Japanese fire while advancing blindly through the jungle.[147] The news would not reach his parents until April 16, nearly a month later. Older now than he had been when the First World War stirred up the fighting blood of the Hubbell men, Roman grieved, "It is just too bad that humans that are supposed to be intelligent cannot iron out their differences except by fighting."[148] With Monnie died the Hubbell grandchild most likely to carry on the family business. Monnie "seemed attuned to trade and Navajo culture," and it was to him that the Hubbell legacy would have passed.[149] Without him the future looked bleak, for his death came almost exactly two years after the Hubbells lost another pillar of strength—Lorenzo, Jr.

### The Passing of "The Second Lorenzo, the Great"

Not long after Adele passed away in 1939, Lorenzo, Jr., began to suffer serious health problems. He had always been a large man, and now his heart, liver, joints, and blood pressure, no doubt aggravated by the unrelenting stress of the last decade, all began to wreak havoc. Lorenzo was not one to take vacations from his work or follow the advice of doctors, and his family and employees anxiously watched him drag obstinately through his days.[150] When his cousin George's wife, Madge, found out how ill Lorenzo was in October 1939, she begged him to see a doctor at once. "We can't any of us spare you just yet, not only Auntie Bob but all of us *need you*," she pleaded.[151]

And they did need him. Even though Lorenzo was hopelessly disorganized, his generous personality was the keystone holding the business together. In November, his health deteriorated so precipitously that he finally gave in and went to see a doctor in Phoenix. For "five long weeks . . . I did not walk any further than fifty feet from my bed," Lorenzo recalled. "The doctor gave me not more than four days to live. When he told me this, I told him that he could plan my death but that I would make my own funeral arrangements."[152] By sheer stubbornness or reluctant cooperation with the doctor's insistence that he give up tobacco, alcohol, and meat, Lorenzo staved off death. But while he was recuperating, rumors began to spread in Navajo country that he had both feet in the grave and would not last two weeks. His relatives, employees, and customers all reacted as if the whole business of Indian trading would surely die with Lorenzo. Thomas S. Hubbell, Lorenzo's cousin, reassured his employees and the Navajos, who had "heard he was dead," that Lorenzo was mending and would be home soon.[153] He convalesced in Phoenix and then at Loma Linda Sanitarium in California until the end of January 1940, but his absence pained him, not only because of the business, which was never far from his mind, but because Navajo country, which he had seldom left in his entire life, was in his blood. He returned with palpable relief: "I am sure glad to get back to this country, and see some more Navajos and Hopis; I like the indian country best of all."[154]

Lorenzo spent the next few years, between bouts of illness, trying to revive his business while his family and friends solicitously sent him care packages of whole wheat bread and vegetables.[155] His illness exacerbated his normal forgetfulness, and he began to mislay papers and quarrel with his employees—which only made him sicker, he hated conflict so much.[156] He knew the state of the business required more of him than it ever had before, but he felt himself unable to do what he needed to do. "If ever I was embarrased [sic] its now, I feel my obligations so greatly, and not any to[o] well to work efficiently, which I have never done before, and now I am more or less helpless; its a terrible pridicament [sic]," he worried.[157]

In the last year of his life, Lorenzo seemed to sense the end was near and began attempting to liquidate as many of his assets as possible: property, rugs, antiques, and even the Ganado homestead and its art collection. The prospect of selling the old family home was not a pleasant one, but after a decade of tooth-and-nail scrabbling, Lorenzo likely saw no other choice. But he wanted a buyer who would understand its intangible qualities, things that could not be quantified on any survey map or bill of sale.

Postcard showing Lorenzo, Jr., in the rug room of his Oraibi trading post, c. 1923. Courtesy of the National Park Service, HUTR 04940.

As he explained to one potential buyer, "It may interest you to know that if the proper parties would like a business or a home and are interested in the pictures and old things at Ganado surrounded by primitive Indians and accessible to Canyon Dechelley and on the road to the Hopi Villages and the Grand Canyon and its self setting in a red valley I would consider it's [sic] sale. Whoever purchases this place will find it one of the most interesting locations in the Southwest, it is on patented land containing about 160 acres, on which stands I believe the oldest business in Arizona located in the same place and run by the same family."[158] The Ganado property was more than a trading post, an old house, and some outbuildings on a 160-acre ranch. It was all of the artists and anthropologists who had sheltered there, all of the Navajos who had ridden to the door on ponies laden with sacks of wool. It was the landscape and the bright blue sky. It was the Hubbell family legacy.

Buyers with cash were scarce in 1941, however, as Lorenzo found out when he tried to sell the Pronto Service Station, Marble Canyon, his property in Gallup, and the fruit ranch at Farmington.[159] The same conditions that made Lorenzo desperate to sell made buyers reluctant, so Ganado and the art collections remained safe and intact. Meanwhile, Lorenzo's health worsened. First his legs, and then his hips and stomach began to swell, and sleeplessness haunted his nights, but rather than leave the business, he corresponded with his doctor in Phoenix, hoping for a cure by mail.[160] He kept meaning to go back to Loma Linda, but could never arrange his affairs to his satisfaction. Soon, he was confined to his bed with Roman at his side, dictating business letters as the war news broke over them. Lorenzo Hubbell, Jr., died at his home in Oraibi on March 2, 1942, of hypertensive heart disease at age 58, not three months after the bombing of Pearl Harbor.[161] The family laid him to rest on Hubbell Hill with those of his family who had gone before him.

Word of Lorenzo's passing left an ache in the hearts of his friends near and far, "Indians and whites alike."[162] At Cedar Springs, a group of Navajos who could not make it to Ganado in time for Lorenzo's funeral gathered to sign with their thumb prints a letter carrying their sympathies and admiration for Lorenzo.[163] The news stunned John Collier, who wrote in Lorenzo's obituary, "It seems impossible. Lorenzo was still within his middle years. . . . So much of America's best, of the best of old Spain, of the Indians' best, was gathered into, fused within, that never-resting creative spirit of his, that he seemed like an ancient Merlin, even eighteen years ago."[164] His reputation was not the larger-than-life frontier legend that J. L.'s had been, but those who knew Lorenzo, who could not picture Oraibi and the Snake Dance without him, mourned him as "one of God's noblemen."[165] Lorenzo's "world wasn't a large world, but in it he was known as a good and fine man and if a man's worth can be measured by the number of people who sincerely mourn his passing, then Lorenzo Hubbell was truly a great man, a man of worth."[166]

## Picking Up the Pieces

Lorenzo, despite his best efforts, did not leave his affairs in any better shape than his father had left his. The Hubbell family frantically tried to settle his estate, all the while keenly feeling his loss, for the business did not pass out of Lorenzo's hands smoothly, but in a bitter struggle. "I've been sitting here in Lorenzo's office at Oraibi," Hubbell Parker, who took over the management of the post after Lorenzo's passing, wrote to one of his uncle's friends, "and wishing that Lorenzo was the one that was writing you this letter."[167] A year after Lorenzo passed, Roman admitted in exhaustion to one of his old

Tours customers, "Lorenzo passed away and certainly left a lot of work for me to do."[168]

Lorenzo, in a will he had signed before Adele's death in 1939, appointed Forrest Parker the executor of his estate and left the J. L. Hubbell Trading Post at Ganado to his sisters, dividing the multitude of other appendages of the business equally among his siblings and his nephews and niece.[169] With Adele dead, her shares went to her husband, and Forrest, now remarried, returned to Navajo country a partial owner of nearly all of the Hubbells' assets. During his stints at the trading post, Forrest seems to have clashed with everyone, even Lorenzo. His position as executor caused tension in the family as he made decisions that did not sit well with those who had been more intimately involved in the business—especially decisions about the Ganado property. Roman, Dorothy, and LaCharles exchanged letters full of bitter frustration and searched for a way to remove Forrest from the business altogether.[170] With Lorenzo's estate in probate, its assets controlled by the court until its debts could be settled, and Forrest holding all the power, they felt helpless. On one occasion, Roman managed to free up enough money to pay Henry Chee Dodge the interest on the mortgage, and thought he could make the next payment at sheep-buying time in the fall, but "after that, the Lord only knows what we can do, everything may be changed."[171] Somehow, after "a continual fight... through lawyers and court orders to prevent their liquidating the estate," Dorothy and Roman managed in the spring of 1943 to buy out Forrest's interests, as well as those of Miles and Hubbell Parker.[172] When the J. L. Hubbell Trading Post incorporated, its officers consisted of Roman as President and Treasurer, LaCharles as Vice-President, Dorothy as Secretary, and John as a member.[173] Having managed to raise enough money to pay off their debts, they operated the Lorenzo Hubbell Trading Company as a separate business.

For the remainder of the war, the Hubbells returned to the normal activities of running the trading business as best they could—selling land, planting alfalfa on the farm, buying what livestock there was to buy. Roman and Dorothy sold their property and business in Gallup and moved to Winslow to manage both businesses from Lorenzo's wholesale office. Barbara, unable to take care of herself as her Parkinson's disease worsened, finally relinquished her duties as the hostess of Hubbell Trading Post and went to live with Dorothy and Roman, while hired managers looked after Ganado whenever LaCharles could not be there.[174] Roman continued to struggle to keep the posts staffed as the draft claimed one employee after another, and he continued to cope with the diminished supply of blankets and curios. He kept his eyes fixed on the end of the war and the revival of Roman Hubbell Navajo Tours—a hope, however faint.

The war finally ended in 1945, but life on the Navajo Reservation would not simply return to the way it had been. The war had brought sweeping changes, and the Hubbell Trading Post was not spared. Edward T. Hall captured the essence of the change in one bleak paragraph:

> The war . . . put a period on the closing sentence of nineteenth-century life on the reservation. After the war, roads were paved, and the big washes . . . were all bridged. Prosperity came to the reservation, bringing four-wheel-drive vehicles and pickup trucks instead of wagons and horses for the Navajos and the Hopis. There was also the Peabody Coal Company ripping the guts out of Black Mesa, and Lake Mead providing access to tourists by the thousands to the once inaccessible Rainbow Bridge. In the Four Corners region, giant power plants produced electricity to light Phoenix and Los Angeles, and the smog choked the Grand Canyon and obscured the view of Mount Taylor. . . . Because all the new roads brought more and more people, the National Park Service had to control access to Canyon de Chelly and the great ruins of Betatakin and Keit Seil. Lorenzo Hubbell's trading post at Oraibi was torn down after his death in 1942, and the Hubbell empire collapsed.[175]

CHAPTER NINE

# A New Era
## Becoming a National Historic Site, 1945–1967

In the spring of 1948, Roman walked out of a meeting between the Navajo Council Advisory Committee and the United Indian Traders Association fuming. A few weeks before, the Tribal Council had passed a landmark resolution known as the Long Range Rehabilitation Act that would call for the appropriation of $90 million to be spent on improving the conditions on the Navajo Reservation—including building roads, hospitals, schools, highways, and irrigation projects—all projects that Roman should have wholeheartedly approved. But attached to the resolution were new regulations for traders. The reforms had been suggested by Max M. Drefkoff, a consultant commissioned by the US Department of the Interior to conduct a study on the Navajos' languishing postwar economy.[1] Drefkoff's report recommended that the Navajo Tribal Council regulate prices and set markup ceilings on the traders' goods, levy a tax on gross sales as a form of rent, and require more stringent bookkeeping.[2] The traders, balking at the idea of increased regulation, blamed Drefkoff for the Navajos' support of his plan, calling him a "stranger" and accusing him of giving the desperate Navajos "a straw in the sea to save themselves."[3] Roman raged about "the methods used by Drefkoff in intimidating and using Communistic methods to poison their [the Navajos'] minds against the traders."[4] But Navajos had been increasingly critical of traders even before the war. Like so many other problems that had been simmering on the back burner on the Navajo Reservation, reform of the trading post system "received a boost from veterans' expectations and demands."[5] After the war, "the pent up feelings of many Diné erupted in a campaign that startled many of the old-time traders, who had grown accustomed to minimal regulation and accountability."[6]

The traders protested. They hoped to find some common ground with the Tribal Council, but when their meeting resulted only in a one percent reduction on the tax to be levied on gross sales, the traders left convinced that they "cannot survive if the Drefkoff plan is carried into operation."[7] Traders argued that the plan would lead to the breakdown of the pawn system, and many feared that the demands of bookkeeping—traditionally a haphazard affair at best—would hobble the traders. As Roman put it, "Between the red tape concerned with all reports and their snoopers and . . . inspectors and records we have to keep it will take an auditor and a Philadelphia lawyer to figure it out—which a great many of the traders cannot afford to hire."[8] The traders claimed that the regulations would hurt the Navajos, too. Roman believed that the Navajos still needed the traders and would for many more years—Drefkoff's plans for Navajo-owned cooperative stores, he thought, were "all projects of the future."[9] The new regulations, he argued, would "knock the props out of the Navajo economy as when they are in need they will not have any where to go for help."[10]

The traders protested loudly enough that Acting Commissioner of Indian Affairs William J. Zimmerman did not approve the resolution, calling instead for more studies. But it was a hollow victory. The Navajos would continue to push back against what many saw as unfair trading practices, winning more substantial reforms year by year, and in the meantime, the other old-time traders could do nothing to stem the deluge of change that swept over the Navajo Reservation in the wake of the war. The influence of the outside world chipped away at the isolation of the traders and their Navajo customers. The Navajo economy was transforming, and the traders, willing or not, had to transform with it.[11]

When World War II ended, the momentum of life on the Navajo Reservation seemed to slow down abruptly, like a machine breaking down after years of furious activity, giving the consequences of the previous two decades' radical changes a chance to catch up. Young Navajo men and women returned from serving their country overseas or from working in the munitions depots to face chronic unemployment. Overgrazing and stock reduction had weakened the traditional economy, slamming the door on the lives that generations of Diné had led, and leaving young Navajos to scramble for insufficient wage work. To make the transition to a peacetime economy even more difficult, severe blizzards struck in the winter of 1947, forcing the Navajos to rely on food and aid distributed by the Red Cross and the federal government.¹² With all the troubles the Navajos had weathered, through depression and the devastation of their herds, it was then, not two years after the close of World War II, that "material life on the Navajo Reservation was at a low point."¹³

Although the federal government, awakened by the press to the Navajos' startling poverty, would dedicate government funds to welfare and unemployment programs, the Navajos themselves "increasingly took charge of the world in which they resided."¹⁴ The war had taken thousands of Navajos off the reservation, increasing their ability to move effectively in the outside world. As Peter Iverson notes, "Empowered by their experiences in wartime, the Navajos sought more political and legal authority as well as full participation in the American political system," turning their attention to developing medical, educational, and economic resources.¹⁵

Indian trading as an institution was as caught up in the whirlwind of change as the Navajos were. In the years immediately following the war, when the Navajo economy stumbled badly, the traders responded by taking in less pawn and extending less credit than had been their custom. Not long after the war ended, Roman advised the clerks in all of his trading posts not to "take any more pawn until further notice" and to give even those Navajos who paid their accounts "very little credit."¹⁶ As he explained to an anthropologist friend, "The Navajos are feeling the economic pressure as they do not seem to be able to find work enough to take the place of the amount their herds of livestock was reduced. Traders are loaded with pawn which the Indians cannot redeem, and accounts which they cannot pay."¹⁷ The collapse of the traditional Navajo economy also drastically reduced business for the traders, and they desperately needed every paying customer who came to the trading post. Roman told his clerks to buy any rug that came through the door, and urged them, "don't let a single lamb go out of your corral to be sold anywhere else regardless of what you have to pay for it."¹⁸ As more Navajos sought work off-reservation or went to work in the mines, as automobiles and paved roads broke the ties between Navajo families and their local trading posts, traders responded by becoming "more businesslike."¹⁹ As Willow Powers states, "Now traders were businessmen who, buying goods wholesale and selling them retail, sought—indeed, needed—to make a profit, to pay the store's bills, the percentage due to the Tribe, and the basic repairs on or even expansions to the trading post buildings. Trading posts were now more like other American businesses, in which economics and culture rested on the foundations of capitalism: working for wages, trying to build up capital or savings in money, doing business in which profit was essential."[20]

As trading posts began to operate more like other businesses, they also began to *look* more like other business as the trappings of modernization seeped in. Fluorescent lights, washing machines, air conditioning units, cash registers, coolers, and linoleum invaded the bullpens. But despite all the changes, both "visible and invisible," for those who stayed on the reservation, the trading post remained an important part of Navajo life a little longer.[21] The trading seasons rolled on around the calendar as they had always done, even if fewer sacks of wool and fewer rugs passed the traders' threshold and gas pumps cropped in the yard.[22] The trading business that Roman explained to a customer in 1946 did not seem so different from the way it had been in his father's day: "The life of an Indian Trader is certainly a varied one and we find that we put aside our correspondence in favor of something that simply cannot wait. These fall months are a terribly busy season for us—sheep and cattle shipping time—when everyone is on the go from morning till dark."[23]

## Old Strategies and New Ventures

During these years of monumental change, Roman and Dorothy ran the business with the Hubbell family's signature element of chaos, heightened by Roman's unchecked imagination and flare for publicity. When Lorenzo, Jr., died, Roman was forced to assume the management of the entirety of what was left of the Hubbell empire—still a considerable undertaking with the Winslow wholesale house, two freight lines, seven trading posts, and the Ganado homestead. In order to preserve the rest of the business, Roman had to sacrifice his treasured Roman Hubbell Navajo Tours, but he never ceased courting publicity and promoting tourism in the Navajo region.[24] Meetings about trading regulations Roman endured; his heart lay elsewhere. Of Roman, one friend wrote, "If Indian trading is unlike other businesses, Roman Hubbell is even more unlike other traders. A handsome man of fifty-six, with dark, graying hair he often wears striking Indian jewelry and colorful, handwoven vests. With flashing brown eyes that light up every time he gets an idea—about once every three minutes during his waking hours—Roman is as busy as a centipede on a hot griddle. . . . To the casual customer, the Hubbell company seems to operate on a principle of pandemonium, a condition resulting from Roman's feeling that he must personally supervise every transaction, a commendable but futile ambition."[25]

One of Roman's schemes was a curio outlet in Phoenix. The population of the Valley of the Sun had grown to a quarter of a million people, many of them newly arrived, building homes and "definitely prejudiced in favor of Western architecture and furnishings," and Roman was convinced that a curio shop could do well there if given a few seasons to establish its name.[26] Roman convinced Bill Greene and his wife, Evelyn, who had been helping run Marble Canyon since the end of the war, to open a shop with Roman supplying the goods on consignment. The couple fixed up an old house on Central Avenue in downtown Phoenix, painted and stocked the shelves, and built a Navajo hogan out front. Roman sent rugs and a weaver, Nanebah Clah, relying on the tried-and-true methods of the Fred Harvey Company to entice winter tourists.[27] The Greenes operated the Sun Valley Trading Post in fits and starts for three years in different locations until the trio finally acknowledged that the scheme was simply not profitable enough to justify keeping the store open.[28] Bill and Evelyn closed their doors in Phoenix and returned to the Navajo Reservation to manage the Oraibi trading post.[29] Despite his vision and aptitude, Roman had had no more luck in establishing a curio outlet in Phoenix than his brother had in California.

Roman's other pet project involved harnessing the potential of the Ganado and Marble Canyon trading posts as guest lodges. Lorenzo had always believed that the Marble Canyon post was perfectly positioned to capitalize on tourist travel along Highway 89 between Flagstaff and the North Rim of the Grand Canyon. As soon as the war ended, Roman, who had far greater aptitude for such a project than Lorenzo ever had, set out to implement it. In 1946, he took two photographers from *Life* and a few local newspapermen to Marble Canyon and down the Colorado River on a motorboat he bought for the occasion, launching his project with a healthy dose of publicity.[30] Over the next few years, he poured money into renovations, and by 1951, Marble Canyon Lodge boasted 20 rooms for rent across the street from the trading post, gas station, and a first-class roadside café.[31]

Meanwhile, the trading post and home at Ganado remained devoid of Hubbells but for brief visits.[32] Longtime Navajo country resident Dora Winnie Balcomb and her son Pete managed the trading post and ranch in the late 1940s and early 1950s, while the Hubbells all resided elsewhere.[33] For the first time in its hospitable history, the Hubbell home was closed to visitors more often than not. With none of the family under the roof, Roman and Dorothy directed travelers, even old friends like anthropologist Margaret Schevill, to "stay overnight at the Ganado Mission."[34] Having the house closed, however, seemed to Roman and Dorothy like a wasted opportunity, for they were convinced that "if we could find the right personnel, Marble Canyon and Ganado could work together very well as motels, and guest lodges."[35] In 1947, they entertained the possibility of turning the homestead into a dude ranch, but they were far more enthusiastic about a 1949 proposition of using the ranch as a summer camp for boys.[36] The site offered "truly a Western atmosphere to thrill the heart of any teen-age boy," Roman wrote to Eugene Clyde Weafer, who proposed the idea.[37] It was steeped in history and Indian culture, and surrounded by a rugged piñon and sagebrush landscape, with the added benefit of having Sage Memorial Hospital as a neighbor to assuage the fears of reluctant parents.[38] Roman thought he could turn an old warehouse he never finished into a dormitory, install shower and toilet facilities with relative ease, and have the place crawling with youngsters before the summer was out. The idea, however, was never actualized, and the Hubbells soon set their sights on other schemes. When a nine million dollar appropriation in 1949 signaled a flurry of road work on the reservation, including a road through Ganado to Tuba City and on to Highway 89 to Marble Canyon, Roman resolved that "some kind of accommodations at Ganado should be made available the traveling public. This might be our chance."[39]

The doors to the Hubbell home reopened to guests the following year when Roman and Dorothy hired Bob and Betty Dillon, who operated a hotel in Scottsdale called the Navajo, to manage the property as a guest lodge while the Balcombs continued to manage the store. From May to November that year, the traveling public could find meals and accommodations for up to fourteen people at Casa Don Lorenzo for $10 a day or $60 a week.[40] Roman capitalized on the site's history to draw guests, churning out romantic publicity with great practice. Not only was the old Hubbell home conveniently located for travel to the Navajo Reservation's most scenic locations, but by staying there, visitors would witness a trading post still in operation, sheep and blanket buying going on as it has always done, and a museum containing "some of the finest examples of Indian arts and crafts, both modern and ancient . . . and a fine anthropological and historical library, as well as priceless relics of the ancient peoples of this country, and a collection of paintings of American Indians by famous artists."[41] Nearby, the Ganado Reservoir offered ample opportunity for fishing, swimming, and boating, and always there was the tantalizing possibility of a traditional Indian dance. Traveling by car in the 1950s in greater numbers than ever before, Americans on vacation could stay in the home of a famous Indian trader that had "housed many of the world's great ... writers, artists and anthropologists," and be treated to the same "charm and warmth of hospitality and stateliness of living in the fine old Spanish tradition" that earlier visitors had enjoyed.[42]

Roman and Dorothy were proud of the venture. They put in a modern gas pump near the entrance of the trading post, and built a picnic area north of the guest Hogan with a stone table and benches, a barbecue pit, and a wagon-wheel light fixture.[43] That summer, they personally conducted fifteen members of the local chapter of the PEO Sisterhood, of which Dorothy was a member, on a tour of Navajo country, with their stay at Casa Don Lorenzo a focal point.[44] Some of their former guests from days past also visited Casa Don Lorenzo. Mahonri Young, who had once delighted a young LaCharles with his animal drawings, was pleased on his visit "to find Ganado so little changed."[45] The venture, however, lasted only two brief summers. The Dillons returned to Scottsdale at the end of the 1950 tourist season, and the following year the Hubbells did not manage to find anyone to run the guest lodge until halfway through the summer.[46] By the 1952 tourist season, disaster had fallen and Casa Don Lorenzo, along with almost everything else, was gone.

## *Bankruptcy*

Despite all of their visions and efforts, Roman and Dorothy's attempts to revive the Hubbell family business after the war failed. Everywhere they turned, from traditional Indian trading to modern tourism, business never matched their investments. The Lorenzo Hubbell Motor Company in Winslow, a venture far outside Roman's area of expertise, may have proved an especially voracious drain on their finances.[47] Business in 1951 was particularly disheartening as Hubbell wool sat unsold in Boston warehouses while the markets dipped, and in the spring of 1952, Roman began asking for loans on the Marble Canyon Lodge.[48] "In the end, Roman's strengths—managing the ranch as farm property and turning his father's guests into paying tourists—were not enough," and the Hubbells were finally forced to do what they had narrowly avoided doing on so many other occasions.[49]

On June 27, 1952, the J. L. Hubbell Trading Post and the Lorenzo Hubbell Trading Company declared bankruptcy and began operating under a receivership.[50] The court appointed I. J. Miller to manage the business, collect on delinquent accounts, sell dead pawn, repossess cars, pay creditors, and liquidate assets. Dorothy and Roman had to stand back while an outsider ran their business. Roman fidgeted and found fault with Miller, frequently driving to Ganado and ignoring Miller's assurances that his help was not needed. Roman also flew to Phoenix to attend creditors' meetings. Through it all his morale dragged. "It was very confusing," he wrote to his son, John, after one meeting in Phoenix, "I do not quite understand what is going on."[51]

The proceedings proved painful to the Hubbells in the extreme as the court sold their assets at staggering losses. In November 1952, the court sold for $125,000 a bundle of properties Roman estimated to be worth $428,000 to Buchanan and Bales: the Marble Canyon Lodge, the Winslow wholesale house, the Lorenzo Hubbell Motor Company, 100 acres of land outside Winslow, the Frontier, and Na-Ah-Tee Canyon. Dorothy harbored a deep-seated resentment toward Bales, whom she remembered greedily sniffing around the Ganado trading post, which, along with Piñon and Oraibi, were all that the Hubbells had left after the sale.[52] The Piñon post was to be sold to the Navajo Tribe, which Roman approved, but he fought to hold onto Oraibi and Ganado, persuading mortgage holders on the Ganado property to withdraw their claims from the bankruptcy proceedings, and preparing to sell some of the art collection, including Burbank's drawings. Roman needed to raise $30,000 to save Oraibi and Ganado, and he figured he could get $100 each for their nearly 200 Burbank Conte crayon Indian portraits, and $25,000 each for their three original Burbank oil paintings.[53] Roman and Dorothy did not immediately follow through with their idea to sell the art collections, but it was a recourse to which they would return in the future.

The estate closed on April 1, 1953, and the Hubbells retained possession of what little was left of their assets: Ganado and Oraibi. Roman and Dorothy moved to Ganado to take up the operation of a much-diminished J. L. Hubbell Trading Post, and Barbara, who had resisted leaving Navajo country for so long, finally agreed to move to Denver with LaCharles.[54] They put Oraibi in the hands of the Babbitts while they waited to see if the Navajo Tribe might buy it for enough money to pay their mortgage on the Ganado property, and even considered selling Ganado to the Navajos for $125,000.[55] By 1955, Oraibi and had been sold, and the Hubbell empire was reduced to its nucleus. Ganado was the only trading post left in the Hubbells' possession.

## *The Closing of an Era*

The ugliness of the bankruptcy proceedings, far more than the devastating results, finally smothered Roman's indefatigable cheerfulness and set him down the path of illness that his siblings had already walked. Roman, like his father and brother, had always prided himself on his generosity and honesty. "You'd be surprised at the people who take the stand at bankruptcy proceedings," Dorothy recalled, "that you're being *crooked*—and it was that idea of being crooked that really *cut,* and I think, *killed* Roman."[56] In the fall of 1953, Roman suffered his first stroke. A series of small strokes followed in the wake of the first, gradually leaving Roman paralyzed on his right side and unable to walk.[57] Dorothy, who had come to Ganado as a schoolteacher, took the reins of the business in her able hands, handling even the sheep and wool trade. By the spring of 1957, Roman was "an invalid" and in great pain.[58] His last months before his death on October 17 of that year were a trial to both of them. Dorothy tried to steel herself against the death of her husband of thirty-six years, but she found in the end that "my own personal loss seems to overshadow all else."[59] As she wrote to a friend, "That one so full of energy, so great an inspiration always to the rest of us, to be cut so quickly, was more than heart-breaking to us. I had many months in which to try to be prepared, but I found that I was not. He was such a big part of my life, adjustment is difficult for me."[60]

Roman's friends across the country received the news of his death as if not merely a man but a part of Navajo country had perished. Senator Barry Goldwater, sitting in his office looking at a map of Arizona, found it "almost impossible . . . to believe that Ramon [*sic*] is no longer with us. He was part and parcel . . . of that section of our State and to say that I will miss him would be an incomplete statement because I'm afraid the experience will be far more than just 'missing.' He was a friend in every good sense of the word."[61] Mrs. O. C. Havens echoed his sentiments, writing, "To me, an era that I truly loved, is fast coming to a close. The past few years have marked the passing of so many people that meant Gallup and the Southwest to me. We know that we cannot cling to loved ones forever yet their departures leave us with a feeling of loss and nostalgia. Some of these people were not close friends, but they were the Southwest that I love so much. To us, Roman was such a grand man and he typified that era of which today's youth is so unaware. A gentleman of the old school."[62]

Roman was buried in the family cemetery on Friday, October 18.[63] Though she was surrounded by family and friends, Dorothy felt burdened by the future she faced. "I cannot begin to describe my feelings as we descended Hubbell Hill, and with each step I could hear the words, over and over again, 'You are alone,'" she remembered. "That night after my descent from Hubbell Hill and after the guests had retired, I sat before the fireplace in the great hall and gazed at the leaping flames. My mind spun like a reel as memories of the past screamed by. I remembered that when I was a young girl alone, I was frightened of the vastness of the country and of what seemed to me then the savage aspect of the Indians."[64] Roman's absence was a gaping hole not only in her heart but in the business that leaned so heavily on the personalities of the Hubbell family to sustain it, and there were no other shoulders but Dorothy's to carry the weight, for John and LaCharles had their own responsibilities away from the reservation, and none of their children had the same indelible ties to Ganado that had kept previous generations of the Hubbell family anchored there. Though the task seemed more than she could confidently face, Dorothy had long since proved herself resourceful and determined. She knew what she had to do: "After much soul searching and counseling, I realized full well I must assume the management of the estate."[65]

As owner and manager of the J. L. Hubbell Trading Post, the Navajos called Dorothy "Tall Woman," or, as her hair turned white, "Mother."[66] She ran the trading post capably, but slowly gave up on more and more facets of the business. After World War II, even before Roman's illness, the managers at Hubbell Trading Post no longer scoured the reservation for lambs, visiting Navajos in their hogans as Roman had once done, but bought only the sheep the Navajos brought them. Trade dropped to fewer than 2,000 head, which they grazed on the farm, and Dorothy bought her last lambs in 1959.[67] The curio business began to wane. At the time of Roman's death,

Dorothy had in stock only pawned jewelry that had gone unredeemed for more than three years, and no Hopi products at all.[68] She discontinued the wholesale curio business altogether by 1958.[69] The mail routes had been sold to Bert Cresto along with Roman Hubbell Navajo Tours, and the post office moved out of the trading post when Barbara resigned.

The farm, too, had been declining slowly for many years. Even though the farms on the Ganado Irrigation Project "produced more crops than any Arizona Navajo project, year after year the project lived on in a deepening twilight until 1954, when authorized funds were diverted finally and entirely."[70] In that year, the BIA shifted seventy-three thousand dollars from the Ganado Irrigation Project for upkeep and repairs to the Hogback Project along the San Juan River. The funds were not meant to be withdrawn permanently, but "it was the era of the Termination policy which rejected the assimilationist paternalism that had been the philosophical and social underpinning of the Indian Irrigation Division, and neither attention nor funds have ever been restored."[71] Dorothy continued to plant alfalfa, irrigating one hundred acres into the mid-1960s, but the weir at the reservoir was plugged sometime later in the decade and the whole works fell into disrepair.[72] As Charles Peterson states, "The 1954 transfer of funds was the symbol of the Ganado Project's decline just as the return of Roman and Dorothy Hubbell to Ganado from Winslow symbolized the declining fortunes of the Hubbell family as traders."[73]

Other changes in the 1960s sprang up even faster than the weeds choked the irrigation works. The modernization that had followed the war paled in comparison to the social and economic changes of the late 1960s, as traders "began to convert trading posts to self-service operations, doing away with the old bull-pens and putting in 'gondolas,' or checkout counters with a cash register."[74] Dorothy loved the old trading post and valued its history too dearly to undertake such a conversion herself. In the whirlwind, she relied on older customers who still did their trading the old fashioned way, and a few unobtrusive modern adaptations of her own. In 1964, for example, she converted a disused extension of the wareroom into a laundromat—but this, too, she saw as "just part of serving the community," as Navajos came from miles around to use the facility in a place where such conveniences were rare.[75] But where other trading posts metamorphosed into supermarkets or were left abandoned among the sage and piñons, Dorothy preserved a tradition, making Hubbell Trading Post "the oldest on the reservation to still be in operation with the same original buildings, the same type of trading."[76] It was a distinction that would later prove essential.

### "Much More Than Just a Collection of Buildings"

Before Roman's death, he and Dorothy reluctantly considered selling the trading post they had fought so hard to preserve through the bankruptcy. Roman's illness and their continued financial difficulties seemed to leave them little choice. As Dorothy explained to a friend, "At first, we could not bring ourselves to consider any kind of sale for we all are so very much attached to the home place. But the facts are these, John (our younger son) is Professor of Spanish at the University of Vermont, and is keenly interested in his own kind of work though he does help us here during the summers; we lost Roman, Jr. in World War II; La Charles has her own family, home, and obligations in Denver. That leaves the responsibilities on my shoulders. . . . physically it is telling on me, and the constant shift in personnel is a great worry."[77] Though she showed a remarkable aptitude and love for trading, LaCharles was a grandmother by this time, with one son in the army in Japan, one married in Connecticut, and the youngest a college student in Boulder, Colorado. "If her obligations didn't keep her in Denver," Dorothy mused, "she certainly would be a most interested and capable business woman here. Too bad she isn't twins."[78] With no heir to take over the family business, Roman and Dorothy were haunted by the fear that Ganado's collections might be scattered to the winds if they sold the trading post to just anybody. When their friends John and Louisa Wetherill passed away and their son sold their Kayenta trading post, the enormous collection of Indian artifacts they had amassed over years of archaeological exploration and Indian trading was lost. Dorothy, who remembered fondly seeing the collection when she was new to Navajo country, was shocked: "The place was sold, everything was gone. *Everything was gone.* Nothing was collected, put into a collection where it could be studied. It was gone. I thought, well, now, what would happen to Ganado if I sold to somebody?"[79]

Though beset by financial difficulties and aware that time was running out, Roman and Dorothy determined "to consider only someone who was interested in the historical significance, the art collection, the welfare of the Indians themselves," and who would understand that the Hubbell Trading Post "was much more than just a collection of buildings."[80] As buyers

Dorothy standing behind the jewelry counter in the trader's office, c. 1963. Courtesy of the National Park Service, HUTR 07130.

interested in the trading post or the art collection approached them, the Hubbells acted cautiously. One buyer who admitted freely that he "would sell all the stuff and convert the place into a liquor store" they rejected out of hand.[81] A few New York art dealers offered them as much as $100 apiece for some of Burbank's drawings, but they could find no one to purchase all of them, and the Hubbells did "not wish to break up the collection, preferring to dispose of it where it can be preserved and available to those interested."[82] And so their plans to sell the artwork and the trading post never bore fruit, giving them time to formulate a plan that would: turning the Hubbell Trading Post into a national historic site.

In mid-July 1957, J. L. Hubbell's old friend, Dr. Harold S. Colton, founder and director of the Museum of Northern Arizona, and his assistant director, Dr. Edward B. Danson, who had stayed a night at Hubbell Trading Post as a boy on family vacation in the 1920s, drove from Flagstaff to Ganado to secure a loan of some of the Hubbells' art collection for an exhibit of Burbank's work.[83] As Danson later recalled, "During the course of our conversation, they asked Dr. Colton, knowing of his interest in conservation and his active work for the National Park Service (he was responsible for getting Sunset Crater and Wupatki National Monuments into the Park Service) if he thought it would be possible to get Hubbell Trading Post into the Park Service. We discussed this on our return home and Dr. Colton asked me to see what could be done."[84] Roman, Dorothy, LaCharles, and John agreed "with one accord we would be most happy to see the Hubbell Trading Post become a National Monument, for that would lend a dignity which we believe it deserves."[85] Upon returning to Flagstaff, Danson went to work talking to anthropologists, historians, and Park Service personnel about how best to proceed. In September, he wrote to Representative Stewart L. Udall and Senators Barry Goldwater and Carl Hayden, all of whom had ties to the trading post. And as Dorothy told him, "There are probably no people who would know the family and the place any better than Senator Hayden and Senator Goldwater, both of whom have been here many times and are friends of long standing."[86] Within a month, all three had written to the Park Service to request the Hubbell Trading Post be investigated as a potential national historic site. And so the wheels began ever so slowly to turn.[87]

## *"Ah Me, the Time It Takes": Hubbell Trading Post in Congress*

Park Service regional historian Robert M. Utley conducted the first study assessing the significance of Hubbell Trading Post for the National Survey of Historic Sites and Buildings in 1958. He spent several days at the trading post, staying in one of the bedrooms as Dorothy's guest and going through a hundred years of family papers and business records that had been crammed into barrels and spoiled by rat droppings in the barn. The resulting 108-page report made the case that "the Hubbell Trading Post was the most important single trading post in the history of Navajo trading."[88] When the document reached Park Service headquarters in 1959, however, it was greeted with a deflating 18-page critique that, in essence, concluded that "Hubbell Trading Post was good enough for the State of Arizona but not good enough to become a unit of the National Park Service."[89] The Park Service considered neither Don Lorenzo nor Indian traders as a breed significant enough to national history to merit distinction. J. L. Hubbell's influence, they argued, extended to only part of the vast Navajo Reservation. Furthermore, "Hubbell Trading Post possessed no exceptional value for commemorating the cultural, political, military, or economic history of the United States; none of the members of the family had any important significance in the history of the United States; the trading post did not appear to have any association with important events which are symbolic of any great idea or ideals of the American people; the buildings at the trading post did not constitute notable works of a master builder, designer, or architect whose individual genius reflected his age; nor were the archeological sites of major significance."[90] The committee grudgingly admitted that the trading post, though not particularly notable, was at least old, and recommended some regional or local agency undertake its preservation.

Danson had, in the meantime, been appointed to the Secretary of the Interior's Advisory Board on National Parks, Historic Sites, Buildings and Monuments, and as soon as Utley's report was available, he presented it in their next board meeting. Whether it was Danson's persuasiveness or the report's enthusiastic assessment of the site, "*something* swayed the Board in the direction of Hubbell Trading Post; on the 22nd day of April they recommended that Hubbell Trading Post be classified as of exceptional value under the terms of the Historic Sites Act."[91] With the ribbon of that "exceptional value" around their necks, in 1959 Carl Hayden introduced to the Senate S.1871, while Stewart Udall introduced to the House H.R. 7279, proposing Hubbell Trading Post be made a national historic site.[92]

For the first few legislative sessions, both bills were largely ignored while necessary reports were gathered and committee meetings held. By the time H.R. 7279 passed committee and made its debut on the House floor, three years had passed since Danson and Colton first discussed the idea with Roman and Dorothy. There, it found a firestorm of opposition, much of it generated by Iowa Representative H. R. Gross, "a thrift-minded ex-newspaperman" who saw the proposition as a shocking waste of government money.[93] Why, he demanded, did the bill ask for $300,000 when the property was assessed at only $9,957? Surely, Gross argued, such a staggering increase could not be explained by "a few paintings and an ethnological collection."[94] Udall attempted to assure the Representatives that the figure of $9,957 was misleading because Arizona tax law assessed property at only one tenth of its value, and that a fair appraisal would be made of the artwork and Indian artifacts before a dime would be spent. But his protests fell on deaf ears. Texan Representative John Dowdy put a period on the discussion by exclaiming, "This is obviously an attempt to bail out the owners of worthless property at the expense of the American taxpayer. It is no wonder that our national budget cannot be balanced."[95] The bill was defeated 208 votes to 171.

Though the House bill suffered an ignominious defeat, the Senate version managed to pass, and if nothing else, the arguments made on the floor convinced its proponents that they could not proceed without a proper inventory of the art and artifacts.[96] This they completed in December 1960. Revised assessments valued the art and ethnological collections at $111,536; the books, house furnishings, gun collection, and other miscellany at $8,464; and the land and buildings at $169,000.[97] But the appraisals did not stop subsequent versions of the bill from floundering in the House in 1961 and 1962. Hubbell supporters finally managed to overcome Gross's opposition by yoking the bill to a proposition to make a site in Gross's home state—President Herbert Hoover's birthplace—a national historic site. But by then the bill had found another dogged enemy in Senator Clinton P. Anderson. This time, objections swirled around rumors that Dorothy had sold some of the artwork, and that Hubbell Trading Post had already been reduced to a shell of its former self. Anderson told Frank McNitt, who had written the senator in Dorothy's defense, that "many people who were very familiar with the old ranch tell me that the best pictures were disposed of, that the library is gone, and that most of the best examples of pottery are gone."[98] He would have favored acquisition, he said, if the post were still intact, but if the situation was indeed as bad as his sources described, he could not countenance spending such a sum on a couple of ranch buildings. McNitt, who was by this time intimately familiar with the trading post from his work on *Indian Traders,* assured Anderson that he had personally seen that the collections were intact and urged him to visit Hubbell Trading Post to see for himself.[99] McNitt pleaded, "Long after the Navajo women stop weaving, won't our people want to see—after seeing the originals in museums—the exact surroundings where the 'Hubbell blankets' had their inception? Tourists come now from every corner of our country and from the countries of Europe to see the Hubbell Trading Post and warehouse, and if they are brassy enough or lucky enough, the great living room of the Hubbell home. As life in the Southwest changes, and as new tides of population sweep in, will not this present concern or interest only increase?"[100] Anderson, however, remained implacable, continuing to resist the bill, challenging the appraisal of the books in the library and the artwork, objecting to the presence of the laundromat and the gas station, and tenaciously clinging to the idea that Dorothy had sold parts of the collection.[101]

For Dorothy, the years of congressional back-and-forth seemed endless. As the process lumbered forward, she consulted frequently with John and LaCharles, mailing them copies of important correspondence to keep them abreast of developments. John came to the trading post occasionally, and LaCharles still "managed a few days in the wool season or when buying lambs, to come to help," but Dorothy was its guardian.[102] The longer she held out the more she seemed heroic in the eyes of her friends. Arizona journalist Don Dedera expressed her supporters' frustrations, writing, "Mrs. Dorothy Hubbell waits patiently, year after year after year, for Congress to do its clear duty. Under the circumstances, nobody could blame her for selling to the highest commercial bidder. She could make much more than she stands to get from the government. And her ordeal of sarcastic inquisition by various congressional committees would be finished. . . . In its agony of inertia, Congress has treated Mrs. Hubbell with ungallantness bordering on insult. She has agreed to sell the place at a conservative price set by disinterested appraisers. In the public interest, she has resisted the temptation to auction off the collections to dealers."[103] Certainly Dorothy could not help but grow weary of the endless deliberations. When the House adjourned in 1961 without considering her bill yet again, she sighed to a friend, "Ah me, the time it takes!!"[104] And when the University of Arizona's Bernard Fontana wrote to ask about the fate of those moldering barrels of records Utley had found in the Hubbell barn, Dorothy's reply showed her palpable frustration at the snail's pace of government. "I really do not know what to tell you. This has been a long drawn-out affair waiting to see what if any action is taken by Congress," she wrote, adding, "Even as late as one day last week, another appraiser came at the request of the government, so it would seem that they are still working on it. We certainly have a long list of names of those who came for various kinds of surveys, inventories, reports, etc."[105]

The reluctance of Congress to acquire the trading post led Ned Danson to pursue local options for its preservation.[106] He wrote to Stewart Udall, wondering "if it might be possible for the people of Arizona to raise part of the needed funds," some quarter of a million dollars.[107] "I believe that Congress," he wrote, "would be more apt to consider the purchase with enthusiasm if the people of the state were to contribute part of the money necessary."[108] Udall put the matter before Bert Fireman of the *Phoenix Gazette*. Fireman thought, based on other failed attempts at fundraising for other causes—even a memorial for the sunken USS *Arizona* in Pearl Harbor—that it would be nigh unto impossible, and that "the best bet might be to find some ailing moneybags with interest in that particular project."[109] He candidly advised, "Through the papers I've watched the growing campaign to make this post a National Historic Site, but have never been able to generate any enthusiasm about it, although I'm a bug on Arizona history. To me it lacks popular appeal. I recognize the Hubbells' great contribution to the development of Navajo crafts and their considerable contribution to better understanding between redmen and white, but even so cannot feel that this project would ever have broad public support."[110] Dorothy even corresponded with the Heard Museum, an American Indian art and history museum in Phoenix that had been founded by old friends and political correspondents of J. L. Hubbell, but the museum wanted to purchase only the collections and move them to Phoenix.[111] Dorothy might have considered selling the post to the Navajo Tribe, but they decided the price tag attached to the old landmark was simply too high.[112] The National Park Service, it seemed, was still Hubbell Trading Post's best hope.

Despite Fireman's feeling that the preservation of Hubbell Trading Post could not produce the groundswell of support necessary to generate enough donations to preserve it, the trading post and the Hubbell family attracted passionate allies. Though many of the artists and writers who had known J. L. Hubbell had passed away by the 1960s, a few remained, and were joined by the legions of travelers who had been shown the Southwest by Lorenzo, Jr., and Roman. When they heard of the trading post's predicament, they wrote their congressmen and Dorothy with their hopes "it will, one day, be made fully available."[113] Some of them visited her there at Ganado to relive old memories. One woman, who "had wanted so very long to see Ganado again," stopped by with her sister in 1965.[114] "To see it again," she told Dorothy, "almost exactly as I remembered it, was like walking back into a wonderful dream. Thank you for making that dream a reality."[115] To those who could not separate Hubbell Trading Post from the Navajo Reservation in their memories and imaginations, preserving it became personal. While Congress batted the bill around in the late 1950s and early 1960s, Arizona's newspapers and magazines filled with articles about Don Lorenzo and his famous trading post, and each time they did, Dorothy received a fresh batch of letters of support from readers and former guests.[116]

A turning point for the project came in 1964 when Anna Kopta received a card in the mail from one of her friends who had just visited the Hubbell Trading Post.[117] She and her husband, Emry Kopta, had lived on the reservation in the 1920s, Anna working as a teacher for the Indian Service, and Emry as a sculptor. They had known J. L. and his trading post at their glorious peak, and had been near neighbors and lifelong friends of Lorenzo, Jr.—in fact, five of Emry's sculptures were part of the Hubbell collections now at risk of dispersal. Emry had passed away in 1952, only a few years before Roman, and his widow was now eighty-two years old. But when that chance card found her mailbox, she was serving as state chairman of monuments and markers for the Arizona chapters of the Daughters of the American Colonists (DAC). Catching the fire of the cause, she presented it to the DAC state regent and the national regent, who happened to be visiting Arizona, explaining "her dream, the dream of many Arizonans—to preserve this olden-day relic for future generations to see."[118] The regents liked the idea, and immediately went to work throwing an Indian-themed luncheon where the women of the Arizona chapters resolved to help preserve the Hubbell Trading Post. It would be their main project for the year of 1965.[119]

They commenced writing letters, starting with every member of the House of Representatives, where the bill had encountered the most resistance before. They wrote letters to other chapters of the DAC, particularly in states whose Congressmen had opposed the bill, asking them to try to sway the opinions of their elected officials.[120] They reached out to newspapers and television and radio stations to arrange for stories about the trading post, for adults and children alike.[121] They asked members of the American Automobile Association, American Indian arts and crafts organizations, the Heard Museum Guild, and even five hundred Boy Scout troops to write and call members of Congress on behalf of the bill.[122] When the bill (now conveniently attached to the Herbert Hoover birthplace bill) finally passed in the House of Representatives that summer only to bog down in the Senate, the DAC began again, this time writing to the senators.

Though it is impossible to measure the exact effect of their efforts, 1965, a year in which "the opposition look[ed] unbeatable," became the year that Congress finally authorized the creation of Hubbell Trading Post National Historic Site.[123] H.R. 3320, with the hefty price tag of $952,000, passed the

Senate on August 17, 1965, and cleared the desk of President Lyndon B. Johnson on August 28.[124] In Arizona, Dorothy heaved a sigh of relief: finally, "after nine long years of congressional debate, some heated, the old Hubbell Trading Post was approved a National Historic Site."[125] The bill's supporters across Arizona, from politicians to the women of the DAC, enjoyed their victory. "The Hubbell Trading Post, which cost more stamp money from Arizona women than any other project so far this year, was saved for posterity."[126]

## *A Living Monument*

Empty rows of folding chairs sat facing a speaker's platform in the parking lot in front of Hubbell Trading Post, their occupants driven inside the store by an exuberant afternoon thundershower that made a boggy mess out of the red Ganado dirt. Water rushed down the hillside to swirl an inch or two deep around the legs of the abandoned chairs and the tires of parked cars. Inside the trading post, a mixed party of Navajos, traders, government officials, and friends of the Hubbell family packed every available inch of the bullpen not taken up by shoes, straw hats, and Pendleton blankets.[127]

"Since this is a trading post," Stewart L. Udall, now Secretary of the Interior, observed from his position behind the counter, "maybe it is fortunate that nature compelled us to hold these ceremonies inside—for this is where the trading was done."[128] It was September 7, 1967, and the ceremony that brought such a crowd to Hubbell Trading Post was its long-awaited and hard-won dedication as a national historic site. Dorothy, John, and LaCharles stood next to Udall as the guests of honor, the ladies with corsages pinned to their shoulders and pleased smiles on their faces.

Like everything else at Hubbell Trading Post, the dedication ceremonies were a unique mixture of Navajo and Anglo influences. The Master of Ceremonies, John E. Cook, Superintendent of both Hubbell Trading Post National Historic Site and Canyon de Chelly National Monument, led the proceedings between both worlds with practice. After Rev. Glen Williamson of the Ganado Mission, the trading post's steadfast neighbor, offered an invocation, and Wescoat S. Wolfe, the Park Service's supervisory historian at Hubbell Trading Post, welcomed the slightly damp audience, Friday Kinlicheenie, a longtime employee of the Hubbells' and a Navajo medicine man, performed a blessing chant.[129] Raymond Nakai, chairman of the Navajo Tribal Council and a gifted orator, then gave an elegant speech celebrating

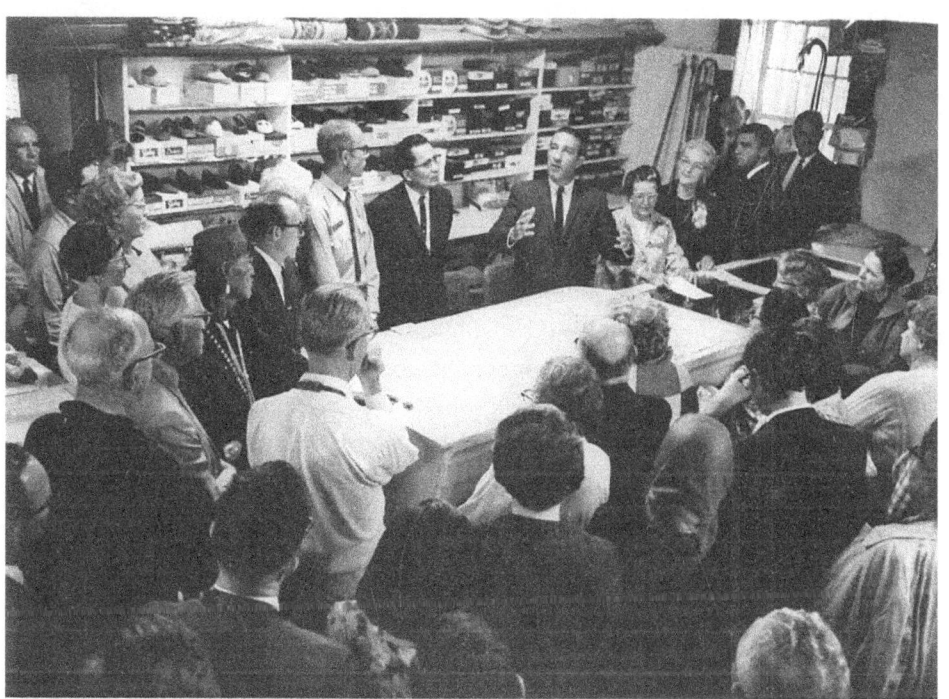

Visitors and guests crowd the bullpen during the dedication ceremonies of Hubbell Trading Post National Historic Site. Dorothy and LaCharles stand next to Secretary of the Interior Stewart Udall. Courtesy of the National Park Service, HUTR 24460.

the life of J. L. Hubbell. "Today we dedicate a monument to a great man, a great people," he said. "We are here to give thanks for the workings of a man—a man noted for his kindness, goodness and sincerity. Just as monuments rise above the earth, so do his good works rise above those of his contemporaries. Just as monuments seem to soar to the heavens so do the deeds of this man soar to the skies above. His hands worked many wondrous miracles for a grateful people. Juan Lorenzo Hubbell was a man of vision."[130] So too, the audience agreed, were the remaining Hubbells people of vision. When it came time for his address, Udall thanked Dorothy, John, and LaCharles sincerely for preserving the old trading post from the decay of time and for persevering when their case seemed hopeless.

The road had not been smooth—nor would it be, for the Park Service had elected to manage Hubbell Trading Post not as a static museum preserved in time, but as a living trading post. From the beginning, Danson and Dorothy had dreamed of running "the post as an active and living museum by having the Park Service sublet the trading activities as a concession," an idea that made a convert out of reluctant Park Service Director George Hartzog.[131] Hartzog told Robert Utley that "he would not countenance another goddamned dead embalmed historic site, that it must be a living trading post," and committed them all to the idea by telling Congress that they hoped not just to *preserve* the trading post, but to *operate* it.[132] Now the Park Service faced the challenge of running a traditional trading post at a time when sheep had become symbols of Navajo life rather than the vital heart of the Navajo economy, when the very institution of Indian trading was under fierce legal attack, when the price of change since the end of the war had been "a widening split between traditional and modern Navajo life."[133] Yet there were still Navajos who traded at Hubbell Trading Post, and the Park Service's intention to continue to operate the business set their minds at ease about the transition as they bade goodbye to Dorothy and welcomed a new element into their community.[134] And still there were tourists, coming now to the reservation and to Hubbell Trading Post in greater numbers than ever before.

It must have been with a bittersweet sense of relief that Dorothy listened to Rev. Emanuel Trockur's benediction at the dedication ceremonies, and led the crowd on a personal tour of the trading post and her one-time home. Her fight was over. Nothing but her iron will and the hopes of her friends had held the place together during the past decade. At the end of the day, the guests held their coats over their heads and dashed through the rain and mud to their cars, pulling away with rumbling motors.[135] Dorothy, John, and LaCharles would follow them before long, leaving the old homestead in the care of the National Park Service.

# Notes

## Abbreviations

| | |
|---|---|
| Brugge Papers | David M. Brugge Manuscript Collection, unprocessed, MSS 770, Center for Southwest Research, University Libraries, University of New Mexico, Albuquerque, NM |
| Colton Family Collection | Colton Family Collection, MS 207-1-124, Museum of Northern Arizona, Flagstaff, AZ |
| Day Family Collection | Day Family Collection, NAU.MS.89, Cline Library, Special Collections and Archives Department, Northern Arizona University, Flagstaff, AZ |
| Historical Files, HUTR | Historical Files, Hubbell Trading Post National Historic Site, Ganado, AZ |
| Hubbell Papers | Hubbell Trading Post Records, 1882–1968 (bulk 1905–1950), AZ 375, University of Arizona Library Special Collections, Tucson, AZ |
| Lorenzo Hubbell, Jr., Papers | Lorenzo Hubbell, Jr., Collection, NAU.MS.453, Cline Library, Special Collections and Archives Department, Northern Arizona University, Flagstaff, AZ |
| McNitt Papers | Frank McNitt Papers, 1973-024, New Mexico Commission of Public Records, State Records Center and Archives, Santa Fe, NM |
| Museum Collections, HUTR | Museum Collections, Hubbell Trading Post National Historic Site, Ganado, AZ |
| Oral Histories, HUTR | Oral Histories, Hubbell Trading Post National Historic Site, Ganado, AZ |

| | |
|---|---|
| Plez Talmadge Reilly Collection | Plez Talmadge Reilly Collection, NAU. MS.275, NAU.OH.52, NAU.PH.97.46, NAU.VT.93.9, and NAU.MI.93.9, Cline Library, Special Collections and Archives Department, Northern Arizona University, Flagstaff, AZ |
| Raymond Nakai Collection | Raymond Nakai Collection, 1963–1988, NAU. MS.386 and NAU.PH.2006.16, Cline Library, Special Collections and Archives Department, Northern Arizona University, Flagstaff, AZ |
| San Juan Oral History Collection | San Juan Oral History Collection, Cline Library, Special Collections and Archives Department, Northern Arizona University, Flagstaff, AZ |
| David K. Udall Papers | David K. Udall Papers, 1947–1988, MS 294, University of Arizona Library Special Collections, Tucson, AZ |
| Stewart L. Udall Papers | Stewart L. Udall Papers, 1950–2010, AZ 372, University of Arizona Library Special Collections, Tucson, AZ |

## Introduction

1. Grace MacGowan Cooke, "Experiences in the Desert," *Lookout*, July 12, 1913. (Subsequent quotations in the first several paragraphs are also drawn from this source.) Hubbell used a variety of names during his life. Born Juan Lorenzo, he later anglicized his name to John Lorenzo, which he usually abbreviated to J. L. Friends also frequently referred to him as Don Lorenzo or Lorenzo. I refer to him in this study primarily as Hubbell or J. L. to distinguish him from his son, whom I refer to as both Lorenzo, Jr., and Lorenzo. Other members of the Hubbell family I refer to by their first names.

2. Grace MacGowan Cooke to J. L. Hubbell, May 29, 1912, Folder "Cooke," Historical Files, HUTR; Cooke, "Experiences in the Desert."

3. Frank C. Lockwood, *Pioneer Portraits: Selected Vignettes* (Tucson: University of Arizona Press, 1968), 144.

4. Ibid., 146.

5. Charles F. Lummis, "The Swallow's-Nest People," *Out West* 26, no. 6 (June 1907): 500–501.

## Chapter 1

1. Agnes C. Laut, *Through Our Unknown Southwest* (New York: McBride, Nast, 1913), 106.

2. Frank McNitt, *The Indian Traders* (Norman: University of Oklahoma Press, 1962), 142.

3. John Lorenzo Hubbell, "Fifty Years an Indian Trader," as told to John Edwin Hogg, *Touring Topics* 22, no. 12 (December 1930): 24. Much of the information about Hubbell's early life comes from this article, which was written by California journalist John Edwin Hogg after he interviewed J. L. in the fall or summer of 1930. J. L. had a flare for the dramatic, and loved to tell stories about his early adventures, sometimes embellishing the details and confusing dates, and Hogg admitted that in writing the piece, "I have endeavored to portray him as the grand old man, and virile character that he has obviously been." John Edwin Hogg to Barbara Goodman, November 1, 1930, Box 40, Folder Hogg, Hubbell Papers. Because of Hogg's admiration and J. L.'s tendency to exaggerate, the reader is cautioned to take the autobiography with a grain of salt when statements cannot be verified by other evidence, but the reader should also remember that, while some details may not be entirely factual, they are certainly true to the spirit of the man who told them.

4. Hubbell, "Fifty Years," 24.

5. Ibid.

6. Gene Haldeman, interview by David M. Brugge, November 29, 1972, interview 62, transcript, Oral Histories.

7. Ibid.

8. Hubbell Parker, interview by Frank McNitt, May 12, 1972, transcript, Box 16-25(18), Folder 7, McNitt Papers.

9. Hubbell, "Fifty Years," 25.

10. Clarence G. Salsbury, with Paul Hughes, *The Salsbury Story: A Medical Missionary's Lifetone of Public Service* (Tucson: University of Arizona Press, 1969), 138. Haldeman had heard this version of the story from others. He told David Brugge that J. L. had never told him about a gunfight and that, "knowing him, I doubt it. He was a peaceful character." Gene Haldeman, interview by David M. Brugge, November 29, 1972, transcript, Oral Histories, HUTR.

11. Gene Haldeman, interview by David M. Brugge, November 29, 1972, interview 62, transcript, Oral Histories, HUTR.

12. Hubbell, "Fifty Years," 25. (The quotations that follow are also drawn from this source.)

13. George Wharton James, *Indian Blankets and Their Makers* (Chicago: A. C. McClurg, 1920), 204–205.

14. Henry B. Coddington, quoted in McNitt, *Indian Traders*, 217.

15. Martha Blue, *Indian Trader: The Life and Times of J. L. Hubbell* (Walnut, CA: Kiva Publishing, 2000), 6; Joseph Emerson Smith, "Navajo Art Patron Dead," *El Palacio* 29 (December 1930): 372.

16. Brian Hamnett, *A Concise History of Mexico*, 2nd ed. (Cambridge: Cambridge University Press, 2006), 72.

17. Lawrence Lane, "The Family History," *La Bandera de la Casa Hubbell-Gutierrez* 4, no. 3 (September 2007): 5.

18. Ibid., 6; Julian G. Baca, "Juliana Hubbell de Gutiérrez Family History and Genealogy," n.d., Box 3, Folder "Baca, Julian G. . . ," Brugge Papers.

19. Thomas E. Sheridan, *Arizona: A History* (Tucson: University of Arizona Press, 1995), 25–26.

20. Ibid., 26.

21. Hal K. Rothman, "From Prehistory to the Twentieth Century," chap. 1 in *Navajo National Monument: A Place and Its People* (Santa Fe, NM: National Park Service, Southwest Cultural Resource Center, 1991), http://www.nps.gov/history/history/online_books/nava/adhi/adhit.htm.

22. David M. Brugge, "Navajo Prehistory and History to 1850," in *Handbook of North American Indians*, vol. 10: *Southwest*, ed. Alfonso Ortiz (Washington, DC: Smithsonian Institution, 1983), 489; Peter Iverson, *Diné: A History of the Navajos* (Albuquerque: University of New Mexico Press, 2002), 12–20. The arguments about when and how the Navajos came to the Southwest are too involved to be encapsulated here. Iverson recommends as a starting point the differing scholarly opinions of the contributors to Ronald H. Towner, ed., *The Archaeology of Navajo Origins* (Salt Lake City: University of Utah Press, 1996). Iverson contends that the scientific explanations should be considered in conjunction with the Navajos' own story of their origins. "In these renditions, the Diné too often lurch onto the Southwestern stage as nomadic vagabonds," he argues. This relegates them to the status of newcomers and second-class citizens among the other native groups. The archaeological and anthropological stories, he argues, "deny the power and the essential truth of the traditional Navajo account of their origins." Iverson, *Diné*, 13–14.

23. Iverson, *Diné*, 14.

24. Jack D. Forbes, *Apache, Navaho, and Spaniard* (Norman: University of Oklahoma Press, 1994), 57–58; Herbert Eugene Bolton, ed., *Spanish Exploration of the Southwest, 1542–1706* (1908; repr., New York: Barnes and Noble, 1946), 183. The first definite reference to the Navajos was not until 1627 when Fray Gerónimo de Zárate Salmerón, a missionary, reported that the "Apaches de Nabajú" were living somewhere north of Jemez pueblo. A second mention came from Fray Alonso de Benavides in 1631. "The Navajos," he wrote, "are very skillful farmers for the word Navajo means 'large cultivated fields.'" Marsha Weisiger, "The Origins of Navajo Pastoralism," *Journal of the Southwest* 46, no. 2 (Summer 2004): 257. David Brugge further explains, "Spanish *Navajó* seems to be a borrowing of Tewa *navahu*, a compound of *nava* 'field' and *hu*, 'wide arroyo, valley' used to designate a large arroyo in which there are cultivated fields. . . . In the nineteenth century *Navajó* became the most common Spanish name for the tribe." Brugge, "Navajo Prehistory," 496.

25. Forbes, *Apache, Navaho, and Spaniard*, 58; David M. Brugge, "Navajo and Western Pueblo History," *Smoke Signal* 25 (Spring 1972): 95. In a noteworthy episode, when Espejo reached the Hopi mesas, he found that they remembered well their bloody encounter with one of Coronado's men, Pedro de Tovar. The Hopis enlisted the help of the Navajos, while Espejo in turn enlisted the help of the Zunis. The encounter ended in a stalemate, and Espejo returned to Mexico. The incident is illustrative of the complicated relationship between the Hopis, the Navajos, and

the Spanish. Like the Navajos, the Hopis allied with whomever best suited their interests, but their reception of Spanish missionaries would always be tenuous at best, and the Hopis participated heartily in the Pueblo Revolt, killing the four or five priests then in their villages. When the Franciscans returned to the Hopis and were received by the village of Awatovi in 1700, the other Hopis attacked and destroyed the pueblo, while the survivors fled to join the Navajos. David M. Brugge, *The Navajo Hopi Land Dispute: An American Tragedy* (Albuquerque: University of New Mexico Press, 1994), 5–9.

26. Bernard L. Fontana, *Entrada: The Legacy of Spain and Mexico in the United States* (Albuquerque: University of New Mexico Press, 1994), 53.

27. Ibid., 63.

28. Weisiger, "Navajo Pastoralism," 254.

29. Ibid., 253.

30. Ibid., 260, 266; Iverson, *Diné*, 23–24.

31. Iverson, *Diné*, 24.

32. William H. Lyon, "Americans and Other Aliens in the Navajo Historical Imagination in the Nineteenth Century," *American Indian Quarterly* 24, no. 1 (Winter, 2000): 143.

33. Iverson, *Diné*, 21.

34. Ibid., 22, 26. For further information on slavery in the Southwest, see David M. Brugge, *Navajos in the Catholic Church Records of New Mexico, 1694–1875* (Tsaile, AZ: Navajo Community College Press, 1985), 127–144; and James F. Brooks, *Captives and Cousins: Slavery, Kinship and Community in the Southwest Borderlands* (Chapel Hill: University of North Carolina Press, 2002).

35. Weisiger, "Navajo Pastoralism," 259.

36. Brugge, "Navajo Prehistory," 491–492.

37. Weisiger, "Navajo Pastoralism," 265; Brugge, "Navajo Prehistory," 491–495.

38. Brugge, "Navajo and Western Pueblo History," 97.

39. Fontana, *Entrada*, 145.

40. Brugge, "Navajo Prehistory," 495.

41. Weisiger, "Navajo Pastoralism," 270.

42. Blue, *Indian Trader*, 7–8.

43. Julian G. Baca, "Juliana Hubbell de Gutiérrez Family History and Genealogy," n.d., Box 3, Folder "Baca, Julian G. . . . ," Brugge Papers. See Lane, "The Family History," for an account of how the Pajarito property was passed down in the Gutiérrez and Baca families.

44. John O. Baxter, *Las Carneradas: Sheep in New Mexico, 1700–1860* (Albuquerque: University of New Mexico Press, 1987), 47; Julian G. Baca, "Juliana Hubbell de Gutiérrez Family History and Genealogy," n.d., Box 3, Folder "Baca, Julian G. . . . ," Brugge Papers.

45. Julian G. Baca, "Juliana Hubbell de Gutiérrez Family History and Genealogy," n.d., Box 3, Folder "Baca, Julian G. . . . ," Brugge Papers; Blue, *Indian Trader*, 8.

46. Julian G. Baca, "Juliana Hubbell de Gutiérrez Family History and Genealogy," n.d., Box 3, Folder "Baca, Julian G. ...," Brugge Papers; Blue, *Indian Trader*, 8.

47. Iverson, *Diné*, 32.

48. Sheridan, *Arizona: A History*, 50.

49. Blue, *Indian Trader*, 9. For James Lawrence Hubbell's military records, see Serial Number 10684, Folder 5, McNitt Papers.

50. Donald Sidney Hubbell, ed., *Hubbell Pioneers* (Downers Grove, IL: Hubbell Family Historical Society, 1989), 335.

51. Marc Simmons, *Albuquerque: A Narrative History* (Albuquerque: University of New Mexico Press, 1982), 161.

52. Blue, *Indian Trader*, 8.

53. Julian G. Baca, "Juliana Hubbell de Gutiérrez Family History and Genealogy," n.d., Box 3, Folder "Baca, Julian G. ...," Brugge Papers; Simmons, *Albuquerque: A Narrative History*, 161; Lane, "The Family History," 4. Santiago's brother, Charles, would go on to serve under Kit Carson in the campaign against the Navajos. John drowned in New Mexico in 1865 in a river crossing (Blue, *Indian Trader*, 9). Sidney Auger Hubbell, who was educated as a criminal lawyer at Yale University, served on the New Mexico Territorial Supreme Court for two terms and as a district attorney. Donald Sidney Hubbell, *Hubbell Pioneers*, 338–340.

54. Blue, *Indian Trader*, 10.

55. Donald Sidney Hubbell, *Hubbell Pioneers*, 336.

56. Sheridan, *Arizona: A History*, 50–52.

57. William H. Lyon, "The Navajos in the Anglo-American Historical Imagination, 1807–1870," *Ethnohistory* 43, no. 3 (Summer 1996): 483.

58. Iverson, *Diné*, 38–39.

59. Amiel Whipple, *A Pathfinder of the Southwest: The Itinerary of Lieutenant A. W. Whipple During His Explorations for a Railway Route from Fort Smith to Los Angeles in the Years 1853 & 1854*, ed. Grant Foreman (Norman: University of Oklahoma Press, 1941), 3–6.

60. James J. Simpson, *Navaho Expedition: Journal of a Military Reconnaissance From Santa Fe, New Mexico, to the Navajo Country, Made in 1849 by Lieutenant James H. Simpson*, ed. Frank McNitt (Norman: University of Oklahoma Press, 1964), 70.

61. Ibid., 96.

62. Lyon, "Anglo-American Historical Imagination," 492.

63. Charles S. Peterson, *Homestead and Farm: A History of Farming at the Hubbell Trading Post National Historic Site* (Globe, AZ: Southwest Parks and Monuments Association, 1986), 17–18. See also Lorenzo Sitgreaves, *Report of an Expedition Down the Zuni and Colorado Rivers* (Washington, DC: Robert Armstrong Public Printer, 1853); Lewis Burt Lesley, ed., *Uncle Sam's Camels: The Journal of Edward Fitzgerald Beale, 1857–1858* (Cambridge, MA: Harvard University Press, 1929); and J. G. Walker and O. L. Shepherd, *The Navajo Reconnaissance: A Military*

*Exploration of the Navajo Country in 1859*, ed. L. R. Bailey (Los Angeles: Westernlore, 1964).

64. Lyon, "Anglo-American Historical Imagination," 497.

65. Ibid. 493.

66. Weisiger, "Navajo Pastoralism," 265.

67. Quoted in Iverson, *Diné*, 34.

68. Iverson provides a good summary of the incarceration of the Navajos at Fort Sumner and the treaties and events that led up to it, but a more detailed account can be found in Gerald Thompson, *The Army and the Navajo: The Bosque Redondo Reservation Experiment, 1863–1868* (Tucson: University of Arizona Press, 1976); and J. Lee Correll, *Through White Men's Eyes: A Contribution to Navajo History*, vols. 1–6 (Window Rock, AZ: Navajo Heritage Center, 1979). Correll's work is a six-volume chronological account of Navajo history up to 1868 and is the most complete source on early Navajo history, containing many original documents and treaties.

69. Quoted in Lyon, "Americans and Other Aliens," 148.

70. Iverson, *Diné*, 41.

71. Jennifer Denetdale, *Reclaiming Diné History: The Legacies of Navajo Chief Manuelito and Juanita* (Tucson: University of Arizona Press, 2007), 65–66.

72. Ibid.

73. Sheridan, *Arizona: A History*, 69.

74. Denetdale, *Reclaiming Diné History*, 67–70.

75. Sheridan, *Arizona: A History*, 69.

76. Andrew Edward Masich, *The Civil War in Arizona: The Story of the California Volunteers, 1861–1865* (Norman: University of Oklahoma Press, 2006), 12.

77. Ibid., 12–13, 53. For additional information on the Civil War in the Southwest, see L. Boyd Finch, *Confederate Pathway to the Pacific: Major Sherod Hunter and Arizona Territory, C. S. A.* (Tucson: Arizona Historical Society, 1996); and Alvin M. Josephy, *The Civil War in the American West* (New York: Knopf, 1991).

78. Masich, *Civil War in Arizona*, 12–14; Howard Roberts Lamar, *The Far Southwest, 1846–1912: A Territorial History*, rev. ed. (Albuquerque: University of New Mexico Press, 2000), 107.

79. Lamar, *The Far Southwest*, 108.

80. Iverson, *Diné*, 48–49.

81. Quoted in Denetdale, *Reclaiming Diné History*, 70.

82. Gerald Thompson, *The Army and the Navajo*, 11. For additional accounts of the Long Walk, see Lynn R. Bailey, *The Long Walk: A History of the Navajo Wars, 1846–1868* (Los Angeles: Westernlore, 1964); Lynn R. Bailey, *Bosque Redondo: An American Concentration Camp* (Pasadena, CA: Socio-Technical Books, 1970); Clifford E. Trafzer, *The Kit Carson Campaign: The Last Great Navajo War* (Norman: University of Oklahoma Press, 1982); and Lawrence C. Kelly, *Navajo Roundup: Selected Correspondence of Kit Carson's Expedition Against the Navajo, 1863–1865*

(Boulder, CO: Pruett, 1970). For a Navajo perspective, see Broderick H. Johnson and Ruth Roessel, eds., *Navajo Stories of the Long Walk Period* (Tsaile, AZ: Navajo Community College Press, 1973).

83. Lane, "The Family History," 4; Blue, *Indian Trader*, 11. See also Darlis A. Miller, "Hispanos and the Civil War in New Mexico: A Reconsideration," *New Mexico Historical Review* 54, no. 2 (April 1979): 105–123; and John Taylor, *Bloody Valverde: A Civil War Battle on the Rio Grande, February 21, 1862* (Albuquerque: University of New Mexico Press, 1995).

84. Lane, "The Family History," 5.

85. Iverson notes that "Although Carson has garnered most of the attention devoted to the effort to force the Diné into exile, he did not act by himself. Carson knew, for example, that the Utes could furnish some of the necessary knowledge of the land, and with the recent animosity between the Utes and the Navajos, he figured correctly that the Utes would be valuable additions to his forces. Other Indian communities, including the Hopis and the Zunis, contributed men and knowledge of the terrain. Carson carefully chose his company commanders, picking experienced soldiers. He generally selected people he knew, those whom he believed he could count on in the heat of battle." Iverson, *Diné*, 51.

86. Denetdale, *Reclaiming Diné History*, 70–74.

87. Ibid., 73–74.

88. Albert H. Schroeder, ed., *The Changing Ways of Southwestern Indians: A Historical Perspective* (Glorieta, NM: Rio Grande, 1973), 162–163; Kathy M'Closkey, *Swept Under the Rug: A Hidden History of Navajo Weaving* (Albuquerque: University of New Mexico Press, 2002), 49; Thompson, *The Army and the Navajo*, 59. Documents pertaining to Charles's role in the campaign can be found in Correll, *Through White Men's Eyes*, vols. 3 and 4.

89. Blue, *Indian Trader*, 14.

90. Baxter, *Las Carneradas*, 330–331. Santiago had had previous encounters with the Navajos. In February 1851, he reported that Navajo raiders descended on Pajarito and "filched livestock belonging to James and his father-in-law. Persistent and bold, James gathered ten men, and the group took out in pursuit of the raiders," but were unsuccessful in regaining their livestock. Blue, *Indian Trader*, 10. When the fleeing Navajos realized that they "could not escape with all of their booty . . . every animal of the cow kind was speared by them, and their escape effected." Correll, *Through White Men's Eyes*, vol. 1, 282, 288. In September 1859, Santiago filed a complaint with the army that Navajos had killed two Mexican herders and driven off their livestock, a report that sparked army retaliations that culminated in the burning of Navajo war leader Manuelito's camp at Pueblo Colorado Wash. Blue, *Indian Trader*, 11; Correll, *Through White Men's Eyes*, vol. 2, 290–293; Frank McNitt, *Navajo Wars: Military Campaigns, Slave Raids, and Reprisals* (Albuquerque: University of New Mexico Press, 1972), 172–173.

91. Correll, *Through White Men's Eyes*, vol. 6, 132.

92. Donald L. Baars, *Navajo Country: A Geology and Natural History of the Four Corners Region* (Albuquerque: University of New Mexico Press, 1995), 187.

93. Denetdale, *Reclaiming Diné History*, 74–75.

94. Ibid., 75–76; Gerald Thompson, *The Army and the Navajo*, 155. The full text of the Treaty Between the United States of America and the Navajo Tribe of Indians can be found in Correll, *Through White Men's Eyes*, vol. 6, as well as Appendix C of David E. Wilkins, *The Navajo Political Experience*, rev. ed. (Lanham, MD: Rowman & Littlefield, 2003), 225–237. Correll also includes the full text of the treaty negotiations.

95. Iverson, *Diné*, 67.

96. John O. Baxter, "Restocking the Navajo Reservation After Bosque Redondo," *New Mexico Historical Review* 58, no. 4 (October 1983): 325–334.

97. Ibid., 335, 340.

98. Willow Roberts Powers, *Navajo Trading: The End of an Era* (Albuquerque: University of New Mexico Press, 2001), 28.

99. Ibid., 27.

100. Blue, *Indian Trader*, 5; Darlis A. Miller, "Hispanos and the Civil War," 105.

101. Blue, *Indian Trader*, 11. Blue takes her impressions of Juliana from an interview with one of Juliana's grandchildren, Phillip Hubbell.

102. Ibid., 5.

103. Ibid.

104. Harriet Mayfield, "Great Southwest Pioneer Passes On," *Santa Fe Magazine* 25, no. 2 (January 1931): 30.

105. Hubbell, "Fifty Years," 24. J. L. remembered the details of his early education differently in various accounts. In this account, he says he went to Farley's Presbyterian School in Santa Fe at age 12, but the records of St. Michaels School list Juan Lorenzo in attendance for thirty-eight months beginning in December 1862, when he was nine years old. Blue, *Indian Trader*, 13.

106. Blue, *Indian Trader*, 16.

107. Peterson, *Homestead and Farm*, 7.

108. Hubbell and Hubbell, *History and Genealogy*, 146.

109. Maurice Frink, *Fort Defiance and the Navajos* (Boulder, CO: Pruett, 1968), 2.

110. Herbert Welsh, *Report of a Visit to the Navajo, Pueblo, and Hualapais Indians of New Mexico and Arizona* (Philadelphia: Indian Rights Association, 1885), 14–15.

111. McNitt, *Indian Traders*, 146.

112. Ibid., 144–145.

113. Ibid., 144. See 150–165 for a detailed telling of the incident.

114. David M. Brugge, *Hubbell Trading Post National Historic Site* (Tucson: Southwest Parks and Monuments Association, 1993), 22; McNitt, *Indian Traders*, 146.

115. Brugge, *Hubbell Trading Post*, 22–23; McNitt, *Indian Traders*, 149; Blue, *Indian Trader*, 21–24; "More About the Murder of the Navajoes," *The Latter-day Saints' Millennial Star* 36, no. 37 (September 1874): 583. The documents that record snapshots of J. L.'s experiences working at Fort Defiance can be found at the National Archives, Letters Received by the Office of Indian Affairs, New Mexico Superintendency, 1874 and 1875. See also Blue's notes to pages 21–24 on page 299 of *Indian Trader*.

116. McNitt, *Indian Traders*, 164–165.

117. Blue, *Indian Trader*, 23.

118. Hubbell, "Fifty Years," 26.

## Chapter 2

1. Blue, *Indian Trader*, 56.

2. Hubbell, "Fifty Years," 29. (The quotations that follow are also drawn from this source.)

3. Ibid. Despite the outcome, this tale would not have been unappreciated by Navajo listeners who may have heard Hubbell tell it. As Martha Blue notes, "Navajos are known for their sense of humor—dry, witty, often self-effacing—and most traders' 'baptismal' tales end with acceptance of the trader by the Indians, who often laughed in appreciation of the trader's besting them." Blue, *Indian Trader*, 57.

4. Hubbell, "Fifty Years," 28.

5. Powers, *Navajo Trading*, 45; Peterson, *Homestead and Farm*, 18. On the change from the name Pueblo Colorado to Ganado, see Will C. Barnes, *Arizona Place Names*, rev. ed. (Tucson: University of Arizona Press, 1960), 12.

6. Peggy Froeschauer-Nelson, *Cultural Landscape Report: Hubbell Trading Post National Historic Site, Ganado, Arizona*, under "Prehistoric and Proto-historic Periods" (Santa Fe, NM: US Department of the Interior, National Park Service, Intermountain Region, 1998), http://www.nps.gov/parkhistory/online_books/hutr/clr/clr.htm; Sheridan, *Arizona: A History*, 4.

7. Brugge, *Hubbell Trading Post*, 5–6.

8. David M. Brugge, "Traditional History of Wide Reeds," in *Wide Reed Ruin: Hubbell Trading Post National Historic Site*, ed. James E. Mount, et al. (Santa Fe, NM: National Park Service, Southwest Cultural Resources Center, 1993), 121; Peterson, *Homestead and Farm*, 16.

9. Froschauer-Nelson, "Spanish Exploration," in *Cultural Landscape Report*.

10. Brugge, "Traditional History of Wide Reeds," 123.

11. Joseph Christmas Ives, *Report upon the Colorado River of the West, Explored in 1857 and 1858 . . .*, 36th Cong., 1st sess., House Executive Document 90 (Washington, DC: Government Printing Office, 1861), 128.

12. Ibid.

13. Teresa J. Wilkins, *Patterns of Exchange: Navajo Weavers and Traders* (Norman: University of Oklahoma Press, 2008), 26.

14. Brugge, "Traditional History of Wide Reeds," 122. LaCharles Eckel also mentions the "gigantic Navajo chieftain" of local legend and "his hapless harem." LaCharles G. Eckel, "History of Ganado, Arizona," *Plateau* 6, no. 10 (April 1934): 47.

15. McNitt, *Navajo Wars*, 393-396; Brugge, "Traditional History of Wide Reeds," 123.

16. Teresa J. Wilkins, *Patterns of Exchange*, 27.

17. Eckel, "History of Ganado, Arizona," 48.

18. Brugge, *Hubbell Trading Post*, 11.

19. Ibid.

20. Ibid., 13.

21. Teresa J. Wilkins, *Patterns of Exchange*, 27-28.

22. Brugge, *Hubbell Trading Post*, 15-16.

23. David M. Brugge, "Trading, Interpretive Note #39," 1975, Historical Files, HUTR.

24. Robert A. Trennert, Jr., *Indian Traders on the Middle Border: The House of Ewing, 1827-54* (Lincoln: University of Nebraska Press, 1981), 3.

25. McNitt, *Indian Traders*, 17.

26. David M. Brugge, "Trading, Interpretive Note #39," 1975, Historical Files, HUTR.

27. McNitt, *Indian Traders*, 15.

28. James S. Calhoun to Luke Lea, February 29, 1852, in *The Official Correspondence of James S. Calhoun While Indian Agent at Santa Fe and Superintendent of Indian Affairs in New Mexico*, ed. Annie Heloise Abel (Washington, DC: Government Printing Office, 1915), 488; McNitt, *Indian Traders*, 45. David Brugge states that the earliest Navajo trader on record was Agustin Lacome, who received a license in 1853. Brugge, *Hubbell Trading Post*, 17.

29. Brugge, *Hubbell Trading Post*, 17.

30. McNitt, *Indian Traders*, 46.

31. W. W. Hill, "Navaho Trading and Trading Ritual: A Study of Cultural Dynamics," *Southwestern Journal of Anthropology* 4, no. 4 (Winter 1948): 373.

32. Klara Kelley and Harris Francis, "Many Generations, Few Improvements: 'Americans' Challenge Navajos on the Transcontinental Railroad Grant, Arizona, 1881-1887," *American Indian Culture and Research Journal* 25, no. 3 (2001): 89-90.

33. McNitt, *Indian Traders*, 46-47, 49-50.

34. Brugge, *Hubbell Trading Post*, 18; Iverson, *Diné*, 76-79.

35. Robert M. Utley, "The Reservation Trader in Navajo History," *El Palacio* 68, no. 1 (Spring 1961): 7.

36. Brugge, *Hubbell Trading Post*, 18.

37. Various sources put traders named Charles Crary, Mr. Stover, William B. "Old Man" Leonard, George M. "Barney" Williams, Mr. Webber, Charlie Hubbell, and J. L. Hubbell at trading posts in the Pueblo Colorado Valley during the 1870s. A clear chronology of their occupation and locations has not been deciphered as the historical record is faint, and each source presents a slightly different account.

As Frank McNitt notes, because the area was not part of the reservation, the early traders did not require licenses and therefore cannot be traced through Indian Office records. McNitt, *Indian Traders*, 201. In addition, as David Brugge states, "the change in personnel at many trading posts is relatively rapid and oral tradition consequently quite subject to error." Brugge, "Navajo and Western Pueblo History," 107. Some of the names associated with early trading posts also show up in histories of St. Johns, especially in connection to the St. Johns Ring, with which Hubbell was involved. See Mark E. Miller, "St. Johns's Saints: Interethnic Conflict in Northeastern Arizona, 1880-85," *Journal of Mormon History* 23, no. 1 (Spring 1997): 66-99. I present here the most commonly accepted theories, noting alternate explanations in the Notes.

38. Brugge, *Hubbell Trading Post*, 19.
39. Ibid., 15.
40. Arthur Woodward, *A Brief History of Navajo Silversmithing* (Flagstaff: Northern Arizona Society of Science and Art, 1938), 48. Not much is known about Crary or Stover. Although they are mentioned in many histories of Hubbell Trading Post, the earliest reference seems to be Charles Avery Amsden's *Navaho Weaving: Its Technic and History* (1934; repr., Glorieta, NM: Rio Grande, 1969), 174–175. Amsden used Hubbell and Hogg's "Fifty Years an Indian Trader," but also interviewed three pioneer traders, S. E. Aldrich, Joseph Lee, and C. N. Cotton, to establish his chronology of post ownership passing from Stover and Crary to Leonard to Hubbell. Amsden, however, admits that the men's memories of that time were dim. McNitt speculated that Amsden's mention of Stover as Crary's partner was probably an error. McNitt, *Indian Traders*, 201. See also Eckel, "History of Ganado, Arizona," 48; Woodward, *Navajo Silversmithing*, 48.
41. Brugge, *Hubbell Trading Post*, 21; Blue, *Indian Trader*, 40; Peterson, *Homestead and Farm*, 19; Amsden, *Navaho Weaving*, 174–175.
42. Peterson, *Homestead and Farm*, 19; Blue, *Indian Trader*, 59.
43. McNitt, *Indian Traders*, 80.
44. Martha Blue, *The Witch Purge of 1878: Oral and Documentary History in the Early Navajo Reservation Years*, Navajo Oral History Monograph Series No. 1 (Tsaile, AZ: Navajo Community College Press, 1988), 2.
45. Blue, *Indian Trader*, 3; Blue, *Witch Purge*, 3; Iverson, *Diné*, 71.
46. Charlie directed his letters to William Leonard, which Blue suggests indicates he was either working for or partnering with him. Blue, *Witch Purge*, 5.
47. Charles Hubbell to William Leonard, May 31, 1878, Box 95, Folder 1878–1895, Hubbell Papers. These are copies of records from the National Archives, Records Group 98, Records of the War Department, Dept. of New Mexico, Letters Received. Interestingly, in his 1884 book *Snake Dance of the Moquis*, John G. Bourke recounts a story told to him in 1881 by Mr. Webber, Barney Williams' trading partner in the Pueblo Colorado Valley. That story recounts the 1878 stoning of sorcerer Ostin-Bijaca (Old Deaf Man) in front of Williams and Webber's store. It bears remarkable resemblance to the Navajo oral histories that Blue examines in *Witch Purge*, down to the name of the victim. Webber claimed that his partner,

Williams, had gone to Fort Wingate, leaving him "the only white man for thirty miles" during the incident. This presents a few possibilities. First, that Williams was operating a trading post separate from the Hubbell's, perhaps even at Hardison's house, that the witch was killed there, and that Webber merely omitted Charlie's presence from his story. Alternatively, Webber could have lifted the story in its entirety from Charlie and presented it as his own. See John G. Bourke, *The Snake Dance of the Moquis of Arizona* (1884; repr., Tucson: University of Arizona Press, 1984), 74–77.

48. Blue, *Witch Purge,* 11–12.

49. Charles Hubbell to William Leonard, May 31, 1878, Box 95, Folder 1878–1895, Hubbell Papers.

50. Blue, *Witch Purge,* 14.

51. Brugge, *Hubbell Trading Post,* 24.

52. J. L. Hubbell to Commanding Officer, Fort Wingate, June 10, 1878, Box 95, Folder 1878–1895, Hubbell Papers.

53. Blue, *Witch Purge,* 20–21.

54. Frank C. Lockwood, "More Arizona Characters," *University of Arizona General Bulletin,* no. 6 (Tucson: University of Arizona, 1943), 60–61; Dorothy Challis Mott, "Don Lorenzo Hubbell of Ganado," *Arizona Historical Review* 4 (April 1931): 45–51. Mott's article is loosely based on the Hogg interview, but she takes a great deal of creative license dramatizing events, inventing stereotypical dialogue full of grunts and pidgin English.

55. Hubbell, "Fifty Years," 29. Given Hubbell's characteristic fuzziness on dates, he could be referring to any number of small smallpox outbreaks before 1900.

56. Ibid.

57. Blue, *Indian Trader,* 41.

58. See William Y. Adams, *Shonto: A Study of the Role of the Trader in a Modern Navaho Community,* Smithsonian Institution, Bureau of American Ethnology, Bulletin 188 (Washington, DC: Government Printing Office, 1963).

59. Iverson, *Diné,* 79.

60. Utley, "Reservation Trader," 6.

61. Hubbell, "Fifty Years," 24.

62. Ibid.

63. Blue, *Indian Trader,* 82–83.

64. Bourke, *Snake Dance,* 89.

65. Ibid., 67–70, 89, 173. Whether he had his own trading post or was an employee of Hubbell's or Leonard's, Barney Williams would not stay in the valley long; by 1883 he was homesteading at Tanner Springs, Arizona, embroiled in a land dispute with the Navajos. See Kelley and Francis, "Many Generations," 75–101.

66. Welsh, *Report of a Visit,* 32. Pillsbury was apparently a hired clerk who worked for Hubbell. Brugge, *Hubbell Trading Post,* 26. See also E. S. Clark, "In the Matter of the Homestead Entry of John Lorenzo Hubbell," April 1908, Box 529, Folder 2, Hubbell Papers; and Julian Scott, "Report on the Moqui Pueblos of

Arizona," in *Moqui Pueblo Indians of Arizona and Pueblo Indians of New Mexico*, ed. Thomas Donaldson (Washington, DC: US Census Printing Office, 1893), 51.

67. Lester L. Williams, *C. N. Cotton and His Navajo Blankets: A Biography of C. N. Cotton* (Albuquerque: Avanyu Publishing, 1989), 3–5; John Kevin Fellin, "The Role of C. N. Cotton in the Development of Northwestern New Mexico," *New Mexico Historical Review* 55, no. 2 (April 1980): 151–153.

68. C. N. Cotton to Collector of Internal Revenue, December 17, 1884, Box 91, Folder 1, Letter 12, Hubbell Papers.

69. Williams, *C. N. Cotton*, 9; Amsden, *Navaho Weaving*, 175; McNitt, *Indian Traders*, 202.

70. David M. Brugge, "Changes in the Building Complex at Hubbell Trading Post and Significance for Development of the Area as a National Historic Site—A Preliminary Evaluation of the Data Available," 1974, Box 3, Folder "Brugge, Changes...," Brugge Papers.

71. William J. Robinson, "A Construction Sequence for Hubbell Trading Post and Residence," *Kiva* 50, no. 4 (1985): 235.

72. Robert S. McPherson, "*Naalye'he Ba' Hooghan*: 'Home of Merchandise,' The Navajo Trading Post as an Institution of Cultural Change, 1900–1930," *American Indian Culture and Research Journal* 16, no. 1 (November 1992): 27.

73. Blue, *Indian Trader*, 82.

74. Teresa J. Wilkins, *Patterns of Exchange*, 29.

75. Ibid. Navajo Agent Charles E. Vandever and US Indian Inspector Arthur W. Tinker both called Cotton's store the best on the reservation. Both cited nearly identical reasons: good stock, reasonable prices, cash business, refusal of credit, no pawn, no liquor, not open on Sundays, and no gambling. The very qualities that made government officials rave about Cotton's operation made him less popular with his Navajo customers than Hubbell, who opened on Sunday, allowed gambling, and operated much of his business on the basis of pawn and credit. Williams, *C. N. Cotton*, 18–19.

76. Blue, *Indian Trader*, 82.

77. See Cotton to John H. Bowman, July 31, 1885, Box 91, Folder 4, Hubbell Papers; Cotton to John H. Bowman, November 12, 1885, Box 91, Folder 6, Hubbell Papers; Cotton to J. J. Patterson, January 12, 1888, Box 92, Folder 15, Hubbell Papers; Cotton to J. J. Patterson, January 20, 1888, Box 92, Folder 15, Hubbell Papers.

78. J. L. Hubbell to Cashier, 1st National Bank, June 22, 1885, Box 91, Folder 3, Hubbell Papers. It is Martha Blue's opinion that since Hubbell sold his interest in the Ganado store to Cotton on June 22, 1885, the eve of the challenge to his position as sheriff in St. Johns, the arrangement was merely political, and Hubbell, in fact, continued to participate in the partnership. Blue, *Indian Trader*, 75, 308. Correspondence between Hubbell and Cotton makes it clear that Hubbell was still involved at some level in the business, even if in a smaller role. C. N. Cotton to C. S. Burch Pub. Co., February 20, 1885, Box 91, Folder 7, Hubbell Papers; C. N. Cotton to S. S. Patterson, February 18, 1888, Box 93, Folder 16, Hubbell Papers.

79. Peterson, *Homestead and Farm*, 26.

80. Blue, *Indian Trader*, 70; McNitt, *Indian Traders*, 203–204; *Notables of the West: Being the Portraits and Biographies of the Progressive Men of the West Who Have Helped in the Development and History Making of This Wonderful Country*, vol. 2, Press Reference Library, Western Edition (New York: International News Service, 1915), 187; J. L. Hubbell to C. Eastman, May 10, 1880, Box 95, Folder 1878–1895, Hubbell Papers.

81. Blue, *Indian Trader*, 67; Peterson, *Homestead and Farm*, 19.

82. Mark E. Miller, "St. Johns's Saints," 67.

83. Blue, *Indian Trader*, 68. See James H. McClintock, *Mormon Settlement in Arizona: A Record of Peaceful Conquest of the Desert* (Phoenix, AZ: Manufacturing Stationers, 1921), 178–182.

84. Blue, *Indian Trader*, 71–72, 81; Peterson, *Homestead and Farm*, 21.

85. John H. Krenkel, ed., *The Life and Times of Joseph Fish, Mormon Pioneer* (Danville, IL: Interstate Printers & Publishers, 1970), 200–201.

86. Ibid., 200.

87. Mark E. Miller, "St. Johns's Saints," 75.

88. Ibid., 74–75.

89. Krenkel, *Joseph Fish, Mormon Pioneer*, 248. In October 1880, J. L. penned a letter on behalf of community leaders to David K. Udall in which he warned the Mormons to cease surveying near St. Johns. "We will not feel it inconvenient to show you that we will place all the means in our power and within our reach to impede the establishment of the Mormons in the surroundings of this town," he wrote, ending with the vaguely threatening suggestion that, should the Mormons desist in settling, they could all "avoid difficulties and disagreeable consequences." J. L. Hubbell et al. to David J. Udell, October 26, 1880, Box 6 Folder 10, David K. Udall Papers. Udall's sedate reply suggested they hold a public meeting to discuss the matter. In response to J. L.'s charges, all Udall wrote was, "As for the insinuating and insulting sentences in your document I will not condescend to reply." D. K. Udall to Mr. Marcus Baca y Padia, and others, October 27, 1880, Box 6, Folder 10, David K. Udall Papers. Notwithstanding his declarations, J. L. would later become quite friendly with the Mormons, especially Udall. Fish would even later nominate J. L. to a position in local politics. Krenkel, *Joseph Fish, Mormon Pioneer*, 361.

90. Larry D. Ball, *Desert Lawmen: The High Sheriffs of New Mexico and Arizona, 1846–1912* (Albuquerque: University of New Mexico Press, 1992), 63, 286. See Mark E. Miller, "St. Johns's Saints," for an account of Hubbell's role in the St. Johns Ring.

91. Hubbell, "Fifty Years," 26. For stories of J. L.'s exploits as sheriff, see Hubbell, "Fifty Years"; *Notables of the West*; Thomas Edwin Farish, *History of Arizona*, vol. 6 (Phoenix, AZ: Manufacturing Stationers, 1918); Lockwood, "More Arizona Characters," 53–79; and Lockwood, *Pioneer Portraits*, 129–159.

92. Hubbell, "Fifty Years," 27.

93. Ibid.

94. Hamlin Garland, "Delmar of Pima," *McClure's Magazine* 18, no. 4 (February 1902): 347. Frank Lockwood said that "Garland himself told me that Hubbell was the hero of the story," and, indeed, the references to Delmar's political savvy, his half-Spanish heritage, and even his brother "Carlos" make Delmar's true identity quite plain. Lockwood, "More Arizona Characters," 64. Some of J. L.'s stories about his time as sheriff also found their way into Dane Coolidge's novel *Lorenzo the Magnificent: The Riders from Texas* (New York: Grosset and Dunlap, 1925).

95. "At a special meeting...," *Arizona Champion*, July 11, 1885.

96. Ibid.

97. "Apache County Imbroglio," *Weekly Arizona Miner*, July 3, 1885; "Sheriff Hubbell has been absent...," *St. Johns Herald*, May 27, 1885.

98. "Apache County Imbroglio," *Weekly Arizona Miner*, July 3, 1885.

99. Ibid.

100. "Disgraceful State of Affairs in Apache County," *Arizona Champion*, July 18, 1885. Ball, *Desert Lawmen*, 64. See Earle R. Forrest, *Arizona's Dark and Bloody Ground*, rev. ed. (Caldwell: Caxton Printers, 1962), chapters 7 and 15, for an account of Owens' tenure as sheriff and the Apache County strife. J. L. usually remembered that he had served two terms as sheriff and had been elected in 1882, but the record shows that Thomas Perez was elected to sheriff that year. J. L. was also accused of claiming as his own the accomplishments of his successor, Owens. Blue, *Indian Trader*, 72–73; Ball, *Desert Lawmen*, 346.

101. Lina and Lucero were married on January 1, 1873. J. L. claimed that Lina's parents were "descended from old Spanish-American families who have lived in this part of the country since the Sixteenth Century. My wife's grandfather, whose name was also Cruz Rubi, fought in the Civil War on the Confederate side." Hubbell, "Fifty Years," 26. Lina's father served with Santiago Hubbell in the New Mexico Volunteers. Blue, *Indian Trader*, 69.

102. Court Proceeding 68, District Court of the Third Judicial District, County of Apache, Lina Rubi de Lucero v. Encarnacion Lucero, December 26, 1885, Box 3, Folder "Hubbell, Lina Rubi, 1884," Brugge Papers. The copies in Brugge's collection were sent to him by Martha Blue. The originals can be found in the collections of the Arizona State Library, Archives and Public Records, Phoenix, AZ.

103. Ibid.

104. Blue, *Indian Trader*, 69; Krenkel, *Joseph Fish, Mormon Pioneer*, 201; Hubbell, "Fifty Years," 26.

105. Court Proceeding 68, District Court of the Third Judicial District, County of Apache, Lina Rubi de Lucero v. Encarnacion Lucero, December 26, 1885, Box 3, Folder "Hubbell, Lina Rubi, 1884," Brugge Papers. Martha Blue speculates that Roman may have been J. L. and Lina's only biological child—but J. L.'s remembering of his wedding date as 1879, the naming of Lorenzo, Jr., after J. L. in 1883, and J. L.'s presence as witness in the court records of Lina's divorce all indicate that his relationship with her was long-standing and that the other children were also likely his.

106. Williams, *C. N. Cotton*, 29.

107. For example, in 1890, Hubbell and Cotton each had their own letterhead for the Ganado store. In his catalog "Indian Traders' Supplies and Navajo Blankets," Cotton later wrote that he sold his business interests on the reservation in 1894, but in an earlier version of the catalog, published in 1896, George Wharton James called the trading post at Ganado Cotton's—without even a nod in J. L.'s direction. Williams, *C. N. Cotton*, 69, 73. In addition, E. S. Clark testified that the Cotton-Hubbell partnership had lasted for about ten years, from 1885 until 1895 or 1896. E. S. Clark, "In the Matter of the Homestead Entry of John Lorenzo Hubbell," April, 1908, Box 529, Folder 2, Hubbell Papers.

108. Iverson, *Diné*, 73; Williams, *C. N. Cotton*, 14. Unlike other Native American reservations, which were whittled away by white settlement, the Navajo Reservation grew in area from about 5,000 square miles in 1868 to roughly 25,000 square miles today. Iverson, *Diné*, 69.

109. C. N. Cotton to A. W. Cleland, January 22, 1887, Box 92, Folder 11, Hubbell Papers.

110. See Peterson, *Homestead and Farm*, 27; and Kelley and Francis, "Many Generations."

111. Adjustment of Rights of Settlers on the Navajo Indian Reservation, Arizona, S. Rep. 2041, 57th Cong. 2 (1902).

112. Ibid.

113. Williams speculates that the legal transfer of the land back to Hubbell might not have taken place until as late as 1902 when Congress passed the law excepting the land and clearing the title. Williams, *C. N. Cotton*, 16–17.

114. C. N. Cotton to Agent Hayzlett, April 24, 1899, quoted in Adjustment of Rights of Settlers on the Navajo Indian Reservation, Arizona, S. Rep. 2041, 57th Cong. 4 (1902).

115. For example, the Senate attached a provision opening the Navajo Reservation to mining. See W. A. Jones to J. L. Hubbell, January 22, 1902, Box 43, Folder Indians, 1873–1905, Hubbell Papers.

116. G. W. Hayzlett to Col. L. B. Henderson, December 2, 1899, quoted in Peterson, *Homestead and Farm*, 36.

117. Peterson, *Homestead and Farm*, 39–40.

## Chapter 3

1. Walter Dyk, ed. *Son of Old Man Hat* (1938; repr., Lincoln: University of Nebraska Press, 1967), 226–231.

2. Blue, *Indian Trader*, 41.

3. Charles S. Peterson, "Big House at Ganado: New Mexican Influence in Northern Arizona," *Journal of Arizona History* 30 (Spring 1989): 52.

4. Dyk, *Son of Old Man Hat*, 231. (The quotations that follow in the same paragraph are also drawn from this source, pages 232–233.)

5. Martha Blue states that Navajos often boasted about besting a trader. Franciscan Father Emanuel Trockur related a story in which a Navajo sold Hubbell a sack of wool with a rock stuffed inside to increase the weight. He did not manage to pull the wool over the trader's eyes, however; Hubbell discovered the rock and told his clerk to put it in a sack of flour which he then sold to the same Navajo. Blue, *Indian Trader*, 49.

6. Brugge, *Hubbell Trading Post*, 36. McNitt states that competition, rather than set prices, encouraged traders' fair behavior toward the Navajos. "Market prices for wool and hides and sheep and horses—the Indians' basic trade commodities—were common knowledge. The traders adjusted their prices accordingly, and where there was any sort of competition, the prices varied by no more than a few cents. It had to be that way. If a trader's prices moved too far out of line the Indians were soon aware of it and took their trade across the mesa." McNitt, *Indian Traders*, 51.

7. Hubbell, "Fifty Years," 28.

8. Brugge, *Hubbell Trading Post*, 38–39; Powers, *Navajo Trading*, 51; McNitt, *Indian Traders*, 84; Blue, *Indian Trader*, 52–53. Because tin money could usually only be spent at the store that minted it (though there were exceptions among friendly traders who would accept each other's tin money and periodically exchange it), the use of trade tokens encouraged Navajos to keep going back to the same trader. The Bureau of Indian Affairs attempted to abolish the use of trade tokens as early as 1878. The Navajos, however, often preferred *seco*. They distrusted paper money, and if they received silver coin they often used it for making jewelry. In fact, some traders even accepted the silver buttons that were once coins that Navajos clipped off their clothes as payment for goods. Tin money was officially abolished in 1935, though its use continued until the Navajo Reservation made the full conversion to a cash economy. McNitt, *Indian Traders*, 84–86.

9. Blue, *Indian Trader*, 43.

10. Dyk, *Son of Old Man Hat*, 236.

11. Powers, *Navajo Trading*, 49.

12. Hubbell, "Fifty Years," 28.

13. Blue, *Indian Trader*, 48.

14. Ibid., 54. As Blue notes, Hubbell's command of Navajo was generally considered quite good, but some Navajos remarked on his deficiencies. His sons, who, unlike their father, grew up on the Navajo Reservation and therefore began speaking the language at a much earlier age, were generally considered better speakers.

15. Hubbell, "Fifty Years," 28.

16. Powers, *Navajo Trading*, 51.

17. Brugge, *Hubbell Trading Post*, 35.

18. Dyk, *Son of Old Man Hat*, 234–236. The quotations that follow in the same paragraph are also drawn from this source, page 236.

19. Blue, *Indian Trader*, 50. While Left Handed's account stresses Hubbell's generosity, his friendliness, and his language skills, Martha Blue points out that the story can also be interpreted as containing a critique of the Navajo cultural gaffes that Hubbell committed by greeting his customers immediately rather than waiting

for them to approach his door, by repeating himself, by being overbearing in his use of directives, and by using inappropriate kinship terms to address Navajos he barely knew.

20. Peterson, "Big House," 62.

21. C. N. Cotton to W. K. P. Wilson, March 3, 1885, Box 91, Folder 2, Hubbell Papers.

22. Some of these stains, in fact, contribute to the difficulty of reconstructing the business before 1900: at least one book containing copies of outgoing letters covering the period has been badly damaged by water, the notations blurring into obscurity in entries up to around 1902. Additionally, the 1880s, when C. N. Cotton had primary charge of the business, yield clearer records than the 1890s, when Hubbell took over the management and ownership again. This period is therefore, by a relative surfeit of surviving evidence, less clear than the complex business that would emerge after 1900.

23. Custom House Appraiser's Office Ledger, 1878–1899, Lorenzo Hubbell, Jr., Papers.

24. Robert M. Utley, *Special Report on Hubbell Trading Post, Ganado, Arizona* (Santa Fe, NM: US Department of the Interior, National Park Service, 1959), 17.

25. McPherson, "Home of Merchandise," 28.

26. See Box 327, Folder 1, Hubbell Papers.

27. Peterson, *Homestead and Farm*, 220.

28. McNitt, *Indian Traders*, 203.

29. Hubbell, "Fifty Years," 26.

30. Ibid.

31. Custom House Appraiser's Office Ledger, 1878–1899, Lorenzo Hubbell, Jr., Papers.

32. Peterson, *Homestead and Farm*, 212; A. Y. Chrisholm to Cotton and Hubbell, October 17, 1884, Box 91, Folder 1, Hubbell Papers.

33. These firms included Oberne, Hosick & Co., Staab & Co., Eiseman Brothers, and Spiegelberg Brothers. See correspondence from Box 91, Folder 1, Hubbell Papers.

34. Peterson, *Homestead and Farm*, 221–222.

35. Sheridan, *Arizona: A History*, 105.

36. C. N. Cotton to A. W. Cleland, May 15, 1886, Box 92, Folder 9, Hubbell Papers.

37. Peterson, *Homestead and Farm*, 220, 225.

38. Williams, *C. N. Cotton*, 27.

39. Hubbell and Cotton to Staab & Co., February 21, 1885, Box 91, Folder 1, Hubbell Papers.

40. Blue, *Indian Trader*, 46.

41. William S. Kiser, "Navajo Pawn: A Misunderstood Traditional Trading Practice," *The American Indian Quarterly* 36, no. 2 (Spring 2012): 153. See also Powers, *Navajo Trading*, 51–52.

42. Ibid., 51; McNitt, *Indian Traders*, 55; Hubbell, "Fifty Years," 28.

43. McNitt, *Indian Traders*, 56.
44. Ibid., 56–57.
45. Ibid.
46. Maynard Dixon, "Chindih," n.d., unpublished manuscript, Folder "Dixon," Historical Files, HUTR.
47. McNitt, *Indian Traders*, 56. According to Kiser, many traders, in fact, chose not to accept pawn "as the profitability of pawn often proved marginal at best, especially when compared to the more lucrative business of straight trading. Pawn required that a trader hold an item for an extended period of time and collect interest, whereas trading consisted of a simple one-time transaction and a more immediate monetary turnaround for traders." Kiser, "Navajo Pawn," 151. Pawn was also "very time consuming, requiring a separate ledger book, individual entries for each transaction, filling out pawn tickets by hand, and the storage and security of pawned items." Kiser, "Navajo Pawn," 153.
48. McNitt, *Indian Traders*, 57.
49. Powers, *Navajo Trading*, 60.
50. Blue, *Indian Trader*, 47.
51. Hubbell, "Fifty Years," 28.
52. Teresa J. Wilkins, *Patterns of Exchange*, 24.
53. C. N. Cotton to A. Grunsfeld, January 22, 1886, Box 92, Folder 11, Hubbell Papers; C. N. Cotton to A. Grunsfeld, January 6, 1886, Box 92, Folder 11, Hubbell Papers.
54. C. N. Cotton to John H. Bowman, April 29, 1886, Box 91, Folder 8, Hubbell Papers.
55. Iverson, *Diné*, 93.
56. Peterson, *Homestead and Farm*, 213. Mormon traders in Tuba City, the Barth Brothers in St. Johns, Henry Springer and W. R. Milligan of Springerville, Henry Huning and C. E. Cooley of the Showlow-Pinetop area, Sam Day, Sr., at St. Michaels, and Thomas Keam all mixed trade, freighting, farming, and mail contracts, most of them before Hubbell. In this light, Peterson argues, Hubbell's operation "was the outgrowth of a well-tried if not always successful business strategy." For information about government mail contracts, see John and Lillian Theobald, *Arizona Territory Post Offices and Postmasters* (Phoenix: Arizona Historical Foundation, 1961), 2–3; and US Postal Service, *The United States Postal Service: An American History, 1775–2006* (Washington, DC: Government Relations, United States Postal Service, 2007), 18.
57. Theobald, *Arizona Territory Post Offices*, 101.
58. Eckel, "History of Ganado, Arizona," 49.
59. Theobald, *Arizona Territory Post Offices*, 101; Froeschauer-Nelson, *Cultural Landscape Report*, under "Hubbell Trading Post as Post Office for Community"; "Post Office Department," January 11, 1895, Box 545, Folder 1, Hubbell Papers.
60. Theobald, *Arizona Territory Post Offices*, 8, 19, 56; US Postal Service, *An American History*, 18–20.

61. Colby, "Persons at Hubbell Trading Posts," 1972, Box 3, Folder "Hubbell Business, Revised Graph...," Brugge Papers; Blue, *Indian Trader,* 268.

62. C. N. Cotton to John H. Bowman, April 29, 1886, Box 91, Folder 8, Hubbell Papers; J. L. Hubbell to C. C. Beam, December 9, 1885, Box 95, Folder 1878–1895, Hubbell Papers; Williams, *C. N. Cotton,* 20; McNitt, *Indian Traders,* 213–214. Cotton's dream revived briefly in the late-1880s when he bought interests in a second Chinle post, but he failed to win the license until 1890. See Williams, *C. N. Cotton,* 20–22.

63. C. N. Cotton to A. Grunsfield, May 15, 1886, Box 92, Folder 9, Hubbell Papers; C. N. Cotton to Charles Hubbell, May 18, 1886, Box 92, Folder 9, Hubbell Papers; Williams, 26–27; Blue, *Indian Trader,* 83.

64. There are few surviving business records from either Blue Canyon or Sin Let Za He. See Box 91, Folders 8 and 9, Hubbell Papers. The early operations at the Chinle store left behind a bit more evidence, including an account book from 1886–1887 and a few orders and inventories from 1890. See Box 321, Folder 7, and Box 242, Folder 1, Hubbell Papers.

65. See Peterson, *Homestead and Farm,* 22–25. As Peterson states, early travelers often referred to Hubbell's trading post as a trading ranch, which, according to Bourke's description, would have included chickens, gardens, and other agricultural improvements. See Bourke, *Snake Dance,* 67–78, 82–84.

66. Peterson, *Homestead and Farm,* 176.

67. Ibid., 181–183.

68. Peterson, "Big House," 68–69; Peterson, *Homestead and Farm,* 7.

69. G. W. Hayzlett to L. B. Henderson, December 2, 1899, quoted in Peterson, *Homestead and Farm,* 48.

70. Charles S. Peterson, "Headgates and Conquest: The Limits of Irrigation on the Navajo Reservation, 1880–1950," *New Mexico Historical Review* 68, no. 3 (July 1993): 269–271.

71. Ibid., 274.

72. Peterson, *Homestead and Farm,* 56–57. See W. C. Brown, *Report Upon Condition of the Navajo Indian Country,* 52nd Cong., 2nd sess., Senate Executive Document 68 (Washington, DC: Government Printing Office, 1893).

73. Peterson, *Homestead and Farm,* 61.

74. Martha Blue, "A View from the Bullpen: A Navajo Ken of Traders and Trading Posts," *Plateau* 57, no. 3 (1986): 12.

75. Robinson, "Construction Sequence," 226.

76. Blue, *Indian Trader,* 83.

77. Froeschauer-Nelson, *Cultural Landscape Report,* under "Early Settlement," and "Zenith Period of the Hubbell Trading Post and Farm (1895–1922)."

78. Robinson, "Construction Sequence," 231–235.

79. Williams, *C. N. Cotton,* 13.

80. The daily life of a Navajo trader has been well documented and offers many opportunities for comparison to the changing character of life around Hubbell Trading Post. See Frances Gillmore and Louisa Wade Wetherill, *Traders to the*

*Navajos: The Story of the Wetherills of Kayenta* (1934; repr. Albuquerque: University of New Mexico Press, 1953); Elizabeth C. Hegemann, *Navaho Trading Days* (Albuquerque: University of New Mexico Press, 1963); Hilda Faunce, *Desert Wife* (Boston: Little, Brown, 1934); Willow Roberts, *Stokes Carson: Twentieth Century Trading on the Navajo Reservation* (Albuquerque: University of New Mexico Press, 1987); and Gladwell Richardson, *Navajo Trader*, ed. Philip Reed Rulon (Tucson: University of Arizona Press, 1986).

81. Blue, *Indian Trader*, 119.
82. Ibid., 83.
83. Peterson, "Big House," 66; Peterson, *Homestead and Farm*, 232.
84. Peterson, *Homestead and Farm*, 233.
85. Blue, *Indian Trader*, 127.
86. Peterson, "Big House," 66.
87. Mrs. White Mountain Smith, "He is our Friend," *The Desert Magazine* 4, no. 1 (November 1940): 7.
88. Ibid., 8.
89. Ibid., 7; Maurice Kildare, "The Second Lorenzo, The Great," *Old West* 9 (Summer 1973): 12.
90. White Mountain Smith, "He is our Friend," 8.
91. Hubbell, "Fifty Years," 27.
92. Blue, *Indian Trader*, 101.
93. White Mountain Smith, "He is our Friend," 8.
94. E. A. Burbank to Roman Hubbell, April 29, 1937, Box 7, Folder 3, Roman Hubbell Papers.
95. J. L. Hubbell to Roman Hubbell, March 7, 1909, Box 95, Folder March 1–9, 1909, Hubbell Papers.
96. Blue, *Indian Trader*, 101.
97. Ibid., 98.
98. Francis E. Leupp to J. L. Hubbell, quoted in Blue, *Indian Trader*, 87. One woman artist, Cornelia Cassidy Davis, sent Lina a painting of Hopi girls.
99. Blue *Indian Trader*, 99.
100. Lorenzo Hubbell, Jr., to LaCharles Eckel, March 31, 1933, Box 107, Folder March, 1933, Hubbell Papers; Blue, *Indian Trader*, 102.
101. Blue, *Indian Trader*, 113–114. These are Yiłxaba, who bore Maude Hubbell in 1906 and Tom McCabe in 1908; Bidáya łaní Bici', who gave birth to John Shirley in 1900; Yiłhanazba', who gave birth to Peter Lee in 1893; Aszá' né z, who bore Mildred Hubbard in 1902; an unnamed woman whose daughter was named Na Kai Sání Bici, or Old Mexican's First Daughter; and another unnamed woman who named her son Roman Hubbell, born in 1904. Blue notes that the list should not be considered exhaustive, and recounts how several of the Navajo oral histories mention J. L.'s relationships with women. Blue also relates how, as she was conducting research for her biography of Hubbell, Navajos would often mention that their grandmother or great-grandmother had a child "for" J. L. Hubbell. Most of these

names, she notes, were not included in the records at St. Michaels. Teresa J. Wilkins includes a fascinating discussion of the "sexual component" of Indian trading in *Patterns of Exchange*, 146–148. She argues that these relationships were a reflection of both Navajo and Hispanic culture. As she writes, "These relationships were entwined with trading post economics in a complex web of gifts, obligations, and expectations. For Hubbell, with his Spanish upbringing, sexual conquest and the ability to take care of a large extended network of people were symbols of the kind of honor befitting a Spanish 'don.' This ideology meshed with Navajo matrilineality and the helping economy," as women bore children for J. L. and he in turn helped them with groceries. Teresa J. Wilkins, *Patterns of Exchange*, 146–147.

102. Blue, *Indian Trader*, 111.

103. Ibid., 113.

104. Blue, "Bullpen," 15–16. For a discussion of the paradoxical nature of Hubbell's relationship with the Navajos, see Blue, *Indian Trader*, 227–237.

105. C. C. Rister, "Harmful Practices of Indian Traders of the Southwest, 1865–1876," *New Mexico Historical Review* 6, no. 3 (July 1931): 232.

106. Hubbell, "Fifty Years," 26.

107. Ibid.

108. Edgar K. Miller, "The Indian and the Trader," *Indian School Journal* 7, no. 9 (July–September 1907): 17.

109. Blue, *Indian Trader*, 235.

110. Peterson, "Big House," 62.

111. Ibid., 61. For a more in-depth analysis of Navajo wealth distribution, see Robert S. McPherson, "*Ricos* and *Pobres*: Wealth Distribution on the Navajo Reservation in 1915," *New Mexico Historical Review* 60, no. 4 (October 1985): 415–434. McPherson argues that an understanding of the Navajos' system of egalitarianism, in which the accumulation of wealth was discouraged and generous distribution of wealth encouraged, must be qualified by an understanding of the role of wealth in social and political power on the reservation. McPherson and others have found that "wealth was concentrated among a few," and those few were often in positions of power. McPherson, "*Ricos* and *Pobres*," 432. Klara B. Kelley and Peter M. Whiteley further argue that "wealth stratification became more pronounced after about 1800" among the Navajos, and that the uneven distribution of livestock predated the incarceration at Bosque Redondo. Klara B. Kelley and Peter M. Whiteley, *Navajoland: Settlement and Land Use* (Tsaile, AZ: Navajo Community College Press, 1989), 39, 49.

112. Blue, "Bullpen," 12.

113. Brugge, *Hubbell Trading Post*, 39.

114. Ibid., 38–39.

115. Blue, "Bullpen," 14.

116. Blue, *Indian Trader*, 232–233. J. L. was known to distribute candy, nuts, oranges, and apples to Indian school children, and tobacco, soap, shoes, and clothing to Navajos who visited the post on Christmas.

117. Blue, "Bullpen," 14; Brugge, *Hubbell Trading Post*, 38.

118. Harold Berresford Hubbell and Donald Sidney Hubbell, eds., *History and Genealogy of the Hubbell Family*, 3rd ed. (Brooklyn, NY: Theo. Gaus, 1980), 37.

119. Ibid. Traders would come to substitute a sack of coins for the chicken in later chicken pulls. Brugge, *Hubbell Trading Post*, 38.

120. Blue, "Bullpen," 14.

121. Hubbell and Hubbell, *History and Genealogy*, 38.

122. Peterson, *Homestead and Farm*, 233.

123. Blue, *Indian Trader*, 129.

## Chapter 4

1. J. L. Hubbell to Charles H. Hubbell, November 19, 1902, Box 95, Folder 1902, Hubbell Papers.

2. See Forrest M. Parker to J. L. Hubbell, February 13, 1902, Box 95, Folder 1902, Hubbell Papers. Though this letter is filed in Folder 1902, the handwriting of the year is unclear, and in my opinion, the letter and engagement date from 1903. In his letter, Forrest states, "We expect to be married about the first of September at the latest & maybe before." Adela and Forrest were, in fact, married in September 1903.

3. Forrest M. Parker to J. L. Hubbell, February 13, 1902, Box 95, Folder 1903, Hubbell Papers.

4. Hubbell Parker, interview by Frank McNitt, May 12, 1972, transcript, Box 16-25(18), Folder 7, McNitt Papers.

5. "Miss Adele Hubbell," *Weekly Arizona Journal-Miner*, September 30, 1903.

6. LaCharles Eckel, interview by Lawrence C. Kelley, June 26, 1979, interview 074, transcript, Oral Histories, HUTR.

7. Hubbell Parker, interview by Frank McNitt, May 12, 1972, transcript, Box 16-25(18), Folder 7, McNitt Papers.

8. See J. L. Hubbell to Lorenzo Hubbell, March 4, 1909, Box 95, Folder March 1-9, 1909, Hubbell Papers.

9. Charles Q. Goodman to J. L. Hubbell, June 17, 1906, Box 95, Folder 1906, Hubbell Papers.

10. Barbara Hubbell to J. L. Hubbell, September 26, 1906, Box 95, Folder 1906, Hubbell Papers. LaCharles Eckel shares an anecdote that sheds further light on Adela and Barbara's differences in temperament. She remembered, "Adela was [a] much more meticulous housekeeper than my mother. She had the girls and every day her bedroom got completely turned out, the rugs taken out and everything. My mother finally said, 'leave my room alone!'" LaCharles Eckel, interview by Lawrence C. Kelley, June 26, 1979, interview 074, transcript, Oral Histories, HUTR.

11. See Barbara Hubbell to J. L. Hubbell, February 16, 1908, Box 95, Folder 1908, Hubbell Papers; and Barbara to J. L. Hubbell, June 16, 1910, Box 96, Folder January-June, 1910, Hubbell Papers.

12. "Charles Goodman Accidentally Shot Dead," *Albuquerque Journal*, January 25, 1909.

13. Ibid.

14. J. L. Hubbell to Ralph Cameron, March 3, 1909, Box 95, Folder March 1–9, 1909, Hubbell Papers.

15. "Charles Goodman Accidentally Shot Dead," *Albuquerque Journal*, January 25, 1909.

16. LaCharles Eckel, interview by Lawrence C. Kelley, June 26, 1979, interview 074, transcript, Oral Histories, HUTR.

17. Ibid.; J. L. Hubbell to Barbara Goodman, April 24, 1912, Box 97, Folder April 22–30, 1912, Hubbell Papers; J. L. Hubbell to Barbara Goodman, June 13, 1912, Box 97, Folder June 1912, Hubbell Papers; Roman Hubbell or Lorenzo Hubbell, Jr., to W. H. Knap, January 31, 1913, Box 97, Folder January 15–31, 1913, Hubbell Papers.

18. LaCharles Eckel, interview by Lawrence C. Kelley, June 26, 1979, interview 074, transcript, Oral Histories, HUTR.

19. Blue, *Indian Trader*, 222–223. In an attempt to cure his deafness, Roman had Miguelito perform a Navajo Nightwater ceremony for him in 1922. Dickson Hartwell described the ceremony in an article about Roman, claiming that it gathered a crowd of 5,000 Navajos "to participate in the united plea to let their beloved friend hear again." Hartwell concluded, "Roman Hubbell is still deaf. But within a year of the sing a marvelous new hearing aid was developed and with it Roman enjoys almost normal hearing. There isn't a Navajo anywhere but knows—as does Hubbell—that the appearance of the device following the sing was more than coincidental." Dickson Hartwell, "White Brother to the Navajo," *Collier's*, April 30, 1949.

20. John Cavanaugh to J. L. Hubbell, August 26, 1908, Box 83, Folder University of Notre Dame, Hubbell Papers.

21. John Cavanaugh to J. L. Hubbell, March 11, 1909, Box 83, Folder University of Notre Dame, Hubbell Papers.

22. Ibid.

23. J. L. Hubbell to Roman Hubbell, March 7, 1909, Box 95, Folder March 1–9, 1909, Hubbell Papers.

24. Lorenzo Hubbell, Jr., to J. L. Hubbell, June 5, 1910, Box 96, Folder January–June 1910, Hubbell Papers.

25. Accounts of J. L.'s political involvement can be found in Blue, *Indian Trader*, 170–188; and *Notables of the West*, 187–188.

26. Hubbell won his seat on the territorial legislature in a race against Democratic candidate John Hunt, 470 votes to 380. "Apache County," *Arizona Republican*, November 26, 1892; James H. McClintock, *Arizona: Prehistoric—Aboriginal—Pioneer—Modern; The Nation's Youngest Commonwealth Within a Land of Ancient Culture*, vol. 2 (Chicago: S. J. Clarke, 1916), 341. A record of Hubbell's doings as a territorial legislator can be found in *Journals of the Seventeenth Legislative Assembly of the Territory of Arizona* (Phoenix, AZ: Herald Book and Job Office, 1893).

27. "Law Makers," *Arizona Republican*, February 12, 1893.

28. Martha Blue notes that while J. L. liked to claim altruistic reasons for his political involvement, he usually followed an agenda aligned closely with his personal interests. Most notably, J. L.'s support of the Navajos often depended on how closely their interests aligned with his own. For example, he opposed the further expansion of the Navajo Reservation, an unsurprising stance given his struggle to obtain title to his land after it had been swallowed up in a previous expansion. And despite his support of woman and Hispanic suffrage, he made no similar moves to support the Navajo vote. However, Hubbell did sometimes support the Navajos with no direct benefit to himself. When he traveled to Washington in 1910 to testify against the Educational Qualification Law, he ended his testimony by asking the members of the committee to disapprove a provision in the law that prohibited the Indians from intermarrying with whites, arguing that "this is a very short-sighted policy on the part of our legislature. . . . I do not think their rights should be curtailed if they should decide to intermarry." *Statehood: Hearing Before the Subcommittee on Territories on the Bill S. 5916*, 61st Cong. 74 (1910) (statement of J. L. Hubbell).

29. Blue, *Indian Trader*, 173.

30. J. L. Hubbell to Charles H. Hubbell, November 19, 1902, Box 95, Folder 1902, Hubbell Papers.

31. "The Republican Territorial Convention . . . ," *Cochise Review and Arizona Daily Orb*, May 12, 1900.

32. See "Hon. Lorenzo Hubbell of Apache," *Coconino Sun*, August 7, 1908; "A. Hubbell has Support of Gov. Kibbey," *Bisbee Daily Review*, August 13, 1908; "Judge Ruiz Bitter Against Accuser Barth," *Weekly Arizona Journal-Miner*, August 19, 1908; and "Hubbell Balks at Nomination Won't Have It," *Bisbee Daily Review*, August 22, 1908.

33. Sheridan, *Arizona: A History*, 174. Hubbell articulated his views on statehood in "Throws up Sponge for Joint Statehood," *Arizona Silver Belt*, September 20, 1906. Hubbell's support for joint statehood, however qualified by his preference for single statehood, would later pit many Arizona residents against him politically. See "Attorney General E. S. Clark . . . ," *Mohave County Miner*, August 8, 1909.

34. Jay J. Wagoner, *Arizona Territory, 1863–1912: A Political History* (Tucson: University of Arizona Press, 1970), 439.

35. Sheridan, *Arizona: A History*, 175.

36. J. L. had previously fought similar legislation while serving as a member of the territorial legislature. He had introduced a bill "amending an act defining the qualifications of officeholders," asking "that a person able to read and write Spanish be entitled to the same privileges as though he also read English." The bill passed. See "One Week's Run," *Arizona Republican*, February 18, 1893; "Washington," *Arizona Republican*, February 24, 1893.

37. J. L. Hubbell to J. U. Lloyd, March 5, 1909, Box 95, Folder March 1–9, 1909, Hubbell Papers.

38. J. L. Hubbell to Ralph Cameron, March 3, 1909, Box 95, Folder March 1–9, 1909, Hubbell Papers.

39. A neat summary of the arguments can be found in "Former Arizona Opponents Now Friends of Territory," *Weekly Journal-Miner,* March 9, 1910.

40. *Statehood: Hearing before the Subcommittee on Territories on the Bill S. 5916,* 61st Cong. 74 (1910).

41. Ralph Emerson Twitchell, *The Leading Facts of New Mexican History,* vol. 2 (Albuquerque: Horn and Wallace, 1963), 579–582.

42. "The Republican Organization," *Bisbee Daily Review,* November 3, 1911; Lorenzo Hubbell, Jr., to J. L. Hubbell, September 18, 1910, Box 96, Folder July–December 1910, Hubbell Papers.

43. Blue, *Indian Trader,* 178. J. L. was elected chairman of the Republican Central Committee on November 6, 1911. See "Republican State Committee Elects Hubbell Chairman," *Weekly Journal-Miner,* November 8, 1911.

44. "The Republican Organization," *Bisbee Daily Review,* November 3, 1911.

45. J. L. Hubbell to David K. Udall, November 17, 1911, Box 96, Folder November 1911, Hubbell Papers.

46. "The Triumph of Democracy at Phoenix," *Bisbee Daily Review,* December 10, 1911. For unknown reason, J. L. was frequently referred to as "Alonzo Hubbell" or "J. A. Hubbell" during his tenure as state senator.

47. McClintock, *Arizona,* 337–338.

48. Lorenzo Hubbell or Roman Hubbell to Maynard Dixon, February 7, 1913, Box 97, February 1–9, 1913, Hubbell Papers.

49. J. L. Hubbell to Roman Hubbell, April 19, 1912, Box 97, Folder April 8–21, 1912, Hubbell Papers.

50. J. L. Hubbell to Lorenzo Hubbell, April 27, 1912, Box 97, Folder April 22–30, 1912, Hubbell Papers.

51. J. L. Hubbell to Charles F. Lummis, May 6, 1912, Box 97, Folder May 1–9, 1912, Hubbell Papers.

52. J. L. Hubbell to Elias Armijo, March 21, 1912, Box 97, Folder March 1912, Hubbell Papers; J. L. Hubbell to Lorenzo Hubbell, Jr., March 21, 1912, Box 97, Folder March 1912, Hubbell Papers.

53. J. L. Hubbell to Lorenzo Hubbell, Jr., March 25, 1912, Box 97, Folder March 1912, Hubbell Papers.

54. Lorenzo Hubbell, Jr., to J. L. Hubbell, May 10, 1913, Box 99, Folder May 1913, Hubbell Papers.

55. It is important to note, however, that the surviving business records from the decade 1890–1900 are very meager, and that the absence of evidence that Hubbell owned other posts at this time does not eliminate the possibility that he did.

56. Brugge, *Hubbell Trading Post,* 52.

57. For estimated dates of operation, see "Persons at Hubbell Trading Post," a list prepared in 1972 by University of Arizona Special Collections archivist Clint Colby while processing the Hubbell Papers. A copy can be found in Box 3, Folder

"Hubbell Business, Revised graph fr. Kathy M'Closkey + one from Clint Colby," Brugge Papers. Lorenzo, Jr., bought the Cedar Springs store from his father, who had purchased it a few years before. He would also later buy the Black Mountain store from his father around 1917—a trend of ownership swapping that demonstrates the interconnected and yet separate nature of the Hubbell family trading posts.

58. McPherson, "Home of Merchandise," 31.

59. Brugge, *Hubbell Trading Post*, 53. The Hubbells' curio trade took off in earnest around 1900 as they began to sell not only to visitors, eastern department stores, and individuals through mail-order catalogues, but to the Southwest tourism giant, the Fred Harvey Company.

60. Keam, like Hubbell, was a man more complicated than his legend. For an excellent biography of Keam, see Laura Graves, *Thomas Varker Keam, Indian Trader* (Norman: University of Oklahoma Press, 1998). See also Lynn R. Bailey, "Thomas Varker Keam, Tusayan Trader," *Arizoniana* 2, no. 4 (Winter 1961): 15–19; and Richard Van Valkenburg, "Tom Keam, Friend of the Moqui," *Desert Magazine* 9, no. 9 (July 1946): 9–12.

61. Graves, *Thomas Varker Keam*, 226–227.

62. Lorenzo Hubbell, Jr., to J. L. Hubbell, June 14, 1902, Box 95, Folder 1902, Hubbell Papers.

63. J. L. Hubbell to Lorenzo Hubbell, Jr., March 22, 1909, Box 95, Folder March 20–31, 1909, Hubbell Papers. Another letter typical of J. L.'s advice to Lorenzo is J. L. Hubbell to Lorenzo Hubbell, Jr., March 19, 1909, Box 95, Folder March 10–19, 1909, Hubbell Papers.

64. Lorenzo Hubbell, Jr., to J. L. Hubbell, May 25, 1902, Box 95, Folder 1902, Hubbell Papers.

65. See Kildare, "The Second Lorenzo"; White Mountain Smith, "He is our Friend"; and Lorenzo Hubbell, Jr., to J. L. Hubbell, September 6, 1904, Box 95, Folder 1904, Hubbell Papers.

66. Lorenzo Hubbell, Jr., to J. L. Hubbell, May 30, 1902, Box 95, Folder 1902, Hubbell Papers.

67. Kildare, "The Second Lorenzo," 12.

68. White Mountain Smith, "He is our Friend," 8.

69. Lorenzo Hubbell, Jr., to J. L. Hubbell, May 25, 1902, Box 95, Folder 1902, Hubbell Papers.

70. J. L. Hubbell to C. E. Wood, May 17, 1902, Box 94, Letter 339, Hubbell Papers. Lorenzo opened a post office at Keams Canyon in early 1905. Lorenzo Hubbell to J. L. Hubbell, April 26, 1905, Box 95, Folder 1905, Hubbell Papers.

71. Peterson, *Homestead and Farm*, 226. (Subsequent citations in this paragraph and the next are to the same source, pp. 226–232.)

72. Blue, *Indian Trader*, 144. See 143–145 for J. L. Hubbell motoring anecdotes. See also Faunce, *Desert Wife*, 66–72; and Lockwood, *Pioneer Portraits*, 148–150.

73. Roman Hubbell to J. J. Kirk, February 19, 1913, Box 97, Folder February 10–28, 1913, Hubbell Papers.

74. Blue, *Indian Trader*, 143.

75. Roman Hubbell to Cousin, February 18, 1913, Box 97, Folder February 10–28, 1913, Hubbell Papers. Even though cars were cheaper than horses—cars did not have to haul hundreds of pounds of feed for the draft animals just for the journey—they did require gasoline and oil, which Hubbell had shipped in tanks by wagon from Gallup to Ganado. J. L. Hubbell to C. N. Cotton, January 16, 1913, Box 97, Folder January 1–14, 1913, Hubbell Papers.

76. After 1900, the Hubbells continued to bid for mail contracts to supplement their income. The Hubbells operated four mail routes between 1900 and 1914 between Ganado and St. Michaels, Keams Canyon, Cedar Springs, and Chin Lee. Mail contracts were awarded for a period of three to four years, and paid between $515.00 and $1,650 per year, depending on the frequency of delivery and the volume of the mail. See Box 82, Folder US—Post Office Department, 1902–1915, Hubbell Papers. The Hubbells also continued to operate the post office out of the Ganado trading post. J. L. gave up the office of postmaster to Charles Bierkemper, a Presbyterian missionary, in 1908. The office of postmaster turned over every few years, with Kathleen M. Neubert, Elias H. Armijo, Walter Codington, and Donald Schillenburg holding the post for about two years each until Barbara Hubbell Goodman was appointed postmistress in 1919, a duty she would fulfill until 1943. Froeschauer-Nelson, *Cultural Landscape Report*, under Hubbell Trading Post as Post Office for Community."

77. J. L. Hubbell to Fourth Assistant Postmaster General, March 3, 1913, Box 99, Folder March 1–11, 1913, Hubbell Papers.

78. J. L. Hubbell to Fourth Assistant Postmaster General, June 24, 1913, Box 99, Folder June 1913, Hubbell Papers.

79. Joseph Schmedding, *Cowboy and Indian Trader* (Albuquerque: University of New Mexico Press, 1974), 311–312.

80. Peterson, *Homestead and Farm*, 248, 235–236.

81. Brugge, "Navajo and Western Pueblo History," 108.

82. Mary May Bailey, interview by Karen Underhill, July 13, 1999, United Indian Traders Association Project, "Traders: Voices from the Trading Post," Cline Library, Special Collections and Archives Department, Northern Arizona University, accessed August 30, 2012, http://library.nau.edu/speccoll/exhibits/traders/oralhistories/bailey.html.

83. Schmedding, *Cowboy and Indian Trader*, 310.

84. J. L. Hubbell to Lorenzo Hubbell, Jr., March 1, 1909, Box 95, Folder March 20–31, 1909, Hubbell Papers.

85. Simeon Schwemberger to Dear Friend, December 5, 1913, Box 99, Folder July–December 1913, Hubbell Papers.

86. Peterson, "Headgates and Conquest," 274–275; Peterson, *Homestead and Farm*, 59–62, 104.

87. Peterson, *Homestead and Farm*, 64.

88. Peterson, "Headgates and Conquest," 275. According to Peterson, Hubbell had many close friends in the Bureau of Indian Affairs, whom he contacted on the irrigation matter frequently, as well as local superintendents of the Navajo

agencies and the Indian Irrigation Service. Key individuals from the latter organization include Samuel Shoemaker, George Butler, Herbert Gregory, and H. F. Robinson. There is also a strong tradition that Theodore Roosevelt used his influence to get the appropriation passed, though Peterson doubts Roosevelt's role as advocate since his tour of the reservation—and Hubbell's irrigation works—would not happen until 1913, after the appropriation had already passed. See Peterson, *Homestead and Farm*, 98–104. In 1909, Herbert E. Gregory made a recommendation that Hubbell's efforts be bolstered by government involvement, "since the water to be stored at this place is for the benefit of the Navajos." Herbert E. Gregory, *The Navajo Country: A Geographic and Hydrographic Reconnaissance of Parts of Arizona, New Mexico, and Utah* (Washington, DC: Government Printing Office, 1916), 110–111.

89. J. L. Hubbell to Lorenzo Hubbell, Jr., April 6, 1912, Box 97, Folder April 1–7, 1912, Hubbell Papers.

90. Peterson, *Homestead and Farm*, 92–94. J. L. reported the costs of the projects differently at various times. See tax assessment records, Box 128, Hubbell Papers; and Ganado Ledger Book, 1902–1907, Box 336, Hubbell Papers.

91. Brugge, *Hubbell Trading Post*, 50; Peterson, *Homestead and Farm*, 106.

92. Brugge, *Hubbell Trading Post*, 50.

93. Peterson, *Homestead and Farm*, 86 (for Navajo views of the construction project, see 87–91); and Oral Histories, HUTR.

94. Peterson, *Homestead and Farm*, 96–97.

95. Ibid., 112–113.

96. The Presbyterians selected Ganado as the site of their mission in 1901, with the help of Hubbell, who had previously attempted to secure a Catholic mission for Ganado. Charles H. Bierkemper, the first missionary, lived at Hubbell Trading Post with his wife while he constructed a two-room adobe residence and chapel on the mission site in 1902. Blue, *Indian Trader*, 164–165. For a history of the mission, see Cora B. Salsbury, *Forty Years in the Desert: A History of Ganado Mission, 1901–1941* (Chicago: Physicians' Record Co., 1941).

97. Peterson, "Headgates and Conquest," 278, 285, 289; Brugge, *Hubbell Trading Post*, 51.

98. Peterson, *Homestead and Farm*, 96–97.

99. J. L. Hubbell to F. M. Covert, December 1907, Box 95, Folder 1907, Hubbell Papers. See also Lorenzo Hubbell, Jr., to Forrest M. Parker, October 19, 1908, Box 95, Folder 1908, Hubbell Papers.

100. J. L. Hubbell to Bank of Commerce, June 1, 1909, Box 96, Folder June 1909, Hubbell Papers; J. L. Hubbell to E. A. Burbank, February 23, 1909, Box 95, Folder February 20–28, 1909, Hubbell Papers.

101. J. L. Hubbell to Frank A. Hubbell, June 1, 1909, Box 96, Folder June 1909, Hubbell Papers.

102. J. L. Hubbell to Lorenzo Hubbell, Jr., March 22, 1909, Box 95, Folder March 20–31, 1909, Hubbell Papers.

103. J. F. Alkire to J. L. Hubbell, June 11, 1910, Box 96, Folder January–October 1911, Hubbell Papers.

104. Blue, *Indian Trader,* 109–110.
105. Ibid., 183.
106. Ibid.
107. Charles Hubbell to Roman Hubbell, March 30, 1913, Box 99, Folder March 12–31, 1913, Hubbell Papers.
108. See Charlie Hubbell to J. L. Hubbell, March 4, 1913, Box 99, Folder March 1–11, Hubbell Papers.
109. Lorenzo Hubbell, Jr., to J. L. Hubbell, May 10, 1913, Box 99, Folder May 1913, Hubbell Papers.
110. In her account of Roman's wedding, Elizabeth Hegemann states that Alma had come to Ganado "as a secretary to Don Lorenzo, Sr., when he held an important appointive position in Washington for a few years." Hegemann, *Navaho Trading Days,* 202–203.
111. "Indian Did Not Tie Knot Tight Enough," *Anaconda Standard,* September 7, 1912. See also "Not Satisfied with Wedding Ceremony," *Evening Telegram,* September 7, 1912; and "Married Under Moki Rite," *Washington Post,* September 7, 1912.
112. J. L. Hubbell to Roman Hubbell, September 27, 1912, Box 96, Folder July–December 1912, Hubbell Papers.
113. Blue, *Indian Trader,* 110.
114. Lorenzo Hubbell, Jr., to J. L. Hubbell, September 24, 1913, Box 98, Letterbook, Hubbell Papers.
115. Roman Hubbell to J. L. Hubbell, September 9, 1913, Box 99, Folder July–December 1913, Hubbell Papers; quoted in Blue, *Indian Trader,* 121.
116. Barbara H. Goodman to J. L. Hubbell, June 16, 1910, Box 96, Folder January–June 1910, Hubbell Papers.
117. Lorenzo Hubbell, Jr., to Roman Hubbell, October 30, 1913, Box 96, Folder January–October 1911, Hubbell Papers.
118. J. L. Hubbell to Lorenzo Hubbell, Jr., March 21, 1912, Box 97, Folder March 1912, Hubbell Papers; J. L. Hubbell to Lorenzo Hubbell, Jr., March 25, 1912, Box 97, Folder March 1912, Hubbell Papers .
119. J. L. Hubbell to Lorenzo Hubbell, Jr., May 7, 1912, Box 97, Folder May 1–9, 1912, Hubbell Papers.
120. Blue, *Indian Trader,* 120.
121. Lorenzo Hubbell, Jr., to LaCharles G. Eckel, March 31, 1933, Box 107, Folder March 1933, Hubbell Papers. Lorenzo would later give the brooch to LaCharles as a gift upon the birth of her first child.
122. Mortgage Deed, March 16, 1914, Box 529, Folder 2, Hubbell Papers; Blue, *Indian Trader,* 183–184, 319.
123. Lockwood, *Pioneer Portraits,* 146.
124. J. L. Hubbell to S. B. Wood, June 21, 1913, Box 99, Folder June 1913, Hubbell Papers.
125. Forrest M. Parker to Thomas B. Getz, October 8, 1914, Box 94, Letterbook, Hubbell Papers.

126. Forrest M. Parker to C. N. Cotton, October 17, 1914, Box 94, Letterbook p. 693, Hubbell Papers.

127. Forrest M. Parker to Carter H. Harrison, October 29, 1914, Box 100, Letterbook, Hubbell Papers.

128. Forrest M. Parker to W. M. Knap, October 28, 1914, Box 100, Letterbook, Hubbell Papers.

129. See James Chace, *1912: Wilson, Roosevelt, Taft, and Debs—The Election That Changed the Country* (New York: Simon & Schuster, 2004).

130. McClintock, *Arizona*, 378.

131. "Republican Misunderstanding," *Arizona Republican*, July 26, 1914; "Pima, Cochise, Pinal, Santa Cruz, and Others Firmly Against Fusion," *Arizona Republican*, July 23, 1914.

132. "Republicans' Second Round in Campaign," *Arizona Republican*, October 24, 1914.

133. McClintock, *Arizona*, 380; "Election Returns as Officially Canvassed by Counties," *Graham Guardian*, December 14, 1914.

134. Blue, *Indian Trader*, 187.

## Chapter 5

1. The purchase and sale of trading post locations does not follow a simple pattern of sale in times of hardship and purchase in times of plenty. Often, the Hubbells opened stores when they seemed the most financially unstable, as if they expected the additional location to save them. It is also possible that they viewed trading posts as long-term investments, buying them whenever they became available, whether or not they had the cash on hand to do so. In either case, even during difficult years, they acquired as many trading posts as they sold; it was not until the last stores opened in 1935 that a clear pattern of loss emerges.

2. By paying off part of the debt, J. L. was able to get the mortgage on his property released, though the stock of goods and the water right were still held against future payments. "Partial Release of Mortgage," April 7, 1917, Box 529, Folder 2, Hubbell Papers. For information about the failure of Sheep Springs and Chinle, see Lorenzo Hubbell, Jr., to Forrest M. Parker, February 25, 1916, Box 101, Folder January–March 1916, Hubbell Papers.

3. Williams, *C. N. Cotton*, 40–41. Schmedding describes his taking possession of "one of the best-known and most influential Indian trading posts in the country" in *Cowboy and Indian Trader*, 313–320.

4. Schmedding, *Cowboy and Indian Trader*, 316. J. L. had bought the Oraibi post in 1906. German-born trader Frederick W. Volz had originally opened it around 1898. Volz used the Oraibi post to facilitate his curio trade and encourage tourism to the Hopi villages, roles that the Hubbells would take over once they bought the post. Richard O. Clemmer, *Roads in the Sky: The Hopi Indians in a Century of Change* (Boulder, CO: Westview, 1995), 94; Peter M. Whiteley, *Deliberate*

*Acts: Changing Hopi Culture Through the Oraibi Split* (Tucson: University of Arizona Press, 1988), 103. For additional information about Volz and his influence on tourism and curio trade, see Tricia Loscher, "The Volz Collection of Hopi Katsina Dolls at the Heard Museum," *American Indian Art Magazine* 30, no. 3 (Summer 2005): 78–88; and McNitt, *Indian Traders*, 270.

5. Garrick Bailey and Roberta Glenn Bailey, *A History of the Navajos: The Reservation Years* (Santa Fe, NM: School of American Research Press, 1986), 118.

6. Ibid; Powers, *Navajo Trading*, 36–38.

7. Powers, *Navajo Trading*, 36.

8. Bailey and Bailey, *History of the Navajos*, 118.

9. For letters and receipts regarding rationing during WWI, see Box 523, Folder 1, Hubbell Papers.

10. See Roman and Lorenzo's draft registration cards, which can be found online at Ancestry.com, *World War I Draft Registration Cards, 1979–1918*, or in the original at United States, Selective Service System, *World War I Selective Service Draft Registration Cards, 1917–1918*, M1509, 4,582 rolls, Washington, DC, National Archives and Records Administration.

11. Forrest M. Parker to Lorenzo Hubbell, Jr., August 24, 1918, Box 101, Folder June–December 1918, Hubbell Papers.

12. Forrest M. Parker to Lorenzo Hubbell, Jr., June 10, 1918, Box 101, Folder June–December 1918, Hubbell Papers.

13. Lorenzo Hubbell, Jr., to Ed Thacker, October 3, 1913, Box 101, Folder June–December 1918, Hubbell Papers.

14. Howard M. Bahr, ed., *The Navajo as Seen by the Franciscans, 1898–1921: A Sourcebook*, Native American Resources Series, no. 4 (Lanham, MD: Scarecrow, 2004), 438. See pages 438–461 for excerpts of firsthand accounts of the influenza epidemic from Franciscan Fathers Berard Haile and Anselm Weber.

15. Ibid. Robert A. Trennert attributes the high death toll among the Navajos to the swiftly overwhelmed and inadequate government facilities, to the illness at the height of the epidemic of both Anglo and Navajo healers, and to the Navajo fear of the dead, which led the Diné to flee from outbreak sites, carrying the disease with them. Robert A. Trennert, *White Man's Medicine: Government Doctors and the Navajo, 1863–1955* (Albuquerque: University of New Mexico Press, 1998), 123. See also Wade Davies, *Healing Ways: Navajo Health Care in the Twentieth Century* (Albuquerque: University of New Mexico Press, 2001); Scott C. Russell, "The Navajo and the 1918 Influenza Pandemic," in *Health and Disease in the Prehistoric Southwest*, ed. Charles F. Merbs, Robert J. Miller, and Elizabeth S. Dyer Alcauskas (Tempe: Arizona State University Press, 1985), 380–390; and Gillmore and Wetherill, *Traders to the Navajos*, 222–229.

16. Bailey and Bailey, *History of the Navajos*, 119.

17. Bahr, *Navajo as Seen*, 438; Iverson, *Diné*, 115.

18. Rose Mitchell, *Tall Woman: The Life Story of Rose Mitchell, A Navajo Woman, c. 1875–1977*, ed. Charlotte J. Frisbie (Albuquerque: University of New

Mexico Press, 2001), 118. See pages 128–135 for a more detailed account of Navajo perceptions of and responses to the epidemic.

19. Ibid., 132; Trennert, *White Man's Medicine*, 123.

20. Bailey and Bailey, *History of the Navajos*, 119–120.

21. Lorenzo Hubbell, Jr., to Ed Thacker, October 8, 1918, Box 101, Folder June–December 1918, Hubbell Papers.

22. Ethel Thacker to Lorenzo Hubbell, Jr., November 4, 1918, Box 101, Folder June–December 1918, Hubbell Papers.

23. Lorenzo Hubbell, Jr., to Ed Thacker, December 1, 1918, Box 101, Folder June–December 1918, Hubbell Papers.

24. Ed Thacker to Lorenzo Hubbell, Jr., November 29, 1918, Box 101, Folder June–December 1918, Hubbell Papers.

25. Lorenzo Hubbell, Jr., to Ed Thacker, December 1, 1918, Box 101, Folder June–December 1918, Hubbell Papers.

26. LaCharles Eckel, interview by Lawrence C. Kelly, June 26, 1979, interview 074, transcript, Oral Histories, HUTR.

27. "Deaths and Funerals," *Gallup Independent*, October 24, 1918. For Alma's previous illnesses, see J. L. Hubbell to Lorenzo Hubbell, Jr., February 3, 1913, Box 9, Folder February 1–9, 1913, Hubbell Papers; Roman Hubbell to Lorenzo Hubbell, February 18, 1913, Box 97, Folder February 10–28, 1913, Hubbell Papers.

28. Dorothy Smith Hubbell, "Arizona," in *Hubbell Pioneers*, ed. Donald Sidney Hubbell (Downers Grove, IL: Hubbell Family Historical Society 1989), 358.

29. "Deaths and Funerals," *Gallup Independent*, October 24, 1918.

30. Blue, *Indian Trader*, 248–249.

31. Billie Williams Yost, *Bread Upon the Sands* (Caldwell, ID: Caxton Printers, 1958), 222. Yost provides a touching personal account of the murder's aftermath on pages 221–238.

32. Ibid., 223–225.

33. Ed Thacker to Lorenzo Hubbell, Jr., March 24, 1919, Box 101, Folder January–July 1919, Hubbell Papers.

34. "Trader at Hopi Post Found Dead," *Salt Lake Telegram*, March 25, 1919.

35. Headlines like these would later move the defense to appeal for a change of venue in the two Navajos' trial, though the request was denied. "Brother of Senator Is Burned to Death," *San Francisco Chronicle*, March 25, 1919; "Indian Slayer of White Barricaded," *Salt Lake Telegram*, April 3, 1919; "Navajo Slayers Standing at Bay," *San Francisco Chronicle*, April 3, 1919; "One of Slayers of Trader Hubbell Very Valuable Navajo Medicine Man; Tribesmen Plead for Clemency," *Santa Fe New Mexican*, April 26, 1919; State of Arizona vs. Adeltoni Bigue No. 1 and Adeltoni Bigue No. 2, Superior Court of Coconino County (no docket number), Coconino County Courthouse, Flagstaff, Arizona. A copy of these court records can also be found in the Brugge Papers, Box 3, Folder "Hubbell, Charles—Killing of," Center for Southwest Research.

36. "Trader Murdered at Trading Post by Indians is Belief," *Gallup Independent*, March 27, 1919.

37. Lorenzo Hubbell, Jr., to Leo Crane, March 29, 1919, Box 101, Folder January–July 1919, Hubbell Papers.

38. Lorenzo Hubbell, Jr., to Hastiin Nez and Adakai, March 29, 1919, Box 101, Folder January–July 1919, Hubbell Papers.

39. Ibid.

40. "Two Indian Murderers Surrounded in Cave," *Mohave County Miner,* April 5, 1919.

41. See Lorenzo Hubbell, Jr., to J. L. Hubbell, April 29, 1919, Box 101, Folder January–July 1919, Hubbell Papers, as well as other letters in the same folder.

42. Yost, *Bread Upon the Sands,* 235.

43. "Life is Jury's Verdict in Hubbell Murder Case; General Disappointment at Verdict," *Coconino Sun,* August 1, 1919. In a letter to Attorney F. M. Gold, Lorenzo stated that the evidence of Charlie's gun had been tampered with—three different Navajos who had had the gun in their possession in the days following the murder each reported a different number of empty shells, chambers, and bullets. Lorenzo Hubbell, Jr., to F. M. Gold, July 10, 1919, Box 101, Folder January–July 1919, Hubbell Papers.

44. McNitt, *Indian Traders,* 322; Blue, *Indian Trader,* 235.

45. "Life is Jury's Verdict in Hubbell Murder Case; General Disappointment at Verdict," *Coconino Sun,* August 1, 1919.

46. Ibid. The brothers were incarcerated at the Arizona state penitentiary in Florence. Adeltoni Bigue No. 1 was considered a model prisoner, learning English during his sentence. "Cheerful Chirps," *Coconino Sun,* May 28, 1920. Both brothers were released on parole by Christmastime, 1920, much to the disappointment of Lorenzo and J. L. See Lorenzo Hubbell, Jr., to J. L. Hubbell, December 12, 1920, Box 102, Folder October–December 1920, Hubbell Papers; Yost, 237.

47. Ed Thacker to Lorenzo Hubbell, Jr., April 4, 1919, Box 101, Folder January–July 1919, Hubbell Papers.

48. Lorenzo Hubbell, Jr., to Ed Thacker, July 31, 1919, Box 101, Folder January–July 1919, Hubbell Papers.

49. Lorenzo Hubbell, Jr., to First National Bank, April 15, 1919, Box 101, Folder January–July 1919, Hubbell Papers.

50. Lorenzo Hubbell, Jr., to Claude Romero, April 11, 1919, Box 101, Folder January–July 1919, Hubbell Papers.

51. Yost, *Bread Upon the Sands,* 233.

52. Blue, *Indian Trader,* 119. See also Leo Crane to Lorenzo Hubbell, Jr., March 27, 1919, Box 101, Folder January–July 1919, Hubbell Papers.

53. Charles Hubbell to J. L. Hubbell, July 3, 1919, Box 96, Folder July–December 1910, Hubbell Papers.

54. McNitt, *Indian Traders,* 338.

55. No surviving correspondence from J. L. preserves his feelings at his brother's death, but an article, "Don't Visit Indians Without Proper Guides," *Coconino Sun,* August 1, 1919, reported him warning travelers "to stay away from the reservation or know just where and who you are going with." Another article, "Case

Against Indians for Hubbell Murder Postponed to July 21," *Coconino Sun,* July 11, 1919, reported him speculating that the murder had been committed not for robbery, but for Charlie's scalp: "There are good and bad Indians, the same as among the people of any other race, and knowing the friendly feeling among the Indians with whom my brother had lived for years, I doubt if any of the older men would ever have thought of murdering him." Lorenzo, Jr.'s, feelings of bitterness are easier to retrieve in the letters he wrote in the days following the murder and the trial. His friend, Gladwell "Toney" Richardson, writing under the pseudonym Maurice Kildare, also wrote in an article that "[d]espite all the love Lorenzo had for the Navajos, one cruel episode bothered him to the end.... Lorenzo could never mention his Uncle Charles without becoming very bitter. During all the long years I knew him this was the only subject I ever heard him discuss with passion." Kildare, "The Second Lorenzo," 52.

56. Blue, *Indian Trader,* 246.

57. Lorenzo Hubbell, Jr., to Ed Thacker, November 12, 1919, Box 101, Folder August–December 1919, Hubbell Papers.

58. Sheridan, *Arizona: A History,* 253; Marsha Weisiger, *Dreaming of Sheep in Navajo Country* (Seattle: University of Washington Press, 2009), 138.

59. See Lorenzo Hubbell, Jr., to J. L. Hubbell, September 11, 1922, Box 102, Folder July–December 1922, Hubbell Papers.

60. See Peter Paquette to Roman Hubbell, December 29, 1922, Day Family Collection; and Teresa J. Wilkins, *Patterns of Exchange,* 121–126.

61. Mortgage Deed, March 5, 1920, Box 529, Folder 2, Hubbell Papers; Mortgage Deed, August 5, 1927, Box 529, Folder 2, Hubbell Papers; Mortgage Deed, October 2, 1928, Box 529, Folder 2, Hubbell Papers; Mortgage—Real Estate, December 3, 1929, Box 529, Folder 2, Hubbell Papers; Mortgage Deed, January 1, 1931, Box 529, Folder 2, Hubbell Papers; J. L. Hubbell to Lorenzo Hubbell, Jr., April 19, 1923, Box 102, Folder January–May 1923, Hubbell Papers.

62. Lorenzo Hubbell, Jr., to Roman Hubbell, March 28, 1926, Box 104, Folder March 1926, Hubbell Papers.

63. Lorenzo Hubbell, Jr., to Forrest M. Parker, quoted in Blue, *Indian Trader,* 256.

64. Blue, *Indian Trader,* 257.

65. Lorenzo Hubbell, Jr., to Adela H. Parker, September 28, 1920, Box 102, Folder January–September 1920, Hubbell Papers.

66. Forrest was one of the better record keepers in the family, and when he left the Ganado post, the written record declined sharply. With J. L. at Gallup and Roman at Ganado, the balance of the record swings sharply to Oraibi.

67. See Forrest M. Parker to Lorenzo Hubbell, Jr., July 4, 1920, Box 102, Folder January–September 1920, Hubbell Papers; Lorenzo Hubbell, Jr., to Forrest M. Parker, August 30, 1920, Box 102, Folder January–September 1920, Hubbell Papers.

68. Lorenzo Hubbell, Jr., to J. L. Hubbell, May 4, 1921, Box 102, Folder May 1921, Hubbell Papers.

69. Forrest M. Parker to Lorenzo Hubbell, Jr., May 4, 1921, Box 102, Folder May1921, Hubbell Papers.

70. Forrest M. Parker to Lorenzo Hubbell, Jr., June 6, 1921, Box 102, Folder June–July 1921, Hubbell Papers.

71. Forrest M. Parker to Lorenzo Hubbell, Jr., September 20, 1921, Box 102, Folder September–December 1921, Hubbell Papers.

72. See correspondence between Lorenzo and Forrest, June 1921–July 1922, Box 102, Hubbell Papers.

73. Forrest M. Parker to Lorenzo Hubbell, May 2, 1923, Box 102, Folder January–May 1923, Hubbell Papers.

74. See correspondence December 1924–January 1925, Box 103, Folders November–December 1924 and January 1925, Hubbell Papers.

75. Forrest M. Parker to Lorenzo Hubbell, Jr., April 26, 1926, Box 104, Folder April 1926, Hubbell Papers.

76. Ibid.

77. Tommy Hubbell to Lorenzo Hubbell, Jr., June 2, 1929, Box 106, Folder June–August 1929, Hubbell Papers. In this letter, Tommy recounts an incident where Forrest lost his temper and launched into a spectacular rant, complaining that Lorenzo would not let him run the Winslow business the way he wanted to, that there was not enough merchandise, and that the whole business was a mess. A month later, when Forrest was working in El Paso, he wrote in apology, "I will write you, Lorenzo, occasionally and hope you will find time to write me. Regardless of our little differences, I will always appreciate what you have done for me and my feeling toward you will never be any different than it has always been." Forrest M. Parker to Lorenzo Hubbell, Jr., July 15, 1929, Box 106, Folder June–August 1929, Hubbell Papers.

78. H. C. Hibben to Lorenzo Hubbell, Jr., September 22, 1926, Box 104, Folder September 1926, Hubbell Papers; H. C. Hibben to Lorenzo Hubbell Jr, October 9, 1926, Box 105, Folder October 1926, Hubbell Papers.

79. See H. C. Hibben to Lorenzo Hubbell, Jr., February 3, 1927, and February 8, 1927, Box 105, Folder February 1927, Hubbell Papers.

80. H. C. Hibben to Lorenzo Hubbell Jr, December 21, 1928, Box 106, Folder October–December 1928, Hubbell Papers.

81. J. L. Hubbell to Lorenzo Hubbell, Jr., April 19, 1923, Box 102, Folder January–May 1923, Hubbell Papers; Lorenzo Hubbell, Jr., to C. L. Walker, January 14, 1928, Box 105, Folder January–April 1928, Hubbell Papers.

82. As Peterson states, "Although construction and maintenance work was often in process, the period after 1923 was the high tide of farming under the Ganado Project." Peterson, *Homestead and Farm,* 117, 153.

83. Roman Hubbell to Lorenzo Hubbell, Jr., March 24, 1926, Box 104, Folder March 1926, Hubbell Papers.

84. Dorothy Hubbell, interview by David M. Brugge, October 13, 1969, interview 052, transcript, Oral Histories, HUTR. See Peterson, *Homestead and Farm,* 159–175; "J. L. Hubbell Property," n.d., Box 529, Folder 1, Hubbell Papers.

85. Peterson, *Homestead and Farm*, 274–281, 292–295.

86. Dorothy Hubbell, interview by David M. Brugge, October 13, 1969, interview 052, transcript, Oral Histories, HUTR. The Hubbells also butchered cattle and sheep on the farm. Dorothy Hubbell, interview by Frank McNitt, May 1, 1972, interview I, transcript, Box 2, Folder 17, Roman Hubbell Papers.

87. J. L. Hubbell to Lorenzo Hubbell, Jr., April 6, 1912, Box 97, Folder April 1–7, 1912, Hubbell Papers.

88. Dorothy S. Hubbell, interview by Ed and Clarinda, July 14, 1990, interview 087, transcript, Oral Histories, HUTR.

89. Peterson, *Homestead and Farm*, 6.

90. Ibid., 302–345.

91. Joe Tippecanoe, interview by David M. Brugge, November 16, 1971, interview 145, transcript, Oral Histories, HUTR; J. L. Hubbell Trading Post to Delco Light Co., December 6, 1930, Box 106, Folder May–December 1930, Hubbell Papers; Roman Hubbell to Lorenzo Hubbell, July 19, 1924, Box 103, Folder July–August 1924, Hubbell Papers; Lorenzo Hubbell, Jr., to Howard, February 17, 1927, Box 105, Folder February 1927, Hubbell Papers.

92. Froeschauer-Nelson, *Cultural Landscape Report*, under "Decline of the Hubbell Trading Post and Farm (1923–1967)."

93. Dorothy S. Hubbell and LaCharles Eckel, interview by unknown, March 22, 1973, interview 053, transcript, Oral Histories, HUTR; Froeschauer-Nelson, *Cultural Landscape Report*, under "Decline of the Hubbell Trading Post and Farm (1923–1967)." Lorenzo, at least, felt that the destruction of the Leonard building was "too bad, but it seems like modern methods is to dispose of old relics, it is strange that such sentiment cannot be preserved." Lorenzo Hubbell, Jr., to Howard, February 17, 1927, Box 105, Folder February 1927, Hubbell Papers.

94. Lorenzo Hubbell, Jr., to Joe, December 15, 1926, Box 105, Folder 1926 and Undated, Hubbell Papers.

95. Lorenzo Hubbell, Jr., to Evelyn Bentley, December 3, 1925, Box 104, Folder November–December 1925, Hubbell Papers.

96. See Box 550, Folder 4, Hubbell Papers. Lorenzo also stated that his father ran a mail route from Gallup to Shiprock, New Mexico. Lorenzo Hubbell, Jr., to Howard, February 17, 1927, Box 105, Folder February 1927, Hubbell Papers; J. C. Koons to Barbara H. Goodman, January 2, 1919, Box 82, Folder US Post Office Dept., Hubbell Papers; Froeschauer-Nelson, *Cultural Landscape Report*, under "Hubbell Trading Post as Post Office for Community."

97. Lorenzo Hubbell, Jr., to Roman Hubbell, March 28, 1926, Box 104, Folder March 1926, Hubbell Papers.

98. Peterson, *Homestead and Farm*, 189.

99. Lorenzo Hubbell, Jr., to J. L. Hubbell, July 14, 1924, Box 103, Folder July–August 1924, Hubbell Papers.

100. Lorenzo Hubbell, Jr., to Ed Thacker, July 29, 1923, Box 102, Folder June–October 1923, Hubbell Papers.

101. Peterson, *Homestead and Farm,* 297.
102. Ibid., 187
103. Ibid., 203–205.
104. Lorenzo Hubbell, Jr., to Roman Hubbell, August 4, 1926, Box 104, Folder August 1926, Hubbell Papers.
105. Peterson, *Homestead and Farm,* 300.
106. Lorenzo Hubbell, Jr., to Emry Kopta, November 13, 1921, Box 103, Folder November–December 1923, Hubbell Papers; Lorenzo Hubbell, Jr., to Charlie, October 19, 1923, Box 102, Folder June–October 1923, Hubbell Papers.
107. Lorenzo Hubbell, Jr., to Howard, February 17, 1927, Box 105, Folder February 1927, Hubbell Papers.
108. LaCharles G. Eckel, interview by Lawrence C. Kelly, June 26, 1979, interview 074, transcript, Oral Histories, HUTR.
109. They also famously kept a blow snake in the bullpen to catch mice. Dorothy S. Hubbell, interview by David M. Brugge, October 13, 1969, interview 052, transcript, Oral Histories, HUTR; see also Dorothy S. Hubbell, interview by Liz Bauer and Terry Nichols, January 8, 1977, interview 077, transcript, Oral Histories, HUTR.
110. LaCharles G. Eckel, interview by Lawrence C. Kelly, June 26, 1979, interview 074, transcript, Oral Histories, HUTR.
111. Donald Sidney Hubbell gives an account of one day in the life of the trading post in *Hubbell Pioneers,* 37–40.
112. Hubbell Parker, interview by Frank McNitt, May 12, 1972, transcript, Box 16-25(18), Serial no. 10684, Folder 7, McNitt Papers.
113. LaCharles G. Eckel, interview by Lawrence C. Kelly, June 26, 1979, interview 074, transcript, Oral Histories, HUTR; "From Other Schools and Agencies," *American Indian* 17, no. 1 (January 8, 1916): 31.
114. Lorenzo Hubbell, Jr., to Barbara H. Goodman, September 28, 1920, Box 102, Folder January–September 1920, Hubbell Papers.
115. Dorothy's account of how she came to Ganado and her life there can be found in Dorothy Smith Hubbell, "Arizona," 347–360; Dorothy Smith Hubbell, "The Days and Nights at a Trading Post," in *This Land, These Voices,* ed. Abe Chanin and Mildred Chanin (Tucson, AZ: Midbar Press, 1977), 105–112; and in several oral histories, including interviews by Frank McNitt, Box 2, Folder 17, Roman Hubbell Papers. Dorothy was born in 1899 to Harry S. Smith and Mabel C. Wanee in Connorsville, Indiana. She received her teaching certification from Indiana University. Dorothy also studied piano from the time she was a young girl through University, a qualification that attracted the notice of Barbara, who wanted a teacher who could also teach piano to LaCharles.
116. Barbara H. Goodman to Dorothy E. Smith, October 18, 1920, Box 102, Folder October–December 1920, Hubbell Papers.
117. Dorothy S. Hubbell, "Days and Nights," 106.
118. Dorothy Hubbell, interview by Frank McNitt, May 1, 1972, interview I, transcript, Box 2, Folder 17, Roman Hubbell Papers.

119. Doug Frerichs, "Navajos Confirm It: She's a Pioneer," *Phoenix Gazette,* July 23, 1980.

120. Dorothy Smith Hubbell, "Days and Nights," 108.

121. Dorothy Hubbell, interview by Frank McNitt, May 2, 1972, interview III, Box 2, Folder 17, Roman Hubbell Papers.

122. Dorothy Hubbell, interview by Frank McNitt, May 2, 1972, interview IV, transcript, Box 2, Folder 17, Roman Hubbell Papers. For more information on the Yeibichai, see Rebecca M. Valette and Jean Paul Valette, *Weaving the Dance: Navajo Yeibichai Textiles (1910–1950)* (Albuquerque, NM: Adobe Gallery, 2000).

123. Dorothy never taught the Parker children, who were sent to school elsewhere as their parents did not live at Ganado during the time Dorothy was teaching there. See LaCharles G. Eckel, interview by Lawrence C. Kelly, June 26, 1979, interview 074, transcript, Oral Histories, HUTR; Dorothy Hubbell, interview by Frank McNitt, May 2, 1972, interview III, transcript, Box 2, Folder 17, Roman Hubbell Papers.

124. Dorothy Hubbell, interview by Frank McNitt, May 2, 1972, interview III, transcript, Box 2, Folder 17, Roman Hubbell Papers.

125. LaCharles G. Eckel, interview by Lawrence C. Kelly, June 26, 1979, interview 074, transcript, Oral Histories, HUTR.

126. Ibid., 24.

127. "Son of Senator J. L. Hubbell Married," *Coconino Sun,* July 29, 1929.

128. Roman Hubbell to Forrest M. Parker, July 25, 1921, Box 102, Folder June–July 1921, Hubbell Papers.

129. LaCharles G. Eckel, interview by Lawrence C. Kelly, June 26, 1979, interview 074, transcript, Oral Histories, HUTR.

130. Dorothy S. Hubbell, interview by Frank McNitt, May 2, 1972, interview IV, transcript, Box 2, Folder 17, Roman Hubbell Papers.

131. Ibid.

132. Donald Sidney Hubbell, *Hubbell Pioneers,* 349.

133. Lorenzo Hubbell, Jr., to Cecelia Barth, October 19, 1926, Box 105, Folder October 1926, Hubbell Papers.

134. Lorenzo Hubbell, Jr., to Howard, February 17, 1927, Box 105, Folder February 1927, Hubbell Papers; Dorothy S. Hubbell, interview by David M. Brugge, October 13, 1969, interview 052, transcript, Oral Histories, HUTR.

135. Cora B. Salsbury, *Forty Years,* 16.

136. Ibid., 18.

137. Barbara writes a section in Salsbury's *Forty Years in the Desert,* in which she names dozens of employees at the mission, when they arrived, and their personal characteristics, from superintendents down to housekeepers, indicating that the social scenes of the trading post and mission were tightly interwoven. See Cora B. Salsbury, *Forty Years,* 16–19.

138. "Grand Old Man of Apache County Presents a Few Political Rules," *Arizona Republican,* February 21, 1921.

139. Lorenzo Hubbell, Jr., to Ed Thacker, November 12, 1919, Box 101, Folder August–December 1919, Hubbell Papers.

140. Lorenzo Hubbell, Jr., to Ed Thacker, August 22, 1923, Box 102, Folder June–October 1923, Hubbell Papers.

141. J. L.'s illness is mentioned in Isabel Corrigan to Lorenzo Hubbell, Jr., April 30, 1929, Box 106, Folder January–March 1929; and Tommy Hubbell to Lorenzo Hubbell, Jr., June 2, 1929, Box 106, Folder June–August 1929, Hubbell Papers.

142. Dorothy S. Hubbell, interview by Frank McNitt, May 4, 1972, interview V, transcript, Box 2, Folder 17, Roman Hubbell Papers.

143. Clarence G. Salsbury, *Salsbury Story*, 140.

144. George and Madge Hubbell to Lorenzo Hubbell, Jr., November 16, 1930, Box 106, Folder May–December 1930, Hubbell Papers.

145. Tommy Hubbell to Lorenzo Hubbell, Jr., November 16, 1930, Box 106, Folder May–December 1930, Hubbell Papers.

146. Lorenzo Hubbell, Jr., to Dane Coolidge, December 2, 1930, Box 106, Folder May–December 1930, Hubbell Papers.

147. "Don Lorenzo Hubbell is Laid At Rest in Ganado Cemetery," November 15, 1930, newspaper clipping, Box 545, Folder 1, Hubbell Papers.

148. Joseph Emerson Smith, "Navajo Art Patron Dead," 372.

## Chapter 6

1. Charles F. Lummis, *Mesa, Cañon and Pueblo* (New York: D. Appleton-Century, 1938), 182.

2. Mott, "Don Lorenzo Hubbell," 49.

3. Lummis, *Mesa, Cañon and Pueblo*, 182.

4. Herman Schweizer to T. E. Purdy, December 4, 1930, Box 38, Folder Harvey, Fred 1928–1930, Hubbell Papers.

5. Joseph Emerson Smith, "Greatest Patron of Navajo Artistry in Rug Weaving Dies," *Denver Post*, November 30, 1930.

6. Erika Marie Bsumek, *Indian-Made: Navajo Culture in the Marketplace, 1868–1940* (Lawrence: University Press of Kansas, 2008), 103–104; Kathleen L. Howard, "Creating an Enchanted Land: Curio Entrepreneurs Promote and Sell the Indian Southwest, 1880–1940" (PhD dissertation, Arizona State University, 2002), 3.

7. Howard, "Creating an Enchanted Land," 3.

8. Lummis, "Swallow's-Nest," 502; Bsumek, *Indian-Made*, 31.

9. Many histories of Navajo weaving discuss the role of Hubbell Trading Post in the development of the art. A few classics include George Wharton James, *Indian Blankets*; Amsden, *Navaho Weaving*; and H. L. James, *Rugs and Posts: The Story of Navajo Weaving and Indian Trading* (West Chester, PA: Schiffer, 1988). Two of the best and most recent studies of weaving deal directly with Hubbell Trading Post: Kathy M'Closkey's *Swept Under the Rug*, which presents an excellent critical quantitative and economic analysis of the role of the blanket trade in the business,

and Teresa J. Wilkins's *Patterns of Exchange*, which provides perhaps the most thorough and human analysis of weaving at Hubbell Trading Post. Elizabeth Bauer, *Research for a Catalog of the Navajo Textiles of Hubbell Trading Post* (Ganado, AZ: US Department of the Interior, National Park Service, Hubbell Trading Post National Historic Site, 1987) is also a good reference work. My summary of Navajo weaving draws mostly from the above sources. For a broader sampling of the voluminous literature on Navajo weaving, see Ann Lane Hedlund, *Beyond the Loom: Keys to Understanding Early Southwestern Weaving* (Boulder, CO: Johnson Books, 1990); Kate Peck Kent, *Navajo Weaving: Three Centuries of Change* (Santa Fe, NM: School of American Research Press, 1985); Marian E. Rodee, *One Hundred Years of Navajo Rugs* (Albuquerque: University of New Mexico Press, 1995); Marian E. Rodee, *Old Navajo Rugs: Their Development from 1900 to 1940* (Albuquerque: University of New Mexico Press, 1981); and Joe Ben Wheat, *The Gift of Spiderwoman: Southwestern Textiles, the Navajo Tradition* (Philadelphia: University Museum, University of Pennsylvania, 1984).

10. For information on traditional Navajo dyes and weaving, see Nonabah Gorman Bryan, Stella Young, and Charles Keetsie Shirley, *Navajo Native Dyes: Their Preparation and Use* (Palmer Lake, CO: Filter, 1978).

11. Laura Jane Moore, "Elle Meets the President: Weaving Navajo Culture and Commerce in the Southwestern Tourist Industry," *Frontiers: Journal of Women Studies* 22, no. 1 (2001): 25; Teresa J. Wilkins, *Patterns of Exchange*, 13. Wilkins provides a concise summary of the history of textiles in southwestern trade on pp. 12–21.

12. Joe Ben Wheat and Ann Lane Hedlund, *Blanket Weaving in the Southwest* (Tucson: University of Arizona Press, 2003), 31.

13. Quoted in M'Closkey, *Swept Under the Rug*, 19–20.

14. For example, James H. Simpson noted in an ethnocentric attitude characteristic of the period, "It seems anomalous to me that a nation living in such miserably constructed mud lodges should, at the same time, be capable of making, probably, the best blankets in the world!" Simpson, *Navaho Expedition*, 96.

15. Scholars of Navajo weaving divide its development into three periods. The classic period lasted from 1650 to 1868, during which "global processes, especially trade between divergent local communities, such as European cloth manufacturers, Mexican traders, and Navajo weavers, occurred," and the textiles from that period often reflect the interaction between Navajo, Spanish, and indigenous Mexican influences. The transitional period stretched from 1868 to 1890, when the market for Navajo blankets shifted to tourists. Textiles from this period show the influence of industrialization and consumption, reflected in the use of Germantown yarn, chemical dyes, new designs, and the weaving of rugs rather than blankets for clothing. The third period is the rug period, 1890 onward, in which trader-introduced designs dominated. Bsumek, *Indian-Made*, 26.

16. Moore, "Elle Meets the President," 27.

17. George Wharton James, *Indian Blankets*, 47.

18. Hubbell and Cotton to Post Trader, June 20, 1885, Box 91, Folder 3, Hubbell Papers.

19. C. N. Cotton to Unknown, November 7, 1885, Box 91, Folder 6, Hubbell Papers.

20. C. N. Cotton to H. F. Douglas, April 24, 1886, Box 91, Folder 8, Hubbell Papers.

21. Rodee, *Old Navajo Rugs*, 65.

22. Williams, *C. N. Cotton*, 24.

23. C. N. Cotton to Arnold Constable and Co., November 2, 1887, Box 92, Folder 15, Hubbell Papers.

24. Ibid.

25. Ibid.; Teresa J. Wilkins, *Patterns of Exchange*, 28; see also correspondence from February 1888, Box 93, Folder 16, Hubbell Papers.

26. Williams, *C. N. Cotton*, 33; Amsden, *Navaho Weaving*, 179.

27. Kerwin L. Klein, "Frontier Products: Tourism, Consumerism, and the Southwestern Public Lands, 1890–1990," *Pacific Historical Review* 62, no. 1 (February 1993): 44.

28. Emily Ballew Neff, *The Modern West: American Landscapes, 1890–1950* (New Haven, CT: Yale University Press in association with the Museum of Fine Arts, Houston, 2006), xiii.

29. Leah Dilworth, *Imagining Indians in the Southwest: Persistent Visions of a Primitive Past* (Washington, DC: Smithsonian Institution Press, 1996), 3.

30. John Collier, copy of speech sent to Lorenzo Hubbell, Jr., Box 18, Folder Collier, Hubbell Papers.

31. Teresa J. Wilkins, *Patterns of Exchange*, 52.

32. Klein, "Frontier Products," 44.

33. Bsumek, *Indian-Made*, 84; Teresa J. Wilkins, *Patterns of Exchange*, 50. For example, Hubbell designed elaborate letterheads that pictured Navajo weavers and proclaimed him as a "Dealer in Navajo Blankets . . . Silverware, Baskets, and Curios" with "old style weavings and patterns a specialty" as early as 1890. The Hubbells toyed on more than one occasion with the idea of making postcards of rugs designs, but ultimately discarded the idea for fear that the designs might fall into the hands of competitors. J. L. did some of his own advertising by talking up the merits of Indian products in his personal and political travels across Arizona and the country, carting displays of blankets around with him. Joann F. Boles, "The Navaho Rug at the Hubbell Trading Post, 1880–1920," *American Indian Culture and Research Journal* 5, no. 1 (1981): 60–61; J. L. Hubbell letterhead, May 14, 1890, Box 95, Folder 1878–1895, Hubbell Papers; Lorenzo Hubbell, Jr., to Roman Hubbell, April 2, 1912, Box 97, Folder April 1–7, 1912, Hubbell Papers; "J. L. Hubbell packed up the remainder of his Navajo blankets today," *Arizona Weekly Journal-Miner*, February 19, 1890.

34. C. N. Cotton and George Wharton James, *Wholesale Catalogue and Price List of Navajo Blankets* (Pasadena, CA: G. Wharton James, 1896). This catalog, along with several later catalogs issued by Cotton, can be found reprinted in Williams, 54–102.

35. Teresa J. Wilkins, *Patterns of Exchange*, 58. Wilkins provides an analysis of catalogs by Cotton, Hubbell, Moore, and the Hyde Exploring Expedition on pages 56–73.

36. See letters from H. G. Maratta in Box 54, Folder Maratta, Hubbell Papers.

37. John Lorenzo Hubbell, *Catalogue and Price List: Navajo Blankets & Indian Curios* (Chicago: Press of Holister Brothers, 1902), 2. A copy of this catalog can be found in Box 545, Folder 13, Hubbell Papers.

38. Ibid. Though Cotton continued to issue catalogs as long as he was in the rug business, the Hubbells did not. As Forrest wrote to one customer, "It is a difficult problem to give ideas of patterns by letter as you probably know that no two blankets are just alike as regards pattern. We issued a catalogue several years ago but it gave such a poor idea of what we carried we have not issued any since." Forrest M. Parker to Jas. Hughes, March 4, 1915, Box 100, Letterbook, Hubbell Papers.

39. McPherson, "Home of Merchandise," 34–35.

40. Ibid.

41. Teresa J. Wilkins, 105; Boles, "The Navaho Rug," 59.

42. Blue, *Indian Trader*, 64.

43. Boles, "The Navaho Rug," 56–57.

44. Teresa J. Wilkins, *Patterns of Exchange*, 53; M'Closkey, *Swept Under the Rug*, 73–79.

45. Quoted in M'Closkey, *Swept Under the Rug*, 95.

46. Boles, "The Navaho Rug," 58.

47. Kathy M'Closkey, "Marketing Multiple Myths: The Hidden History of Navajo Weaving," *Journal of the Southwest* 36, no. 3 (Autumn 1994): 191.

48. Ibid.

49. Teresa J. Wilkins, *Patterns of Exchange*, 97; Lorenzo Hubbell, Jr., to Tom Hubbell, April 20, 1920, Box 102, Folder January–September 1920, Hubbell Papers; Lorenzo Hubbell, Jr., to R. E. L. Daniel, August 12, 1920, Box 102, Folder January–September 1920, Hubbell Papers.

50. M'Closkey, *Swept Under the Rug*, 135–136.

51. Teresa J. Wilkins, *Patterns of Exchange*, 103.

52. Ibid., 98.

53. Lorenzo Hubbell, Jr., to Forrest M. Parker, September 4, 1921, Box 102, Folder September–December 1921, Hubbell Papers.

54. Teresa J. Wilkins, *Patterns of Exchange*, 112.

55. Forrest M. Parker to Carter H. Harrison, October 29, 1914, Box 100, Letterbook, Hubbell Papers; Forrest M. Parker to Alexander Squibb, January 3, 1916, Box 101, Folder January–March 1916, Hubbell Papers.

56. Bsumek, *Indian-Made*, 63–68. This practice was known as overstocking.

57. Forrest M. Parker to Jas. Hughes, March 4, 1915, Box 100, Letterbook, Hubbell Papers; Teresa J. Wilkins, *Patterns of Exchange*, 106.

58. Better access to Hopi goods must have formed a good part of J. L.'s motivation for locating his son at Keams Canyon. As he wrote to C. E. Wood on the day

he bought the trading post, "I think that I can supply you with what Moqui [Hopi] goods you may need at reasonable prices." J. L. Hubbell to C. E. Wood, May 17, 1902, Box 94, Letterbook, Hubbell Papers. Lorenzo, Jr., also took frequent collecting trips to the Hopi mesas. Lorenzo Hubbell, Jr., to J. L. Hubbell, August 4, 1902, Box 95, Folder 1902, Hubbell Papers.

59. J. L. Hubbell to Hugh B. E. Brown, Box 95, Folder March 1–9, 1909, Hubbell Papers. See also J. L. to Ind. Trader, Osage Agency, January 21, 1902, Box 94, Letterbook, Hubbell Papers.

60. George Wharton James, *Indian Blankets*, 204.

61. The extent of J. L. and other traders' influence on Navajo textiles has been debated extensively in the literature on weaving. See JoAnn F. Boles, "The Development of the Navaho Rug, 1890–1920, As Influenced by Trader J. L. Hubbell," 2 vols. (PhD dissertation, Ohio State University, 1977). Most accounts tend to emphasize the traders' influence on design, color, materials, and quality. See, for example, George Wharton James, *Indian Blankets*, 204. M'Closkey, however, argues that the traders' impact has been greatly overestimated. As she states, "One could argue that standards were imposed concerning quality (i.e., clean wool, straight edges), excepting special orders, and preferences for conservative versus innovative designs. The inducement to place borders around the perimeter of the rug took nearly a generation to effect. There is no question that traders were responsible for this change, as the niche for the Navajo wearing blanket had vanished. For the most part, although Hubbell encouraged the production of oversized textiles, weavers held their own matters of color, design, and size." M'Closkey, *Swept Under the Rug*, 169–170. Hubbell's influence on other Native arts and crafts has been less studied. Some sources, however, attribute a role to Cotton and Hubbell in the early development of Navajo silverwork. See Woodward, *Navajo Silversmithing*, 72–73; John Adair, *The Navajo and Pueblo Silversmiths* (Norman: University of Oklahoma Press, 1946), 8, 13–15; and Williams, *C. N. Cotton*, 26.

62. Hubbell, *Catalogue*, 2.

63. Hubbell compromised with Cotton on the matter or dyes, allowing the sale of black and blue dyes at the trading post on the grounds that they were traditional Navajo colors that were simply much easier to achieve using commercial dyes. Williams, *C. N. Cotton*, 23.

64. Boles, "The Navaho Rug," 55.

65. J. L. Hubbell to H. E. Skinner Co., October 3, 1901, Box 94, Letterbook, Hubbell Papers.

66. J. L. Hubbell to Fred Harvey, September 21, 1901, Box 94, Letterbook, Hubbell Papers. In his catalog, Hubbell claimed that he had on a few occasions "unraveled some of the old genuine Navajo blankets to show these modern weavers how the pattern was made." Hubbell, *Catalogue*, 2. Bauer states, "These blanket styles, using classic period designs in combination with Germantown yarns, came to be known as the 'Hubbell Revival.'" Bauer, *Research for a Catalog*, 47.

67. J. L. Hubbell to H. E. Skinner Co., October 3, 1901, Box 94, Letterbook, Hubbell Papers.

68. Bauer, *Research for a Catalog*, 25.

69. Boles, "The Navaho Rug," 52. Amsden states that, as Hubbell and other traders bowed to the tastes of their customers, there "crept in that tendency toward standardization of pattern, with the white man's preferences consecrated in such items as the border and the use of isolated geometric figures in the field thus enclosed—for the Navaho seldom or never employed these graphic devices in earlier times." Amsden, *Navaho Weaving*, 190.

70. Boles, "The Navaho Rug," 54; M'Closkey, *Swept Under the Rug*, 92–93.

71. Bauer states that "The Ganado regional style comes closest to what most people think a Navajo rug should look like, that is . . . strong geometric patterns, bold and clean cut, with good solid colors." She states that Ganado Red rugs typically feature crosses and diamonds with a main central element and smaller motifs in each corner, on a solid background (usually red) with a border. Bauer, *Research for a Catalog*, 184. Along a similar vein, C. N. Cotton has been credited with introducing the "floating element style" into weaving in his 1896 catalog. This style, which featured geometric figures in red, black, and gray on a solid background of gray or white, "came to dominate blanket design and was found all over the reservation between the mid-1890s to about 1915." Bauer, *Research for a Catalog*, 25.

72. Amsden, *Navaho Weaving*, 193. Hubbell had a rug measuring 12 ft. × 18 ft. woven in 1885, now in the Gladin Collection in the Museum of Northern Arizona in Flagstaff. Williams, *C. N. Cotton*, 24–25. Later, Lorenzo, Jr., had an even larger rug woven, 21 ft. × 37 ft., which he boasted was the "world's largest Navajo rug." He displayed it around the country and in his Winslow showroom. Jack DeVere Rittenhouse, *A Guide Book to Highway 66* (Albuquerque: University of New Mexico Press, 1946), 98.

73. M'Closkey, *Swept Under the Rug*, 83–84. See also Teresa J. Wilkins, *Patterns of Exchange*, 82–106 for a thorough discussion of the paintings and their origins, use, and influence.

74. George Wharton James, *Indian Blankets*, 125; see also Amsden, *Navaho Weaving*, 189–190.

75. M'Closkey, *Swept Under the Rug*, 99.

76. Boles, "The Navaho Rug," 52.

77. M'Closkey, *Swept Under the Rug*, 158.

78. Alice Kaufman and Christopher Selser, *The Navajo Weaving Tradition: 1650 to the Present* (New York: Dutton, 1985), 64.

79. George Wharton James, *Indian Blankets*, 204.

80. M'Closkey, "Marketing Multiple Myths," 188–189.

81. J. L. Hubbell to Charlie Hubbell, March 21, 1912, Box 97, Folder March 1912, Hubbell Papers.

82. Lorenzo Hubbell, Jr., to J. L. Hubbell, November 16, 1913, Box 98, Letterbook, Hubbell Papers.

83. Teresa J. Wilkins, *Patterns of Exchange*, 83–85.

84. Ibid., 98, 102; M'Closkey, *Swept Under the Rug*, 140.

85. Lorenzo Hubbell, Jr., to Roman Hubbell, March 20, 1925, Box 104, Folder March 1925, Hubbell Papers.

86. Lorenzo Hubbell, Jr., to Nobby Harness Co., December 26, 1940, Box 112, Folder December 1940, Hubbell Papers. J. L. also once wrote to assure the Mandel Brothers of Chicago, "The facts are that I have five stores on the Navajo Reservation, away from the railroad, where the Indians are not exploited, and do not hesitate to bring me the best of their output." J. L. Hubbell to Mandel Bros., March 1, 1913, Box 99, Folder March 1–22, 1913, Hubbell Papers.

87. Marguerite S. Shaffer, *See America First: Tourism and National Identity, 1880–1940* (Washington, DC: Smithsonian Books, 2001), 25.

88. Sheridan, *Arizona: A History*, 237.

89. Bsumek, *Indian-Made*, 32.

90. See, for example, Victoria E. Dye, *All Aboard for Santa Fe: Railway Promotion in the Southwest, 1890s to 1930s* (Albuquerque: University of New Mexico Press, 2005); Dilworth *Imagining Indians*; T. C. McLuhan and William E. Kopplin, *Dream Tracks: The Railroad and the American Indian, 1890–1930* (New York: Abrams, 1985); and Shelby J. Tisdale, "Railroads, Tourism, and Native Americans in the Greater Southwest," *Journal of the Southwest* 38, no. 4 (Winter 1996): 433–462.

91. Shaffer, *See America First*, 21.

92. Bsumek, *Indian-Made*, 46.

93. Howard, "Creating an Enchanted Land," 1.

94. Bsumek, *Indian-Made*, 46.

95. Charles F. Lummis, "The Artist's Paradise," *Out West* 29, no. 3 (September 1908): 191.

96. Marta Weigle, "From Desert to Disney World: The Santa Fe Railway and the Fred Harvey Company Display the Indian Southwest," *Journal of Anthropological Research* 45, no. 1 (Spring 1989): 115. One of the most recent histories of the Fred Harvey Company is Marisa Kay Brandt, "'Necessary Guidance': The Fred Harvey Company Presents the Southwest" (PhD dissertation, University of Minnesota, 2011). An excellent collection of scholarly essays on the Harvey Company can be found in Marta Weigle and Barbara A. Babcock, eds., *The Great Southwest of the Fred Harvey Company and the Santa Fe Railway* (Phoenix, AZ: Heard Museum, 1996). Other histories include Keith L. Bryant, *History of the Atchison, Topeka, and Santa Fe Railway* (New York: Macmillan, 1974); Lesley Poling-Kempes, *The Harvey Girls: Women Who Opened the West* (New York: Paragon House, 1989); Stephen Fried, *Appetite for America: How Visionary Businessman Fred Harvey Built a Railroad Hospitality Empire that Civilized the Wild West* (New York: Bantam Books, 2010); and Diane Thomas Darnall, *The Southwestern Indian Detours: The Story of the Fred Harvey/Santa Fe Railway Experiment in Detourism* (Phoenix, AZ: Hunter, 1978).

97. Kathleen L. Howard and Diana F. Pardue, *Inventing the Southwest: The Fred Harvey Company and Native American Art* (Flagstaff, AZ: Northland, 1996), 1.

98. Bsumek, *Indian-Made*, 32.

99. Howard and Pardue, 9.

100. Brandt, "'Necessary Guidance,'" 80–81.

101. Howard and Pardue, *Inventing the Southwest*, 10.

102. Ibid., 11.

103. Ibid., 10.

104. 1904 brochure, quoted in Howard and Pardue, *Inventing the Southwest*, 18.

105. Brandt, "'Necessary Guidance,'" 92.

106. See Fred Harvey Company to J. L. Hubbell, May 24, 1902, Box 36, Folder Harvey, Fred 1902–1904, Hubbell Papers.

107. Brandt, "'Necessary Guidance,'" 93.

108. J. L. Hubbell to Fred Harvey Company, January 22, 1902, Box 94, Letterbook, Hubbell Papers.

109. Forrest M. Parker to Alexander Squibb, January 3, 1916, Box 101, Folder January–March 1916, Hubbell Papers; Blue, *Indian Trader*, 150.

110. Brandt, "'Necessary Guidance,'" 93.

111. Dorothy Hubbell, interview by Frank McNitt, May 2, 1972, interview III, transcript, Box 2, Folder 17, Roman Hubbell Papers.

112. Howard and Pardue, *Inventing the Southwest*, 41–42.

113. Ibid.

114. See, for example, Herman Schweizer to J. L. Hubbell, August 19, 1908, Box 37, Folder Harvey, Fred 1908, Hubbell Papers; Herman Schweizer to J. L. Hubbell, January 15, 1909, Box 37, Folder Harvey, Fred 1909–1910, Hubbell Papers.

115. Herman Schweizer to Lorenzo Hubbell, Jr., February 1, 1917, Box 37, Folder Harvey, Fred 1916–1919, Hubbell Papers.

116. Ibid.

117. Forrest M. Parker to Lorenzo Hubbell, Jr., December 13, 1921, Box 102, Folder September–December 1921, Hubbell Papers. The dash in this quote is as Forrest wrote it.

118. Howard and Pardue, *Inventing the Southwest*, 42.

119. For example, Schweizer once wrote to J. L. asking him to send to the Grand Canyon a silversmith and a couple of Navajo forges made from "a piece of steel rail or whatever there may be that is homemade and a homemade bellows." He wrote that he would also "like for the Navahos at the Canyon to have and *use* some of their homemade pots to cook in as [we] would not want them to use a stove there." Herman Schweizer to J. L. Hubbell, November 17, 1904, Box 36, Folder Harvey, Fred 1902–1904, Hubbell Papers.

120. Moore, "Elle Meets the President," 28, 32.

121. J. F. Huckel to J. L. Hubbell, May 23, 1905, Box 36, Folder Harvey, Fred, January–June 1905, Hubbell Papers; J. F. Huckel to J. L. Hubbell, July 1, 1905, Box 36, Folder Harvey, Fred July–December 1905, Hubbell Papers.

122. Moore, "Elle Meets the President," 34–35.

123. Herman Schweizer to J. L. Hubbell, September 13, 1905, Box 36, Folder Harvey, Fred July–December 1905, Hubbell Papers.

124. J. F. Huckel to J. L. Hubbell, April 21, 1905, Box 36, Folder Harvey, Fred January–June 1905, Hubbell Papers.

125. J. F. Huckel to J. L. Hubbell, April 26, 1905, Box 36, Folder Harvey, Fred January–June 1905, Hubbell Papers.

126. J. F. Huckel to J. L. Hubbell, May 23, 1905, Box 36, Folder Harvey, Fred January–June 1905, Hubbell Papers; Lorenzo Hubbell, Jr., to J. L. Hubbell, June 7, 1905, Box 95, Folder 1905, Hubbell Papers.

127. Blue, *Indian Trader*, 151.

128. The two companies also helped each other out by serving as each other's bill collectors. J. L. sometimes sent to the Harvey Company individuals who owed him money on their store accounts, requesting that Huckel pay part of the demonstrators' wages to him. J. L. also honored the Harvey Company's requests to "re-recruit demonstrators who still owed them money." Blue, *Indian Trader*, 154.

129. Moore, "Elle Meets the President," 28–29; J. F. Huckel to J. L. Hubbell, March 23, 1905, Box 36, Folder Harvey, Fred 1902–1904, Hubbell Papers.

130. Blue, *Indian Trader*, 155.

131. Howard and Pardue, 2 *Inventing the Southwest*, 3.

132. Nancy J. Parezo and Don D. Fowler, *Anthropology Goes to the Fair: The 1904 Louisiana Purchase Exposition* (Lincoln: University of Nebraska Press, 2007), 3–4.

133. Ibid., 5; Don D. Fowler, *A Laboratory for Anthropology: Science and Romanticism in the American Southwest, 1846–1930* (Albuquerque: University of New Mexico Press, 2000), 204.

134. Fowler, *Laboratory for Anthropology*, 205.

135. "J. L. Hubbell," *Arizona Silver Belt*, January 25, 1890; "J. L. Hubbell packed up," *Arizona Weekly Journal-Miner*, February 19, 1890.

136. "Fine Navajo Blankets," *Arizona Weekly Republican*, February 23, 1893.

137. Bruce Hilpert, "Arizona Goes to the Fair: The World's Columbian Exposition of 1893," *Arizona and the West* 25, no. 3 (Autumn 1983): 272; Fowler, *Laboratory for Anthropology*, 209.

138. J. B. Parke, "Great is Evolution," *Cedar Rapids Evening Gazette*, September 8, 1893.

139. Fried, *Appetite for America*, 206.

140. Howard and Pardue, *Inventing the Southwest*, 62–63; Fried, *Appetite for America*, 205.

141. S. M. McCowan to J. L. Hubbell, March 23, 1904, Box 43, Folder Indians 1873–1905, Hubbell Papers; S. M. McCowan to J. L. Hubbell, November 2, 1903, Box 43, Folder Indians 1873–1905, Hubbell Papers.

142. S. M. McCowan to J. L. Hubbell, March 23, 1904, Box 43, Folder Indians 1873–1905, Hubbell Papers.

143. Dorothy Hubbell, interview by David M. Brugge, October 13, 1969, interview 052, transcript, Oral Histories, HUTR.

144. Howard and Pardue, *Inventing the Southwest*, 71–76; Phoebe S. Kropp, "'There is a little sermon in that': Constructing the Native Southwest at the San

Diego Panama-California Exposition in 1915," in Weigle and Babcock, *Great Southwest*, 40.

145. Herman Schweizer to J. L. Hubbell, September 8, 1914, Box 37, Folder Harvey, Fred 1913-1914, Hubbell Papers.

146. Herman Schweizer to T. E. Purdy, December 4, 1930, Box 38, Folder Harvey, Fred 1928-1930, Hubbell Papers.

147. Fred Harvey Company to J. L. Hubbell, October 20, 1909, Box 37, Folder Harvey, Fred 1909-1910, Hubbell Papers; H. A. Bassett to J. L. Hubbell, April 29, 1919, Box 8, Folder Bassett, Hubbell Papers; H. A. Bassett to J. L. Hubbell, May 15, 1919, Box 8, Folder Bassett, Hubbell Papers; Roman Hubbell to Harry Carey, April 6, 1931, Box 106, Folder April 1931, Hubbell Papers.

148. Dorothy Hubbell, interview by David M. Brugge, October 13, 1969, interview 052, transcript, Oral Histories, HUTR

149. Lorenzo Hubbell, Jr., to E. K. Miller, May 29, 1924, Box 103, Folder May-June 1924, Hubbell Papers; Lorenzo Hubbell, Jr., to Fredric Snyder, June 16, 1927, Box 105, Folder June-July 1927, Hubbell Papers; Fletcher Corrigan to Mary Russell Ferrell Colton, October 23, 1930, Box 106, Folder May-December 1930, Hubbell Papers. The Hubbells may also have exhibited at the Exposition of Indian Tribal Arts at Grand Central Art Galleries New York City in 1931. See Box 27, Hubbell Papers. The Hubbells were so busy with their business and supplying exhibits almost constantly that they sometimes even had to pass up exhibition opportunities. For example, Lorenzo just missed sending an exhibit to London in 1939. Lorenzo Hubbell, Jr., to Delphine Dawson, March 7, 1939, Box 111, Folder March 1939, Hubbell Papers.

150. "Industrial Arts and Handicrafts," pamphlet, Box 2, Folder American Federation of Arts, Hubbell Papers; Helen H. Cambell to Lorenzo Hubbell, Jr., May 31, 1934, Box 2, Folder American Federation of Arts, Hubbell Papers; American Federation of Arts to Lorenzo Hubbell, Jr., July 21, 1931, Box 2, Folder American Federation of Arts, Hubbell Papers.

151. Lorenzo Hubbell, Jr., to American Federation of Arts, August 5, 1931, Box 106, Folder August 1931, Hubbell Papers.

152. The Indian Arts and Crafts Board was a government agency formed by John Collier and Harold Ickes to combat counterfeit Indian products marketed as genuine. Lorenzo, Jr., was appointed to the board in 1938. For a history of the Indian Arts and Crafts Board, see Susan Labry Meyn, *More Than Curiosities: A Grassroots History of the Indian Arts and Crafts Board and Its Precursors, 1920-1942* (Lanham, MD: Lexington Books, 2001), and for information on Lorenzo, Jr.'s, involvement, see "Lorenzo Hubbell Named On Indian Crafts Board," *Tucson Star*, July 11, 1938; correspondence in Box 2, Folder American Indian Defense Association, Hubbell Papers; and correspondence in Box 43, Folder Indian Arts and Crafts Board, 1938—, Hubbell Papers. Eastern mills had been selling imitation "Indian" blankets for decades, and the Hubbells and others involved in the blanket and curio trade became concerned that the public were being duped into believing the manufactured knockoffs were in fact genuine Navajo blankets. In 1910, Huckel

sent a spurious advertisement to J. L., asking him to consider using his position as a well-known Indian trader and politician to bring the matter to the attention to the federal government. It was not until the 1930s, however, when the threat worsened as "mass-produced rugs bearing Navajo patterns flooded eastern markets [and T]raders were forced to stop acquiring rugs from weavers because consumers now purchased a 'crude substitute,'" that the Indian Arts and Crafts Board was formed. Teresa J. Wilkins, *Patterns of Exchange*, 130; J.F. Huckel to J. L. Hubbell, November 22, 1910, Box 37, Folder Harvey, Fred 1909–1910, Hubbell Papers.

153. John Collier to Roman Hubbell and Dorothy Hubbell, December 20, 1933, Box 7, Folder 9, Roman Hubbell Papers; Roman Hubbell to John Collier, December 27, 1933, Box 7, Folder 9, Roman Hubbell Papers.

154. C. B. Wood to J. L. Hubbell, June 10, 1913, Box 3, Folder Arizona State, Hubbell Papers; Vernon L. Clark to J. L. Hubbell, October 28, 1905, Box 3, Folder Arizona State, Hubbell Papers.

155. Dorothy Hubbell, interview by David M. Brugge, October 13, 1969, interview 052, transcript, Oral Histories, HUTR; Lorenzo Hubbell, Jr., to John B. Brown, December 31, 1924, Box 103, Folder November–December 1924, Hubbell Papers.

156. "Gallup Will Have Big Indian Ceremonial in September," *Gallup Independent*, August 3, 1922; M. F. Kirk to Lorenzo Hubbell, Jr., August 8, 1922, Box 45, Folder Inter-Tribal Indian Ceremonial Association, Hubbell Papers.

157. "Gallup Will Have Big Indian Ceremonial in September," *Gallup Independent*, August 3, 1922; Dorothy Hubbell, interview by David M. Brugge, October 13, 1969, interview 052, transcript, Oral Histories, HUTR; Roman Hubbell to Lorenzo Hubbell, Jr., September 3, 1924, Box 103, Folder September–October 1924, Hubbell Papers; Lorenzo Hubbell, Jr., to Inter Tribal Ceremonial Association, August 6, 1927, Box 105, Folder August–September 1927, Hubbell Papers.

158. Unknown to Grace M. Sparks, June 18, 1932, Box 107, Folder June 1932, Hubbell Papers; Roman Hubbell to M. L. Woodard, August 5, 1944, Box 115, Folder July–August 1944, Hubbell Papers.

159. "For Immediate Release," April 27, 1948, Box 11, Folder 11/10, Roman Hubbell Papers.

160. Ibid.

161. Bert Fireman, "Under the Sun," *Phoenix Gazette*, April 13, 1948; Roman Hubbell to Gladys Reichard, April 22, 1948, Box 119, Folder April 1948, Hubbell Papers; Angus Macpherson to Roman Hubbell, April 7, 1948, Box 4, Folder Arizona Unlimited, Hubbell Papers.

162. Roman Hubbell to W. R. Leigh, April 26, 1948, Box 119, Folder April 1948, Hubbell Papers; Roman Hubbell to W. R. Leigh, June 29, 1948, Box 119, Folder June 1948, Hubbell Papers.

163. Angus Macpherson to Roman Hubbell, May 27, 1948, Box 4, Folder Arizona Unlimited, Hubbell Papers.

164. M'Closkey, *Swept Under the Rug*, 267. The Hubbells also sold blankets to the Hyde Exploring Expedition, an archaeological party from the American Museum of Natural History that excavated the ruins at Pueblo Bonito and operated

several trading posts and retail stores in New York, Boston, and Philadelphia. Bauer, *Research for a Catalog*, 48; Amsden, *Navaho Weaving*, 193.

165. For example, Lorenzo, Jr., assisted Nils-Gustaf Skiöld of the Swedish Technical Dying Association during his visit in 1934. Swedish Technical Dying Association to Lorenzo Hubbell, Jr., September 24, 1934, Box 79, Folder Svenska, Hubbell Papers.

166. *The Twenty-first Year Book of The Brooklyn Institute of Arts and Sciences, 1908–1909* (Brooklyn, NY: Brooklyn Institute of Arts and Sciences, 1909), 256; Brooklyn Institute of Arts and Sciences to J. L. Hubbell, November 21, 1903, Box 12, Folder Brooklyn Institute of Arts and Sciences, Hubbell Papers.

167. Bsumek, *Indian-Made*, 120. All of the exhibits and demonstrations, from museums to world's fairs, were fraught with contradictions. The displays in Culin's museum were meant to be scientific and to preserve American Indian history, but they also "helped legitimize whites' construction and racialization of Navajo identity," portraying Indians as primitive peoples. Bsumek, *Indian-Made*, 146. At the world's fairs, in the Harvey Company's demonstrations, and even the Gallup Ceremonial, which was billed as "for, of, and by the Indian," the presentation of Navajos' lives was carefully staged. The organizers asked Lorenzo, Jr., to "tell the Indians to come to Gallup in their Native costumes—to leave everything of the white man at home, so far as is possible." Charles A. Williamson to Sir (probably Lorenzo Hubbell, Jr.), July 22, 1925, Box 45, Folder Inter-Tribal Indian Ceremonial Association, Hubbell Papers; "Gallup, New Mexico, invites you to attend its Inter-Tribal Indian Ceremonial," pamphlet, 1925, Box 45, Folder Inter-Tribal Indian Ceremonial Association, Hubbell Papers. The displays simultaneously celebrated modern progress and offered an escape from it, portraying Indians as a fragile population on the brink of vanishing while promoting their crafts as a way to help them survive. Kropp, "'There is a little sermon,'" 38; Bsumek, 94. Indians, tourists, and traders alike were caught up in a web of commercialism, profit, exploitation, and the very genuine desire for preservation and scientific understanding. Bsumek, *Indian-Made*, 140.

168. "Annual Report of the Director," *Annual Report of the Director to the Board of Trustees for the Year 1910* 4, no. 1, Publication 150 (Chicago: Field Museum of Natural History, 1910): 15; S. C. Simms to Lorenzo Hubbell, Jr., May 7, 1934, Box 28, Folder Field Museum of Natural History, Hubbell Papers.

169. This collection of pottery may be the same collection referred to by James Mooney as the second largest and most important archaeologic find in the history of the area. He referred to it as the "cave deposit, consisting of about one hundred and sixty pieces, discovered north of St. John's about six years ago [1886 or 1887], and now in the possession of Mr. Lorenzo Hubbell, of that place." James Mooney, "Recent Archaeologic Find in Arizona," *American Anthropologist* 6, no. 3 (July 1893): 283. In 1889, Cotton tried to sell the pottery for $1.00 to $5.00 apiece. Hubbell listed them in his catalog in 1901 for $2.50 to $10.00 each. He offered the whole lot of 700 pieces to Stephen Van Rensselaer for $1,500 or 5 pieces for $20.00. See

C. N. Cotton to James L. Shields, April 22, 1889, Box 93, Folder 20, Hubbell Papers; J. L. Hubbell to Stephen Van Rensselaer, November 11, 1903, Box 94, Letterbook, Hubbell Papers; and Hubbell, *Catalogue*.

170. "Recent Progress in Anthropology: George G. Heye," *American Anthropologist* 8, no. 3 (July–September 1906): 537-539.

171. Joseph Emerson Smith, "Navajo Art Patron Dead," 374.

172. Martin Padget, *Indian Country: Travels in the American Southwest, 1840-1935* (Albuquerque: University of New Mexico Press, 2004), 169-170.

173. Bsumek, 57.

174. McNitt, *Indian Traders*, 217.

175. Henry B. Coddington, quoted in McNitt, *Indian Traders*, 217.

## Chapter 7

1. Hamlin Garland, *A Daughter of the Middle Border* (New York: The Macmillan, 1922), 126.

2. Ibid., 125.

3. Ibid., 127. See also Neff, *The Modern West*, 129.

4. Garland, *Daughter of the Middle Border*, 128.

5. Ibid.

6. Lonnie Underhill and Daniel F. Littlefield, Jr., eds. *Hamlin Garland's Observations on the American Indian, 1895-1905* (Tucson: University of Arizona Press, 1976), 29.

7. Garland, *Daughter of the Middle Border*, 128.

8. Neff, *The Modern West*, 135.

9. Joseph Emerson Smith, "Navajo Art Patron Dead," 371. The Hopi Snake Dance in particular became a great magnet for southwestern tourism. See Graves, *Thomas Varker Keam*, 147-149; and Dilworth, *Imagining Indians*, 21-75.

10. See, for one of many examples, James H. Ferris, "The Navajo Nation," *The Nautilus* 34, no. 1 (July 1920): 1-14.

11. Brugge, *Hubbell Trading Post*, 44.

12. Frank M. Palmer, "Among the Cliff Dwellers," *Bulletin of the Archaeological Institute of America* 3 (1907): 39.

13. Laut, *Unknown Southwest*, 105.

14. Hubbell, "Fifty Years," 29, 51. Dorothy Hubbell, interview by Frank McNitt, May 1, 1972, interview II, transcript, Box 2, Folder 17, Roman Hubbell Papers. Frank Lockwood reported that once, Indian Agent Leo Crane "sat in the old man's office and vigorously took him to task for lavish and indiscriminate outlay on transient guests. He said, 'I venture that you spend five thousand dollars a year entertaining bums, coffee salesmen, and other traveling men of that sort with only now and then a distinguished man.' He admitted that he spent that much and probably more in providing for strangers. But his intense Spanish pride made it impossible for him to do otherwise." Lockwood, *Pioneer Portraits*, 156.

15. Laut, *Unknown Southwest*, 105.

16. Dane Coolidge, *California Cowboys* (Tucson: University of Arizona Press, 1939), 47.

17. Maynard Dixon quoted in Donald J. Hagerty, *The Life of Maynard Dixon* (Layton, UT: Gibbs Smith, 2010), 68.

18. See Blue, *Indian Trader*, 169. Hubbell was adamant that he did *not* run a tour business. When a woman wrote to him without reference to any mutual friend in 1909 asking him to conduct her and her party around Navajo country, he referred her to Harry Coddington and told her, "I have never taken parties in this visits, or rather trips, but they were friends who could stand the discomforts of the trip without complaint. I have noticed, so many parties that come out here, and while they enjoy the trip, yet they will as a rule always complain of the party who has them in charge." He invited the woman to stop by Ganado, and then, as if he could not help himself, offered to take her to Canyon de Chelly after all, but for the price of twenty dollars a day, so long as she understood "that it is a rough trip. I on my part will treat you the same as I do my personal friends." J. L. Hubbell to M. A. Drake, June 16, 1909, Box 96, Folder June 1909, Hubbell Papers.

19. Discovering every guest of fame and influence that the Hubbells entertained over a period of more than fifty years is an impossible task. As Dorothy Hubbell stated, J. L. "had many most interesting guests, but he wouldn't allow us to keep a guest book." Dorothy Hubbell, interview by Frank McNitt, May 1, 1972, interview II, transcript, Box 2, Folder 17, Roman Hubbell Papers. The Hubbells' roster of illustrious guests must therefore be pieced together using oral history interviews, newspaper articles, literature, surviving correspondence in the Hubbell Papers, and the Hubbell Trading Post's own collection of artwork and books. In this chapter I do not attempt to mention every visitor who is suspected or even known to have visited. I mention only a few to give a general picture of the trading post as a destination for travelers.

20. Hamlin Garland, "The Bad Medicine Man," *Independent*, December 6, 1900, 2899–2904; Hamlin Garland, "Big Mogassen," *Independent*, November 1, 1900, 2622–2624; and Garland, "Delmar of Pima." "The Bad Medicine Man" is the story of a Navajo witch, Gray Eagle, and the Navajo policeman, Aglar, who takes justice into his own hands by killing the old man. The story contains echoes of the 1878 witch scare in Ganado, and Hubbell probably told Garland about that incident from two decades earlier. "Delmar of Pima" relates many of the incidents Hubbell loved to recall about his tenure as sheriff, and the main character, Andrew Delmar, bears an obvious resemblance to a younger J. L. Hubbell.

21. Garland, "Delmar of Pima," 341.

22. Lockwood, *Pioneer Portraits*, 154.

23. Dilworth, *Imagining Indians*, 24.

24. Fowler, *Laboratory for Anthropology*, 71. For a history of the development of anthropology, see Curtis M. Hinsley Jr., *Savages and Scientists: The Smithsonian Institution and the Development of Anthropology, 1846–1910* (Washington, DC: Smithsonian Institution Press, 1981); and Fowler, *Laboratory for Anthropology*.

25. Dilworth, *Imagining Indians*, 24.

26. Barbara A. Babcock and Nancy J. Parezo, *Daughters of the Desert: Women Anthropologists and the Native American Southwest, 1880–1980* (Albuquerque: University of New Mexico Press, 1988), 7.

27. Graves, *Thomas Varker Keam*, 139.

28. Fowler, *Laboratory for Anthropology*, 138.

29. The traders' role in facilitating southwestern archaeology and anthropology was not without negative effects for the individuals studied. The published reports of ceremonies often promoted racial stereotypes. The Snake Dance, for example, was billed variously as the "Weird Arizona Snake Dance" and "Hideous Rites." Dilworth, *Imagining Indians*, 21. Martha Blue notes that J. L. Hubbell himself sometimes enticed visitors to the Snake Dance by describing it as the "most astonishing and gruesome dance." Blue, *Indian Trader*, 192. Many Hopis resented the presence of intruders in their ceremonies. As Dilworth states, "Ethnographers made it their business to 'discover' and then publicize Hopi ritual knowledge. Consequently, the men who recorded their rituals . . . most thoroughly—Voth, Stephen, and Fewkes—were and still are not well regarded among Hopis." Dilworth, *Imagining Indians*, 42. Other damage came in the form of the stripping of ancient archaeological sites. Traders, eager to make a profit on the trade in curios, modern and ancient, sometimes denuded the land of pottery and other artifacts. J. L. was among those traders who sometimes collected ancient pottery with the intention of selling it.

30. See Graves, *Thomas Varker Keam*, 139–170; and McNitt, *Indian Traders*, 190–191.

31. Graves, *Thomas Varker Keam*, 152.

32. Joseph Emerson Smith, "Navajo Art Patron Dead," 374.

33. For example, Hubbell arranged horses, pack animals, and staff for archaeologist Alfred V. Kidder's excavations near Kayenta and Chinle in 1914. Alfred V. Kidder to J. L. Hubbell, February 16, 1914, Box 48, Folder Kidder, Hubbell Papers; Alfred V. Kidder to J. L. Hubbell, March 11, 1914, Box 48, Folder Kidder, Hubbell Papers.

34. Graves, *Thomas Varker Keam*, 142.

35. Palmer, "Cliff Dwellers," 39.

36. Jimmy H. Miller, *The Life of Harold Sellers Colton: A Philadelphia Brahmin in Flagstaff* (Tsaile, AZ: Navajo Community College Press, 1991), 62–63.

37. Harold S. Colton to J. L. Hubbell, October 28, 1913, Box 18, Folder Colton, Hubbell Papers.

38. Jimmy H. Miller, *Harold Sellers Colton*, 63.

39. Blue, *Indian Trader*, 170–171.

40. Dorothy Hubbell, interview by Frank McNitt, May 1, 1972, interview II, transcript, Box 2, Folder 17, Roman Hubbell Papers.

41. Hubbell, "Fifty Years," 27.

42. Blue states that J. L.'s "presidential contacts were generally quite superficial —'Thank you' notes on White House stationery in return for a Navajo blanket or

J. L.'s formal letters encouraging the appointment of this person or that person to a position constitute most of these 'intimate contacts.' Teddy Roosevelt's 1913 visit to Hubbell's trading ranch was the only true personal contact J. L. had with any of the country's presidents." Blue, *Indian Trader,* 170.

43. J. L. Hubbell to Charles F. Lummis, May 6, 1912, Box 97, Folder May 1–9, 1912, Hubbell Papers.

44. Nicholas Roosevelt to J. L. Hubbell, May 26, 1913, Box 71, Folder Roosevelt, Hubbell Papers.

45. Nicholas Roosevelt to J. L. Hubbell, June 17, 1913, Box 71, Folder Roosevelt, Hubbell Papers.

46. Roosevelt wrote about his experiences in Arizona in three articles: Theodore Roosevelt, "Cougar Hunt on the Rim of the Grand Canyon," *Outlook,* October 4, 1913, 259–266; Theodore Roosevelt, "Across the Navajo Desert," *Outlook,* October 11, 1913, 309–317; and Theodore Roosevelt, "The Hopi Snake Dance," *Outlook,* October 18, 1913, 365–373.

47. Roosevelt, "The Hopi Snake Dance," 371. In return for the favor of being shown the ceremony, Roosevelt asked the Hopis what he could do to show his appreciation. They requested that he send them some cowrie shells, which they used as decorations for the dance. He made good on his promise in 1916 when he sent 300 cowrie shells and a bottle of Atlantic seawater to the Hopis, care of J. L. Hubbell. Anthony Fiala to J. L. Hubbell, February 4, 1916, Box 71, Folder Roosevelt, Hubbell Papers.

48. Natalie Curtis, "Theodore Roosevelt in Hopi-Land: Another Personal Reminiscence," *Outlook,* September 17, 1919, 87.

49. Jimmy H. Miller, *Harold Sellers Colton,* 62.

50. Hubbell, "Fifty Years," 28.

51. Roosevelt, "The Hopi Snake Dance," 373.

52. Hubbell, "Fifty Years," 27.

53. Hubbell Parker, interview with Frank McNitt, May 12, 1972, transcript, Box 16-25(18), Folder 7, McNitt Papers.

54. Roosevelt wrote a thank you note to J. L., in which he said, "This is just a line to say how much obliged I am to you for all you have done for us. I appreciate it to the full—and so do my three companions, including my horse-dealing son and nephew! Will you give my warm regards to your daughter, our hostess. We shall always remember the day at your house." Theodore Roosevelt to J. L. Hubbell, September 12, 1913, Box 71, Folder Roosevelt, Hubbell Papers.

55. Jimmy H. Miller, *Harold Sellers Colton,* 62–63.

56. Roosevelt, "The Hopi Snake Dance," 373.

57. Blue, *Indian Trader,* 197.

58. J. L. Hubbell to Roman Hubbell, August 28, 1913, Box 99, Folder July–December 1913 and Undated, Hubbell Papers.

59. Neff, *The Modern West,* xiii.

60. Weigle and Babcock, *Great Southwest,* 3.

61. Neff, 5 *The Modern West*, 3.

62. Blue, *Indian Trader*, 207.

63. The portrait was painted by Harold Harrington Betts, who must have taken great pleasure in painting the portrait of the "most interesting man I have ever met." Betts, however, said of the portrait, "I was not satisfied with [it] and wish now that I had done it over better." Harold Harrington Betts to Lorenzo Hubbell, Jr., November 14, 1930, Box 9, Folder Betts, Hubbell Papers.

64. Frank P. Sauerwein to J. L. Hubbell, February 9, 1910, Box 73, Folder Sauerwein, Hubbell Papers.

65. Frank P. Sauerwein to J. L. Hubbell, September 2, 1908, Box 73, Folder Sauerwein, Hubbell Papers.

66. Frank P. Sauerwein to J. L. Hubbell, February 9, 1910, Box 73, Folder Sauerwein, Hubbell Papers.

67. Dorothy Hubbell, interview by Frank McNitt, May 1, 1972, interview II, transcript, Box 2, Folder 17, Roman Hubbell Papers.

68. LaCharles, interview by Lawrence C. Kelly, June 26, 1979, interview 074, transcript, Oral Histories, HUTR.

69. Ibid.

70. Padget, *Indian Country*, 141; Charles Francis Browne, "Elbridge Ayer Burbank: A Painter of Indian Portraits," *Brush and Pencil* 3, no. 1 (October 1898): 16–35.

71. Judith A. Barter, *Window on the West: Chicago and the Art of the New Frontier, 1890–1940* (Chicago: Art Institute of Chicago, 2003), 21; Padget, *Indian Country*, 137. For more information about Edward E. Eyer, see Padget, *Indian Country*, 151–155; and Frank C. Lockwood, *The Life of Edward E. Ayer* (Chicago: A. C. McClurg, 1929). For more on E. A. Burbank, see Susan Marie Sullivan, "Many Brushes: Elbridge Ayer Burbank, Painter of Indian Portraits" (master's thesis, University of San Diego, 1983).

72. Barter, *Window on the West*, 24.

73. E. A. Burbank, Earnest Royce, and Frank J. Taylor, *Burbank Among the Indians* (Caldwell, ID: Caxton Printers, 1944), 22.

74. E. A. Burbank, quoted in Navajo Nation Museum, *Diné Ndaashch'ąągo Beelyaa, Portraits of the People: E. A. Burbank at Hubbell Trading Post* (Window Rock, AZ: Navajo Nation Museum, 2001), 2.

75. Padget, *Indian Country*, 138; Bill Mercer, introduction to *American Indian Portraits: Elbridge Ayer Burbank in the West, 1897–1910*, by M. Melissa Wolfe (Youngstown, OH: Butler Institute of American Art, 2000), 9. Dorothy Hubbell gave J. L. credit for inspiring Burbank's project by asking the artist "to make a red drawing of a head from every tribe in the United States." Dorothy Hubbell, interview by Frank McNitt, May 1, 1972, interview II, transcript, Box 2, Folder 17, Roman Hubbell Papers.

76. Mercer, introduction to *American Indian Portraits*, 9; Padget, *Indian Country*, 143, 148.

77. George Wharton James, "A Noted Painter of Indian Types," *The Craftsman* 7, no. 3 (December 1904): 281.

78. M. Melissa Wolfe, *American Indian Portraits: Elbridge Ayer Burbank in the West, 1897–1910* (Youngstown, OH: Butler Institute of American Art, 2000), 14.

79. Charles F. Lummis, "Painting the First Americans: Burbank's Indian Portraits," *Land of Sunshine* 12, no. 6 (May 1900): 340.

80. According to Burbank, the Indians themselves kept him committed to accuracy. He kept a scrapbook of his portraits that were reproduced in magazines and newspapers, and he would show this scrapbook to American Indians he met as a sort of introduction. "They would sit," he wrote, "and examine the pictures by the hour and criticize the detail of the costumes. I soon learned to be very careful of details so that the Indians would know that my pictures were faithful reproductions." Burbank, Royce, and Taylor, *Burbank Among the Indians*, 37–38.

81. Mercer, introduction to *American Indian Portraits*, 11. Burbank's work, however, is not without a degree of ambiguity. As Martin Padget states, "Burbank's art belongs to an era in which Indians across the West were being physically incorporated into American society through the reservation system. He traveled extensively in search of diverse Native American tribes only to participate in the process of absorbing them into American society; he considered himself a friend of Native Americans but could be dismissive of those people he did not think sufficiently 'Indian'; and he spent copious amounts of time among Native people, claiming them as friends, while working for patrons who thought tribal cultures must inevitably come to an end." Padget, *Indian Country*, 140.

82. Navajo Nation Museum, *Diné Ndaashch'ąągo Be'elyaa* 3.

83. Burbank, Royce, and Taylor, *Burbank Among the Indians*, 41.

84. Ibid., 42.

85. Ibid.

86. Burbank, Royce, and Taylor, *Burbank Among the Indians*, 43. This incident illustrates well Burbank's perspective on what he thought his subjects ought to wear. Burbank intended to paint Indians unaffected by European culture, viewing those whose dress reflected cultural syncretism as less authentic than those in more traditional costume. Burbank reported that he was at the trading post when Many Horses passed away, and helped J. L. bury him on top of Hubbell Hill.

87. J. L. Hubbell to E. A. Burbank, March 27, 1909, Box 95, Folder March 20–31, 1909, Hubbell Papers; Roman Hubbell to Edward Eberstadt and Sons, March 20, 1956, Box 121, Folder 1955–1956, Hubbell Papers. Burbank was not the only artist to work for Hubbell. Photographer Simeon Schwemberger clerked in several of Hubbell's trading posts, and artist Julian Scott also reportedly worked there. Doris Ostrander Dawdy, *Artists of the American West: A Biographical Dictionary* (Chicago: Sage Books, 1974), 208. Burbank and Nettie also tried to sell curios for Hubbell in Burbank's hometown of Harvard, Illinois, and worked as a middleman for Hubbell's sale of curios to Marshall Field's and other Chicago department stores. Padget, *Indian Country*, 160; Wolfe, *American Indian Portraits*, 15–16.

88. Hubbell Parker, interview with Frank McNitt, May 12, 1972, transcript, Box 16-25(18), Folder 7, McNitt Papers.
89. Navajo Nation Museum, Diné Ndaashch'ąągo Be'elyaa, 3.
90. J. L. Hubbell to Sam S. Porter, March 4, 1909, Box 95, Folder March 1-9, 1909, Hubbell Papers; E. A. Burbank to J. L. Hubbell, June 19, 1906, Box 12, Folder Burbank, Hubbell Papers; Dorothy Hubbell, interview by Frank McNitt, May 1, 1972, interview II, transcript, Box 2, Folder 17, Roman Hubbell Papers. As dearly as he loved Burbank's work, it was not immune from sale when J. L. needed cash. In early 1915, just after his defeat in the race for the senate and when his business was deeply in debt, he consigned several of Burbank's drawings to the Fred Harvey Company to sell at the El Tovar at the Grand Canyon. One of the drawings sold for $20.00, $10.75 of which went back to the Hubbells. Fred Harvey Company to J. L. Hubbell, July 1, 1915, Box 37, Folder Harvey, Fred 1915, Hubbell Papers.
91. E. A. Burbank to J. L. Hubbell, April 10, 1902, Box 12, Folder Burbank, Hubbell Papers.
92. Padget, *Indian Country*, 159.
93. E. A. Burbank to Edward Ayer, November 5, 1902, quoted in Wolfe, 17.
94. Wolfe, *American Indian Portraits*, 16.
95. Padget, *Indian Country*, 161.
96. Roman Hubbell to E. A. Burbank, January 12, 1944, Box 116, Folder January–February 1945, Hubbell Papers.
97. Hagerty, *Life of Maynard Dixon*, 9.
98. Dixon, "Arizona in 1900," *Arizona Highways* 18, no. 2 (February 1942): 17.
99. Thomas Brent Smith and Donald J. Hagerty, *A Place of Refuge: Maynard Dixon's Arizona* (Tucson: Tucson Museum of Art and Historic Block, 2008), 13; Hagerty, *Life of Maynard Dixon*, 13.
100. Hagerty, *Life of Maynard Dixon*, 12.
101. Ibid., 66.
102. Ibid., 70–71.
103. Bernard L. Fontana, ed., *Querido Patron: Letters from Maynard Dixon to Lorenzo Hubbell* (Tucson: Friends of the University of Arizona Library, 1987), ii.
104. Hagerty, *Life of Maynard Dixon*, 80.
105. Ibid., 69–70. Hagerty notes that Dixon's time in Ganado had an important impact on his development as an artist: "There, he experimented seriously with oil painting, developed his pastels and watercolors, and absorbed the lonely shimmering land of color into his imagination."
106. Dixon, "Arizona in 1900," 40. Dixon would visit again in 1905, 1915, and 1923. Hagerty, *Life of Maynard Dixon*, 80, 149.
107. Out of a jumble of notes under the title "Navajo Burial," Dixon wrote a semi-fictional short story called "Chindih," which he never published. A copy of the story can be found in the collections of Hubbell Trading Post. Dixon also memorialized Hubbell and his trading post in an article called "Arizona in 1900" for *Arizona Highways*.

108. Maynard Dixon, "Chindih," n.d., unpublished manuscript, Folder "Dixon," Historical Files, HUTR.

109. Hagerty, *Life of Maynard Dixon*, 113.

110. Dixon, "Arizona in 1900," 40.

111. Ibid., 2.

112. Ibid., 19–20. Dixon was quoting from Spanish poet Ramón de Campoamor, though he mixed up the order of the first two lines of the famous poem.

113. Ibid., 20. Hagerty writes that "Dixon remembered the words and wrote them down, integrating their meaning into his personal and artistic journey." Hagerty, *Life of Maynard Dixon*, 81.

114. Hagerty, *Life of Maynard Dixon*, 70–71.

115. Ibid., 83.

116. Fontana, *Querido Patron*, 14, 15.

117. Ibid., 15.

118. Hagerty, *Life of Maynard Dixon*, 66.

119. Ibid., 180.

120. Frank P. Sauerwein to J. L. Hubbell, February 9, 1910, Box 73, Folder Sauerwein, Hubbell Papers.

121. Neff, *The Modern West*, xiii.

122. Richard W. Etulain, *Re-Imagining the Modern American West: A Century of Fiction, History, and Art* (Tucson: University of Arizona Press, 1996), 68. For an overview of Southwestern regional literature, see Mark Busby, "Texas and the Great Southwest," in *A Companion to the Regional Literatures of America*, ed. Charles L. Crow (Malden, MA: Blackwell, 2003), 422–457; and Frank J. Dobie, *Guide to Life and Literature of the Southwest* (Austin: University of Texas Press, 1943).

123. D. H. Lawrence, "The Spirit of Place," quoted in Neff, *The Modern West*, 134.

124. Neff, *The Modern West*, 134.

125. Dorothy Hubbell, interview by Frank McNitt, May 4, 1972, interview V, transcript, Box 2, Folder 17, Roman Hubbell Papers. See also Allen H. Anderson, *The Chief: Ernest Thompson Seton and the Changing West* (College Station: Texas A&M University Press, 1986), 181–182.

126. Fowler, *Laboratory for Anthropology*, 249; Padget, *Indian Country*, 118.

127. Lummis, "Swallow's-Nest," 501–502.

128. Padget, *Indian Country*, 116.

129. Fowler, *Laboratory for Anthropology*, 247.

130. Ibid.

131. Mark Thompson, *American Character: The Curious Life of Charles Fletcher Lummis and the Rediscovery of the Southwest* (New York: Arcade, 2001), 16; Fowler, *Laboratory for Anthropology*, 247.

132. Lummis's travel writings were later published as *A Tramp Across the Continent* (New York: Charles Scribner's Sons, 1892).

133. Mark Thompson, *American Character*, 20.

134. Lummis was unimpressed by the Navajos. By the time he reached Arizona, his tramp had become more of a trudge of endurance, and there was little in the wintery landscape to relieve his misery. He called them "dirty, thievish, treacherous, and revoltingly licentious" in his weekly dispatch, a criticism which he softened only slightly for *A Tramp Across the Continent,* where he called them "the most savage aborigines of the West." Quoted in Mark Thompson, *American Character*, 45; Lummis, *Tramp*, 212. His opinion of the people later improved markedly.

135. Fowler, *Laboratory for Anthropology*, 250. For an excellent critical assessment of Lummis's role as creator of the Southwest, see Padget, *Indian Country*, 115–136.

136. In June 1906, Lummis gave J. L. a collection of inscribed books. Inside *The Awakening of a Nation: Mexico Today,* Lummis wrote an inscription in Spanish, part of which translates, "To Senor Don J. L. Hubbell with the most grateful memories . . . of August, 1890." Charles F. Lummis, *The Awakening of a Nation: Mexico of Today* (New York: Harper and Brother Publishers, 1904), HUTR 1712, Museum Collections, HUTR.

137. Lummis, "Swallow's-Nest," 500.

138. Blue quotes a letter from Hubbell to Lummis in which J. L. offered to provide "material assistance to any of the members [of the Sequoyah League] who may visit this region," and praised Lummis for his work "with the poor unfortunate Indians in California . . . who have no friends." Quoted in Blue, *Indian Trader*, 200.

139. Lummis, "Swallow's-Nest," 501; Charles F. Lummis to J. L. Hubbell, February 7, 1905, Box 53, Folder Lummis, Hubbell Papers; Charles F. Lummis to J. L. Hubbell, January 1, 1907, Box 53, Folder Lummis, Hubbell Papers; and Mark Thompson, 309.

140. Lummis, "Swallow's-Nest," 500.

141. Dorothy Hubbell, interview by David M. Brugge, October 13, 1969, interview 052, transcript, Oral Histories, HUTR. For more information about the life of Charles Lummis, see Edwin R. Bingham, *Charles F. Lummis: Editor of the Southwest* (San Marino, CA: Huntington Library, 1955); and Turbesé Lummis Fiske and Keith Lummis, *Charles F. Lummis: The Man and His West* (Norman: University of Oklahoma Press, 1975).

142. Peter Wild, *George Wharton James,* Boise State University Western Writers Series, No. 93 (Boise, ID: Boise State University, 1990), 26.

143. Ibid., 13–15; Kevin Starr, *Inventing the Dream: California through the Progressive Era* (New York: Oxford University Press, 1985), 110. For more information on George Wharton James, see Paul R. Arreola, "George Wharton James and the Indians," *Masterkey* 60, no. 1 (Spring 1986): 11–18; Roger Joseph Bourdon, "George Wharton James: Interpreter of the Southwest," (PhD dissertation, University of California, Los Angeles, 1965); Enrique Cortés, "George Wharton James: Advocate for the Golden State," *Masterkey* 60, no. 1 (Spring 1986): 19–25; and Stephen G. Maurer, "In the Heart of the Great Freedom: George Wharton James and the Desert Southwest," *Masterkey* 60, no. 1 (Spring 1986): 4–10.

144. Wild, *George Wharton James*, 17.

145. Starr, *Inventing the Dream*, 111.

146. George Wharton James to J. L. Hubbell, March 9, 1908, Box 46, Folder James, George Wharton, Hubbell Papers; George Wharton James to J. L. Hubbell, September 5, 1912, Box 46, Folder James, George Wharton, Hubbell Papers.

147. George Wharton James to J. L. Hubbell, September 14, 1914, Folder James, George Wharton, Hubbell Papers. James also offered to publish an article about J. L. called "A Day with a Navaho Indian Trader" in *Out West*, but the article never made it to print. George Wharton James to J. L. Hubbell, July 11, 1913, Folder James, George Wharton, Hubbell Papers.

148. George Wharton James, *New Mexico: Land of the Delight Makers* (Boston: Page, 1920), 405.

149. Ibid. James also related a version of this story in George Wharton James, *Our American Wonderlands* (Chicago: A. C. McClurg, 1915), 41–43.

150. George Wharton James, *New Mexico*, 405.

151. Ibid., 406; George Wharton James, *Our American Wonderlands*, 43.

152. Interestingly, James was not remembered fondly by the Hubbell family. Dorothy related the following: "My sister-in-law was very mad a George Wharton James. Mr. Hubbell had a very rare manuscript that he was proud of. It disappeared about the time that James was here. Later when he came back, she asked him if he had the manuscript. He said, 'Yes, what are you going to do about it?' We never got it back." Dorothy Hubbell, interview by David M. Brugge, October 13, 1969, interview 052, transcript, Oral Histories, HUTR. When Frank McNitt questioned her further about this statement, she said did not know any additional information, but referred him to LaCharles. Dorothy Hubbell, interview by Frank McNitt, May 6, 1972, interview VI, transcript, Box 2, Folder 17, Roman Hubbell Papers. In his brief biography of James, Peter Wild also mentions a rumor of James having borrowed "a valuable 'Spanish document' that he never returned." Wild, *George Wharton James*, 23.

153. Owen Ulph, "A Dedication to the Memory of Dane Coolidge, 1873–1940," *Journal of the Southwest* 23, no. 1 (Spring 1981): 2.

154. Ibid., 3. See also Dane Coolidge and Mary Roberts Coolidge, *The Navajo Indians* (Boston: Houghton Mifflin, 1930).

155. Ulph, "Dedication," 2.

156. Hagerty, *Life of Maynard Dixon*, 105.

157. Ibid., 96.

158. Dane Coolidge, *Texas Cowboys* (New York: E. P. Dutton, 1937); Dane Coolidge, *Arizona Cowboys* (New York: E. P. Dutton, 1938); and Dane Coolidge, *Old California Cowboys* (New York: E. P. Dutton, 1939).

159. Dane Coolidge to Mr. Hubbell, December 5, 1913, Folder Dane Coolidge, Historical Files, HUTR.

160. Ulph, "Dedication," 3.

161. Coolidge, *Lorenzo the Magnificent*, 3.

162. Coolidge, *Lorenzo the Magnificent*, HUTR 1654, Museum Collections, HUTR.

163. Dane Coolidge to Mr. Hubbell, December 5, 1913, Folder Dane Coolidge, Historical Files, HUTR.

164. Coolidge, *California Cowboys*, 49.

165. "Don Lorenzo Hubbell, Beloved Character of Old Arizona, Is Dead," newspaper article, title unknown, November 13, 1930, Box 545, Folder 1, Hubbell Papers.

166. Joseph Emerson Smith, "Navajo Art Patron Dead," 371.

167. Harold Harrington Betts to Lorenzo Hubbell, Jr., November 14, 1930, Box 9, Folder Betts, Hubbell Papers.

168. Henry Fountain Ashurst, *A Many Colored Toga: The Diary of Henry Fountain Ashurst* (Tucson: University of Arizona Press, 1962), 298–299.

169. White Mountain Smith, "He is our Friend," 10. Roman continued to help all sorts of people interested in the Diné. For example, he took conductor Leopold Stokowski and Carlos Chavez, Mexican composer and director of the Mexican symphonic orchestra, who incorporated native instruments into his symphonies, to several Navajo sings so they could study Navajo music. Dorothy Hubbell, interview by David M. Brugge, October 13, 1969, interview 052, transcript, Oral Histories, HUTR.

170. Louise Lamphere, introduction to *Spider Woman: A Story of Navajo Weavers and Chanters*, by Gladys A. Reichard (Albuquerque: University of New Mexico Press, 1997), viii.

171. Louise Lamphere, "Gladys Reichard Among the Navajo," *Frontiers: A Journal of Women Studies* 12, no. 3 (1992): 79.

172. Ibid., 88.

173. Lamphere, introduction to *Spider Woman*, xi.

174. Lamphere, "Gladys Reichard," 91.

175. Ibid., 92.

176. Reichard, *Spider Woman*, xxix.

177. Ibid., xxx.

178. Quoted in Lamphere, "Gladys Reichard," 93.

179. See Dorothy Hubbell, interview by Frank McNitt, May 4, 1972, interview V, transcript, Box 2, Folder 17, Roman Hubbell Papers.

180. Gladys Reichard, *Navajo Shepherd and Weaver* (New York: J. J. Augustin, 1936); Gladys Reichard, *Dezbah: Woman of the Desert* (New York: J. J. Augustin, 1939).

181. Laura Adams Armer, *In Navajo Land* (New York: David McKay, 1962), 18. (Subsequent citations in this paragraph are to the same source, pp. 41, 45, and 97.)

182. Lorenzo Hubbell, Jr., to Barbara Goodman and Roman Hubbell, October 6, 1927, Box 105, Folder October–December 1927, Hubbell Papers.

183. Fowler, *Laboratory for Anthropology*, 359.

184. Laura Adams Armer, *Southwest* (London: Longmans, Green, 1935), 207.

185. Gladys A. Reichard to Mr. Hubbell, October 17, 1928, Box 69, Folder Reichard, Hubbell Papers; Fowler, *Laboratory for Anthropology*, 359.

186. Laura Adams Armer, *Waterless Mountain* (New York: Junior Literary Guild, 1931), v.

187. Armer, *Southwest*, 207. The Hubbell name was as good as gold among the Navajos for years to come. Ann Axtell Morris, the archaeologist, "got one of the biggest 'kicks' in my life" one summer when talking to an old Navajo man named Charlie Mitchell at a Navajo Indian Council at Fort Wingate. She introduced to him two women—the first he barely took notice of, but the second was LaCharles Goodman. When Morris introduced her as "the granddaughter of Lorenzo Hubbell," Mitchell "was overjoyed and tremendously interested at once. I myself only rated his attention because I was the cousin of Bruce Barnard, also a trader—I felt that the first families of the Southwest had scored beautifully over New England social prominence." Ann Axtell Morris, *Digging in the Southwest* (Garden City, NY: Doubleday, Doran, 1934), 181–182.

188. Dorothy Hubbell, interview by David M. Brugge, October 13, 1969, interview 052, transcript, Oral Histories, HUTR.

189. Louise Swinnerton to Lorenzo, Jr., September 18, 1940, Box 79, Folder Swinnerton, Hubbell Papers.

## Chapter 8

1. The mortgages were held by Henry Chee Dodge. Lorenzo Hubbell, Jr., to Roman Hubbell, September 16, 1930, Box 106, Folder May–December 1930, Hubbell Papers; A. S. Gibbons to J. L. Hubbell, October 23, 1930, Box 3, Folder 1, Hubbell Papers.

2. Lorenzo Hubbell, Jr., to Kirk Brothers, November 19, 1930, Box 106, Folder May–December 1930, Hubbell Papers. Lorenzo, Jr., continued to operate his business, the Lorenzo Hubbell Trading Company, separately from the J. L. Hubbell Trading Post, even though he managed both businesses. Forrest regularly sent invoices and other formal business correspondence to the Lorenzo Hubbell Trading Company, indicating that the Hubbells tried to keep the two as financially and legally distinct as possible. See Lorenzo Hubbell, Jr., to R. G. Dun & Co., July 15, 1931, Box 106, Folder July 1931, Hubbell Papers.

3. Forrest Parker to Lorenzo Hubbell, Jr., January 31, 1931, Box 106, Folder January–February 1931, Hubbell Papers.

4. Bailey and Bailey, *History of the Navajos*, 182–183.

5. Roman Hubbell to Lorenzo Hubbell, Jr., February 18, 1932, Box 107, Folder February 1932, Hubbell Papers.

6. Bailey and Bailey, *History of the Navajos*, 183.

7. Lorenzo Hubbell, Jr., to George Hubbell, May 31, 1932, Box 107, Folder May 1932, Hubbell Papers.

8. Donald L. Parman, *The Navajos and the New Deal* (New Haven, CT: Yale University Press, 1976), 23–24.

9. Lorenzo Hubbell, Jr., to Roman Hubbell, May 3, 1932, Box 107, Folder May 1932, Hubbell Papers.

10. Lorenzo Hubbell, Jr., to Frank H. Hitchcock, October 27, 1932, Box 107, October 1932, Hubbell Papers.

11. Lorenzo Hubbell, Jr., to Roman Hubbell, April 27, 1935, Box 109, Folder April 1935, Hubbell Papers.

12. Lorenzo Hubbell, Jr., to George Hubbell, August 17, 1932, Box 107, Folder July–August 1932, Hubbell Papers; Lorenzo Hubbell, Jr., to Tom, August 17, 1932, Box 107, Folder July–August 1932, Hubbell Papers.

13. Lorenzo Hubbell, Jr., to Standard Overall Co., February 20, 1933, Box 107, Folder February 1933, Hubbell Papers; Lorenzo Hubbell, Jr., to The Rice-Thomas Manufacturing Co., March 15, 1932, Box 107, Folder March 1932, Hubbell Papers.

14. Forrest M. Parker to Lorenzo Hubbell, Jr., January 13, 1931, Box 106, Folder January–February 1931, Hubbell Papers.

15. Lorenzo Hubbell, Jr., to Roman Hubbell, June 29, 1931, Box 106, Folder June 1931, Hubbell Papers; Roman Hubbell to Lorenzo Hubbell, Jr., June 27, 1931, Box 106, Folder June 1931, Hubbell Papers.

16. Peterson, *Homestead and Farm*, 199.

17. Gladwell Richardson, *Navajo Trader*, 119.

18. Laura Adams Armer, "The Big Snow," *Desert Magazine* 24, no. 4 (April 1961): 18.

19. Gladwell Richardson, *Navajo Trader*, 119.

20. Parman, *Navajos and the New Deal*, 24.

21. Armer, "Big Snow," 119.

22. Ibid.

23. See correspondence between the Hubbells and John Collier, 1931–1932, Box 7, Folder 8, Roman Hubbell Papers.

24. Weisiger, *Dreaming of Sheep*, 163; Lorenzo Hubbell, Jr., to Helen Corcoran, February 1, 1932, Box 107, Folder February 1932, Hubbell Papers.

25. Bailey and Bailey, *History of the Navajos*, 183; Weisiger, *Dreaming of Sheep*, 163.

26. Peterson, *Homestead and Farm*, 199.

27. Ibid., 198.

28. "Memorandum," n.d., Box 18, Folder Collier, Hubbell Papers; "Indians Want John Collier Bureau Chief," *New Mexico State Tribune*, December 31, 1932; and "The Indian Commission," *New Mexico State Tribune*, January 3, 1933.

29. Quoted in Iverson, *Diné*, 146.

30. Marsha Weisiger, "Gendered Injustice: Navajo Livestock Reduction in the New Deal Era," *Western Historical Quarterly* 38, no. 4 (Winter 2007): 441; Powers, *Navajo Trading*, 38–39.

31. Parman, *Navajos and the New Deal*, 22–23.

32. Weisiger, "Gendered Injustice," 339–440.

33. Parman, *Navajos and the New Deal*, 3.

34. Iverson, *Diné*, 142. As Marsha Weisiger states, "In their haste to respond to an environmental crisis, Collier and his conservationists unwitting made matters worse, ecologically and culturally. Among their many mistakes, they ignored the importance of long-established cultural patterns, disparaged local knowledge and cultural understandings of nature, and refused to listen to Navajos' advice in implementing the livestock reduction program." Weisiger, "Gendered Injustice," 441.

35. Jennifer McLerran, *A New Deal for Native Art: Indian Arts and Federal Policy, 1933–1943* (Tucson: University of Arizona Press, 2009), 15.

36. Ibid., 232.

37. Powers, *Navajo Trading*, 39.

38. Iverson, *Diné*, 153; Weisiger, *Dreaming of Sheep*, 25.

39. Quoted in Iverson, *Diné*, 153.

40. Dorothy Hubbell, interview by David M. Brugge, October 13, 1969, interview 052, transcript, Oral Histories, HUTR.

41. Ibid. In a letter to Gladys Reichard, Dorothy explained the Navajos' reluctance to comply with stock reduction. "The Indians have so much less since our bad winters of two and three years ago, (and if we get no rain pretty pronto, there will be plenty of stock reduction)—they know of the seriousness of erosion, I'm sure, but don't understand or care much of any result to the Boulder Dam,—and they hesitate to give up something they know and understand for something they hear about. It is all very well for these government officials to speak of the thousands, even millions of dollars which will be paid out to the Navajos for these various emergency conservation projects, which, also, they claim will amount to several times what they will lose in this reduction of sheep and goats,—but still, they are skeptical. They claim they don't all get some of this new work, and want assurance that the money really will be spent, etc." Dorothy Hubbell to Gladys Reichard, March 27, 1934, Box 7, Folder 9, Roman Hubbell Papers.

42. Roman Hubbell to John Collier, April 23, 1933, Box 7, Folder 9, Roman Hubbell Papers.

43. Roman Hubbell to Henry A. Wallace, August 8, 1934, Box 7, Folder 9, Roman Hubbell Papers; John Collier to Roman Hubbell, August 22, 1934, Box 7, Folder 9, Roman Hubbell Papers.

44. Lorenzo Hubbell, Jr., to John Collier, September 10, 1941, Box 113, Folder September 1941, Hubbell Papers.

45. Ibid.

46. Brugge, *Hubbell Trading Post*, 71.

47. Lorenzo Hubbell, Jr., to J. A. Mahoney, January 22, 1942, Box 114, Folder January 1942, Hubbell Papers.

48. Iverson, *Diné*, 145, 155.

49. Roman Hubbell to John Collier, February 19, 1939, Box 7, Folder 10, Roman Hubbell Papers.

50. Powers, *Navajo Trading*, 39.

51. William S. Collins, *The New Deal in Arizona* (Phoenix: Arizona State Parks Board, 1999), 238.

52. Brugge, *Hubbell Trading Post*, 70–71. Other New Deal projects benefited the Navajos only indirectly, but focused on recording and preserving Navajo culture. The government hired Anglo anthropologists to study Navajo culture and society, and the Hubbells became involved in some of Collier's other programs. Roman, for example, provided the names of Navajo sand painters and weavers to participate in a project decorating public buildings with Navajo artwork. See Nina Collier to Dorothy and Roman Hubbell, December 20, 1933, Box 7, Folder 9, Roman Hubbell Papers; and Roman Hubbell to Nina Collier, December 27, 1933, Box 7, Folder 9, Roman Hubbell Papers. Around the same time, Lorenzo, Jr., became involved with the Indian Arts and Crafts Board, which hoped to promote a revival of native arts that would serve the dual purposes of "encouraging cultural preservation and promoting economic development." Collins, *New Deal in Arizona*, 260.

53. Peterson, *Homestead and Farm*, 118–119.

54. Ibid.

55. Ibid., 120.

56. McLerran, *New Deal for Native Art*, 232.

57. Mortgage Deed, January 1, 1931, Box 529, Folder 2, Hubbell Papers; Mortgage Deed, February 1936, Box 529, Folder 2, Hubbell Papers; Quitclaim Deed, 1941, Box 529, Folder 2, Hubbell Papers; Lorenzo Hubbell, Jr., to Merchant's Bank, January 20, 1932, Box 107, Hubbell Papers.

58. Lorenzo Hubbell, Jr., to Herman W. Atkins, July 3, 1933, Box 108, Folder June–July 1933, Hubbell Papers.

59. A. B. Frank Company v. J. Lorenzo Hubbell, Jr., June 11, 1932, Day Family Collection; Lorenzo Hubbell, Jr., to Roman Hubbell, August 13, 1933, Box 108, Folder August 1933, Hubbell Papers.

60. Lorenzo Hubbell, Jr., to Roman Hubbell, January 24, 1935, Box 108, Folder January 1935, Hubbell Papers.

61. Bailey and Bailey, *History of the Navajos*, 183.

62. Lorenzo Hubbell, Jr., to Barbara H. Goodman, May 18, 1935, Box 109, Folder May 1935, Hubbell Papers.

63. Lorenzo Hubbell, Jr., to Flora Sandoval, September 5, 1935, Box 109, Folder September 1935, Hubbell Papers.

64. Lorenzo Hubbell to John G. Hunger, August 1, 1931, Box 106, Folder August 1931, Hubbell Papers; Lorenzo Hubbell, Jr., to Hub Store, April 16, 1934, Box 108, Folder February–May 1934, Hubbell Papers; "Terms of Sale of Cow Springs Trading Post," June 30, 1935, Box 109, Folder June 1935, Hubbell Papers; and Lorenzo Hubbell, Jr., to Tourists News, July 15, 1935, Box 109, Folder July 1935, Hubbell Papers.

65. Lorenzo Hubbell, Jr., to Goodyear Tire and Rubber Co., January 10, 1936, Box 109, Folder January–February 1936, Hubbell Papers; Lorenzo Hubbell, Jr., to Miles Parker, June 6, 1939, Box 111, Folder June 1939, Hubbell Papers.

66. Lorenzo Hubbell, Jr., to Joe Hillier, April 4, 1935, Box 109, Folder April 1935, Hubbell Papers.

67. Lorenzo Hubbell, Jr., to Leslie Murray, May 6, 1938, Box 110, Folder May–June 1938, Hubbell Papers; Lorenzo Hubbell, Jr., to Leslie Murray, May 1, 1937, Box 110, Folder May–June 1937, Hubbell Papers.

68. Lorenzo Hubbell, Jr., to Herman W. Atkins, June 11, 1939, Box 111, Folder June 1939, Hubbell Papers; Lorenzo Hubbell to Miles Parker, October 24, 1939, Box 11, Folder October 1939, Hubbell Papers.

69. Helen Corcoran to Lorenzo Hubbell, Jr., January 12, 1940, Box 112, Folder January 1940, Hubbell Papers.

70. Edward T. Hall, *West of the Thirties: Discoveries Among the Navajo and Hopi* (New York: Doubleday, 1994), 161.

71. Ibid.

72. Establishing a clear chronology of clerks in the trading post is difficult. The written record provides some information, but the recollections of family members and employees are often vague or even contradictory about dates. According to Clint Colby, traders at the Ganado post in the 1930s included Forrest Parker, Ed Morris, Epimenio Armijo, A. A. Romero, and Charles E. Rubi. Clint N. Colby, "Persons at Hubbell Trading Post," 1972, Box 3, Folder "Hubbell Business, Revised graph fr. Kathy M'Closkey + one from Clint Colby," Brugge Papers.

73. Hall, *West of the Thirties*, 161.

74. Ibid; LaCharles Eckel, interview by Lawrence C. Kelly, June 26, 1979, interview 074, transcript, Oral Histories, HUTR.

75. Brugge, *Hubbell Trading Post*, 72.

76. Froeschauer-Nelson, *Cultural Landscape Report*, under "Decline of the Hubbell Trading Post and Farm (1923–1967)."

77. Peterson, *Homestead and Farm*, 117. See Lorenzo Hubbell, Jr., to Roman Hubbell, March 14, 1936, Box 109, Folder March 1936, Hubbell Papers.

78. Roman Hubbell to Lorenzo Hubbell, Jr., June 14, 1937, Box 110, Folder May–June 1937, Hubbell Papers.

79. Roman Hubbell to Lorenzo Hubbell, Jr., May 17, 1937, Box 110, Folder May–June 1937, Hubbell Papers.

80. LaCharles Eckel, interview by Lawrence C. Kelly, June 26, 1979, interview 074, transcript, Oral Histories, HUTR.

81. See LaCharles Eckel to Lorenzo Hubbell, Jr., February 16, 1932, Box 107, Folder February 1932, Hubbell Papers.

82. One local newspaper wrote, "A high school romance climaxed in the elopement and marriage at Holbrook, Ariz., this week of Dorothy Ketner and Roman Hubbell Jr, children of Gallup's most prominent pioneer families. Hubbell graduated last year from the Gallup high school, was a football star and president of his class." "Children of Pioneer Gallup Families Wed," *Clovis Evening News-Journal*, October 19, 1933.

83. Lorenzo Hubbell, Jr., to Flora Sandoval, July 31, 1935, Box 109, Folder July 1935, Hubbell Papers.

84. Hall, *West of the Thirties*, 159.

85. Lorenzo Hubbell, Jr., to Flora Sandoval, March 22, 1935, Box 108, Folder February–March 1935, Hubbell Papers.

86. Flora Sandoval to Lorenzo Hubbell, Jr., May 24, 1936, Box 109, Folder May 1935, Hubbell Papers.

87. Ibid.

88. Lorenzo Hubbell, Jr., to Roman Hubbell and Family, August 10, 1936, Box 110, Folder August 1936, Hubbell Papers.

89. LaCharles Eckel, interview by Lawrence C. Kelly, June 26, 1979, interview 074, transcript, Oral Histories, HUTR.

90. Helen Corcoran to Lorenzo Hubbell, Jr., April 23, 1937, Box 110, Folder March–April 1937, Hubbell Papers. See also Barbara H. Goodman to Lorenzo Hubbell, Jr., and Flora Sandoval, January 7, 1938, Box 110, Folder January–February 1938, Hubbell Papers; Lorenzo Hubbell, Jr., to Sir, June 30, 1939, Box 111, Folder June 1939, Hubbell Papers.

91. Forrest Parker to Roman Hubbell, March 1, 1938, Box 3, Folder 5, Roman Hubbell Papers.

92. Ibid.

93. Lorenzo, Jr., wrote a touching account of his sister's passing in a letter to a friend: "No doubt before leaving Winslow you heard of the death of my sister, she died Monday morning July third, and we buried her next day on top of Hubbell Hill, where mother, father and my father's Navajo friend Many Horses are buried. Many of our relatives, and friends were there for the funeral, all of them who Adel had enjoyed thru life, she was so good and valued her acquaintances so much, that the tribute of flowers and the presence of her friends is just as she might have wanted it. The poor girl has been sick for three years, the last three months bedfast, and the last three days unconscious, so your beautiful letter and message helped as a spiritual gesture. We all read your letter to her, and Forrest was very much moved." Lorenzo Hubbell, Jr., to Mr. Robertson, July 11, 1939, Box 111, Folder July 1939, Hubbell Papers.

94. "Mrs. Parker Dies at Ganado, Ariz.," *Gallup Independent*, July 3, 1939. After Adele's death, Forrest returned to Phoenix to continue working for the Indian Service. He remarried, but stayed in touch with the Hubbell family.

95. Hall, *West of the Thirties*, 160.

96. "Agreement," December 30, 1938, Box 8, Folder 9, Roman Hubbell Papers.

97. White Mountain Smith, "He is our Friend," 10.

98. See, for example, J. L. Hubbell to Mrs. G. G. Trask, April 17, 1915, Box 100, Letterbook, Hubbell Papers.

99. Padget, *Indian Country*, 171. For more information about the Indian Detours, see Padget, *Indian Country*, 169–210; Darnall, *Southwestern Indian Detours*; and Weigle and Babcock, *Great Southwest*.

100. Padget, *Indian Country*, 197–198.

101. Fred Harvey Company, *Indian-Detours: Most Distinctive Motor Cruise Service in the World* (Chicago: Rand McNally, 1930), 1.

102. Roman charged between twenty and forty dollars per person per day, depending on the number of people booked in a single car, while the Indian Detours ranged from twenty-five to seventy dollars per person per day in 1930. "Roman Hubbell Navajo Tours," brochure, n.d., a copy of which can be found in Box 6, Folder 10, Roman Hubbell Papers; Fred Harvey Company, *Indian Detours*, 36.

103. Memorandum, n.d., Box 4, Folder 2, Roman Hubbell Papers.

104. "Roman Hubbell Navajo Tours," brochure, n.d., Box 6, Folder 10, Roman Hubbell Papers.

105. Ibid.

106. Dorothy Hubbell, interview by Frank McNitt, May 2, 1972, interview IV, transcript, Box 2, Folder 17, Roman Hubbell Papers.

107. Roman Hubbell to Earnest B. Bearnarth, January 20, 1939, Box 4, Folder 1, Roman Hubbell Papers.

108. N. Ziebolz to Roman Hubbell, October 10, 1941, Box 6, Folder 12, Roman Hubbell Papers.

109. See, for example, Roman Hubbell to R. W. Birdseye, March 31, 1938, Box 4, Folder 2, Roman Hubbell Papers; T. B. Gallaher, August 25, 1938, Box 4, Folder 2, Roman Hubbell Papers.

110. For a sampling of this publicity, see O. C. Havens, "Transportation Pioneers," *Arizona Highways* 14 (November 1938): 24–25; and Gladys Reichard, "Fifty Thousand Signposts," *New Mexico Magazine* 17 (March 1939): 18–19, 32–33.

111. Jim Welsh to Roman Hubbell, n.d., Box 5, Folder 9, Roman Hubbell Papers.

112. Roman Hubbell to Jim Welsh, March 25, 1941, Box 5, Folder 9, Roman Hubbell Papers.

113. Mrs. E. B. Kellam, "My Indian Detour," n.d., Box 3, Folder 3, Roman Hubbell Papers.

114. Theodore Cronyn to Roman Hubbell, May 27, 1940, Box 6, Folder 6, Roman Hubbell Papers.

115. Brugge, *Hubbell Trading Post*, 69.

116. Dorothy provides a fascinating account of the time Roman Hubbell Navajo Tours worked with the movies in Dorothy Hubbell, interview by Frank McNitt, May 2, 1972, interview IV, transcript, Box 2, Folder 17, Roman Hubbell Papers. She recalls that Roman not only provided transportation, but also Navajos to play "Indian" in films. "Sometimes," Dorothy remembered, "they'd call me at maybe two or three o'clock in the morning and say, 'Mrs. Hubbell, will you see that we have so many people, or so many Indians, or Indians with moccasins, or whatever they wanted, by six o'clock tomorrow morning?' Oh, Roman really worked at it, and one of the Indians . . . had to wear feathers in his hair, you know. Like white people expect Indians to wear. And he was to drive a bunch of cattle in that redrock district there . . . And he had to make I don't know how many starts because either the sun shone on the buckles or the silver conchos he was wearing, or his body didn't glisten just right. So they put glycerin on, you know, so it would look like he was perspiring. Finally . . . this Navajo had to do it so much, that he went up to the director and he took off

his feathers and he said, 'I quit. I'm tired of playing Indian.' And he was an Indian." According to Dorothy, the work Roman Hubbell Navajo Tours did for the movies was among the most lucrative because the rates were determined by the unions.

117. Roman Hubbell to Byron L. Harvey, September 25, 1939, Box 4, Folder 9, Roman Hubbell Papers. Roman Hubbell Navajo Tours, for example, led a total of only six trips from Gallup to points in New Mexico (not including trips to points in Arizona) in 1938. By 1939, the total increased dramatically to twenty-two trips, with a more modest increase to twenty-seven trips in 1940. Untitled fare schedule 1938–1940, n.d. Box 9, Folder 4, Roman Hubbell Papers.

118. Mildred E. Baker to Roman Hubbell, December 11, 1941, Box 4, Folder 3, Roman Hubbell Papers.

119. Roman Hubbell to E. G. Schmiedell, June 4, 1943, Box 114, Folder June 1943, Hubbell Papers.

120. Dorothy Hubbell, interview by David M. Brugge, October 13, 1969, interview 052, transcript, Oral Histories, HUTR.

121. Lorenzo Hubbell, Jr., to Tom and Nell Hubbell, April 25, 1940, Box 112, Folder April 1940, Hubbell Papers.

122. Helen Corcoran to Lorenzo Hubbell, Jr., October 1, 1941, Box 113, Folder October 1941, Hubbell Papers.

123. Tom and Nell Hubbell to Lorenzo Hubbell, Jr., November 12, 1941, Box 113, Folder November 1941, Hubbell Papers.

124. Robert Young quoted in Powers, *Navajo Trading*, 101.

125. Iverson, *Diné*, 182.

126. Ibid.

127. Ibid., 186. For more information about the Navajos in defense industries, see John Westerlund, *Arizona's War Town: Flagstaff, Navajo Ordnance Depot, and World War II* (Tucson: University of Arizona Press, 2003); and John Westerlund, "Bombs from Bellemont: Navajo Ordnance Depot in World War II," *Journal of Arizona History* 42, no. 3 (Autumn 2001): 321–350. For more information about the Navajos' involvement in World War II, see Broderick H. Johnson, *Navajos and World War II* (Tsaile, AZ: Navajo Community College Press, 1977).

128. See rationing records in Box 523, Folder 1; Box 534, Folders 10–11; and Box 535, Folders 1–4, Hubbell Papers.

129. O. Lomavitu to Timothy, January 1, 1942, Box 114, Folder January 1942, Hubbell Papers.

130. M'Closkey, *Swept Under the Rug*, 137; O. Lomavitu to H. Eiser Boot and Saddlery, October 20, 1942, Box 114, Folder September–October 1942, Hubbell Papers; O. Lomavitu to H. L. Hebman's, November 9, 1942, Box 114, Folder November–December, 1942, Hubbell Papers.

131. Roman Hubbell to Selective Service Office, March 11, 1944, Box 115, Folder March 1944, Hubbell Papers.

132. Roman Hubbell to Selective Service System, February 20, 1945, Box 116, Folder January–February 1945, Hubbell Papers.

133. Roman Hubbell to Local Board No. 1, Navajo Country, May 8, 1945, Box 116, Folder May–June 1945, Hubbell Papers.

134. Dorothy Hubbell to Philip, September 27, 1943, Box 115, Folder September–October 1943, Hubbell Papers.

135. Roman Hubbell to Carl Hayden, December 24, 1941, Box 2, Folder 12, Roman Hubbell Papers. The Selective Service called John in March 1941, but rejected him because of his weight and an old heart ailment. After his rejection, John went to school in Buenos Aires, Argentina. See correspondence in Box 1, Folder 5, Roman Hubbell Papers. John returned to Arizona in November 1943 and helped in the family business in early 1944 before he went into the army. See John L. Hubbell to Mrs. Garfield Paltenghe, January 21, 1944, Box 115, Folder January 1944, Hubbell Papers.

136. Dorothy Hubbell to LaCharles Goodman Eckel, June 8, 1944, Box 1, Folder 2, Roman Hubbell Papers.

137. LaCharles Goodman Eckel to Dorothy and Roman Hubbell, December 25, 1944, Box 1, Folder 2, Roman Hubbell Papers.

138. LaCharles Goodman Eckel to Dorothy and Roman Hubbell, December 31, 1944, Box 1, Folder 2, Roman Hubbell Papers.

139. Roman Hubbell to LaCharles Goodman Eckel, March 27, 1944, Box 1, Folder 2, Roman Hubbell Papers.

140. LaCharles Goodman Eckel to Dorothy and Roman Hubbell, December 25, 1944, Box 1, Folder 2, Roman Hubbell Papers.

141. LaCharles Eckel, interview by Lawrence C. Kelly, June 26, 1979, interview 074, transcript, Oral Histories, HUTR.

142. Ibid.

143. Ibid.

144. Dorothy Hubbell, interview by David M. Brugge, October 13, 1969, interview 052, transcript, Oral Histories, HUTR.

145. Iverson, *Diné*, 183–185. Much has been written about Navajo Code Talkers, especially for a popular audience. A good starting point is the classic work, Doris Atkinson Paul, *The Navajo Code Talkers* (Philadelphia: Dorrance, 1973). See also the more recent Adam Adkins, "Secret War: The Navajo Code Talkers in World War II," *New Mexico Historical Review* 72, no. 4 (October 1997): 319–345.

146. Dorothy Hubbell, interview by David M. Brugge, October 13, 1969, interview 052, transcript, Oral Histories, HUTR.

147. For an account of the battle in which Monnie was killed, see Center for Military History, *The Admiralties, Operations of the 1st Cavalry Division, 29 February–18 May 1944* (Washington, DC: Center of Military History, US Army, 1990), 97–117.

148. Roman Hubbell to Jack Verkamp, April 24, 1944, Box 115, Folder April 1944, Hubbell Papers.

149. Blue, *Indian Trader*, 270.

150. Forrest Parker to Lorenzo Hubbell, Jr., April 6, 1936, Box 109, Folder April 1936, Hubbell Papers.

151. Madge Hubbell to Lorenzo Hubbell, Jr., October 25, 1939, Box 111, Folder October 1939, Hubbell Papers.

152. Lorenzo Hubbell, Jr., to Andy Romero, May 2, 1940, Box 112, Folder May 1940, Hubbell Papers.

153. Thomas S. Hubbell to Kee Shelton, November 11, 1939, Box 111, Folder November 1939, Hubbell Papers. See also Thomas S. Hubbell to Emry Kopta, November 9, 1939, Box 111, Folder November 1939, Hubbell Papers.

154. Lorenzo Hubbell, Jr., to Kee Shelton, February 10, 1940, Box 112, Folder February 1940, Hubbell Papers.

155. Helen Corcoran to Lorenzo Hubbell, Jr., January 14, 1941, Box 113, Folder January 1941, Hubbell Papers.

156. Lorenzo described his state of health and mind to Madge Hubbell as follows: "Excuse this short letter, and lack of news, but an honest confession is good for the soul. I hesitate speaking of my self, but I have not and am not well, I lack strength, and swell up as of old but not so much, I get very irritable when I request anything to be done and is not, the Lord knows that I want everything for the greatest number, it irritates me both ways, as most people only figure on commercial values, I want everything to be of human importance, and only wish I bring happiness. I get dizzy at times, so that seldom I can write, as I miss the keys, today I am feeling pretty good, and it pleases that I am able to write this, not so well, but am making a good stab of it." Lorenzo Hubbell to Madge Hubbell, March 19, 1941, Box 113, Folder March 1941, Hubbell Papers. See also Lorenzo Hubbell, Jr., to Treasurer of Coconino County, February 23, 1940, Box 112, Folder 1940, Hubbell Papers; Lorenzo Hubbell, Jr., to Thomas Hubbell, August 15, 1940, Box 112, Folder August 1920, Hubbell Papers.

157. Lorenzo Hubbell, Jr., to L. H. Jr., August 15, 1940, Box 112, Folder August 1940, Hubbell Papers.

158. Lorenzo Hubbell, Jr., to San Diago Rawsin, March 26, 1941, Box 113, Folder March 1941, Hubbell Papers.

159. Lorenzo Hubbell, Jr., to E. Z. Vogt, April 8, 1941, Box 113, Folder April 1941, Hubbell Papers; Lorenzo Hubbell, Jr., to E. Z. Vogt, June 7, 1941, Box 113, Folder June 1941, Hubbell Papers.

160. Lorenzo Hubbell, Jr., to Louis Dysart, July 11, 1941, Box 113, Folder July 1941, Hubbell Papers; Lorenzo Hubbell, Jr., to Louis Dysart, January 2, 1942, Box 114, Folder January 1942, Hubbell Papers

161. Lorenzo Hubbell, Jr., Death Certificate, Box 1, Folder 4, Roman Hubbell Papers.

162. Katherine A. W. to Roman Hubbell, March 7, 1942, Box 1, Folder 4, Roman Hubbell Papers.

163. Wilson J. Nez et. al. to Roman Hubbell, March 4, 1942, Box 1, Folder 4, Roman Hubbell Papers.

164. John Collier, "Lorenzo Hubbell Is Dead," *Indians At Work* 9, no. 7 (March 1942): 3.

165. C. F. Dutton to Roman Hubbell, March 6, 1942, Box 1, Folder 4, Roman Hubbell Papers.

166. Raymond Carlson, "Lorenzo Hubbell, Trader to the Hopi and the Navajo," *Arizona Highways* 13, no. 4 (April 1942): 2.

167. Hubbell Parker to Ned, April 1, 1942, Box 114, Folder April 1942, Hubbell Papers.

168. Roman Hubbell to Dr. Paul M. Wherrit, July 10, 1943, Box 114, Folder June 1943, Hubbell Papers.

169. A copy of Lorenzo's will can be found in Box 1, Folder 4, Roman Hubbell Papers.

170. One letter from LaCharles to Dorothy and Roman in particular hints at the troubles, though it does not enumerate them fully. LaCharles writes, "I agree with you that Forrest's reason for selling a carload of wool all by himself better be good. He'll have a very glib story to tell you—but I'll be a cookie he did it just to prove he doesn't have to consult anybody about anything. I think, too, that he is going to make things as hard as he can for Ganado. If things at Ganado are as bad as they look—it would be a darn good thing if Harry does go after wool season—there is something pretty haywire there. It seems to me much anyone you could get might be better than the present set up—no records of anything seem to have been kept there—so it will be a job to arrive at any figure that is anywhere near right. . . . Personally, I feel that we've been in pretty much of a fog about a whole lot of things. One thing is clear in my mind—if it is decided that Forrest should be thrown out—my vote is certain in favor of it." LaCharles Goodman Eckel to Dorothy and Roman Hubbell, April 27, 1942, Box 114, Folder April 1942, Hubbell Papers. See also Roman Hubbell to C. B. Wilson, May 22, 1942, Box 114, Folder May 1942, Hubbell Papers.

171. Roman Hubbell to LaCharles Goodman Eckel, May 12, 1942, Box 114, Folder May 1942, Hubbell Papers.

172. Roman Hubbell to John Collier, February 21, 1943, Box 7, Folder 10, Roman Hubbell Papers. See also Tomas Hubbell to Dorothy and Roman Hubbell, April 7, 1943, Box 114, Folder April 1943, Hubbell Papers.

173. Roman Hubbell to Lyle and Perry, Attorneys-at-Law, July 19, 1943, Box 114, Folder July 1943, Hubbell Papers.

174. Dorothy Hubbell, interview by David M. Brugge, October 13, 1969, interview 052, transcript, Oral Histories, HUTR.

175. Hall, *West of the Thirties*, 176–177.

## Chapter 9

1. "Traders Face Disaster," *Winslow Mail*, April 2, 1948.

2. Iverson, *Diné*, 217; Powers, *Navajo Trading*, 135. See also Julius A. Krug, *The Navajo: A Long Range Program for Rehabilitation* (Washington, DC: Department of the Interior, 1948).

3. Roman Hubbell to Mr. R. G. Harris, April 2, 1948, Box 119, Folder April 1948, Hubbell Papers.

4. Ibid.

5. Iverson, *Diné*, 216.

6. Ibid.

7. "Traders Face Disaster," *Winslow Mail*, April 2, 1948.

8. Ibid; Roman Hubbell to Mr. R. G. Harris, April 2, 1948, Box 119, Folder April 1948, Hubbell Papers; Roman Hubbell to Sir, April 13, 1948, Box 119, Folder April 1948, Hubbell Papers. Pawn would later come under particular scrutiny with the passage of the Truth in Lending Act in 1969, culminating in a series of lawsuits in the 1970s. See Kiser, "Navajo Pawn," 157–170.

9. Roman Hubbell to Sir, April 13, 1948, Box 119, Folder April 1948, Hubbell Papers.

10. Roman Hubbell to Mr. R. G. Harris, April 2, 1948, Box 119, Folder April 1948, Hubbell Papers.

11. Iverson, *Diné*, 217.

12. The Hubbells were involved in distributing relief goods to the Navajos across the reservation, transporting truckloads of groceries and other goods to trading posts and missions. See Roman Hubbell to Mr. Paul Coze, November 25, 1947, Box 118, Folder November 1947, Hubbell Papers; Roman Hubbell to Paul Jones, December 15, 1947, Box 118, Folder December 1947, Hubbell Papers; Roman Hubbell to Mr. Gordon L'Allemand, December 17, 1947, Box 118, Folder December 1947, Hubbell Papers.

13. Powers, *Navajo Trading*, 106.

14. Iverson, *Diné*, 188. Bailey and Bailey argue that the welfare and other government programs effectively brought "an end to the era of self-sufficiency.... From this time on, the Navajos would in large part be economically dependent on the largess of the United States Congress and the federal bureaucracy." Bailey and Bailey, *History of the Navajos*, 184. See also Powers, *Navajo Trading*, 106–107.

15. Iverson, *Diné*, 189.

16. Roman Hubbell to All Lorenzo Hubbell Trading Posts, May 13, 1946, Box 117, Folder May 1946, Hubbell Papers.

17. Roman Hubbell to Mrs. M. E. Schevill, January 29, 1948, Box 118, Folder January 1948, Hubbell Papers.

18. Roman Hubbell to Clyde Winans, September 27, 1947, Box 118, Folder September 1947, Hubbell Papers.

19. Powers, *Navajo Trading*, 139. For personal accounts from members of the United Indian Traders Association on how trading changed in the second half of the twentieth century, see the online exhibit "Traders: Voices from the Trading Post."

20. Powers, *Navajo Trading*, 139.

21. Ibid., 113.

22. Ibid., 104, 107, 110.

23. Roman Hubbell to Victoria Gift Shop, October 14, 1946, Box 117, Folder October 1946, Hubbell Papers.

24. Roman tried for a while after the war to run the Gallup-based Tours remotely from his new base of operations at Lorenzo's Winslow warehouse, driving for tourists and the Warner Brothers' Western noir picture, *Pursued*, but the Tours required a personal touch and failed to thrive in his absence. Dorothy Smith Hubbell, "Arizona," 348–349; Roman Hubbell to Col. F. Marion Barker, October 5, 1946, Box 117, Folder October 1946, Hubbell Papers.

25. Hartwell, "White Brother," 64.

26. Parker T. Van de Mark to Roman Hubbell, May 10, 1947, Box 118, Folder May 1947, Hubbell Papers.

27. Evelyn Greene, interview by Sandy Nevills Reiff, February 10, 2001, NAU. OH.101.1, transcript, San Juan Oral History Collection.

28. The Sun Valley Trading Post operated mostly in the winter months—Phoenix's tourist season. In 1947, it was located on Central Avenue between Van Buren and Monroe Streets, less than a block from the popular Adams Hotel. In 1948, the trading post reopened on Van Buren, and in 1949 on Harvard Street. See Bill Greene to Roman, November 17, 1947, Box 118, Folder November 1947, Hubbell Papers; Bill Greene to Roman Hubbell, April 17, 1948, Box 119, Folder April 1948, Hubbell Papers; Dorothy Hubbell to A. D. Cochran, April 28, 1948, Box 119, Folder April 1948, Hubbell Papers; Roman to Mrs. A. H. Greene, Jr., June 18, 1948, Box 119, Folder June 1948, Hubbell Papers; Bill Greene to Roman Hubbell, August 8, 1948, Box 119, Folder August 1948, Hubbell Papers; Roman to Bill Greene, Jr., January 26, 1949, Box 119, Folder January 1949, Hubbell Papers; Bill Greene to Roman Hubbell, February 2, 1949, Box 119, Folder February 1949, Hubbell Papers.

29. As Evelyn recalled, after the Greenes closed the shop in Phoenix, Roman asked them to take over the store at Oraibi, which had been left in a monumental mess; it had never been cleaned up properly after Lorenzo's death. She remembers finding piles of Burbank drawings in the corners, gnawed on by mice. Evelyn Greene, interview by Sandy Nevills Reiff, February 10, 2001, NAU.OH.101.1, transcript, San Juan Oral History Collection.

30. Roman Hubbell to A. H. Greene, April 17, 1946, Box 117, Folder April 1946, Hubbell Papers; Roman to Chris Stritzinger, April 26, 1946, Box 117, Folder April 1946, Hubbell Papers.

31. Roman Hubbell to Pat Kelly, March 17, 1951, Box 121, Folder January–March 1951, Hubbell Papers; Roman Hubbell to Robert C. White, June 27, 1950, Box 120, Folder July–August 1950, Hubbell Papers.

32. LaCharles and John both continued to help when possible. See LaCharles Eckel to Dorothy Hubbell, August 19, 1947, Box 118, Folder August 1947, Hubbell Papers; Roman Hubbell to LaCharles Eckel, July 23, 1948, Box 1, Folder 2, Roman Hubbell Papers; Roman Hubbell to John Hubbell, July 7, 1947, Box 118, Folder July 1947, Hubbell Papers.

33. Roman Hubbell to LaCharles Eckel, July 8, 1946, Box 1, Folder 2, Roman Hubbell Papers. Barbara lived there briefly with Mrs. Balcomb and Mrs. Harmon

when she was sick, but lived mostly with Roman and Dorothy at Winslow. Roman Hubbell to LaCharles Eckel, June 15, 1946, Box 1, Folder 2, Roman Hubbell Papers; Roman Hubbell to LaCharles Eckel, July 8, 1946, Box 1, Folder 2, Roman Hubbell Papers.

34. Roman Hubbell to Karl L. Gardner, June 17, 1949, Box 120, Folder June 1949, Hubbell Papers; Roman Hubbell to Margaret Schevill, September 15, 1946, Box 6, Folder 2, Roman Hubbell Papers.

35. Dorothy Hubbell to LaCharles Eckel, July 15, 1952, Box 1, Folder 2, Roman Hubbell Papers.

36. See Roman Hubbell to Mrs. William Hackert, December 20, 1947, Box 118, Folder December 1947, Hubbell Papers; Roman Hubbell to Mr. Eugene Clyde Weafer, May 14, 1949, Box 120, Folder May 1949, Hubbell Papers.

37. Roman Hubbell to Mr. Eugene Clyde Weafer, May 14, 1949, Box 120, Folder May 1949, Hubbell Papers.

38. Roman Hubbell to LaCharles Eckel, June 2, 1949, Box 1, Folder 2, Roman Hubbell Papers.

39. Roman Hubbell to LaCharles Eckel, July 25, 1949, Box 1, Folder 2, Roman Hubbell Papers.

40. "Casa Don Lorenzo, American Plan Only" ephemera, n.d., Box 545, Folder 13, Hubbell Papers.

41. "Casa Don Lorenzo form letter," n.d., Box 121, Folder November–December 1950, Hubbell Papers.

42. Ibid. See also "Casa Don Lorenzo Open to Public This Summer," *Arizona Republic*, May 28, 1950.

43. Froeschauer-Nelson, *Cultural Landscape Report*, under "Decline of the Hubbell Trading Post and Farm (1923–1967)."

44. "Roman Hubbell's Entertain PEO Members At Ganado," *Winslow Mail*, June 9, 1950.

45. "Famous Sculptor Plays Tribute to Arizona," *Winslow Mail*, September 9, 1950.

46. See Roman Hubbell to John F. Jennings, April 21, 1951, Box 121, Folder April–July 1951, Hubbell Papers; Roman Hubbell to Edna E. May, June 30, 1951, Box 121, Folder April–July 1951, Hubbell Papers. When Bob and Betty returned to Scottsdale, the Hubbells continued a business relationship with them in which the Lorenzo Hubbell Trading Company furnished the Dillons with Navajo curios on consignment. Consignment Agreement between Lorenzo Hubbell Company and Robert G. Dillon and Ann E. Dillon, October 1950, Box 10, Folder 3, Roman Hubbell Papers.

47. Evelyn Greene remembered that she and her husband left Roman's employ in 1951 to work for Clarence Wheeler because Roman only paid them $150 a month, plus room and board, as a couple. "He was about to go bankrupt," she said, "but we didn't know that. Of course that had nothing to do with us. He had gone into the car selling business in Winslow and he knew nothing whatsoever about cars, and that's what got him in trouble." Evelyn Greene, interview by Sandy

Nevills Reiff, February 10, 2001, NAU.OH.101.1, transcript, San Juan Oral History Collection.

48. Dorothy Hubbell to LaCharles Eckel, March 11, 1952, Box 1, Folder 2, Roman Hubbell Papers; Roman Hubbell to Connecticut Mutual, March 18, 1952, Box 121, Folder 1952, Hubbell Papers.

49. Blue, *Indian Trader*, 277.

50. I. J. Miller to J. A. Poncel, August 6, 1952, Box 121, Folder 1952, Hubbell Papers. At the time of bankruptcy, the Hubbell assets consisted of the Ganado post and homestead; the Winslow store, including its land, and the Hubbells' residential property there; the Piñon store; the Oraibi store; the Na-Ah-Tee Canyon store and its land; the Marble Canyon store, including 160 acres of land; the Lorenzo Hubbell Motor Company and its land; the Frontier and its land; placer claims in Yavapai; 100 acres of grazing land east of Winslow; and land in St. Johns and Casa Grande. Other assets included various automobiles, furnishings, and equipment, a detailed list of which can be found in "Estate of Roman Hubbell, et al., Bankrupt Partnership Operations Financial Statement," April 1, 1953, Box 499, Folder 2, Hubbell Papers.

51. Roman Hubbell to John Hubbell, November 1, 1952, Box 1, Folder 2, Roman Hubbell Papers.

52. Dorothy Hubbell, interview by Frank McNitt, May 6, 1972, interview VI, transcript, Box 2, Folder 17, Roman Hubbell Papers.

53. Roman Hubbell to Oliver Leland, January 20, 1953, Box 121, Folder 1953–1954, Hubbell Papers. Enrico Menapace, owner of a Buick agency in Gallup, held a twenty thousand dollar mortgage on Ganado at the time of the bankruptcy, and Roman drew up agreements to pay the mortgage in three years from the profits at Ganado.

54. Dorothy Hubbell, interview by David M. Brugge, October 13, 1969, interview 052, transcript, Oral Histories, HUTR.

55. Roman Hubbell to LaCharles Eckel and John Hubbell, April 30, 1953, Box 1, Folder 2, Roman Hubbell Papers.

56. Dorothy Hubbell, interview by Frank McNitt, May 6, 1972, interview VI, transcript, Box 2, Folder 17, Roman Hubbell Papers.

57. Dorothy Hubbell to Mrs. Bagwell, August 20, 1958, Box 121, Folder 1955–1956, Hubbell Papers.

58. Dorothy to Neal G. Trasente, State Tax Commission, March 19, 1957, Box 121, Folder 1957–1959, Hubbell Papers. See also Dorothy to Mrs. B. A. Marx, January 7, 1956, Box 121, Folder 1955–1956, Hubbell Papers.

59. Dorothy Hubbell to Mr. E. Brayton Huguenin, November 15, 1957, Box 121, Folder 1957–1959, Hubbell Papers.

60. Dorothy Hubbell to Mrs. Bagwell, August 20, 1958, Box 121, Folder 1955–1956, Hubbell Papers.

61. Barry Goldwater to Dorothy Hubbell, October 17, 1957, Box 1, Folder 7, Roman Hubbell Papers.

62. Mrs. O. C. Havens to Dorothy Hubbell, October 25, 1957, Box 1, Folder 7, Roman Hubbell Papers.

63. "Famous Indian Trader, Don L. Hubbell, Dies," *Gallup Daily Independent*, October 16, 1957.
64. Dorothy Smith Hubbell, "Arizona," 349.
65. Ibid.
66. Judy Hille, "Sun City Woman Looks Back on 50 Years at Trading Post," newspaper clipping, n.d., Box 9, Folder 134, Plez Talmadge Reilly Collection.
67. Peterson, *Homestead and Farm*, 203–204.
68. Dorothy Hubbell to Mrs. McLeod, November 14, 1957, Box 121, Folder 1957–1959, Hubbell Papers; Dorothy Hubbell to Dora Brahms, December 21, 1957, Box 121, Folder 1957–1959, Hubbell Papers.
69. Dorothy Hubbell to Social Security Administration, January 18, 1963, Box 1221, Folder 1960–1965, Hubbell Papers.
70. Peterson, "Headgates and Conquest," 289.
71. Peterson, *Homestead and Farm*, 121.
72. Dorothy Hubbell to Social Security Administration, January 18, 1963, Box 121, Folder 1960–1965, Hubbell Papers.
73. Peterson, *Homestead and Farm*, 122.
74. Powers, *Navajo Trading*, 131, 125.
75. Dorothy Hubbell to Robert Utley, July 26, 1965, Box 8, Folder 3, Roman Hubbell Papers; Albert L. Platz to Benjamin K. Hess, July 6, 1964, Folder Laundromat, Historical Files, HUTR; Froeschaur-Nelson, *Cultural Landscape Report*, under "Decline of the Hubbell Trading Post and Farm (1923–1967)."
76. Dorothy Smith Hubbell, "Arizona," 351.
77. Dorothy Hubbell to Mrs. Bagwell, August 20, 1958, Box 121, Folder 1955–1956, Hubbell Papers.
78. Ibid.
79. Dorothy Hubbell, quoted in Albert D. Manchester and Ann Manchester, *Hubbell Trading Post National Historic Site: An Administrative History* (Santa Fe, NM: National Park Service, Southwest Cultural Resources Center, 1993), under "The Birth of an Idea," last updated January 22, 2001, http://www.nps.gov/hutr/historyculture/upload/HUTR_adhi.pdf.
80. Dorothy Smith Hubbell, "Arizona," 351.
81. Ibid.
82. Roman Hubbell to David B. Findlay Gallery, March 20, 1956, Box 121, Folder 1955–1956, Hubbell Papers. See also Roman Hubbell to Mr. Charles Eberstadt, June 8, 1955, Box 121, Folder 1955–1956, Hubbell Papers; Roman Hubbell to Mr. Lindley Eberstadt, July 2, 1955, Box 121, Folder 1955–1956, Hubbell Papers; Roman Hubbell to Enrico Menapace, March 17, 1956, Box 121, Folder 1955–1956, Hubbell Papers; Roman Hubbell to Edward Eberstadt and Sons, March 20, 1956, Box 121, Folder 1955–1956, Hubbell Papers; Roman Hubbell to Royal B. Hassrick, March 20, 1956, Box 121, Folder 1955–1956, Hubbell Papers; and Roman Hubbell to Rico Menapace, March 28, 1956, Box 121, Folder 1955–1956, Hubbell Papers.
83. Manchester and Manchester, *Hubbell Trading Post*, under "The Birth of an Idea." Manchester and Manchester provide a fuller account of the process leading

up to the designation of Hubbell Trading Post as a National Historic Site than can be provided here.

84. Edward B. Danson, "Report on the Hubbell Trading Post," June 21, 1965, Folder "H" Miscellaneous, Colton Family Collection. Manchester and Manchester relate a slightly different version of events based on a 1991 interview with Danson. They recount that the Hubbells asked Colton if the Museum of Northern Arizona might be interested in preserving the trading post, and that Colton told them that would be outside the museum's purview. It was only on the drive home that it occurred to Danson that it might be a candidate for the Park Service. Manchester and Manchester, *Hubbell Trading Post*, under "The Birth of an Idea." However, the account in which Danson credits the idea to the Hubbells stems from earlier sources. See Edward B. Danson to Stewart Udall, September 11, 1957, Box 26, Folder 2, Stewart L. Udall Papers.

85. Dorothy Hubbell to Edward B. Danson, August 20, 1957, Box 26, Folder 2, Stewart L. Udall Papers; Dorothy Hubbell to Mrs. Bagwell, August 20, 1958, Box 121, Folder 1955–1956, Hubbell Papers.

86. Dorothy Hubbell to Edward B. Danson, August 20, 1957, Box 26, Folder 2, Stewart L. Udall Papers.

87. Manchester and Manchester, *Hubbell Trading Post*, under "Ned Danson Looks for Help."

88. Utley, *Special Report*, 89. Utley's reasons for recognizing the trading post as a National Historic Site can be found on pp. 89–91.

89. Manchester and Manchester, *Hubbell Trading Post*, under "Robert Utley's Special Report of Hubbell Trading Post, Ganado, Arizona, for The National Survey of Historic Sites and Buildings."

90. Ibid.

91. Ibid.

92. Ibid., under "S. 1871 and H.R. 7279."

93. Ben Cole, "Arizona Loses on Two Attempts to Establish National Monuments," *Arizona Republic*, October 7, 1962.

94. 86 Cong. Rec., 6,150 (March 21, 1960).

95. 86 Cong. Rec., 6,152 (March 21, 1960).

96. Manchester and Manchester, *Hubbell Trading Post*, under "Opposition Arises to the Hubbell Trading Post Legislation."

97. Ibid., under "Inventories and Appraisals."

98. Clinton P. Anderson to Frank McNitt, August 5, 1963, Box 2, Folder 17, Roman Hubbell Papers.

99. Frank McNitt to Clinton P. Anderson, August 9, 1963, Box 2, Folder 17, Roman Hubbell Papers.

100. Frank McNitt to Clinton P. Anderson, August 1, 1963, Box 2, Folder 17, Roman Hubbell Papers.

101. Dorothy wrote Anderson directly in an attempt to correct some of his misconceptions and to invite him personally to visit as her guest. Dorothy Hubbell

to Clinton P. Anderson, July 23, 1965, Box 8, Folder 3, Roman Hubbell Papers. As Manchester and Manchester note, Senator Anderson's objections carried particular weight because he "knew a lot more than the average senator might about Indian arts and crafts and trading posts. And rumor had it that either Anderson himself or a friend of his had been taken advantage of in the purchase of an Indian blanket collection," a rumor that certainly accounts for his reluctance to take the word of the appraisers at face value. Manchester and Manchester, *Hubbell Trading Post*, under "Success."

102. Dorothy Smith Hubbell, "Arizona," 351.

103. Don Dedera, "Ways of Congress Confusing to Many," *Arizona Republic*, July 14, 1965.

104. Dorothy Hubbell to Mrs. Baily, September 28, 1961, Box 121, Folder 1960–1965, Hubbell Papers.

105. Dorothy Hubbell to Bernard L. Fontana, May 25, 1961, Box 121, Folder 1960–1965, Hubbell Papers.

106. Manchester and Manchester, *Hubbell Trading Post*, under "The National Park Service Goes to Work—Roman Hubbell Dies."

107. Edward B. Danson to Stewart Udall, December 2, 1958, Box 26, Folder 2, Stewart L. Udall Papers.

108. Ibid.

109. Bert to Stew, December 8, 1958, Box 26, Folder 2, Stewart L. Udall Papers.

110. Ibid. See also Stewart L. Udall to Edward B. Danson, December 9, 1958, Box 26, Folder 2, Stewart L. Udall Papers.

111. Read Mullan to Dorothy Hubbell, April 14, 1960, Box 8, Folder 3, Roman Hubbell Papers.

112. Manchester and Manchester, *Hubbell Trading Post*, under "Robert Utley's Special Report of Hubbell Trading Post, Ganado, Arizona, for The National Survey of Historic Sites and Buildings."

113. Lester N. Innskeep, July 6, 1962, Box 2, Folder 13, Roman Hubbell Papers. See also correspondence in Box 8, Folders 1–3, Roman Hubbell Papers.

114. Mrs. Linda G. Walker to Dorothy Hubbell, June 19, 1965, Box 3, Folder 5, Roman Hubbell Papers.

115. Ibid.

116. See Harold S. Colton, "The Hubbell Trading Post at Ganado," *Plateau* 30 (April 1958): 85–88; Ed Ellinger, "The Hubbell Trading Post at Ganado," *Arizona Highways* 34 (August 1958): 34–39; Bud DeWald, "The Heritage of Don Lorenzo," *Arizona Days and Ways*, August 3, 1958, 28–31; Edward B. Danson, "Last of the Frontier Merchants: Navajo Still Barter at Ganado, Arizona Trading Post," *National Parks Magazine* (May 1960): 7–9; and Dorothy E. Albrecht, "Vignettes of Arizona Pioneers: John Lorenzo Hubbell, Navajo Indian Trader," *Arizonian* 4, no. 3 (Fall 1963): 33–41. When Ellinger's article was published, Dorothy wrote to Mr. Ralph Lowell that "One of the most pleasant results of the article which appeared in the Arizona Highways is to hear from those who visited here and knew the family in

the early years." Dorothy Hubbell to Mr. Ralph Lowell, August 27, 1958, Box 121, Folder 1957–1959, Hubbell Papers.

117. Mary DuMond, "How the West Is Won—Today," *Arizona Republic*, October 24, 1965.

118. Ibid.

119. Florence Roth, "Work of DAC Pays Off As Hubbell Post To Be Park," *Tempe Daily News*, September 30, 1965; "Women Backing Hubbell Bill," *Phoenix Gazette*, March 5, 1965.

120. "Fine Job," *Arizona Republic*, September 25, 1965; Florence Roth, "Work Of DAC Pays Off As Hubbell Post To Be Park," *Tempe Daily News*, September 30, 1965.

121. For example, Edna Levine, editor of the *Boys and Girls Sunday Republic*, working in cooperation with the DAC, created a Hubbell-themed crossword puzzle and story in May, urging Arizona's youth to help Roy and Rita, the Republic twins, save Hubbell Trading Post by solving the puzzle on a "Magic Olla," and sending in their drawings. Edna Levine, "Save Old Trading Post, Landmark of the West! Clever Puzzle Tale Solvers Please Do Your Best," *Arizona Republic*, May 23, 1965. When the prizes were awarded for the best answers, Levine wrote, "It would have done Don Lorenzo's heart good . . . if he could have seen the hundreds of drawings and posters, the poems and letters that came in response to the call for help to save the old Hubbell Trading Post near Ganado. He would have realized that the memory of his hospitality to all travelers, and the memory of his understanding kindness toward the Indian peoples with whom he dealt, has not been lost in the Arizona land he loved so dearly." Edna Levine, "Prize Winners," *Arizona Republic*, June 27, 1965. See also Orien Fifer, Jr., "Let's Give This Lady A Few Bouquets, Too," *Arizona Republic*, September 29, 1965.

122. DuMond, "How the West Is Won."

123. Don Dedera, "Ways of Congress Confusing to Many," *Arizona Republic*, July 14, 1965.

124. Manchester and Manchester, *Hubbell Trading Post*, under "Success." By this time, the bill had been in Congress so long that it had new champions. With Stewart Udall, Barry Goldwater, and Carl Hayden no longer in Congress, the torch had been taken up by Arizona's new elected officials, Representative George F. Senner, Representative Morris K. Udall, and Senator Paul Fannin.

125. Dorothy Hubbell, "Arizona," 352.

126. DuMond, "How the West Is Won." The DAC placed a bronze plaque at Hubbell Trading Post honoring J. L. Hubbell and marking the site as a National Historic Site in 1969. "Contributions of Hubbell Recognized by New Plaque," *Gallup Independent*, May 21, 1969; "DAC Writes Final Chapter In Saga To Make Hubbell Post Historic Site," *Tempe Daily News*, June 5, 1969.

127. Howard Bryan, "Historic Trading Post Is Dedicated By Udall Who Lauds Hubbell Family," *Albuquerque Tribune*, September 8, 1967.

128. Ibid.

129. Manchester and Manchester, *Hubbell Trading Post*, under "Dedication Ceremony, September 7, 1967." A copy of the program for the dedicatory ceremonies, along with photographs of the proceedings, can be found in Box 137, Folder 5, Stewart L. Udall Papers.

130. Raymond Nakai, "Dedication of Ganado Trading Post," September 7, 1967, Box 5, Folder 48, Raymond Nakai Collection.

131. Edward B. Danson to Stewart Udall, September 11, 1957, Box 26, Folder 2, Stewart L. Udall Papers.

132. Manchester and Manchester, *Hubbell Trading Post*, under "The Origin of the Live Trading Post Concept."

133. Powers, *Navajo Trading*, 127.

134. John Cook recalled that the Navajos reacted to the National Park Service takeover of Hubbell Trading Post in a variety of ways. "There were probably several sets and levels of reactions. The ones affected the most [Dorothy Hubbell's regular customers], very little to no reaction. Primarily because of the fact that Mrs. Hubbell reassured them that, one, their lines of credit would be maintained, that things bad would not happen to them. Secondly, bringing Bill Young along . . . he was no stranger to many of the individuals. Then you had the reaction of some of the tribal leadership, some of whom, as we were in the era of civil rights and the beginning of resurgence of American Indian rights, you got some people really kind of objecting to traders at all. And the National Park Service, the federal government, getting involved in this onerous thing [trading posts] that rips off the American Indian. So you had some negative feelings there. And then you had the Navajo Tribe itself . . . Raymond Nakaai, and later Peter MacDonald . . . who felt that another national park area on or near the reservation would create jobs and bring in money. The chapter people, the Ganado Chapter, they were concerned because they weren't sure what kind of neighbors we were going to be." Quoted in Manchester and Manchester, *Hubbell Trading Post*, under "An Island in the Middle of the Vast Navajo Reservation."

135. Howard Bryan, "Historic Trading Post Is Dedicated by Udall Who Lauds Hubbell Family," *Albuquerque Tribune*, September 8, 1967.

# Bibliography

## Manuscript Collections

Bentley Home Demonstration Papers and Photographs, MS1195. Arizona Historical Society, Tucson, AZ.

Brugge, David M., Manuscript Collection, unprocessed, MSS 770. Center for Southwest Research, University Libraries, University of New Mexico, Albuquerque, NM.

Colton Family Collection, MS 207-1-124. Museum of Northern Arizona, Flagstaff, AZ.

Day Family Collection, NAU.MS.89 and NAU.PH.120.1-88. Cline Library, Special Collections and Archives Department, Northern Arizona University, Flagstaff, AZ.

Ganado Mission Photographs and Sketches f. 1916-1917, PC168. Arizona Historical Society, Tucson, AZ.

Ephemera Files. Arizona Historical Society, Tucson, AZ.

Historical Files. Hubbell Trading Post National Historic Site, Ganado, AZ.

Hubbell Family Papers, 1848-1972, 1975-045. New Mexico Commission of Public Records, State Records Center and Archives, Santa Fe, NM.

Hubbell Family Photograph Collection, Photo 101. New Mexico Commission of Public Records, State Records Center and Archives, Santa Fe, NM.

Hubbell Trading Post Records, 1882-1968 (bulk 1905-1950), AZ 375. University of Arizona Library Special Collections, Tucson, AZ.

Lorenzo Hubbell Collection, MS 133. Museum of Northern Arizona, Flagstaff, AZ.

Lorenzo Hubbell, Jr., Collection, NAU.MS.453. Cline Library, Special Collections and Archives Department, Northern Arizona University, Flagstaff, AZ.

McNitt, Frank, Papers, 1973-024. New Mexico Commission of Public Records, State Records Center and Archives, Santa Fe, NM.

Museum Collections. Hubbell Trading Post National Historic Site, Ganado, AZ.

National Park Service, Denver Service Center, Technical Information Center, Denver, CO.

Navajo Traders Collection, NAU.MS.351. Cline Library, Special Collections and Archives Department, Northern Arizona University, Flagstaff, AZ.
Newcomer Photographs, Indian series, 1926–1968, and Newcomer Portraits, A–L, 1926–1976 (bulk 1950–1969), PC196. Arizona Historical Society, Tucson, AZ.
Oral Histories. Hubbell Trading Post National Historic Site, Ganado, AZ.
Photographs. Hubbell Trading Post National Historic Site, Ganado, AZ.
Plez Talmadge Reilly Collection, NAU.MS.275, NAU.OH.52, NAU.PH.97.46, NAU.VT.93.9, and NAU.MI.93.9. Cline Library, Special Collections and Archives Department, Northern Arizona University, Flagstaff, AZ.
Raymond Nakai Collection, 1963–1988, NAU.MS.386 and NAU.PH.2006.16. Cline Library, Special Collections and Archives Department, Northern Arizona University, Flagstaff, AZ.
Roman Hubbell Family Papers, 1899–1982, MS 322. University of Arizona Library Special Collections, Tucson, AZ.
San Juan Oral History Collection, NAU.OH.101.1. Cline Library, Special Collections and Archives Department, Northern Arizona University, Flagstaff, AZ.
Udall, David K., Papers, 1847–1988, MS 294. University of Arizona Library Special Collections, Tucson, AZ.
Udall, Stewart L., Papers, 1950–2010, AZ 372. University of Arizona Library Special Collections, Tucson, AZ.

## Newspapers

*Albuquerque Journal*
*Albuquerque Tribune*
*Anaconda Standard*
*Arizona Champion*
*Arizona Republic*
*Arizona Republican*
*Arizona Silver Belt*
*Arizona Weekly Journal-Miner*
*Arizona Weekly Republican*
*Bisbee Daily Review*
*Cedar Rapids Evening Gazette*
*Clovis Evening News*
*Cochise Review and Daily Orb*
*Coconino Sun*
*Evening Telegram*
*Gallup Daily Independent*
*Gallup Independent*
*Graham Guardian*

*Latter-day Saints' Millennial Star*
*Lookout*
*Mohave County Miner*
*New Mexico State Tribune*
*New York Times*
*Oakland Tribune*
*Phoenix Gazette*
*Rio Abajo Weekly Press*
*Salt Lake Telegram*
*San Francisco Chronicle*
*Tempe Daily News*
*Tucson Star*
*Washington Post*
*Weekly Arizona Journal-Miner*
*Weekly Arizona Miner*
*Winslow Mail*

### Books and Articles

Abel, Annie Heloise, ed. *Official Correspondence of James S. Calhoun While Indian Agent at Santa Fe and Superintendent of Indian Affairs in New Mexico.* Washington, DC: Government Printing Office, 1915.

Adair, John. *The Navajo and Pueblo Silversmiths.* Norman: University of Oklahoma Press, 1946.

Adams, William Y. *Shonto: A Study of the Role of the Trader in a Modern Navaho Community.* Smithsonian Institution, Bureau of American Ethnology, Bulletin 188. Washington, DC: Government Printing Office, 1963.

Adkins, Adam. "Secret War: The Navajo Code Talkers in World War II." *New Mexico Historical Review* 72, no. 4 (October 1997): 319–345.

Albrecht, Dorothy E. "Vignettes of Arizona Pioneers: John Lorenzo Hubbell, Navajo Indian Trader." *Arizonian* 4, no. 3 (Fall 1963): 33–41.

Amsden, Charles A. *Navaho Weaving: Its Technic and History.* 1934. Reprint, Glorieta, NM: Rio Grande, 1969.

Anderson, Allen A. *The Chief: Ernest Thompson Seton and the Changing West.* College Station: Texas A&M University Press, 1986.

Anderson, Kath M. *Hubbell Trading Post.* Tucson: Southwest Parks and Monuments Association, 1988.

"Annual Report of the Director." *Annual Report of the Director to the Board of Trustees for the Year 1910* 4, no. 1, Publication 150. Chicago: Field Museum of Natural History, 1910.

Armer, Laura Adams. "The Big Snow." *Desert Magazine* 24, no. 4 (April 1961): 18–19.

———. *In Navajo Land.* New York: David McKay, 1962.

———. *Southwest*. London: Longmans, Green, 1935.

———. *Waterless Mountain*. New York: Junior Literary Guild, 1931.

Arreola, Paul R. "George Wharton James and the Indians." *Masterkey* 60, no. 1 (Spring 1986): 11–18.

Ashurst, Henry Fountain. *A Many Colored Toga: The Diary of Henry Fountain Ashurst*. Tucson: University of Arizona Press, 1962.

Baars, Donald L. *Navajo Country: A Geology and Natural History of the Four Corners Region*. Albuquerque: University of New Mexico Press, 1995.

Babbitt, James E. "Trading Posts Along the Little Colorado River." *Plateau* 57, no. 3 (September 1986): 2–9.

Babcock, Barbara A., and Nancy J. Parezo. *Daughters of the Desert: Women Anthropologists and the Native American Southwest, 1880–1980*. Albuquerque: University of New Mexico Press, 1988.

Bahr, Howard M., ed. *The Navajo as Seen by the Franciscans, 1898–1921: A Sourcebook*. Native American Resources Series, no. 4. Lanham, MD: Scarecrow, 2004.

Bailey, Garrick, and Roberta Glenn Bailey. *A History of the Navajos—The Reservation Years*. Santa Fe, NM: School of American Research Press, 1986.

Bailey, Lynn R. *Bosque Redondo: An American Concentration Camp*. Pasadena, CA: Socio-Technical Books, 1970.

Bailey, Lynn R. *The Long Walk: A History of the Navajo Wars, 1846–1868*. Los Angeles: Westernlore, 1964.

———. "Thomas Varker Keam, Tusayan Trader." *Arizoniana* 2, no. 4 (Winter 1961): 15–19.

Ball, Larry D. *Desert Lawmen: The High Sheriffs of New Mexico and Arizona, 1846–1912*. Albuquerque: University of New Mexico Press, 1992.

Barnes, Will C. *Arizona Place Names*. Rev. ed. Tucson: University of Arizona Press, 1960.

Barter, Judith A. *A Window on the West: Chicago and the Art of the New Frontier, 1890–1940*. Chicago: Art Institute of Chicago, 2003.

Bauer, Elizabeth. *Research for a Catalog of the Navajo Textiles of Hubbell Trading Post*. Ganado, AZ: US Department of the Interior, National Park Service, Hubbell Trading Post National Historic Site, 1987.

Baxter, John O. *Las Carneradas: Sheep in New Mexico, 1700–1860*. Albuquerque: University of New Mexico Press, 1987.

———. "Restocking the Navajo Reservation After Bosque Redondo." *New Mexico Historical Review* 58, no. 4 (October 1983): 325–345.

Benedek, Emily. *The Wind Won't Know Me: A History of the Navajo-Hopi Land Dispute*. New York: Knopf, 1992.

Bingham, Edwin R. *Charles F. Lummis: Editor of the Southwest*. San Marino, CA: Huntington Library, 1955.

Blue, Martha. *Indian Trader: The Life and Times of J. L. Hubbell*. Walnut, CA: Kiva, 2000.

———. "A View from the Bullpen: A Navajo Ken of Traders and Trading Posts." *Plateau* 57, no. 3 (September 1986): 10–17.

———. *The Witch Purge of 1878: Oral and Documentary History in the Early Navajo Reservation Years*. Navajo Oral History Monograph Series, no. 1. Tsaile, AZ: Navajo Community College Press, 1988.

Boles, Joann F. "The Development of the Navaho Rug, 1890–1920, As Influenced by Trader J. L. Hubbell." Vols. 1–2. PhD diss., Ohio State University, 1977.

———. "The Navaho Rug at the Hubbell Trading Post, 1880–1920." *American Indian Culture and Research Journal* 5, no. 1 (1981): 47–63.

Boles, Joann, and Lois E. Dickey. "Navajo Rugs: Evolution of the Ganado Style, 1890–1920." *Home Economics Research Journal* 11, no. 1 (September 1982): 98–105.

Bolton, Herbert Eugene, ed. *Spanish Exploration of the Southwest, 1542–1706*. 1908. Reprint, New York: Barnes and Noble, 1946.

Bourdon, Roger Joseph. "George Wharton James: Interpreter of the Southwest." PhD diss., University of California, Los Angeles, 1965.

Bourke, John G. *The Snake Dance of the Moquis of Arizona*. 1884. Reprint, Tucson: University of Arizona Press, 1984.

Boyce, George A. *When the Navajos Had Too Many Sheep: The 1940s*. San Francisco: Indian Historian, 1974.

Boyd, Dennis. "Trading Posts and Weaving: An American-Navajo Symbiosis." Master's thesis, University of Colorado, 1979.

Brinkman, Grover. "Restoration of the Southwest." *Desert Magazine* 41, no. 3 (March 1978): 20–21.

Brandt, Marisa K. "'Necessary Guidance': The Fred Harvey Company Presents the Southwest." PhD diss., University of Minnesota, 2011.

Brooks, James F. *Captives and Cousins: Slavery, Kinship and Community in the Southwest Borderlands*. Chapel Hill: University of North Carolina Press, 2002.

Brown, W. C. *Report Upon Condition of the Navajo Indian Country*. 52nd Cong. 2nd sess. Senate Executive Document 68. Washington, DC: Government Printing Office, 1893.

Browne, Charles Francis. "Elbridge Ayer Burbank: A Painter of Indian Portraits." *Brush and Pencil* 3, no. 1 (October 1898): 16–35.

Brownstein, Elizabeth Smith. *If This House Could Talk: Historic Homes, Extraordinary Americans*. New York: Simon & Schuster, 1999.

Brugge, David M. *Furnishing Study for Historic Building-2, the Hubbell Home*. Ganado, AZ: Hubbell Trading Post National Historic Site, 1972.

———. *Hubbell Trading Post National Historic Site*. Tucson: Southwest Parks and Monuments Association, 1993.

———. "Navajo and Western Pueblo History." *Smoke Signal* 25 (Spring 1972): 89–112.

———. *The Navajo Hopi Land Dispute: An American Tragedy.* Albuquerque: University of New Mexico Press, 1994.

———. *Navajo Pottery and Ethnohistory.* Window Rock, AZ: Navajo Tribal Museum, 1963.

———. "Navajo Prehistory and History to 1850." In *Handbook of North American Indians,* vol. 10: *Southwest,* edited by Alfonso Ortiz, 489–501. Washington, DC: Smithsonian Institution, 1983.

———. *Navajos in the Catholic Church Records of New Mexico, 1694–1875.* Tsaile, AZ: Navajo Community College Press, 1985.

———. "Traditional History of Wide Reeds." In *Wide Reed Ruin: Hubbell Trading Post National Historic Site,* edited by James E. Mount, et al., 121–124. Santa Fe, NM: National Park Service, Southwest Cultural Resources Center, 1993.

Brundige-Baker, Joan. "Restoration and Preservation of Historic Trading Posts." *Plateau* 57, no. 3 (September 1986): 26–31.

Bryan, Nonabah Gorman, Stella Young, and Charles Keetsie Shirley. *Navajo Native Dyes: Their Preparation and Use.* Palmer Lake, CO: Filter, 1978.

Bryant, Kathleen. "Building a Style: Twentieth Century Architecture on the Colorado Plateau." *Plateau* 7, no. 1 (September 2003): 20–39.

Bryant, Keith L. *History of the Atchison, Topeka, and Santa Fe Railway.* New York: Macmillan, 1974.

Bsumek, Erika Marie. *Indian-Made: Navajo Culture in the Marketplace, 1868–1940.* Lawrence: University Press of Kansas, 2008.

Burbank, E. A., Earnest Royce, and Frank J. Taylor. *Burbank Among the Indians.* Caldwell, ID: Caxton, 1944.

Busby, Mark. "Texas and the Great Southwest." In *A Companion to the Regional Literatures of America,* edited by Charles L. Crow, 422–457. Malden, MA: Blackwell, 2003.

Carlson, Raymond. "Lorenzo Hubbell: Trader to the Hopi and the Navajo." *Arizona Highways* 13, no. 4 (April 1942): 2.

Center for Military History. *The Admiralties, Operations of the 1st Calvary Division, 29 February—18 May 1944.* Washington, DC: Center of Military History, US Army, 1990.

Chace, James. *1912: Wilson, Roosevelt, Taft, and Debs: The Election That Changed the Country.* New York: Simon & Schuster, 2004.

Clemmer, Richard O. *Roads in the Sky: The Hopi Indians in a Century of Change.* Boulder, CO: Westview, 1995.

Collier, John. "Lorenzo Hubbell Is Dead." *Indians At Work* 9, no. 7 (March 1942): 3–4.

Collins, William S. *The New Deal in Arizona.* Phoenix: Arizona State Parks Board, 1999.

Colton, Harold S. "The Hubbell Trading Post at Ganado." *Plateau* 30, no. 4 (April 1958): 85–88.

Coolidge, Dane. *Arizona Cowboys*. New York: E. P. Dutton, 1938.
———. *California Cowboys*. Tucson: University of Arizona Press, 1939.
———. *Lorenzo the Magnificent: The Riders from Texas*. New York: E. P. Dutton, 1925.
———. *Texas Cowboys*. New York: E. P. Dutton, 1937.
Coolidge, Dane, and Mary Roberts Coolidge. *The Navajo Indians*. Boston: Houghton Mifflin, 1930.
Correll, J. Lee. *Through White Men's Eyes: A Contribution to Navajo History*. Vols. 1–6. Window Rock, AZ: Navajo Heritage Center, 1979.
Cortés, Enrique. "George Wharton James: Advocate for the Golden State." *Masterkey* 60, no. 1 (Spring 1986): 19–25.
Cotton, C. N., and George Wharton James. *Wholesale Catalogue and Price List of Navajo Blankets*. Pasadena, CA: G. Wharton James, 1896.
Cousins, Jean, Bill Cousins, and Mary Tate Engels. *Tales from Wide Ruins: Jean and Bill Cousins, Traders*. Lubbock: Texas Tech University Press, 1996.
Cowan, John L. "Bedouins of the Southwest." *Out West* 3 (February 1912): 107–116.
Culin, Stewart. "Report on a Collecting Expedition Among the Indians of New Mexico and Arizona." Brooklyn, NY: Department of Primitive Art and New World Cultures, Brooklyn Museum, 1902–1905.
Curtis, Natalie. "Theodore Roosevelt in Hopi-Land: Another Personal Reminiscence." *Outlook*, September 17, 1919, 87–88, 92–93.
Danson, Edward B. "Last of the Frontier Merchants: Navajo Still Barter at Ganado, Arizona Trading Post." *National Parks Magazine* (May 1960): 7–9.
Darnall, Diane Thomas. *The Southwestern Indian Detours: The Story of the Fred Harvey/Santa Fe Railway Experiment in Detourism*. Phoenix, AZ: Hunter, 1978.
Dary, David. *Entrepreneurs of the Old West*. New York: Knopf, 1986.
Davies, Wade. *Healing Ways: Navajo Health Care in the Twentieth Century*. Albuquerque: University of New Mexico Press, 2001.
Dawdy, Doris Ostrander. *Artists of the American West: A Biographical Dictionary*. Chicago: Sage Books, 1974.
DeLauer, Marjel. "A Century of Indian Traders and Trading Posts." *Arizona Highways* 51, no. 3 (March 1975): 6–14.
Denetdale, Jennifer. *Reclaiming Diné History: The Legacies of Navajo Chief Manuelito and Juanita*. Tucson: University of Arizona Press, 2007.
DeWald, Bud. "The Heritage of Don Lorenzo." *Arizona Days and Ways*, August 3, 1958, 28–31.
Dillon, Richard. "Hubbell's Trading Post." *Outdoor Arizona* 48 (August 1976): 21–23.
———. "A Meeting of Two Cultures—Hubbell's Trading Post." *Phoenix* 12 (April 1977): 50–51.
Dilworth, Leah. *Imagining Indians in the Southwest: Persistent Visions of a Primitive Past*. Washington, DC: Smithsonian Institution Press, 1996.

Dixon, Maynard. "Arizona in 1900." *Arizona Highways* 18, no. 2 (February 1942): 16–19, 40.
Dobie, Frank J. *Guide to Life and Literature of the Southwest*. Austin: University of Texas Press, 1943.
Dye, Victoria E. *All Aboard for Santa Fe: Railway Promotion in the Southwest, 1890s to 1930s*. Albuquerque: University of New Mexico Press, 2005.
Dyk, Walter, ed. *Son of Old Man Hat*. 1938. Reprint, Lincoln: University of Nebraska Press, 1967.
Dyk, Walter, and Ruth Van Dyke, eds. *Lefthanded: A Navajo Autobiography*. New York: Columbia University Press, 1980.
Eckel, LaCharles G. "History of Ganado, Arizona." *Plateau* 6, no. 10 (April 1934): 47–50.
Ellinger, Ed. "The Hubbell Trading Post at Ganado." *Arizona Highways* 34, no. 8 (August 1958): 34–39.
Etulain, Richard W. *Re-Imagining the Modern American West: A Century of Fiction, History, and Art*. Tucson: University of Arizona Press, 1996.
Evans, Will. *Along Navajo Trails: Recollections of a Trader, 1898–1948*. Edited by Susan E. Woods and Robert S. McPherson. Logan: Utah State University Press, 2005.
Farish, Thomas Edwin. *History of Arizona*. Vol. 6. Phoenix, AZ: Manufacturing Stationers, 1918.
Faunce, Hilda. *Desert Wife*. Boston: Little, Brown, 1934.
Federal Writers' Project. *Arizona: A State Guide*. 3rd ed. New York: Hastings House, 1940.
Fellin, John Kevin. "The Role of C. N. Cotton in the Development of Northwestern New Mexico." *New Mexico Historical Review* 55, no. 2 (April 1980): 151–156.
Ferriss, James H. "The Navajo Nation." *The Nautilus* 34, no. 1 (July 1920): 1–14.
Fewkes, Jesse Walter. "Archaeological Investigations in New Mexico, Colorado, and Utah." *Smithsonian Museum Collections* 68, no. 1 (May 1917): 1–71.
———. "Tusayan Migration Traditions." In *Nineteenth Annual Report of the Bureau of American Ethnology*, 573–633. Washington, DC: Government Printing Office, 1900.
———. "Two Summers' Work in Pueblo Ruins." In *Twenty-Second Annual Report of the Bureau of American Ethnology*, 1–195. Washington, DC: Government Printing Office, 1904.
Finch, L. Boyd. *Confederate Pathway to the Pacific: Major Sherod Hunter and Arizona Territory, C. S. A*. Tucson: Arizona Historical Society, 1996.
Fiske, Turbese Lummis, and Keith Lummis. *Charles F. Lummis: The Man and His West*. Norman: University of Oklahoma Press, 1975.
Fletcher, Maurine S. *The Wetherills of Mesa Verde: Autobiography of Benjamin Alfred Wetherill*. London: Associated University Press, 1977.
Fontana, Bernard. *Entrada: The Legacy of Spain and Mexico in the United States*. Albuquerque: University of New Mexico Press, 1994.

———. *Querido Patron: Letters from Maynard Dixon to Lorenzo Hubbell.* Tucson: Friends of the University of Arizona Library, 1987.
Forbes, Jack. *Apache, Navaho, and Spaniard.* Norman: University of Oklahoma Press, 1994.
Forrest, Earle R. *Arizona's Dark and Bloody Ground.* Rev. ed. Caldwell: Caxton, 1962.
Fowler, Don D. *A Laboratory for Anthropology: Science and Romanticism in the American Southwest, 1846–1930.* Albuquerque: University of New Mexico Press, 2000.
Franziskaner-Vätern."Die Franziskaner-Mission unter den Navajo-Indianern." *Der Sendbote des Göttlichen Herzens Jesu* 34, no. 4 (April 1907): 313–318.
———. "Die Franziskaner-Mission unter den Navajo-Indianern." *Der Sendbote des Göttlichen Herzens Jesu* 34, no. 5 (May 1907): 410–414.
Fred Harvey Company. *Indian-Detours: Most Distinctive Motor Cruise Service in the World.* Chicago: Rand McNally, 1930.
Fried, Stephen. *Appetite for America: How Visionary Businessman Fred Harvey Built a Railroad Hospitality Empire that Civilized the Wild West.* New York: Bantam Books, 2010.
Frink, Maurice. *Fort Defiance and the Navajos.* Boulder, CO: Pruett, 1968.
Froeschauer-Nelson, Peggy. *Cultural Landscape Report: Hubbell Trading Post National Historic Site, Ganado, Arizona.* Santa Fe, NM: US Department of the Interior, National Park Service, Intermountain Region, 1998. http://www.nps.gov/parkhistory/online_books/hutr/clr/clr.htm.
"From Other Schools and Agencies." *American Indian* 17, no. 1 (January 8, 1916): 30–32.
Garland, Hamlin. "The Bad Medicine Man." *Independent,* December 6, 1900, 2899–2904.
———. "Big Mogassen." *Independent,* November 1, 1900, 2622–2904.
———. *A Daughter of the Middle Border.* New York: Macmillan, 1922.
———. "Delmar of Pima." *McClure's Magazine* 18, no. 4 (February 1902): 340–348.
Gillmor, Frances, and Louisa Wade Wetherill. *Traders to the Navajos: The Story of the Wetherills of Kayenta.* 1934. Reprint, Albuquerque: University of New Mexico Press, 1953.
Gilpin, Laura. *The Enduring Navajo.* Austin: University of Texas Press, 1974.
Goodman, C. W. "In the Hopi Country." *The Native American* 5, no. 35 (October 1908): 332–334.
Graves, Laura. *Thomas Varker Keam: Indian Trader.* Norman: University of Oklahoma Press, 1998.
Gregory, Herbert E. *The Navajo Country: A Geographic and Hydrographic Reconnaissance of Parts of Arizona, New Mexico, and Utah.* Washington, DC: Government Printing Office, 1916.
Hagerty, Donald J. *The Life of Maynard Dixon.* Layton, UT: Gibbs Smith, 2010.
Hall, Edward T. *West of the Thirties: Discoveries Among the Navajo and Hopi.* New York: Doubleday, 1994.

Hamnett, Brian. *A Concise History of Mexico*. 2nd ed. Cambridge: Cambridge University Press, 2006.
Hannum, A. P. *Spin a Silver Dollar: The Story of a Desert Trading Post*. New York: Viking, 1945.
Hartwell, Dickson. "White Brother of the Navajo." *Collier's*, April 30, 1949, 30, 64–65.
Havens, O. C. "Transportation Pioneers." *Arizona Highways* 14, no. 11 (November 1938): 24–25.
Hedlund, Ann Lane. *Beyond the Loom: Keys to Understanding Early Southwestern Weaving*. Boulder, CO: Johnson Books, 1990.
Hegemann, Elizabeth C. *Navajo Trading Days*. Albuquerque: University of New Mexico Press, 1963.
Henderson, Esther, and Church Abbott. "Along The Trading Post Trail." *Arizona Highways* 19, no. 6 (June 1943): 12–19, 41–42.
Herringshaw, Thomas William. *Herringshaw's National Library of American Biography*. Vol. 3. Chicago: American Publishers' Association, 1914.
Hill, Willard Williams. "Navajo Trading and Trading Ritual: A Study of Cultural Dynamics." *Southwestern Journal of Anthropology* 4, no. 4 (Winter 1948): 371–396.
Hilpert, Bruce. "Arizona Goes to the Fair: The World's Columbian Exposition of 1893." *Arizona and the West* 25, no. 3 (Autumn 1983): 261–276.
Hinsley, Curtis M. Jr. *Savages and Scientists: The Smithsonian Institution and the Development of Anthropology, 1846–1910*. Washington, DC: Smithsonian Institution Press, 1981.
Howard, Kathleen L. "Creating an Enchanted Land: Curio Entrepreneurs Promote and Sell the Indian Southwest, 1880–1940." PhD diss., Arizona State University, 2002.
Howard, Kathleen L., and Diana F. Pardue. *Inventing the Southwest: The Fred Harvey Company and Native American Art*. Flagstaff, AZ: Northland, 1996.
Hubbell, Donald Sidney, ed. *Hubbell Pioneers*. Downers Grove, IL: Hubbell Family Historical Society, 1989.
Hubbell, Dorothy Smith. "Arizona." In *Hubbell Pioneers*, edited by Donald Sidney Hubbell, 347–360. Downers Grove, IL: Hubbell Family Historical Society, 1989.
———. "The Days and Nights at the Trading Post." In *This Land, These Voices*, edited by Abe Chanin and Mildred Chanin, 105–111. Tucson, AZ: Milbar Press, 1977.
Hubbell, Harold Berresford, and Donald Sidney Hubbell, eds. *History and Genealogy of the Hubbell Family*. 3rd ed. Brooklyn, NY: Theo. Gaus, 1980.
Hubbell, J. L. *Catalogue and Price List: Navajo Blankets & Indian Curios*. Chicago: Press of Holister Brothers, 1902.
Hubbell, John Lorenzo. "Fifty Years an Indian Trader." As told to John Edwin Hogg. *Touring Topics* 22, no. 12 (December 1930): 24–29, 51.

Hubbell, Mrs. James L. "My Life on a Sheep Ranch." *New Mexico Stockman* 28 (December 1963): 30–31.

Hubbell, Walter. *History of the Hubbell Family, Containing a Genealogical Record.* New York: J. H. Hubbell, 1881.

Iverson, Peter. *Diné: A History of the Navajos.* Albuquerque: University of New Mexico Press, 2002.

———. *For Our Navajo People: Diné Letters, Speeches & Petitions, 1900–1960.* Albuquerque: University of New Mexico Press, 2002.

Ives, Joseph Christmas. *Report upon the Colorado River of the West, Explored in 1857 and 1858. . . .* 36th Cong., 1st sess., House Executive Document 90. Washington, DC: Government Printing Office, 1861.

"J. Lorenzo Hubbell." *Arizona Historical Review* 3, no. 4 (January 1931): 112.

James, George Wharton. *Indian Blankets and Their Makers.* Chicago: A. C. McClurg, 1920.

———. *New Mexico: Land of the Delight Makers.* Boston: Page, 1920.

———. "A Noted Painter of Indian Types." *The Craftsman* 7, no. 3 (December 1904): 280–283.

———. *Our American Wonderlands.* Chicago: A. C. McClurg, 1915.

James, H. L. *Rugs and Posts: The Story of Navajo Weaving and Indian Trading.* West Chester, PA: Schiffer, 1988.

Jeffers, Jo. "Hubbell Trading Post National Historic Site." *Arizona Highways* 43, no. 9 (September 1967): 2–13, 37.

Johnson, Broderick H. *Navajos and World War II.* Tsaile, AZ: Navajo Community College Press, 1977.

Johnson, Broderick H., and Ruth Roessel, eds. *Navajo Stories of the Long Walk Period.* Tsaile, AZ: Navajo Community College Press, 1973

Johnson, Burke. "The Story of Don Lorenzo." *Arizona Days and Ways,* December 26, 1965, 4–11.

Josephy, Alvin M. *The Civil War in the American West.* New York: A. A. Knopf, 1991.

*Journals of the Seventeenth Legislative Assembly of the Territory of Arizona.* Phoenix, AZ: Herald Book and Job Office, 1893.

Judd, Neil M. *Men Met Along the Trail: Adventures in Archaeology.* Norman: University of Oklahoma Press, 1968.

Kastner, Carolyn. "The Trade in Navajo Textiles and Culture at the Hubbell Trading Post." *American Indian Art* 26, no. 2 (Spring 2001): 54–61.

———. "Unraveling a Collection of Nineteenth-Century Navajo Textiles: A Narrative History." PhD diss., Stanford University, 1999.

Kaufman, Alice, and Christopher Selser. *The Navajo Weaving Tradition: 1650 to the Present.* New York: Dutton, 1985.

Kelley, Klara, and Harris Francis. "Indian Giving: Allotments on the Arizona Navajo Railroad Frontier, 1901–1937." *American Indian Culture and Research Journal* 25, no. 2 (2001): 63–91.

———. "Many Generations, Few Improvements: 'Americans' Challenge Navajos on the Transcontinental Railroad Grant, Arizona, 1881–1887." *American Indian Culture and Research Journal* 25, no. 3 (2001): 75–101.

Kelley, Klara B., and Peter M. Whiteley. *Navajoland: Settlement and Land Use*. Tsaile, AZ: Navajo Community College Press, 1989.

Kelly, Lawrence C. *The Navajo Indians and Federal Indian Policy, 1900–1935*. Tucson: University of Arizona Press, 1968.

———. *Navajo Roundup: Selected Correspondence of Kit Carson's Expedition Against the Navajo, 1863–1865*. Boulder, CO: Pruett, 1970.

Kennedy, Mary Jeanette. *Tales of a Trader's Wife: Life on the Navajo Reservation, 1913–1918*. Albuquerque: Valliant, 1965.

Kent, Kate Peck. *Navajo Weaving: Three Centuries of Change*. Santa Fe, NM: School of American Research Press, 1985.

Kildare, Maurice [Gladwell "Toney" Richardson, pseud.]. "The Second Lorenzo, the Great." *Old West* 9 (Summer 1973): 10–13.

Klein, Kerwin L. "Frontier Products: Tourism, Consumerism, and the Southwestern Public Lands, 1890–1990." *Pacific Historical Review* 62, no. 1 (February 1993): 44.

Kluckhohn, Clyde, and Dorothea Leighton. *The Navaho*. Rev. ed. Cambridge, MA: Harvard University Press, 1974.

Knezevic, Srebrica. "Lorenzo Hubbell: Navajo Indian Trader and Friend." In *North American Indian Studies: European Contributions*, edited by Pieter Hovens and Yulia Averkieva, 145–155. Göttingen: Edition Herodot, 1981.

Krenkel, John H., ed. *The Life and Times of Joseph Fish, Mormon Pioneer*. Danville, IL: Interstate, 1970.

Kroeber, A. L. "Native Culture of the Southwest." In *University of California Publications in American Archaeology and Ethnology*, vol. 23, edited by A. L. Kroeber and Robert H. Lowie, 375–398. 1928. Reprint, Berkeley: University of California Press, 1965.

Kropp, Phoebe S. "'There is a little sermon in that': Constructing the Native Southwest at the San Diego Panama-California Exposition in 1915." In *The Great Southwest of the Fred Harvey Company and the Santa Fe Railway*, edited by Marta Weigle and Barbara A. Babcock, 36–46. Phoenix, AZ: Heard Museum, 1996.

Krug, Julius A. *The Navajo: A Long Range Program for Rehabilitation*. Washington, DC: Department of the Interior, 1948.

Lamar, Howard Roberts. *The Far Southwest, 1846–1912: A Territorial History*. Rev. ed. Albuquerque: University of New Mexico Press, 2000.

Lamphere, Louise. "Gladys Reichard Among the Navajo." *Frontiers: A Journal of Women Studies* 12, no. 3 (1992): 78–115.

———. Introduction to *Spider Woman: A Story of Navajo Weavers and Chanters*, by Gladys A. Reichard, v–xxvii. Albuquerque: University of New Mexico Press, 1997.

Lane, Lawrence. "The Family History." *La Bandera de la Casa Hubbell-Gutierrez* 4, no. 3 (September 2007): 1, 4–6, 8–9.
Laut, Agnes C. *Through Our Unknown Southwest.* New York: McBride, Nast, 1913.
Lee, Albert H. *Gaamaliitsoh, Indian Trader: An Autobiography of Albert Hugh Lee, 1897–1976.* Mesa, AZ: Lofgreens, 1982.
Lesley, Lewis Burt. *Uncle Sam's Camels: The Journal of May Humphreys Stacey, Supplemented by the Report of Edward Fitzgerald Beale, 1857–1858.* Cambridge, MA: Harvard University Press, 1929.
Levy, Jerrold E. *In the Beginning: The Navajo Genesis.* Berkeley: University of California Press, 1998.
Lockwood, Frank C. "More Arizona Characters." *University of Arizona General Bulletin*, no. 6. Tucson: University of Arizona, 1943.
———. *Pioneer Portraits: Selected Vignettes.* Tucson: University of Arizona Press, 1968.
———. *The Life of Edward E. Ayer.* Chicago: A. C. McClurg, 1929.
Loscher, Tricia. "The Volz Collection of Hopi Katsina Dolls at the Heard Museum." *American Indian Art Magazine* 30, no. 3 (Summer 2005): 78–88.
Lowell, Susan. *Navajo Rug Designs.* Look West Series. Tucson: Rio Nuevo, 2005.
Lummis, Charles F. "The Artist's Paradise." *Out West* 29, no. 3 (September 1908): 173–192.
———. *Mesa, Cañon and Pueblo.* New York: D. Appleton-Century, 1938.
———. "Painting the First Americans: Burbank's Indian Portraits." *Land of Sunshine* 12, no. 6 (May 1900): 332–343.
———. "The Swallow's-Nest People." *Out West* 26, no. 6 (June 1907): 485–506.
———. *A Tramp Across the Continent.* New York: Charles Scribner's Sons, 1892.
Lyon, William H. "Americans and Other Aliens in the Navajo Historical Imagination in the Nineteenth Century." *American Indian Quarterly* 24, no. 1 (Winter 2000): 142–161.
———. "The Navajos in the Anglo-American Historical Imagination, 1807–1870." *Ethnohistory* 43, no. 3 (Summer 1996): 483–509.
Manchester, Albert D., and Ann Manchester. *Hubbell Trading Post National Historic Site: An Administrative History.* Santa Fe, NM: National Park Service, Southwest Cultural Resources Center, 1993. Last updated January 22, 2001. http://www.nps.gov/hutr/historyculture/upload/HUTR_adhi.pdf.
Masich, Andrew Edward. *The Civil War in Arizona: The Story of the California Volunteers, 1861–1865.* Norman: University of Oklahoma Press, 2006.
Maurer, Stephen G. "In the Heart of the Great Freedom: George Wharton James and the Desert Southwest." *Masterkey* 60, no. 1 (Spring 1986): 4–10.
Mayfield, Harriet. "Great Southwest Pioneer Passes On." *The Santa Fe Magazine* 25, no. 2 (January 1931): 29–33.
McClintock, James H. *Arizona: Prehistoric—Aboriginal—Pioneer—Modern; The Nation's Youngest Commonwealth Within a Land of Ancient Culture.* Vol. 2. Chicago: S. J. Clarke, 1916.

———. *Mormon Settlement in Arizona: A Record of Peaceful Conquest of the Desert.* Phoenix, AZ: Manufacturing Stationers, 1921.
McLerran, Jennifer. *A New Deal for Native Art: Indian Arts and Federal Policy, 1933–1943.* Tucson: University of Arizona Press, 2009.
M'Closkey, Kathy. "Marketing Multiple Myths: The Hidden History of Navajo Weaving." *The Journal of the Southwest* 36, no. 3 (Autumn 1994): 185–220.
———. *Swept Under the Rug: A Hidden History of Navajo Weaving.* Albuquerque: University of New Mexico Press, 2002.
———. Kathy. "Weaving and Mothering: Reframing Navajo Weaving as Recursive Manifestations of K'e." In *Transgressing Borders: Critical Perspectives on Gender, Household, and Culture,* edited by Susan Ilcan and Lynne Phillips, 115–128. Westport, CT: Bergin & Garvey, 1998.
McLuhan, T. C., and William E. Kopplin. *Dream Tracks: The Railroad and the American Indian, 1890–1930.* New York: Abrams, 1985.
McNitt, Frank. *The Indian Traders.* Norman: University of Oklahoma Press, 1962.
———. *Navajo Wars: Military Campaigns, Slave Raids and Reprisals.* Albuquerque: University of New Mexico Press, 1972.
———. *Richard Wetherill: Anasazi.* Albuquerque: University of New Mexico Press, 1957.
McPherson, Robert S. "*Naalye'he Ba' Hooghan:* 'Home of Merchandise,' The Navajo Trading Post as an Institution of Cultural Change, 1900–1930." *American Indian Culture and Research Journal* 16, no. 1 (November 1992): 23–44.
———. "*Ricos* and *Pobres:* Wealth Distribution on the Navajo Reservation in 1915." *New Mexico Historical Review* 60, no. 4 (October 1985): 415–434.
Mercer, Bill. Introduction to *American Indian Portraits: Elbridge Ayer Burbank in the West, 1897–1910,* edited by M. Melissa Wolfe, 9–11. Youngstown, OH: Butler Institute of American Art, 2000.
Meyn, Susan L. *More Than Curiosities: A Grassroots History of the Indian Arts and Crafts Board and Its Precursors, 1920–1942.* Lanham, MD: Lexington Books, 2001.
Miller, Darlis A. "Hispanos and the Civil War in New Mexico: A Reconsideration." *New Mexico Historical Review* 54, no. 2 (April 1979): 105–123.
Miller, Edgar K. "The Indian and the Trader." *Indian School Journal* 7, no. 9 (July–September 1907): 11–19.
———. "Pen and Camera in Tusayan: Part I." *Indian School Journal* 7, no. 2 (December 1906): 11–20).
———. "Pen and Camera in Tusayan: Part II." *Indian School Journal* 7, no. 4 (February 1907): 11–27.
Miller, Jimmy H. *The Life of Harold Sellers Colton: A Philadelphia Brahmin in Flagstaff.* Tsaile, AZ: Navajo Community College Press, 1991.
Miller, Mark E. "St. Johns's Saints: Interethnic Conflict in Northeastern Arizona, 1880–85." *Journal of Mormon History* 23, no. 1 (Spring 1997): 66–99.

Mitchell, Rose. *Tall Woman: The Life Story of Rose Mitchell, A Navajo Woman, c. 1874–1977.* Edited by Charlotte J. Frisbie. Albuquerque: University of New Mexico Press, 2001.
Mooney, James. "Recent Archaeologic Find in Arizona." *American Anthropologist* 6, no. 3 (July 1893): 283–284.
Moore, Laura Jane. "Elle Meets the President: Weaving Navajo Culture and Commerce in the Southwestern Tourist Industry." *Frontiers: A Journal of Women Studies* 22, no. 1 (2001): 21–44.
Morris, Ann Axtell. *Digging in the Southwest.* Garden City, NY: Doubleday, Doran, 1934.
Mott, Dorothy Challis. "Don Lorenzo Hubbell of Ganado." *Arizona Historical Review* 4 (April 1931): 45–51.
Mount, James E., et al. *Wide Reed Ruin: Hubbell Trading Post National Historic Site.* Santa Fe, NM: National Park Service, Southwest Cultural Resources Center, 1993.
Munk, J. A. "The Moqui Snake Dance." *California Eclectic Medical Journal* 8, no. 10 (October 1915): 247–249.
———. *Southwest Sketches.* New York: G. P. Putnam's Sons, 1920.
Navajo Nation Museum. *Diné Ndaashchąągo Beʼelyuu, Portraits of the People: E. A. Burbank at Hubbell Trading Post.* Window Rock, AZ: Navajo Nation Museum, 2001.
Neff, Emily Ballew. *The Modern West: American Landscapes, 1890–1950.* New Haven, CT: Yale University Press in association with the Museum of Fine Arts, Houston, 2006.
*Notables of the West: Being the Portraits and Biographies of the Progressive Men of the West Who Have Helped in the Development and History Making of This Wonderful Country.* Vol. 2. Press Reference Library, Western Edition. New York: International News Service, 1915.
Olsen, Stanley J., and John Beezley. "Domestic Food Animals from Hubbell Trading Post." *Kiva* 41, no. 2 (Winter 1975): 201–206.
O'Neill, Colleen M. *Working the Navajo Way: Labor and Culture in the Twentieth Century.* Lawrence: University Press of Kansas, 2005.
Padget, Martin. *Indian Country: Travels in the American Southwest, 1840–1935.* Albuquerque: University of New Mexico Press, 2004.
Palmer, Frank M. "Among the Cliff Dwellers." *Bulletin of the Archaeological Institute of America* 3 (1907): 32–40.
Parezo, Nancy J., and Don D. Fowler. *Anthropology Goes to the Fair: The 1904 Louisiana Purchase Exposition.* Lincoln: University of Nebraska Press, 2007.
Parman, Donald L. *The Navajos and the New Deal.* New Haven, CT: Yale University Press, 1976.
Paul, Doris Atkinson. *The Navajo Code Talkers.* Philadelphia: Dorrance, 1973.
Patera, Alan H., and John S. Gallagher. *Arizona Post Offices.* Lake Grove, OR: Depot, 1988.

Pearson, J. Diane. "Developing Reservation Economies: Native American Teamsters, 1857–1921." *Journal of Small Business and Entrepreneurship* 18, no. 2 (Spring 2005): 153–170.

Peterson, Charles S. "Big House at Ganado: New Mexican Influence in Northern Arizona." *Journal of Arizona History* 30 (Spring 1989): 51–72.

———. *Farmlands History, Part One: Water, Crops; Hubbell Trading Post National Historic Site, Arizona*. Globe, AZ: Southwest Parks and Monuments Association, 1983.

———. "Headgates and Conquest: The Limits of Irrigation on the Navajo Reservation, 1880–1950." *New Mexico Historical Review* 68, no. 3 (July 1993): 269–290.

———. *Homestead and Farm: A History of Farming at the Hubbell Trading Post National Historic Site*. Globe, AZ: Southwest Parks and Monuments Association, 1986.

Pharo, Agnes M. "Don of Ganado," *Old West* 9 (Summer 1973): 6–9.

Poling-Kempes, Lesley. *The Harvey Girls: Women Who Opened the West*. New York: Paragon House, 1989.

Powers, Willow Roberts. *Navajo Trading: The End of an Era*. Albuquerque: University of New Mexico Press, 2001.

"Recent Progress in Anthropology: George G. Heye." *American Anthropologist* 8, no. 3 (July–September 1906): 537–539.

Reeve, Frank D. "The Government and the Navajo, 1878–1883." *New Mexico Historical Review* 16, no. 3 (July 1941): 275–312.

———. "The Government and the Navajo, 1883–1888." *New Mexico Historical Review* 18, no. 1 (January 1943): 17–51.

Reeve, Frank D., Eleanor B. Adams, and John L. Kessell. *Navajo Foreign Affairs, 1795–1846*. Tsaile, AZ: Navajo Community College Press, 1983.Reichard, Gladys A. *Dezbah: Woman of the Desert*. New York: J. J. Augustin, 1939.

———. "Fifty Thousand Signposts." *New Mexico Magazine* 17 (March 1939): 18–19, 32–33.

———. *Navajo Shepherd and Weaver*. New York: J. J. Augustin, 1936.

———. *Navajo Trader*. Edited by Philip Reed Rulon. Tucson: University of Arizona Press, 1986.

———. *Spider Woman: A Story of Navajo Weavers and Chanters*. Albuquerque: University of New Mexico Press, 1997.

Richardson, Gladwell. "Bonanza in the Ghost Post." *Desert Magazine* 29 (July 1966): 12–15.

Richardson, Toney. "Pioneer Trader to the Navajo." *Desert Magazine* 12 (December 1948): 26–29.

Rigby, Elizabeth. "Blue Canyon." *Arizona Highways* 35, no. 8 (August 1959): 30–39.

Rister, C. C. "Harmful Practices of Indian Traders of the Southwest, 1865–1876." *New Mexico Historical Review* 4, no. 3 (July 1931): 231–248.

Rittenhouse, Jack D. *A Guide Book to Highway 66*. Albuquerque: University of New Mexico Press, 1946.

Roberts, Willow. *Stokes Carson: Twentieth-Century Trading on the Navajo Reservation.* Albuquerque: University of New Mexico Press, 1987.
Robinson, William J. "A Construction Sequence for Hubbell Trading Post and Residence." *Kiva* 50, no. 4 (1985): 219–236.
Rodee, Marian E. *Old Navajo Rugs: Their Development from 1900 to 1940.* Albuquerque: University of New Mexico Press, 1981.
———. *One Hundred Years of Navajo Rugs.* Albuquerque: University of New Mexico Press, 1995.
Roosevelt, Theodore. "Across the Navajo Desert." *Outlook,* October 11, 1913, 309–317.
———. "Cougar Hunt on the Rim of the Grand Canyon." *Outlook,* October 4, 1913, 259–266.
———. "The Hopi Snake Dance." *Outlook,* October 18, 1913, 365–373.
Rothman, Hal K. *Navajo National Monument: A Place and Its People.* Santa Fe, NM: National Park Service, Southwest Cultural Resources Center, 1991.
Russell, Scott C. "The Navajo and the 1918 Influenza Pandemic." In *Health and Disease in the Prehistoric Southwest,* edited by Charles F. Merbs, Robert J. Miller, and Elizabeth S. Dyer Alcauskas, 380–390. Tempe: Arizona State University Press, 1985.
Salsbury, Cora B. *Forty Years in the Desert: A History of Ganado Mission, 1901–1941.* Chicago: Press of Physicians' Record, 1941.
Salsbury, Clarence G., with Paul Hughes. *The Salsbury Story: A Medical Missionary's Lifetime of Public Service.* Tucson: University of Arizona Press, 1969.
Saunders, Charles Francis. *Finding the Worth While in the Southwest.* New York: Robert M. McBride, 1918.
Schmedding, Joseph. *Cowboy and Indian Trader.* Albuquerque: University of New Mexico Press, 1974.
Schroeder, Albert H., ed. *The Changing Ways of Southwestern Indians: A Historical Perspective.* Glorieta, NM: Rio Grande, 1973.
Scott, Julian. "Report on the Moqui Pueblos of Arizona." In *Moqui Pueblo Indians of Arizona and Pueblo Indians of New Mexico,* edited by Thomas Donaldson, 51–68. Washington, DC: US Census Printing Office, 1893.
Shaffer, Marguerite S. *See America First: Tourism and National Identity, 1880–1940.* Washington, DC: Smithsonian Books, 2001.
Sheridan, Thomas E. *Arizona: A History.* Tucson: University of Arizona Press, 1995.
Simmons, Marc. *Albuquerque: A Narrative History.* Albuquerque: University of New Mexico Press, 1982.
Simpson, James H. *Navaho Expedition: Journal of a Military Reconnaissance From Santa Fe, New Mexico, to the Navajo Country, Made in 1849 by Lieutenant James H. Simpson.* Edited by Frank McNitt. Norman: University of Oklahoma Press, 1964.
Sitgreaves, Lorenzo. *Report of an Expedition Down the Zuni and Colorado Rivers.* Washington, DC: Robert Armstrong Public Printer, 1853.

Smith, Joseph Emerson. "Navajo Art Patron Dead." *El Palacio* 29 (December 1930): 371–377.
Smith, Mrs. White Mountain. "He is our Friend." *Desert Magazine*, 4, no. 1 (November 1940): 7–10.
Smith, Thomas Brent, and Donald J. Hagerty. *A Place of Refuge: Maynard Dixon's Arizona*. Tucson, AZ: Tucson Museum of Art and Historic Block, 2008.
Starr, Kevin. *Inventing the Dream: California through the Progressive Era*. New York: Oxford University Press, 1985.
Sullivan, Susan Marie. "Many Brushes: Elbridge Ayer Burbank, Painter of Indian Portraits." Master's thesis, University of San Diego, 1983.
Szuter, Christine R. "A Faunal Analysis of Home Butchering and Meat Consumption at the Hubbell Trading Post, Ganado, Arizona." In *Images of the Recent Past: Readings in Historical Archaeology*, edited by Charles E. Orser, Jr., 333–354. Walnut Creek, CA: AltaMira, 1996.
Taylor, John. *Bloody Valverde: A Civil War Battle on the Rio Grande, February 21, 1862*. Albuquerque: University of New Mexico Press, 1995.
Theobald, John and Lillian. *Arizona Territory Post Offices and Postmasters*. Phoenix: Arizona Historical Foundation, 1961.
Thompson, Gerald. *The Army and the Navajo: The Bosque Redondo Reservation Experiment, 1863–1868*. Tucson: University of Arizona Press, 1976.
Thompson, Mark. *American Character: The Curious Life of Charles Fletcher Lummis and the Rediscovery of the Southwest*. New York: Arcade, 2001.
Tisdale, Shelby J. "Railroads, Tourism, and Native Americans in the Greater Southwest." *Journal of the Southwest* 38, no. 4 (Winter 1996): 433–462.
Towner, Ronald H., ed. *The Archaeology of Navajo Origins*. Salt Lake City: University of Utah Press, 1996.
Trafzer, Clifford E. *The Kit Carson Campaign: The Last Great Navajo War*. Norman: University of Oklahoma Press, 1982.
———. "Sam Day and His Boys: Good Neighbors to the Navajos." *Journal of Arizona History* 18, no. 1 (Spring 1977): 1–22.
Travis, Tara. "Spider Woman's Grand Design: Making Native American Women Visible in Southwestern History Sites." In *Her Past Around Us: Interpreting Sites for Women's History*, edited by Polly Welts Kaufman and Katharine T. Corbett, 69–86. Malabar, FL: Krieger, 2003.
Trennert, Robert A. *Indian Traders on the Middle Border: The House of Ewing, 1827–54*. Lincoln: University of Nebraska Press, 1981.
———. *White Man's Medicine: Government Doctors and the Navajo, 1863–1955*. Albuquerque: University of New Mexico Press, 1998.
*The Twenty-first Year of the Brooklyn Institute of Arts and Sciences, 1908–1909*. Brooklyn, NY: Brooklyn Institute of Arts and Sciences, 1909.
Twitchell, Ralph Emerson. *The Leading Facts of New Mexican History*. Vol. 2. Albuquerque: Horn and Wallace, 1963.
Ulph, Owen. "A Dedication to the Memory of Dane Coolidge, 1873–1940." *Journal of the Southwest* 23, no. 1 (Spring 1981): 1–4.

United Indian Traders Association. "Traders: Voices from the Trading Post." Cline Library, Special Collections and Archives Department, Northern Arizona University. Accessed August 30, 2012. http://library.nau.edu/speccoll/exhibits/traders/index.html.

Underhill, Lonnie E., and Daniel F. Littlefield Jr., eds. *Hamlin Garland's Observations on the American Indian, 1895–1905.* Tucson: University of Arizona Press, 1976.

Underhill, Ruth. *The Navajos.* Norman: University of Oklahoma Press, 1956.

US Postal Service. *The United States Postal Service: An American History 1775–2006.* Washington, DC: Government Relations, United States Postal Service, 2007. https://about.usps.com/publications/pub100.pdf.

Utley, Robert M. *Special Report on Hubbell Trading Post, Ganado, Arizona.* Santa Fe, NM: US Deptartment of the Interior, National Park Service, 1959.

———. "The Reservation Trader in Navajo History." *El Palacio* 68, no. 1 (1961): 5–27.

Van Valkenburg, Richard F. "Tom Keam, Friend of the Moqui." *Desert Magazine* 9, no. 9 (July 1946): 9–12.

Weston, Mary Ann. *Native Americans in the News: Images of Indians in the Twentieth Century Press.* Westport, CT: Greenwood, 1996.

Wagner, Sallie. *Wide Ruins: Memories From a Navajo Trading Post.* Albuquerque: University of New Mexico Press, 1997.

Wagoner, Jay J. *Arizona Territory, 1863–1912: A Political History.* Tucson: University of Arizona Press, 1970.

Walker, J. G., and O. L. Shepherd. *The Navajo Reconnaissance: A Military Exploration of the Navajo Country in 1859.* Edited by L. R. Bailey. Los Angeles: Westernlore, 1964.

Warner, Ted J., ed. *The Dominguez-Escalante Journal: Their Expedition Through Colorado, Utah, Arizona, and New Mexico in 1776.* Salt Lake: University of Utah Press, 1995.

Weigle, Marta. "From Desert to Disney World: The Santa Fe Railway and the Fred Harvey Company Display the Indian Southwest." *Journal of Anthropological Research* 45, no. 1 (Spring 1989): 115–137.

Weigle, Marta, and Barbara A. Babcock. *The Great Southwest of the Fred Harvey Company and the Santa Fe Railway.* Phoenix, AZ: Heard Museum, 1996.

Weisiger, Marsha. *Dreaming of Sheep in Navajo Country.* Seattle: University of Washington Press, 2009.

———. "The Origins of Navajo Pastoralism." *Journal of the Southwest* 46, no. 2 (Summer 2004): 253–282.

———. "Gendered Injustice: Navajo Livestock Reduction in the New Deal Era." *Western Historical Quarterly* 38, no. 4 (Winter 2007): 437–455.

Weiss, Lawrence David. *The Development of Capitalism in the Navajo Nation: A Political-Economic History.* Minneapolis: MEP, 1984.

Welsh, Herbert. *Report of a Visit to the Navajo, Pueblo, and Hualapais Indians of New Mexico and Arizona.* Philadelphia: Indian Rights Association, 1885.

"The West Went East: The Hubbell Trading Post at NYC's Gallery 10." *Journal of the West* 22, no. 4 (October 1983): 84–85.

Westerlund, John. *Arizona's War Town: Flagstaff, Navajo Ordnance Depot, and World War II.* Tucson: University of Arizona Press, 2003.

———. "Bombs from Bellemont: Navajo Ordnance Depot in World War II." *Journal of Arizona History* 42, no. 3 (Autumn 2001): 321–350.

Wheat, Joe Ben. *The Gift of Spiderwoman: Southwestern Textiles, the Navajo Tradition.* Philadelphia: University Museum, University of Pennsylvania, 1984.

Wheat, Joe Ben, and Ann Lane Hedlund. *Blanket Weaving in the Southwest.* Tucson: University of Arizona Press, 2003.

Whipple, Amiel. *A Pathfinder of the Southwest: The Itinerary of Lieutenant A. W. Whipple During His Explorations for a Railway Route from Fort Smith to Los Angeles in the Years 1853 & 1854.* Edited by Grant Foreman. Norman: University of Oklahoma Press, 1941.

Whiteley, Peter M. *Deliberate Acts: Changing Hopi Culture Through the Oraibi Split.* Tucson: University of Arizona Press, 1988.

Wild, Peter. *George Wharton James.* Boise State University Western Writers Series, no. 93. Boise, ID: Boise State University, 1990.

Wilkins, David E. *The Navajo Political Experience.* Rev. ed. Lanham, MD: Rowman & Littlefield, 2003.

Wilkins, Teresa J. *Patterns of Exchange: Navajo Weavers and Traders.* Norman: University of Oklahoma Press, 2008.

Williams, Lester L. *C. N. Cotton and His Navajo Blankets: A Biography of C. N. Cotton.* Albuquerque: Avanyu, 1989.

Winslowe, John R. "Navajo Traders for Many Moons." *True West* 16 (March–April 1969): 10–14, 63–69.

Wolfe, M. Melissa. *American Indian Portraits: Elbridge Ayer Burbank in the West (1897–1910).* Youngston, OH: Butler Institute of American Art, 2000.

Woodward, Arthur. *A Brief History of Navajo Silversmithing.* Flagstaff: Northern Arizona Society of Science and Art, 1938.

Yost, Billie Williams. *Bread upon the Sands.* Caldwell, ID: Caxton, 1958.

# Index

Adakai (Navajo), 105
Advertising: and curio trade development, 125–30; and southwestern tourism, 124, 136, 144–45; and Hubbell Trading Post, 12, 129, 176, 216–19, 277n33, 278n38, 281n86; and Roman Hubbell Navajo Tours, 201–2
Albuquerque, N.Mex., 10; and C. N. Cotton, 43; Hubbell home in, 66–68, 74–76, 96, 151; and J. L., 10–11, 31; as shipping hub, 58; as tourist destination, 137, 140–41, 143
Aldrich, Stephen E., 246n40
Altnaba (Miguelito's daughter), 181
Alvarado Hotel, 137–38, 140, 143. *See also* Fred Harvey Company
American Anthropological Association, 158
American Museum of Natural History, 181–82, 285n164
Ancestral Puebloans, 35, 64
Anderson, Clinton P., 228–29, 314n101
anthropology: and cultural relativism, 180; and evolutionary theories, 155–56, 180; exhibits of Indian life, 142–43, 147; negative impact of, 289n29; of Southwestern Indians, 155–59, 180–83, 283n22, 301n52
antimodernism, 127–29, 135, 185

Apache County, Ariz., 46–49, 250n100; politics, 78, 80, 146. *See also* St. Johns, Ariz.
Apaches, 14, 24, 35, 143, 165; conflicts with Navajos, 35
Apaches de Nabajó, 15, 238n24. *See also* Navajos
Arbuckle coffee, 57, 71
archaeology, 173; negative impact of, 286n169, 289n29; in the Southwest, 14, 33–35, 155, 224, 238n22, 285n164, 289n33
*Arizona Highways*, 147
Arizona Navajo Indian Rug Co., 109–10, 117
Arizona Republican Central Committee, 80
Arizona statehood, 78–81, 260n33
Arizona Territorial and State Fair, 146
Arizona Unlimited, 146–47
Armer, Laura Adams, 180, 182–83; and Big Snow, 188; *The Mountain Chant*, 182; *Waterless Mountain*, 183
Armijo, Elias H., 89, 263n75
Armijo, Rafael (nephew), 115, 117
Arny, William F. M., 30, 38
art collection, 3–5, 153–54, 163–64, 167, 226; efforts to sell, 208–9, 220, 224–25, 227–28, 293n90; rug paintings, 133, 167

artists: as employees and blanket dealers, 133, 164, 167, 292n87; as Hubbell guests, 68, 122, 152, 154, 159, 163–65, 172, 183; and tourism development, 135–36, 152. *See also* Burbank, Elbridge Ayer; Dixon, Maynard
Arts and Crafts Movement, 128
Ashi (Navajo), 182
Ashurst, Henry Fountain, 180, 189
assimilation, 21, 24, 26, 45, 52, 64, 190, 223
Aszá' né z (Navajo wife), 256n101
Atchison, Topeka & Santa Fe Railway: advertising, 135–36; and Fred Harvey Company, 137, 141, 145, 200
Athabaskans. *See* Navajos; Apaches
Atlantic and Pacific Railway, 43, 58
Austin, Mary, 169
automobiles, 104; and Hubbell freight business, 87–90, 263n75; and modernization of Indian trading, 112–13, 183, 215; and tourism, 148–49, 152, 154, 183, 200–202, 219
Awatovi, Ariz., 239n25
Ayer, Edward E., 165, 168

Babbitt Brothers, 87, 221
Baca, Cristóbal, 13
Baca, Luis, 13
Balcomb, Dora Winnie, 217–18, 310n33
Balcomb, Pete, 217–18
Bandelier, Adolph, 154, 158
Barboncito (Navajo), 23, 25–26
Barnart, Miss (teacher), 115
Barth, Solomon, 47
Barth Brothers, 254n56
baskets. *See* Navajo arts and crafts
Benavides, Alonso de, 238n24
Benjamin, Harry, 76
Betts, Harold Harrington, 179, 291n63
BIA. *See* Bureau of Indian Affairs

Bidáya łaní Bici' (Navajo wife), 256n101
Bierkemper, Charles H., 263n76, 264n96
Big Snow, the, 187–89
Bigue, Adeltoni No. 1, 106–7, 269n46
Bigue, Adeltoni No. 2, 106–7, 269n46
Black Mountain post, 83, 87, 101, 262n57
blankets. *See* Navajo rugs and blankets
Blue Canyon, Ariz., 182
Blue Canyon post, 63, 255n64
Board of Supervisors of Apache County, 48
Boas, Franz, 180
book collection, 155, 158, 295n136
Bosque Redondo, 12, 24–26, 35; effects on Navajo economy, 12, 26–28, 37, 42, 125
Bourke, John Gregory, 43, 156, 246n47, 255n65
Bowman, John H., 61–62
Bratton, Sam G., 189
Brooklyn Museum (Brooklyn Institute of Arts and Sciences), 147–48, 158, 286n167. *See also* Culin, Stewart
Browne, Charles Francis, 165
Buchanan and Bales, 220
bullpen, 42, 44, 55, 57, 232, 273n109
Burbank, Elbridge Ayer, 67; artwork in Hubbell collection, 220–21, 225–26, 310n29; background, 165; death of, 168; at Hubbell Trading Post, 154, 165–68; lifework, 165–66, 291n75; Navajo name of, 167; relationship with subjects, 292n81, 292n86; rug paintings, 133, 167
Burbank, Nettie B. Taber, 292n87
Bureau of Indian Affairs, 113, 140, 214, 252n8; assimilation policy, 21, 24, 26, 45, 52, 64, 223; J. L.'s employment with, 31; regulation of traders, 50, 252n8; self-determination policy, 192; termination policy, 223. *See also* Navajo Indian Agency; Indian Irrigation Service

Burgdorff, Ferdinand, 183
Butler, George, 264n88

Calhoun, James S., 37
California Gold Rush, 20
Cameron, Ralph, 76, 80, 160
Canby, Edward R. S., 23
Canyon de Chelly, 39–41, 66, 143; archaeology in, 143, 148, 158; Hubbell tours to, 159, 177, 201, 203, 288n18; National Monument, 203, 212, 232; as Navajo stronghold, 17–18, 24; as tourist attraction, 152, 169, 203
Canyon del Muerto, 17
Carleton, James H., 23–24
Carson, Christopher "Kit," 24, 35, 240n53, 242n85
Casa Don Lorenzo, 218 19
cash economy, 100, 108, 252n8
Catlin, George, 166
Cedar Springs post, 83, 86–87, 90, 101, 262n57, 263n76; and Charlie's murder, 104–8
Century of Progress Exposition, 145
Chaco Canyon, 35, 201
Chain, Charlotte (teacher), 115
Changing Woman, 15
Chaves, Manuel, 23
Chavez, Carlos, 297n169
Chicago World's Columbian Exposition (Chicago World's Fair), 142–43
chicken pull, 67, 70–71, 255n62, 255n64, 258n119
Chinle, 102, 177, 183, 289n33
Chinle posts (Chin Lee), 63, 99, 255n64, 263n76, 266n2
Civil War, 23–24, 250n101
Clah, Nanebah, 217
Cleveland, Grover, 160
Coconino County, Ariz., 106
Coddington, Harry, 288n18
Codington, Walter J., 263n76

Collier, John, 154, 160, 175; and Big Snow, 189; on Indian arts and crafts, 128, 146, 284n152; and livestock reduction, 190, 192–93, 300n34 301n52; on Lorenzo, Jr., 210
Colorado Plateau, 21, 28. See also Navajo country
Colorado River, 11, 217
Colton, Harold S.: at Hubbell Trading Post, 159, 161–63; and Museum of Northern Arizona, 159, 225; preservation of Hubbell Trading Post, 225–27, 314n84
Colton, Marry-Russell Ferrell: and Hopi Craftsmen Exhibition, 145, 159; at Hubbell Trading Post, 159, 161–63
Comanches, 16, 165
Cook, John E., 232, 317n134
Cooke, Grace MacGowan, 3, 5, 177; *The Joy Bringer,* 5
Cooley, C. E., 254n56
Coolidge, Dane, 153, 169; background of, 177–78; *Lorenzo the Magnificent,* 178–79, 250n94; at Hubbell Trading Post, 154, 178–79
Coolidge, Mary Roberts, 177
Corcoran, Helen, 195, 204
cornfields, 41
cornfields post, 83, 86, 87
Cotton, Clinton Neal, 166, 246n40; background of, 43; business relationship with Hubbells, 82, 94, 97–99, 130; and curio trade, 127, 278n38, 286n169; influence on Navajo arts and crafts, 125–30, 279n61, 279n63, 280n71; marriage to Mary Alice Crain, 43; Navajo name of, 44; partnership with J. L., 44, 50, 51–52, 58–59, 61–66, 253n22; as sole owner of Hubbell Trading Post, 45–46, 48, 248n78, 251n107; trading philosophy of, 44–45, 61, 248n75

Cotton, Mary Alice Crain, 43, 65
Coulter, Fred T., 80
Crane, Leo, 105, 287n14
Crary, Charles, 39, 245n37; 246n40
credit, system of, 59–61, 86, 91–92, 133, 164, 188, 215, 317n134; extended to traders, 61, 93, 130–31, 185–87, 194. *See also* pawn
Cresto, Bert, 223
Cresto Transfer, 203
Culin, Stewart: curator of Brooklyn Museum, 147, 286n167; at Hubbell Trading Post, 158
Cummings, Byron, 154
curios. *See* Navajo arts and crafts
Curtis, Edward S., 154

Dam Store, 83, 87, 92, 195
Danson, Edward B. "Ned," 225–27, 229, 233, 314n84
Daughters of the American Colonists, 231–32, 316n121, 316n126
Day, Sam, 87, 201, 254n56
de Benavides, Alonso. *See* Benavides, Alonso de
Dedera, Don, 229
de Espejo, Antonio. *See* Espejo, Antonio de
de Oñate, Juan. *See* Oñate, Juan de
de Tovar, Pedro. *See* Tovar, Pedro de
Dillon, Anne E. "Betty," 218–19, 311n46
Dillon, Robert G. "Bob," 218–19, 311n46
Diné. *See* Navajos
Diné Bikéyah, 25–26, 124. *See also* Navajos: traditional homeland of
Dinétah, 15. *See also* Navajos: traditional homeland of
Dixon, Maynard, 59–60, 81, 154, 175; background of, 168–69; at Hubbell Trading Post, 154, 169–72, 293n105, 293n107, 294n113; Navajo name of, 169

Dodge, Henry Chee, 87, 189; and Hubbell mortgages, 97, 99, 108, 194, 211, 266n2
Doniphan, Alexander W., 20, 22
Dorr, Alma Juliette. *See* Hubbell, Alma Juliette Dorr (daughter-in-law)
Dowdy, John, 228
Drefkoff, Max M., 213–14

Eckel, Edwin B. (grandson-in-law): marriage to LaCharles, 197; in World War II, 205
Eckel, LaCharles Goodman (granddaughter), 103, 109, 119, 298n187; birth of, 76; childhood at Hubbell Trading Post, 77, 82, 114–15, 117, 164–65; dedication of Hubbell Trading Post National Monument, 232–34; education, 110, 117, 197; interest in Hubbell business, 211, 222, 224, 226, 308n170, 310n32; manager of Hubbell Trading Post, 205, 211, 229
Educational Qualification Law, 79–80, 260n28, 260n36
Elle of Ganado, 142
El Navajo Hotel, 116
El Tovar Hotel, 140–41, 293n90. *See also* Fred Harvey Company
Espejo, Antonio de, 14–15, 238n25
Exposition of Indian Tribal Arts, 284n149

Fannin, Paul, 316n124
farm at Ganado, 52, 211, 222, 271n82, 272n86; crops, 111–14; decline of, 223; in Great Depression, 196–97, 203; irrigation of, 63–64, 90–93, 111, 193, 197, 223, 263n88, 264n90, 271n82. *See also* Ganado Irrigation Project
Farmington fruit ranch, 111, 209

Fewkes, Jesse Walter, 158, 289n29
Field Museum of Natural History, 147, 165–66
Fireman, Bert, 230
First Man and First Woman, 26
Fish, Joseph, 46–47, 49, 249n89
Flagstaff, Ariz., 58, 106, 159, 204, 217
Fontana, Bernard, 229
Fort Defiance, 23, 38–39, 41, 45, 150, 152; J. L.'s employment at, 30–31, 33
Fort Sumner. *See* Bosque Redondo
Fort Wingate, 22, 25, 31, 41, 43, 247n47, 298n187
Fort Worth Frontier Centennial Exposition, 145
Frazier, Lynn Joseph, 189
Fred Harvey Company: hotels, 137–38; Indian arts and crafts demonstrators, 136, 138, 140–45, 181, 217, 282n119; Indian Department, 123, 137; Indian Detours, 200–201, 304n102; museum contributions, 147; partnership with Hubbell Trading Post, 138–42, 262n59, 283n128, 293n90; tourism promotion, 136–38, 143–45; world's fairs displays, 143–45
freighting business, 52, 62, 86, 91, 203, 216; by automobile, 87–90, 112–13, 263n75; government contracts, 59, 87, 92; by rail, 58; in St. Johns, 46; teamsters, 65–66, 72, 89, 120; by wagon 57–58, 87, 89–90, 111
Frontier Curio, 220, 312n50

Gallup Inter-Tribal Indian Ceremonial Association, 146, 286n167
Gallup, N.Mex., 116, 166; as shipping center, 58, 87, 89, 91–92, 113, 263n75; as travel hub, 116–17, 150, 166, 201–3, 305n117

Gallup wholesale house, 83, 86, 99, 109, 120, 184, 196, 211
Ganado, Ariz., 53, 119, 156; origin of name, 31, 62. *See also* Hubbell Trading Post; Pueblo Colorado Valley
Ganado Irrigation Project, 91–93, 111, 119, 223, 263n88; in the Great Depression, 193, 197
Ganado Lake, 39, 72, 91; and dam, 72, 91–92, 193, 219
Ganado Mucho (Tótsohnii Hastiin, Man of the Big Water Clan), 30–31, 33, 36, 41, 62
Ganado Red style, 132–33, 280n71
Ganado Trading Post, 109
Garland, Hamlin, 165; "Delmar of Pima," 48, 154, 250n94, 288n20; at Hubbell Trading Post, 150–53, 155
Geronimo, 165
Goddard, Pliny Earle, 181
Gold, F. M., 269n43
Goldwater, Barry, 221, 226, 316n124
Goodman, Barbara Hubbell ("Auntie Bob"; daughter), 49, 66, 115, 117, 207, 273n115; caretaker for Lina, 75–77, 96; education of, 67; hostess of Hubbell Trading Post, 162, 179–82, 196, 211, 290n54; illness of, 196, 205, 211, 220–21, 310n33; marriage to A. B. Myers, 119; marriage to Charles Q. Goodman, 75–76; personal characteristics of, 258n10; as postmistress, 62, 113, 196, 223, 263n76; and Spanish Influenza, 103; and World War I, 100–101; and World War II, 205
Goodman, Charles Q. (son-in-law), 75–76, 79–80
Goodman, LaCharles. *See* Eckel, LaCharles Goodman (granddaughter)

Grand Canyon, 14, 140–41, 145, 160, 217, 282n119
Great Depression, 199; effects on Hubbell business, 185–87, 194–95; effects on Navajo economy, 130, 185, 190; and Public Works of Art, 146
Greene, Art H. "Bill," 217, 310n29, 311n47
Greene, Evelyn, 217, 310n29, 311n47
Gregory, Herbert E., 264n88
Grey, Zane, 154, 177
Gross, H. R., 227–28
Gutiérrez, Clemente, 18
Gutiérrez, Juliana. *See* Hubbell, Juliana Gutiérrez (mother)
Gutiérrez, Lorenzo Antonio, 18
Gutiérrez family, 13–14, 18–19

Haldeman, Gene, 11, 237n10
Hall, Edward T., 196, 199, 212
Hamblin, Jacob, 30–31
Harding, Warren G., 160
Hardison, Charles, 39–40, 247n47
Harmon, Mrs. (Hubbell Trading Post resident), 310n33
Hartzog, George, 234
Harvey, Byron, 137
Harvey, Ford, 137–38
Harvey, Frederick Henry, 136–37
Harvey Company. *See* Fred Harvey Company
Hastiin Biwosi (Navajo witch), 39–41
Hastiin Jéékha Díjólí (Little Deaf Man) (Navajo witch), 39
Hastiin Neé'y (Loco) (Navajo cook), 68, 160
Hastiin Nez (Navajo), 105
Havens, Mrs. O. C., 222
Hayden, Carl, 154, 160; and preservation of Hubbell Trading Post, 226–27, 316n124
Hayzlett, G. W., 64
Heard Museum, 230–31

Hero Twins, 15
Hesse, Jerome, 122
Hewett, Edgar L., 158
Heye, George G., 148
Hibben, H. C. "Dad," 110–11
Hispanics. *See* Mexicans
Hoffman, Malvina, 147
Hogback Project, 223
Hogg, John Edwin, 69, 161, 237n3
Holbrook, Ariz., 58, 87, 302n82
Hollywood curio store, 110–11
Holmes, Yazzie (Navajo), 193
Hoover, Herbert, birthplace of, 228, 231
Hopi Craftsman Exhibition, 145, 159
Hopi House. *See* El Tovar Hotel
Hopis, 116, 143, 156, 289n29, 250n47; arts and crafts, 83, 86, 109, 131, 138, 153, 164, 278n58; arts and crafts demonstrators, 140–43, 145–48; encounters with Spanish, 14, 35, 238n25; J. L.'s stay with, 11; and Lorenzo, Jr., 84, 99, 141, 156; pueblos as tourist attraction, 3, 148, 152, 161, 169, 200–201, 209, 266n4; relationship with Navajos, 35, 238n25, 242n85. *See also* Snake Dance ceremony
hospitality tradition, 5, 123, 202, 219; and anthropologists and archaeologists, 147, 155–59, 180–83, 289n33; and artists, 163–72; and business, 154, 158; costs of, 153, 178–79, 287n14; decline of, 218; and politicians, 159–63, 180; and Navajo customers, 54–56, 112; Spanish roots of, 153, 219, 287n14; and tourists, 230–31; and writers, 172–79
Hotevilla, 148
Howard, M. V., 48
Hubbard, David, 193
Hubbard, Mildred (Navajo daughter), 256n101

## Index

Hubbell, Adele. *See* Parker, Adele Hubbell "Lala" (daughter)
Hubbell, Alma Juliette Dorr (daughter-in-law), 99, 117, 265n110; birth of children, 99; death of, 103–4; marriage to Roman, 95–96, 181
Hubbell, Barbara. *See* Goodman, Barbara Hubbell ("Auntie Bob"; daughter)
Hubbell, Charles (uncle), 19, 240n53; and Long Walk, 24–25
Hubbell, Charles H. (cousin), 73
Hubbell, Charles M. "Charlie" (brother): at Cedar Springs post, 101, 107–8; clerk for J. L., 42–43, 63, 65, 94, 134, 245n37; murder of, 104–8, 268n35, 269n43, 269n46; Navajo name of, 65; personal characteristics of, 65, 107; witch purge of 1878, 39–41, 247nn46–47
Hubbell, Donald Sidney (cousin), 70, 115
Hubbell, Dorothy E. Smith (daughter-in-law), 120, 181–82; background, 115, 273n115; bankruptcy, 219–21; designation of Hubbell Trading Post National Historic Site, 117, 224–30, 232–34, 314n101; and Gallup wholesale house, 184, 196, 211; interest in Hubbell business, 211, 216–19; manager of Hubbell Trading Post, 221–24; marriage to Roman, 117–19; and Monnie's death, 206–7; Navajo names of, 117, 222; and Roman Hubbell Navajo Tours, 199, 201–3; on Roman's death, 221–22; teacher at Hubbell Trading Post, 115–17, 274n123
Hubbell, Dorothy Ketner (granddaughter-in-law), 197, 302n82
Hubbell, Felipe (brother), 47
Hubbell, Flora Sandoval (daughter-in-law), 197–98

Hubbell, Frank A. (brother), 47
Hubbell, George (nephew), 109, 115, 120–21, 185, 207
Hubbell, James Lawrence "Santiago Lorenzo" (father), 37; adoption of Hispanic culture, 19–20; business, 19; in Civil War, 24; marriage to Juliana Gutiérrez, 18–19; in Mexican-American War, 18–19; and Native Americans, 24–25, 242n90
Hubbell, John (uncle), 19, 240n53
Hubbell, John Lorenzo (J. L.; Juan Lorenzo; Don Lorenzo): in Arizona State Senate, 80–82, 91; in Arizona Territorial House of Representatives, 64, 78, 90, 142, 259n26; attitudes toward Native Americans, 11, 33, 171, 269n55; and automobiles, 87, 262n72; bilingualism of, 28, 30, 57; on Board of Fair Commissioners, 146; and Charlie's death, 105–6, 269n55; childhood and youth of, 10–11, 28–30; children of, 49, 250n105; as clerk at other trading posts, 10, 31; dealer in Indian curios, 12, 129, 131, 176, 286n169; death of, 120–22; descriptions of, 5–6, 46–47, 78, 151, 158–59, 163, 171, 233; education of, 29, 243n105; and Fred Harvey Company, 138–42, 262n59, 283n128, 293n90; at Gallup wholesale house, 109, 120; and gambling, 67, 70, 163; and Ganado farm, 63–64, 112, 120; and grandchildren, 114–15; as guide and outfitter, 152, 158, 177, 288n18, 289n33; and Hispanic voting rights, 79–80, 260n36; hospitality of, 5, 12–13, 152–55, 219, 287n14; illness of, 108, 119–20; on Indian rights, 159, 260n28, 295n138; influence on Navajo arts and crafts, 12, 123–35, 279n61, 279n63, 279n66, 280n69,

Hubbell, John Lorenzo (*continued*)
280n71; knowledge of Navajo language and culture, 53–56, 252n14, 252n19; marriage to Lina Rubi, 49–50, 96–97; and Mormons, 11, 30–31, 46–47, 249n89; multicultural heritage of, 5, 13–14, 18, 28–30, 42, 153; names of, 42, 56, 236n1; Navajo perceptions of, 56, 68, 252n19; Navajo wives and children of, 68, 256n101; neglect of business for politics, 78, 81–82, 93–98, 131; partnership with C. N. Cotton, 44, 50, 58–59, 61–66, 248n78, 253n22, 279n63; as politician, 12, 78–82, 93–95, 97–98, 119–20, 260n28, 260n33, 261n43; portrait of, 164, 291n63; as post office clerk, 10, 62; presidential contacts of, 160–63, 289n42; relationship with Navajos, 32–33, 41–42, 60, 68–70, 141, 248n75, 260n28, 269n55; as sheriff of Apache County, 47–49, 73, 155, 250n94, 250n100; in smallpox epidemic, 41–42, 247n55; stay with Hopis, 11; in St. Johns, 44, 46–49; as storyteller, 10–11, 32–33, 41–42, 47–48, 120, 152–54, 169, 178, 237n3, 237n10; as supplier of Indian arts and crafts demonstrators, 140–48, 282n119, 283n128; trading philosophy of, 42, 69; as translator at Fort Defiance, 30–31; US Senate campaign of, 97–99; in Utah Territory, 10–11; and witch purge of 1878, 41; and World War I, 100–101

Hubbell, John Lorenzo "Jack" (grandson), 99, 104, 224; childhood at Hubbell Trading Post, 114–15, 117; and dedication of Hubbell Trading Post National Monument, 232–34; education, 196; interest in Hubbell business, 222, 229, 310n32; in World War II, 205, 306n135

Hubbell, Juliana Gutiérrez (mother), 13, 18; as village matriarch, 28

Hubbell, Lina Rubi (wife), 256n98; ancestry of, 250n101; birth of children, 49–50, 250n105; descriptions of, 68; first marriage and divorce, 49–50; home in Albuquerque, 66–68, 74–76, 96, 151; illness and death of, 75–77, 82, 96–97, 122, 180; marriage to J. L., 49–50, 66; Navajo name of, 68; views on education and gambling, 67

Hubbell, Lorenzo, Jr. "Lorencito" (son), 49, 97; and Big Snow, 187–88; business relationship with Hubbell Trading Post, 84, 86–87, 94, 99, 108, 179, 262n57; on Charlie's death, 105–8, 270n55; childhood of, 66; and curio trade, 109–10, 134, 311n46; education of, 67, 83–84; estate of, 210–12, 308n170; and Fred Harvey Company, 140–41; hospitality tradition of, 13, 149, 156, 180, 182–83, 196; illness and death of, 204, 207–10, 307n156; on Indian Arts and Crafts Board, 146, 284n152; and Indian arts and crafts exhibitions, 145–46, 286n165; at Keams Canyon, 67, 83–86, 89, 96, 131, 138, 141; knowledge of Navajo language and customs, 13, 180, 252n14; on livestock reduction, 192; manager of J. L. Hubbell Trading Post, 184, 194, 199; marriage to Flora Sandoval, 197–98; Navajo name of, 84, 182; at Oraibi, 99, 102, 184–85, 196; nieces and nephews of, 77, 115; personal characteristics, 84, 108, 194–95; relationship with

Navajos and Hopis, 84, 105–6; relationship with Roman, 77, 199; on Spanish Influenza, 102–3; trading philosophy of, 134–35, 194–95; and World War I, 100–101. *See also* Lorenzo Hubbell Trading Company

Hubbell, Madge (George's wife), 120–21, 207, 307n156

Hubbell, Maude (Navajo daughter), 256n101

Hubbell, Nell (Tom's wife), 203

Hubbell, Roman (Navajo son), 256n101

Hubbell, Roman (son), 50; and Arizona Unlimited Exhibition, 146–47; away from Hubbell Trading Post, 96; and bankruptcy, 219–21, 312n53; and Big Snow, 187–89; on Charlie's death, 105; childhood of, 67; deafness of, 77, 100, 259n19; descriptions of, 216–17; education of, 67, 77; efforts to sell Hubbell Trading Post, 224–25; and Ganado farm, 111–12, 196–97; and Gallup wholesale house, 99, 184, 196, 211; hospitality tradition of, 180–82; illness and death of, 221; and Indian arts and crafts, 146, 301n52; interest in the Hubbell business, 211, 216–19; knowledge of Navajo language and customs, 13, 180, 201, 252n14; and Lorenzo, Jr.'s estate, 210–11; on livestock reduction, 192–93; manager of Hubbell Trading Post, 82, 94, 109, 187; marriage to Alma Dorr, 95–96, 104; marriage to Dorothy Smith, 117–19; on Monnie's death, 207; Navajo name of, 77; personal characteristics of, 77, 216–17; relationship with J. L., 77; relationship with Lorenzo, Jr., 77, 199; as tour guide, 95, 149, 180, 199–200, 297n169; and World War I, 100–101. *See also* Roman Hubbell Navajo Tours

Hubbell, Roman Dorr "Monnie" (grandson), 104; childhood at Hubbell Trading Post, 114–15, 117; education, 196; marriage to Dorothy Ketner, 197, 302n82; trader, 187; in World War II, 205–7, 224

Hubbell, Santiago Lorenzo. *See* Hubbell, James Lawrence "Santiago Lorenzo" (father)

Hubbell, Sidney Auger (uncle), 19, 25, 240n53

Hubbell, Thomas (brother), 47

Hubbell, Thomas S. "Tommy" (nephew), 122, 203, 208, 271n77

Hubbell Hill, 97, 122, 180, 199, 210, 222, 292n86, 303n93

Hubbell Trading Post: accommodations at, 148, 164; Anglo and Hispanic employees at, 65–66, 70, 72, 90, 92, 302n72; bankruptcy of, 219–21, 312n50, 312n53; bookkeeping at, 57, 74, 138, 214, 253n22, 254n47, 270n66; branch stores, 63, 83–86, 99, 109–11, 195, 255n64, 262n57, 266n11; bullpen, 55; clerks at, 43, 247n65; curio trade in business, 130–31, 286n28; decline of, 222–23; descriptions of, 3, 5, 169–71; early Navajo rug trade at, 125–27; early trade at, 56–62; effects of politics on business, 78, 81–82, 93–94, 97–98, 131; efforts to sell, 208–9, 224–25; founding of, 11, 39, 50; gas station, 183, 229; guest lodge and camp, 218–19; hired managers at, 196, 211, 217–19, 302n72; Hubbell family at, 66–67; Hubbell home, 65, 73; improvements to, 64–65, 112–13, 183, 197, 219; laundromat, 223,

Hubbell Trading Post (*continued*) 229; livestock reduction at, 192; and local community, 70, 119, 257n116, 274n137; Navajo employees at, 66, 68, 72, 91–92, 111, 153, 160, 196; ownership of, 43, 245n37, 246n40, 247n65; pets at, 273n109; post office, 62, 263n76; role in Navajo community, 70–72; Roman's management of, 82, 94, 109, 187; school at, 115, 117; suppliers of, 57–58; title and ownership of, 50–52, 78, 251n113, 260n28; trading ranch, 63, 255n65; trading ritual at, 53–56. *See also* farm at Ganado; freighting business; hospitality tradition; Hubbell Trading Post National Historic Site; *names of individual posts*

Hubbell Trading Post National Historic Site, 117; dedication of, 232–34; designation process for, 226–32; as living trading post, 233–34; Navajo views of, 317n134; oppositions to designation, 226–30; publicity for, 229–31, 315n116, 316n121; proposal of, 225–26, 314n84

Huckel, John Frederick, 137, 140–41, 283n128, 284n152

Huckel, Minnie Harvey, 137

Huning, Henry, 254n56

Hunt, George W. P., 160–61

Hunt, John, 259n26

Hwéeldi. *See* Bosque Redondo

Hyde Exploring Expedition, 285n164

Ickes, Harold, 160, 284n152

Indian Appropriation Act, 91. *See also* irrigation

Indian Arts and Crafts Board, 146, 284n152, 301n52

Indian arts and crafts demonstrators, 136, 138, 140–42, 217; employed by Fred Harvey Company, 138, 140–45, 181, 217, 236, 282n119, 283n128; Hubbells' role in supplying, 140–48, 282n119, 283n128; at world's fairs, 142–45

Indian Civilian Conservation Corps. *See* Indian New Deal

Indian Irrigation Service, 64, 91–93, 193, 223, 263n88

Indian New Deal, 192–93, 301n52

Indian Reorganization Act, 190, 192–93

Indians. *See names of individual tribes*

Indians, American attitudes toward, 24, 128, 165, 286n167. *See also* assimilation

Indian trading: regulation of, 36, 38, 50, 61, 252n8; history of, 36; and Spanish, 15, 36–37. *See also* Navajo Indian trading

industrialization, 124, 127, 142, 156, 276n15

International Travel and Vacation Exhibition, 146–47

irrigation. *See* farm at Ganado: irrigation of; Indian Irrigation Service

Ives, Joseph Christmas, 21, 35

James, George Wharton, 125, 133, 251n107; background, 175–76; conflict with Hubbell family, 296n152; on E. A. Burbank, 166; on J. L, 12, 131; *Indian Blankets and Their Makers*, 176; promotion of Navajo arts and crafts, 128, 176; at Hubbell Trading Post, 154, 176–77

J. L. Hubbell Trading Post, 184, 211, 298n2; bankruptcy of, 220–21, 312n50, 312n53; incorporation of, 184; sale of Roman and Dorothy's shares, 199. *See also* Hubbell Trading Post: bankruptcy of

jewelry. *See* Navajo jewelry

Johnson, Lyndon B., 232

Kanab, Utah, 10
Keam, Thomas Varker, 30–31, 83–84, 138, 142, 254n56, 262n60; and visitors, 156, 168
Keams Canyon post (Tusayan Trading Post): and Hopi curio trade, 83, 86, 131, 138, 278n58; Lorenzo, Jr., at 67, 83–86, 89, 96, 131, 138, 141; and mail routes, 263n76; post office, 262n70; sale of, 99, 179, 266n3; and scientists, 156
Kearny, Stephen Watts, 19, 20, 22
Kellam, Mrs. E. B. (tourist), 202
Kibbey, Joseph H., 78
Kidder, Alfred V., 289n33
Kin Dah Łichíí (Red Upon the House), 35
Kinlichee, 39, 43
Kinlicheenie, Friday, 232
Kopta, Anna, 231
Kopta, Emry, 231
Kykotsmovi post. *See* Oraibi post

Lacome, Agustin, 245n28
La Fonda Hotel, 140. *See also* Fred Harvey Company
Largos, Zarcillos, 22
Latter-day Saints, Church of Jesus Christ of, 10–11, 56, 254n56; and Native Americans, 30–31; in St. Johns, 46–47, 249n89
Laut, Agnes C., 153
Lawrence, D. H., 172
Lee, Albert H., 109
Lee, Joseph, 66, 246n40
Lee, Peter (Navajo son), 256n101
Lee's Ferry, Ariz., 160
Left Handed (Navajo), 53–57, 69
Leigh, William R., 147
Leonard, William B., 39, 43–44, 50, 245n37, 246n40, 246n46, 247n65
Leonard buildings, 44; as art studio, 164, 167; demolition of, 112, 272n93

Levine, Edna, 316n121
Little, Bertha, 133
Little Gambler (Navajo), 104
livestock: in Great Depression, 185; and Hubbell business, 63–64, 113, 125, 187–89, 197; and Navajos, 15–17, 26, 35; and Spanish Influenza, 102; trade in, 38, 83. *See also* Big Snow, the; livestock reduction; sheep
livestock reduction, 108, 190–94; effect on Hubbell business, 192; effect on Navajos, 192–94, 214, 300n34, 300n41
Lók'aahnteel (Place of the Wide Reeds), 35
London, Jack, 169
Long Walk, 21–25, 35. *See also* Bosque Redondo
Long Beach curio store. *See* Arizona Navajo Indian Rug Co.
Long Range Rehabilitation Act, 213–14
Lorenzo Hubbell Motor Company, 219–20, 311n47, 312n50
Lorenzo Hubbell Trading Company, 147, 211, 298n2, 311n46; bankruptcy of, 220–21, 312n50, 312n53
*Lorenzo the Magnificent. See under* Coolidge, Dane
Louisiana Purchase Exposition, 143–44
Lucero, Encarnacion, 49
Luhan, Mabel Dodge, 148
Lummis, Bertha, 175
Lummis, Charles Fletcher: on E. A. Burbank, 166; on J. L., 3, 5–6, 123; at Hubbell Trading Post, 154, 173–75, 295n138, promotion of Indian arts and crafts, 128, 173–75; *A Tramp Across the Continent*, 173–74, 294n132, 295n134

MacDonald, Peter, 317n134
MacNeil, Herman A., 165
Macpherson, Angus, 147

mail, 57, 108; delivery contracts, 46, 62, 86, 88–90, 111, 113, 223, 254n56, 263n76, 272n96; Ganado post office, 62, 223, 263n76; Keams Canyon post office, 262n70; in World War II, 203
Manuelito (Navajo), 23, 25–26, 33, 41, 242n90
Manuelito, N.Mex., 58
Many Horses, 33, 41, 292n86; burial on Hubbell Hill, 122, 180, 303n93; portrait by E. A. Burbank, 167
Maratta, H. G., 129, 133
Marble Canyon Lodge, 111, 209, 217–20, 312n50
Maria Antonia (Miguelito's wife), 181
Marie (Miguelito's daughter), 181
Martinez, Julian, 141
Martinez, Maria, 141
McCabe, Tom (Navajo son), 256n101
McCowan, Samuel M., 143–44
McNitt, Frank, 228
Menapace, Enrico, 312n53
Mexican-American War, 18–20, 37
Mexicans: independence from Spain, 17–18; relationship with Navajos, 17
Miguelito (Red Point; Navajo medicine man), 95, 181–82, 259n19
Miller, I. J., 220
Milligan, W. R., 254n56
Mitchell, Miss (teacher), 115
Mitchell, Rose, 102
Monsen, Frederick, 169
Moore, J. B., 128
Morley, Sylvanus G., 158
Mormons. *See* Latter-day Saints, Church of Jesus Christ of
Morris, Ann Axtell, 181, 298n187
Morris, Earl, 116
Morrison, Robert E., 80
*Mountain Chant, The* (Armer), 182–83
Mud Springs post, 83
Muir, John, 169

Museum of Northern Arizona, 225, 280n72, 314n84
museums: Hubbell contributions to, 123, 147–48, 158, 285n164; Indian cultural displays in, 147, 286n167. *See also names of individual museums*
Myers, A. B., 119

Na-Ah-Tee Canyon, 220, 312n50
Nakai, Raymond, 232–33, 317n134
Na Kai Sání Bici (Old Mexican's First Daughter; Navajo daughter), 256n101
Nampeyo (Hopi-Tewa potter), 142
Narbona (Navajo headman), 22–23
Narbona, Antonio (Spanish lieutenant), 17–18
National Museum of the American Indian, 148
National Park Service: acquisition of Hubbell Trading Post, 226–34, 314n84, 317n134; and Canyon de Chelly National Monument, 203, 232; Sunset Crater National Monument, 226; Wupatki National Monument, 226. *See also* Hubbell Trading Post National Historic Site
National Survey of Historic Sites and Buildings, 226
Native Americans. *See names of individual tribes*
Navajo arts and crafts: advertising of, 12, 125–30, 176, 216–19, 277n33, 278n38; authenticity and counterfeit products, 132, 145–46, 284n152; in Hubbell business, 83, 86, 109–11, 130–31, 222–23, 262n59; Hubbell collections of, 99, 153, 164, 180, 227–28; market development for, 83, 127–30, 132, 141, 143, 158; trade in, 124–25, 266n4. *See also* Fred Harvey Company; Indian arts and crafts

demonstrators; Navajo jewelry; Navajo rugs and blankets
Navajo City, 39, 41; Hubbell trading post in, 63
Navajo Council Advisory Committee, 213
Navajo country: American exploration of, 20, 125; climate and conditions of, 27, 58, 91, 108, 188, 190, 214–15; roads in, 58, 87–89, 113, 152–53, 218
Navajo Indian Agency, 30–31, 140, 150. *See also* Bureau of Indian Affairs
Navajo Indian trading: decline of, 213–16; early American period, 37–38; goods, 36–37, 55, 57, 95, 149, 180, 199–200, 297n169; origins of, 12, 28; trade practices, 53–56, 252n5; risks of, 61–62, 93, 108, 189; seasonal cycle of, 58–61, 130, with other Indian tribes, 37. *See also* Indian trading
Navajo jewelry: as currency, 53, 55, 59–60, 252n8; role of Hubbell and Cotton in development of, 12, 279n61; silversmithing, 28, 140–41, 143, 147; trade in, 124, 129, 138. *See also* pawn
Navajo Reservation: boundaries of, 36, 48, 50, 251n108, 260n28; conditions on, 27, 58, 91, 108, 188, 190, 214–15; creation of, 26; irrigation of, 64, 91–93, 111; modernization of, 112–13, 183, 212–16, 223–24, 234
Navajo rugs and blankets: aniline dyes and Germantown yarn used in, 127, 132, 276n15, 279n63; commercialization and development of, 125, 132–33, 276n15; early trade in, 125–26; development of market for, 12, 83, 129–30; influences on, 28, 125–30, 132–33, 279n61, 280n69, 280n71; J. L. and Cotton in development of, 12, 123

124–32; J. L.'s influence on, 131–35; in Hubbell business, 3, 84, 86, 93, 109–11, 154, 164, 187, 204, 212; market value of, 134–35; in Navajo economy, 124, 130, 135, 185, 192; origins of, 15, 124–25; reputation of, 20–21, 125, 276n14; trade in, 108, 134, 138; weaving of, 124, 133; world's largest Navajo rug, 147, 280n72
Navajos: American attitudes toward, 21, 105, 107, 125, 276n14; attitudes toward traders, 41–42, 44–45, 69, 213, 244n3; ceremonies of, 95, 101, 116–17, 180, 182–83, 201, 259n19; cultural influences on, 14–15, 17, 125; customs of, 26, 39, 55, 69–70, 267n15, 257n111; early American encounters with, 20–21, 125; early Spanish encounters with, 14–15, 238n24; employed by Hubbell, 66, 68, 72, 91–92, 111, 153, 160, 196; and government aid, 26–27, 114–15, 189, 309n12, 309n14; influence on trading post practices, 53–56; language of, 14, 55–56; origins of, 14, 238n22, 238n24; raiding and warfare, 15–18, 21–23, 35, 238n25, 242n90; relationship with Hopis, 35, 238n25, 242n85; relationship with J. L., 32–33, 41–42, 60, 68–70, 141, 248n75, 260n28, 269n55; and social welfare customs, 69–70, 257n101, 257n111; traditional homeland of, 11–12, 15, 25–26, 124; treaties with, 20, 22–23, 26; and wage work, 204, 214–15; women and J. L., 68, 256n101. *See also* Navajo arts and crafts; Navajo Indian trading
Navajo Tribal Council, 213–14, 232
Navajo Tribal Fair, 146
Navajo Tribe, 220–21, 230, 317
Nazlini post, 99

Neubert, Kathleen M., 263n76
New Deal. *See* Indian New Deal

O'Dwyer, William, 147
Oñate, Juan de, 13, 15
Oraibi, 3, 102
Oraibi post (Kykotsmovi post), 86–87, 101, 212, 217, 312n50; after Lorenzo, Jr.'s death, 310n29; curio trade at, 83, 109–10, 166n4; hospitality at, 149, 196; and Lorenzo, Jr., 99, 102, 184–85; sale of, 220–21
Owens, Commodore Perry, 49, 250n100

Paiutes, 11, 14
Pajarito, N.Mex., 18–19, 28, 76, 242n90
Palmer, Frank M., 158–59
Panama-California Exposition, 144–45
Panama-Pacific International Exhibition, 144–45
Panic of 1893, 62, 135
Panic of 1907, 93
Parker, Adele Hubbell "Lala" (daughter), 49, 66; birth of children, 74; education of, 67; at Hubbell Trading Post, 74, 97, 181–82, 199, 284; illness and death of, 198–99, 303n93; marriage of, 74, 258n2; personal characteristics of, 76, 258n10; and World War I, 100–101; life away from Hubbell Trading Post, 93, 109–10, 196
Parker, Forrest Miles (son-in-law), 171; conflict over Lorenzo, Jr.'s estate, 211, 308n170; as Hubbell employee, 74, 97–98, 109, 184, 270n66; and Ganado Irrigation Project, 193; and Long Beach curio shop, 109, 117; marriage of, 74, 258n2; relationship with Hubbell family members, 74, 109–10, 211, 271n77; work outside Hubbell Trading Post, 93, 110, 184, 196, 198, 303n93; and World War I, 100–101
Parker, Forrest Miles, Jr., "Mudgy" or "Mudge" (grandson), birth of, 74; childhood at Hubbell Trading Post, 114–15; education of, 274n123; interest in Hubbell business, 211
Parker, Lorenzo Hubbell "Hub" (grandson), 109, 161; birth of, 74; childhood at Hubbell Trading Post, 114–15; education of, 110, 274n123; interest in Hubbell business, 211; manager at Oraibi, 210
pawn, 59–61, 185, 223, 248n75, 254n47; decline of practice, 194, 214–15, 309n8
PEO Sisterhood, 219
Perez, Thomas, 250n100
Phoenix, Ariz., 110, 196, 198, 208, 210, 220; curio outlet in, 217; J. L. in, 78, 94, 96–97, 120, 143
Pillsbury, Mr. (early trader in Pueblo Colorado Valley), 43, 247n66
Piñon post, 87, 99, 101, 109, 220, 312n50
Piñon Springs post, 99; bean farm, 111
Pioneer liquor store (Winslow, Ariz.), 195
Porter, James E., 48–49
Powell, John Wesley, 64
Presbyterian Mission, 92, 119, 218, 232, 264n96, 274n137. *See also* Sage Memorial Hospital
Prescott, Ariz., 49, 67
primitivism, 12, 124, 128–29, 150, 201 286n167; in Indian arts and crafts demonstrations, 282n119, 286n167. *See also* antimodernism
Progressive Party, 98, 160
Pronto Service Station, 195, 209
Pueblo Colorado River, 11, 64, 91
Pueblo Colorado Valley, 11, 31–32, 37; early traders in, 38–39, 43, 245n37,

246n40, 246nn46–47, 247nn65–66; European and American exploration and warfare in, 35–36; irrigation survey of, 64; Navajo community in, 33–36, 92–93; Navajo history of, 35–36, 245n14; origin of name, 35; prehistory and archaeology of, 33, 35, 64; and witch purge of 1878, 39–41
Pueblo Indians, 14, 143; cultural influence on Navajos, 17, 125; warfare with Spanish, 14–15, 17, 238n24. *See also* Pueblo Revolt of 1680
Pueblo Revolt of 1680, 14, 17, 125, 239n25

railroads, 20–21, 58, 87. *See also* Atlantic and Pacific Railway; Atchison, Topeka & Santa Fe Railway
*Rajolaro* (newspaper), 117
range war, 47–48, 178
Red Cross, 214–15
Redit, Gertrude, 175
Red Point. *See* Miguelito (Red Point; Navajo medicine man)
Reed, Henry, 31
Reichard, Gladys Amanda, 180–83
Remington, Frederic, 168
Rensselaer, Stephen Van, 286n169
Republican Central Committee, 261n43
Republican Party, 79–80, 98, 160, 162; Hubbell's involvement in, 12, 78–82, 93–95, 97–98, 119–20, 260n28, 260n33, 261n43
Reyes, Tafayo (mother-in-law), 49, 250n101
Rhodes, Eugene Manlove, 177
Richardson, Gladwell ("Toney"; "Maurice Kildare"), 270n55
Richardson, Hubert, 110
Robinson, H. F., 64, 91, 264n88
Rogers, Miss (teacher), 115

Roman Hubbell Navajo Tours, 199–203, 212, 304n102, 305n117, 310n24; advertising for, 201–2; driving movie crews, 203, 304n116, 310n24; sale of, 216, 223; and World War II, 203
Romero, Andy, 90, 302n72
Roosevelt, Archie, 160
Roosevelt, Franklin D., 189
Roosevelt, Nicholas, 160
Roosevelt, Quentin, 160
Roosevelt, Theodore, 78, 98, 148, 264n88; description of J. L., 163; at Hopi Snake Dance, 160–61, 290n47; at Hubbell Trading Post, 154, 160–63, 290n54
Rubi, Cruz (father-in-law), 49, 250n101
Rubi, Lina. *See* Hubbell, Lina Rubi (wife)
rug paintings, 133, 167
rugs. *See* Navajo rugs and blankets

Sacred Mountains, 25–26
Sage Memorial Hospital, 119–20, 218
Salmerón, Gerónimo de Zárate, 238n24
Salsbury, Clarence G., 120
Santa Fe, N.Mex., 18–19, 22, 37; artistic and literary colony in, 163, 172; J. L.'s education in, 29, 243n105
Santa Fe Railway. *See* Atchison, Topeka & Santa Fe Railway
Santa Fe Trail, 19, 37, 58
Sauerwein, Frank P., 164, 172
Schevill, Margaret, 218
Schillenburg, Donald, 263n76
Schmedding, Joe, 89, 99, 266n3
schools, Indian, 26, 30, 70, 83, 87, 111, 119, 117
Schweizer, Herman, 137–41, 145, 282n119; on J. L. Hubbell, 123
Schwemberger, Simeon, 90, 292n87
Scott, Julian, 292n87
Senner, George F., 316n124
Seton, Ernest Thompson, 172–73

sheep: in Hubbell business, 63, 98, 108, 113, 187–89, 190, 197; and James Lawrence Hubbell, 19–20; Navajo attitudes toward, 15–17, 55, 190–91, 300n34; role in Navajo economy, 15, 26–27, 124–25, 192; trade in, 12, 28, 57. *See also* Big Snow, the; livestock; livestock reduction
Sheep Springs post. *See* Steamboat Canyon post (Sheep Springs)
shipping. *See* freighting business
Shoemaker, Samuel, 264n88
silverwork. *See* Navajo jewelry
Simpson, James H., 21, 276n14
Sin Let Za He post, 63, 255n64
Skiöld, Nils-Gustaf, 286n165
slave trade, 16–17, 22–24, 36
smallpox epidemic, 41–42
Smith, Dorothy E. *See* Hubbell, Dorothy E. Smith
Smith, Harry S., 273n115
Smith, Joseph Emerson, 148, 158, 179
Smith, Mabel C. Wanee, 273n115
Smith, Marcus A., 98
Smith, Shine, 202
Smithsonian Institution, 148, 166
Snake Dance ceremony: and anthropologists, 156; and J. L., 11; and Lorenzo, Jr., 66, 210; stereotypes of, 289n29; and tourism, 95, 148–49, 152, 156, 159–61, 200
Southwest Society of the Archaeological Institute of America, 158
Spanish: encounters and warfare with Navajos, 14–18; settlement of New Mexico, 13–15; slave trade, 16–17; trade with Indians, 36–37. *See also* Gutiérrez family
Spanish Influenza Pandemic of 1918, 101–4; and Navajos, 101–2, 267n15; and Hubbell family, 102–4

Springer, Henry, 254n56
Steamboat Canyon post (Sheep Springs), 83, 86, 89, 99, 266n2
Stephen, Alexander McGregor, 289n29
Stiles, Jot Barnett, 90
St. Johns, Ariz., 44, 46–50, 63, 65–66, 82, 125, 156, 178, 246n37, 248n78, 249n89, 286n169, 312n50
St. Johns Ring, 47, 246n37, 249n90
St. Michaels, 88, 243n105, 254n56, 263n76
St. Michaels Mission, 68, 87, 122, 257n101
Stokowski, Leopold, 297n169
Stover, Mr. (early trader in the Pueblo Colorado Valley), 39, 245n37, 246n40
Sun Valley Trading Post, 217, 310n28
Suplee, E. M., 64
Swedish Technical Dying Association, 286n165
Swinnerton, Louise, 183

Taft, William Howard, 80–81, 98, 160
Taft, Zulime, 150, 152
Tanner Springs, Ariz., 247n65
Taos (Navajo silversmith), 141
Taos art colony, 163–64, 172
Thacker, Ethel, 102
Thacker, Thomas Edward "Ed," 101–2, 105, 107, 113; Charlie Hubbell's murder, 105, 107; death of, 114; and Spanish Influenza, 102–3
Tinker, Arthur W., 248n75
tin money (*seco*), 54–55, 71, 108, 252n8
Tippecanoe, Joe, 66, 187, 205
tourism in Navajo country, 12–13, 135–36; advertising, 124, 144–45; and automobiles, 148–49, 152, 183, 200–202, 219; Hubbell promotion of, 216–19; and J. L., 152, 158, 177, 288n18, 289n33; and Roman, 95,

149, 180, 199–200, 297n169. *See also* Fred Harvey Company; Roman Hubbell Navajo Tours
Tovar, Pedro de, 238n25
traders, 19, 28, 36–39, 254n56; and families, 67–68; influence on Navajo weaving, 125–30, 132–33; isolation of, 57, 65, 90, 107–8; and Navajo language, 55–56; regulation of, 36, 38, 50, 61, 213–15, 246n37, 252n8; relationship with Navajos, 32, 41–42, 44–45, 69, 213–14, 244n3; reputation of, 42, 69; as tour guides and outfitters, 154, 156; violence against, 107
trade tokens. *See* tin money
trading posts: competition among, 61–62, 94, 109, 113, 252n6, 277n33; cross-cultural contact at, 42, 53–56; as Navajo community centers, 42, 70–71; design and layout of, 44, 216; modernization of, 183, 223–24, 234. *See also names of individual trading posts*
trading ranches, 38, 43, 63, 254n56, 255n65
transportation. *See* freighting business; automobiles
Trockur, Emanuel, 234, 252n5
Truth in Lending Act, 309n8
Tschudy, Herbert B. (Judy), 133
Tusayan Trading Post. *See* Keams Canyon post (Tusayan Trading Post)

Udall, David K., 80, 249n89
Udall, Morris K., 316n124
Udall, Stewart L., 226–27, 229–30, 232–33, 316n124
United Indian Traders Association, 213, 309n19
US Postal Service. *See* mail

Utah, 10–11, 20, 30, 36, 204
Utes, 14, 16–17, 24, 242n85
Utley, Robert M., 226–27, 229, 234, 314n88

Vandever, Charles E., 248n75
Volz, Frederick W., 266n4
Voth, Heinrich Richert, 289n29
Vroman, Adam Clark, 148

Walpi, 161
Washington, John M., 21–22
*Waterless Mountain* (Armer), 183
Weafer, Eugene Clyde, 218
weaving. *See* Navajo rugs and blankets
Webber, Mr. (early trader in the Pueblo Colorado Valley), 43, 245n37, 246n47
Welsh, James, 202
Wetherill, John, 224
Wetherill, Louisa, 224
Wetherill, Milton, 202
Wetherill, Richard, 128, 142
Wheeler, Burton K., 189
Wheeler, Clarence, 311n47
Williams, Frederick Allen "Fritzie," 164
Williams, George M. "Barney," 39, 43, 245n37, 246n47, 247n65
Williams, William F., 104
Williamson, Glen (Rev.), 232
Winslow, Ariz., 58, 87, 105–6, 108, 110, 146–47, 195, 219, 223, 311n47
Winslow wholesale house, 110–11, 211, 216, 220, 271n77, 310n24, 312n50; showroom, 280n72
Wister, Owen, 177
witch purge of 1878, 39–41, 246n47, 288n20
Wolfe, Wescoat S., 232
wool trade, 38, 63, 108, 192, 197, 216; trade in Great Depression, 185, 190; at Hubbell Trading Post, 58, 219

world's fairs, Indian demonstrators at, 142–45. *See also names of fairs and expositions*
world's largest Navajo rug, 147, 280n72
World War I, 100–101, 127, 207; effects on Hubbell business, 100, 108, 130; effects on Navajo economy, 100, 130; and Hubbell family, 100–101
World War II, 194; effects on Hubbell business, 204–7; effects on Navajo economy, 204, 212, 213–16, 309n14; Navajos in, 204; Navajo Code Talkers, 207

Young, Bill, 317n134
Young, Mahonri, 164–65, 219
Yiłxaba (Navajo wife), 256n101

Zimmerman, William J., 214
Zunis, 14, 35, 238n25, 242n85

www.ingramcontent.com/pod-product-compliance
Lightning Source LLC
Chambersburg PA
CBHW020731160426
43192CB00006B/186